GREAT LIBRARIES

ENDPAPERS: *Taken from the engraving of the chained library at Leyden University in 1610, by Cornelis Woudhanus.*
FRONTISPIECE: *'The Librarian' by Arcimboldo from Skokloster Castle, Stockholm.*

GREAT LIBRARIES

Anthony Hobson

G. P. PUTNAM'S SONS NEW YORK

Filmset by Keyspools Limited, Golborne, Lancs.
Printed in England by D. H. Greaves, Limited, Scarborough, Yorks.
Library of Congress Catalog Card Number: 79–115032

ACKNOWLEDGEMENTS

My thanks are due in the first place to the librarians of the libraries which figure in this book. I am most grateful for the help and kindness I received from them. I must also thank His Grace the Duke of Wellington for showing me the books presented to the first Duke by Ferdinand VII; the Earl of Crawford and Balcarres for allowing me to examine and quote from his grandfather's and great-grandfather's library correspondence; Mgr A. Paredi, Prefect of the Biblioteca Ambrosiana, for permission to quote from the correspondence of Cardinal Federigo Borromeo; the Trustees of the John Rylands Library for permission to quote from an album of papers on the library's history; the Institut de France and Monsieur Roger Pierrot for permission to quote from Spoelberch de Lovenjoul's correspondence; and the Trustees of the Pierpont Morgan Library for permission to examine and quote from the library's file of correspondence. For help on specific points I am indebted to Dr H.A. Feisenberger, Mr P.J. Croft, Mr Andreas Mayor and Mr J.F. Hayward – all of Sotheby's, and Mr H.M. Nixon, Mr George Painter, Dr Dennis Rhodes, Mr John Rowlands and Mr Ian Willison – of the British Museum. Finally my grateful thanks are due to Mrs C. Collingwood for typing nearly the whole of the manuscript, as well as for several valuable suggestions.

ANTHONY HOBSON

The author and publishers wish to thank the Directors and Trustees of the libraries represented in this book for permission to reproduce books and manuscripts in their charge. In particular thanks are due to the Dean and Chapter of Durham, to the Exmo Cabildo de la Catedral de Sevilla and the Exmo Sr Director de la Biblioteca Colombina, to the Board of Trinity College, Dublin, to the Master and Fellows of Magdalene College, Cambridge (for material in the Pepys Library), and to the Rector and the Director of the library of the University of Coimbra for permission to reproduce material in their collections. The view on p. 239 appears by courtesy of the Director of the Library, Mafra. Material in the Biblioteca de Palacio, Madrid, and the Monastero de San Lorenzo el Real, El Escorial, is reproduced by permission of the Patrimonio Nacional. The view of the Vatican Library by Francesco Pannini on pp. 82–3 is © Anthony Hobson.

Staatsbibliothek Bamberg; **37**, 38, 39/1, 39/2, 40/1, 40/2, 40/3, 40/4, 41/1, 41/2, 42/1, 42/2, 42/3, 43/1; Walter Barnes Studio; 306, 308/1, 308/2, 308/3, 309/1, 309/2, 310, 311; James Blewitt; 104, 105, 106/1, 106/2, 106/3, 107, 108/1, 108/2, 108/3, 109/1, 150, **151** 152, 153, 154–5, 155, **156**, **157**, 158, 159, **160**, 161/1, 161/2, 234, 235, 236/1, 236/2, 236/3, 237/1, 237/2, 237/3, 238/1, 238/2, 239/1, 239/2, **240**, **241**; Bodleian Library; 167, 168, **169**, 170/1, 170/2, 171/1, 171/2, 172, 173; British Museum; 65/2, 206/1, 242, 244/1, 244/2, 245/1, 246, 246–7; Bibliothèque Royale, Brussels; 92/1, 92/2, 93, 94, 95, 96, 97, **99**, 100, 101, **102**; Dean and Chapter, Durham; 54, 56/1, 56/2, 56/3, 57/1, 57/2, 58/1, 58/2, 59/1, 59/2; John Freeman; 206/1, 243, 246, 246–7; Green Studios, Dublin; 175, 177, 176/1, 176–7/2, 178, 179, 180, 181, **182**, 183, **184**, 185; Henry E. Huntington Library and Art Gallery; 298, **300**, 301, 302, 303, 304,

305/1; Roger Lalance; 260, 264/2, 266; Edward Leigh; 212, 213, 215/1, 215/2, 216/1, 216/2, 217/1, 217/2, 218/1, 218/2, 219/1, 219/2, 220–1; Bill Malone; 307; John Rylands Library, Manchester; 268, 270, 271, **272**, 274, 275, 276/1, 276/2, 277, 278; Mas Barcelona; 109/2, 162–3; Staatsbibliothek, Munich; 132, 133, 135, 136, 136–7, 138–9, 138/2, 139/2, 140, 141/1; National Portrait Gallery; 243, 245/2; Bibliothèque Nationale, Paris; 120, 121, **122**, **123**, 124, 125, 127, 128, 129, 130, 259; Pierpont Morgan Library; **289**, 290, 291, 292, 293, 294/1, 294/2, 295, 296; Ramsey and Muspratt; 221; Scala; 78/2, 84; Toni Schneiders; 34/2, **35**, 44, 142; Edwin Smith; 55, 247, 269, 279; Ezra Stoller Associates; 288, 296–7; Thomas-Photos; 164, 165; Penny Tweedie; 214; Uffizi; 79/1; Biblioteca Vaticana; 79/2; Oesterreichische Nationalbibliothek; 143, 144, **145**, 146/1, 146/2, 146/3, 146–7, 148/1, 148/2, 149; Tanya Vinogradov; 16, 17, **18**, 19/1, 19/2, 20–1, 22, 23, 36, 43/2, 45, 46/1, 46/2, 47/1, 47/2, 47/3, **48**, **49**, 50, 51/1, 51/2, 52–3, 60–61, 62/1, 62/2, 63, 64, 65/1, 66/1, 67, **68**, 69/1, 69/2, **70**, **71**, 72/1, 72/2, 73, 74, 75/1, 75/2, 76, 77, 78, 80, 81/1, 81/2, 85, **86**, 87/1, 87/2, 88/1, 88/2, 89, 90–1, 103, 110, 111, 112/2, 112/3, 113/1, 113/2, 114/1, 114/2, 115/1, 115/2, 116/1, 116/2, 116/3, 117/1, 117/2, 118/1, 118/2, 118/3, **119**, 131, **134**, 141/2, 174, 186, 187, 188, 189, 190/1, 190/2, 191/1, 191/2, 192, 193, 194, **195**, 196, 197, 198/1, 198/2, 199, 200/1, 201/2, 222, 223, 224/1, **225**, 226, 227, **228**, **229**, 231, 232–3, 248, 249, 250/1, 250/2, 251/1, 251/2, **252**, 253, 254, 255, 256, 256–7, 257, 258, **261**, 262, 263/1, 263/2, 264/1, 265, 267, 280, 281, 282, 283, 284/1, 284/2, 285, 286, 287/1, 287/2, 299, 305/2, 311/2; Derrick Witty; **82–3**; Herzog-August Bibliothek, Wolfenbüttel; 202, 203, 204/1, 204/2, **205**, 206/2, 207, **208**, 209/1, 209/2, 210, 211; Yale University Art Gallery (A.P. Stokes Collection) 224/2; Photo Zumbuhl; 25, 26, 28, 29, 30, 31, 32–3, 34/1.

CONTENTS

GLOSSARY

(Quotations marked *ABC* are from John Carter's *ABC for Book-Collectors*, 4th edition, Rupert Hart-Davis).

Aldines. Books printed in Venice by the scholar-printer Aldus Manutius (1495–1515), his father-in-law Andrea de Asola (1515–29), his son Paulus Manutius (1533–74) and grandson, the younger Aldus (1574–97).

Amerbach, Johann. Printer in Basle 1478–1513. At times in partnership with Johann *Froben* (q.v.).

Antiphoner. The principal chant-book for the Divine Office. Usually of large size so that several choristers could use the same volume.

Association copy. A copy of a book having a special value for collectors from having once belonged to a person of interest, usually a person connected with the book or its author; e.g. Fanny Brawne's copy of Keats's *Endymion*, Shakespeare's copy of Bandello's *Novelle*.

Autograph. In the handwriting of the author.

Bade, Josse. Native of Asch, in Belgium. Humanist printer in Paris 1503–35. His press is illustrated on p. 112.

Baskerville Press. The printing establishment of Robert Baskerville of Birmingham, active 1757–75. The most distinguished English printer of the eighteenth century.

Bestiary. A collection of moralised descriptions of animals. The accounts of their behaviour are mostly fabulous. Often accompanied by illustrations of great charm. Versions also circulated in Persia and the Arab countries.

Bible. Gutenberg Bible. The *Vulgate* (q.v.) text of the Bible printed in Mainz by Johann Gutenberg in partnership with Johann Fust and Peter Schoeffer in 1454–5. The first printed book of any size, the first edition of the Bible and the *ne plus ultra* of a great library's possessions.

    Thirty-six Line Bible. The second edition of the *Vulgate* text, thought to have been printed in Bamberg about 1458. Only thirteen copies are recorded, of which all but four are imperfect.

    1462 Bible. The fourth edition of the *Vulgate* text, printed in Mainz by Fust and Schoeffer in 1462. The first edition to contain the date of printing.

    Polyglot Bible of Alcalá. Latin, Greek, Hebrew and Chaldaean texts of the Bible in parallel columns. Printed in Alcalá de Henares (Spain) in 1514–17 under the patronage of Cardinal Francisco Ximénez de Cisneros, Archbishop of Toledo.

    Plantin Polyglot Bible. Bible in the same four languages as well as Syriac, edited by Arias Montano and printed in Antwerp by Christophe Plantin in 1569–72.

Bindery. A bookbinder's establishment.

Binding. A binding (generally of morocco, calf, pigskin or other leather, cloth, buckram, boards or *wrappers*) consists of an upper (1) and a lower (2) cover, both attached to the *spine* (3). In modern books the title is normally blocked or printed on the *spine*.

Blockbook. Book printed from carved wooden blocks, without movable type. Most blockbooks are later than the earliest books printed with movable type, but the late Allan Stevenson established from watermark evidence that one blockbook (now in the John Rylands Library) dates from 1451.

Book of Hours. A collection, either manuscript or printed, of prayers, psalms and offices, for the private use of the laity.

Book of St Albans. 'The Book of Hawking, Hunting and Blasing of Arms [i.e. heraldry]', attributed to Dame Juliana Berners, printed by the *St Albans Press* in 1486. The first English sporting book.

Book-breaker. A dealer who breaks up a bound volume in order to make a profit by selling parts of it (titlepage, plates, etc.) separately.

Breviary. Book containing the daily offices, either for use in church or for priests' private recitation.

Broadside. 'A large sheet of paper printed on one side only' *SOED*, produced in this form so that it could be fixed to a wall.

Calligraphy. Elegant penmanship, often with elaborate flourishes, produced for its decorative effect.

Capitulary. A collection of ordinances made by Charlemagne or other kings of the Franks.

Caroline minuscule. The beautiful script diffused through Western Europe by Charlemagne's Empire. For examples see pp. 18 and 19. It was revived in the fifteenth century (cf. *humanistic script*). Modern roman letter is a direct descendant.

Cartulary. Volumes containing copies of the charters or other records of a particular monastery.

Catholicon. An encyclopaedia by a thirteenth-century Dominican from Genoa, Johannes Balbus, printed in Mainz in 1460, probably by Johann Gutenberg. The first printed book on any branch of secular learning.

Caxton, William. Printer in Bruges in partnership with Colard Mansion 1475–6 and in Westminster *c.* 1477–91. The first English printer. *Three Caxtons*: three books printed by C.

Chained library. A library where the books are attached by chains, usually to desks or shelves. *Chained folio*: a *folio* volume so attached.

Chapbooks. 'Small pamphlets of popular, sensational, juvenile, moral or educational character, originally distributed by chapmen or hawkers, not by booksellers' *ABC*.

Codex. Manuscript in the same form as a modern printed book as opposed to a *roll* (q.v.). From the fourth century AD onwards the *codex* tended to replace the *roll*.

Colophon. A note at the end of some manuscripts and most incunabula, often giving the date and place of printing (or writing) and the printer's (or scribe's) name. This information was generally transferred to the titlepage in the sixteenth century.

Computus. Set of tables used in the Middle Ages to calculate astronomical events and the movable dates of the calendar.

Corsellis's Oxford press. In the seventeenth century it was mistakenly believed that a certain Frederick Corsellis had printed in Oxford before Caxton set up his press in Westminster.

De Bry's Voyages. Two collections of accounts of voyages to America and the Orient, handsomely illustrated with engravings by Theodore de Bry and his sons, published 1590–1634.

Deposit copies. Copies of a new book which the publisher or printer is required by law to deliver to the national library (or libraries).

Editio princeps. First edition, especially of Greek and Roman authors.

Elzevirs. Pocket-sized books printed by various members of the Elzevir family in Holland in the seventeenth century.

Estiennes. Family of printers in Paris and Geneva. The most famous are Henri (1502–20) and Robert (1525–59).

Exemplar. A manuscript from which one or more copies were made.

Facsimile. Facsimile signature: copy or imitation of someone's signature. *Type facsimile:* 'a reprint which approximates to . . . the typographical style of the original . . .' *ABC*.

First Folio. The first collected edition of Shakespeare's works, a *folio* volume printed in 1616. With the second (1632), third (1663/4) and fourth (1685) collected editions it makes up the *Four Folios*.

Folio. The largest size of book, from about the size of a foolscap sheet upwards.

Fore-edge. The edge of a book on your right as you read the title page. This arrow points to the fore-edge →.

Froben, Johann. Humanist printer in Basle 1491–1527. The press was continued by his son and grandson.

Frontispiece. 'An illustration facing the titlepage of a book' *ABC*. Arcimboldo's *The Librarian* is the frontispiece of this book.

Gloss. Comment, interpretation. In manuscript *glossed books of the Bible* the text was written in a large script in the centre of the page and the commentary in a smaller script all round.

Gothic script. The angular script which began to replace the roman-esque script descended from *Caroline minuscule* in the late twelfth century. Most *incunabula*, the majority of English sixteenth-century books and most German books up to the present century were printed in *black letter* or *Fraktur* derived from *gothic script*.

Gradual. Service-book containing the sung parts of the Mass; usually provided with musical notation.

Herbal. Book consisting of descriptions of herbs and other plants, generally with their medical uses; normally illustrated.

Historiated initial. Illuminated initial in a manuscript or printed book containing a representation of a person or scene.

Humanistic script. The roman script used by most European humanists in the fifteenth century: an adaptation of *Caroline minuscule* (q.v.) revived by Poggio Bracciolini in the early years of the century.

Illumination. Decoration in gold and colours of a manuscript, or more rarely a printed book. The volume decorated is usually on *vellum*. The illumination may take the form of a scene (*miniature* or *historiated initial*) or of abstract or naturalistic ornament.

Imprimatur. Licence to print a book. It may be official, ecclesiastical or a polite convention.

Imprint. 'A notification . . . of the person or persons responsible for the production of a book' *ABC. Three Pfister imprints:* three books printed by P.

Incunable (pl. *incunabula*). Book printed in the fifteenth century.

Interlinear translation. Translation written between the lines of the original text.

Jest-book. Book containing a collection of jokes and funny stories.

Kelmscott Press. Founded by William Morris to 'produce books which it would be a pleasure to look upon as pieces of printing and arrangement of type'. Active in London 1891–98.

Machlinia, William de. Printer in London 1482–*c.* 1490.

Mainz Cicero. Cicero's *De officiis* and *Paradoxa* printed in Mainz by Johann Fust and Peter Schoeffer in 1465. Either this or an undated Cicero printed at Subiaco was the first printed classic.

Mainz Psalter of 1457 (and of 1459). Psalters printed in Mainz by Johann Fust and Peter Schoeffer in these two years. The former is the first printed book with a colophon giving the date of printing. Ten copies are known of the former and thirteen of the latter.

Marbled calf. Calf 'stained to a stylised pattern something like marble' *ABC,* 2nd edn. Commonly used for bindings in France and Spain in the eighteenth century.

Miniature. Illuminated picture in a manuscript or printed book.

Missal. Service-book containing the recited and chanted parts of the Mass. A combination of *sacramentary* and *gradual*.

Movable type. Type cast in single letters, or combinations of letters, which can be arranged to print any text. Invented by Johann Gutenberg in the 1450s.

Muniments. Documents belonging to a family or corporation, usually mostly concerned with the ownership or tenure of land.

Octavo. The size of the average modern novel; 'the commonest size of book' *ABC.*

Palaeography. The study of ancient writing, particularly with a view to establishing the date and origin of manuscripts.

Palimpsest. A manuscript written on re-used vellum, the original text having been washed away and a new text written on top. Common among manuscripts of the Dark Ages.

Paper. An Arab invention, introduced into Spain and Sicily in the twelfth century, but not generally used elsewhere in Europe until the fourteenth century.

Papyrus. The normal writing material of classical antiquity, made from the papyrus reed which then grew abundantly in the Nile delta. Rarely used in Europe after the sixth century. *Demotic papyri:* papyrus manuscripts in ancient Egyptian demotic script.

Pfister, Albrecht. Printed nine popular works in German in Bamberg *c.* 1460–2. All but one contain woodcuts. They are the earliest illustrated printed books. Almost all the few surviving Pfister imprints are in three libraries: Wolfenbüttel, John Rylands and Bibliothèque Nationale, Paris.

Plaquette. Pamphlet (French). Used particularly of French black letter pamphlets of the first half of the sixteenth century, usually of literary content and decorated with one or two woodcuts.

Poetical commonplace-book. A notebook in which the owner has copied poems he wanted to record.

Pre-caroline minuscule. The collective name for the national scripts which evolved between the fall of the Roman Empire and the reign of Charlemagne. The English and Irish version is known as *insular minuscule*.

Presentation copy. A copy of a book presented by the author to a patron or friend. The fact of presentation is generally indicated by an inscription or accompanying letter, less often by other means (stamp on the title, lettering on the binding, etc.).

Press. A cupboard for storing books in. *Printing press:* the machine or machines on which books are printed; a printing house.

Pressmark. A sign or number denoting a volume's position in a library.

Privilege. The sole right of printing a book, normally granted to the printer or publisher for a specified number of years.

Pynson, Richard. Printer in London *c.* 1490–1530.

Quarto. A variable size of book intermediate between *octavo* and *folio*, and of square shape. This book is a large *quarto*.

Roll. Manuscript written on a continuous piece of vellum, papyrus or paper. Rare after the fourth century AD, though used in the Middle Ages for genealogical trees, chronicles in the form of extended genealogies, collections of coats of arms and some records.

Sacramentary. Service-book for use by the priest celebrating the Mass. Replaced by the *missal* in the later Middle Ages.

St Albans Press. Press operated by an anonymous schoolmaster at St Albans *c.* 1480–86, which printed eight books.

Scriptorium. The room where a number of scribes were employed in copying manuscripts. In antiquity usually a commercial enter-prise; in the Middle Ages, especially before *c.* 1200, almost invariably in a monastery. Also used to mean any such body of scribes.

Shakespeare quartos. The earliest separate editions of Shakespeare's plays. The text often differs substantially from that in the *First Folio* (q.v.).

Spine. See *Binding*.

Stalls system. A form of library arrangement with bookshelves and attached desks projecting from the walls. The books were usually *chained*. For an example see p. 166.

Subiaco Lactantius. The works of Lactantius (d. *c.* AD 340) printed by Sweynheim and Pannartz in the abbey of Subiaco in 1465. The third book printed in Italy, but the second of which copies have survived.

Sweynheim and Pannartz. The first Italian printers. Two Germans – S. had probably worked for Fust and Schoeffer in Mainz – who set up a press in the Benedictine abbey of Subiaco in about 1464 and printed four books there. In 1467 they moved to Rome where they produced a further forty-eight books in partnership.

Type specimen. 'A sheet, booklet or piece of demonstration printing designed to display the various "sorts" and sizes of a fount or founts of type . . .' *ABC.*

Typography. The art of printing.

Uncials. The rounded capital letters used by both Greek and Latin scribes in antiquity. Examples may be seen on pp. 17 and 22. There are no gaps between words in *uncial* manuscripts.

Uncut. With the edges untrimmed by the binder; the leaves of an *uncut* book are therefore of their full original size.

Vellum. Writing material made from specially prepared animal skins, usually of calf, goat or sheep. Used in Europe throughout the Middle Ages for the more valuable or richly decorated manu-scripts. Some copies of many printed books were struck off on vellum, initially for church use, later for a bibliophilic market.

Vulgate Bible. The Latin translation of the Bible by St Jerome, completed in AD 404.

Watermark. 'A distinguishing mark or device incorporated in the wire mesh of the tray in which the pulp settles during the process of papermaking, and visible in the finished product when held against the light' *ABC.* Often providing valuable evidence to date an undated book or manuscript.

Woodcut. An illustration printed from a wooden block.

Worde, Wynkyn de. Caxton's foreman and successor. Printer in London *c.* 1491–1534.

Wrappers. Paper covers. The modern paperback is issued in *wrappers*.

Introduction

The most obvious change in libraries in the past fifteen centuries has been in their size. It was believed in the Middle Ages that the Alexandrian Library had owned 40,000 volumes in antiquity. To contemporaries the figure was evidently unimaginably vast. The Papal Library at Avignon was probably the only Christian collection of the West to exceed one twentieth of this total before the invention of printing, and St Gall's 316 volumes or Durham's 436 were large numbers by the standards of their time. It was not until the seventeenth century that the supposed Alexandrian total was exceeded. This contrasts with the annual intake of the British Museum in 1968 – 128,706 volumes.

The increase in knowledge which these figures reflect has been accompanied by its almost complete secularisation. But this process, as it affected the contents and the administration of libraries, has been subject to continual ups and downs. The libraries of the early Middle Ages were all ecclesiastical, for the Church was the only literate institution to survive the crumbling of the Empire. These ancient libraries were of two sorts, cathedral or monastic. The former, more important in the early part of the period, were liable to have a wide range of books. This was partly because bishops were chosen by popular election in the early centuries; the successful candidate was often a cultivated layman, steeped in the Roman literary tradition, who might bring a selection of his own books to his diocese. The most venerable cathedral collections succumbed to war and invasion, with two miraculous exceptions, Lyons and Verona, which still preserve uncial manuscripts written inside their walls.

Charlemagne's encouragement of education and his revival of the culture of Christian antiquity had their effect on cathedral chapters; an example is the great programme of copying and correcting texts carried out by the Archdeacon Pacificus at Verona. But the Emperor's policy was even more influential in monasteries. The ninth century and the eleventh-twelfth centuries were both highly productive for Benedictine libraries – the earlier period here represented by St Gall, the later by Admont and Durham. A convent's basic needs however were modest: the Bible, the Church fathers, service books for the church, lives of saints and anchorites for reading aloud at meals. Some history seems always to have been present, and monks were prominent among the authors of chronicles; but secular works in any number were rare.

Great changes took place from the thirteenth century onwards. The cathedral and monastic schools declined as intellectual life gravitated to the new universities, and the abbey scriptoria for

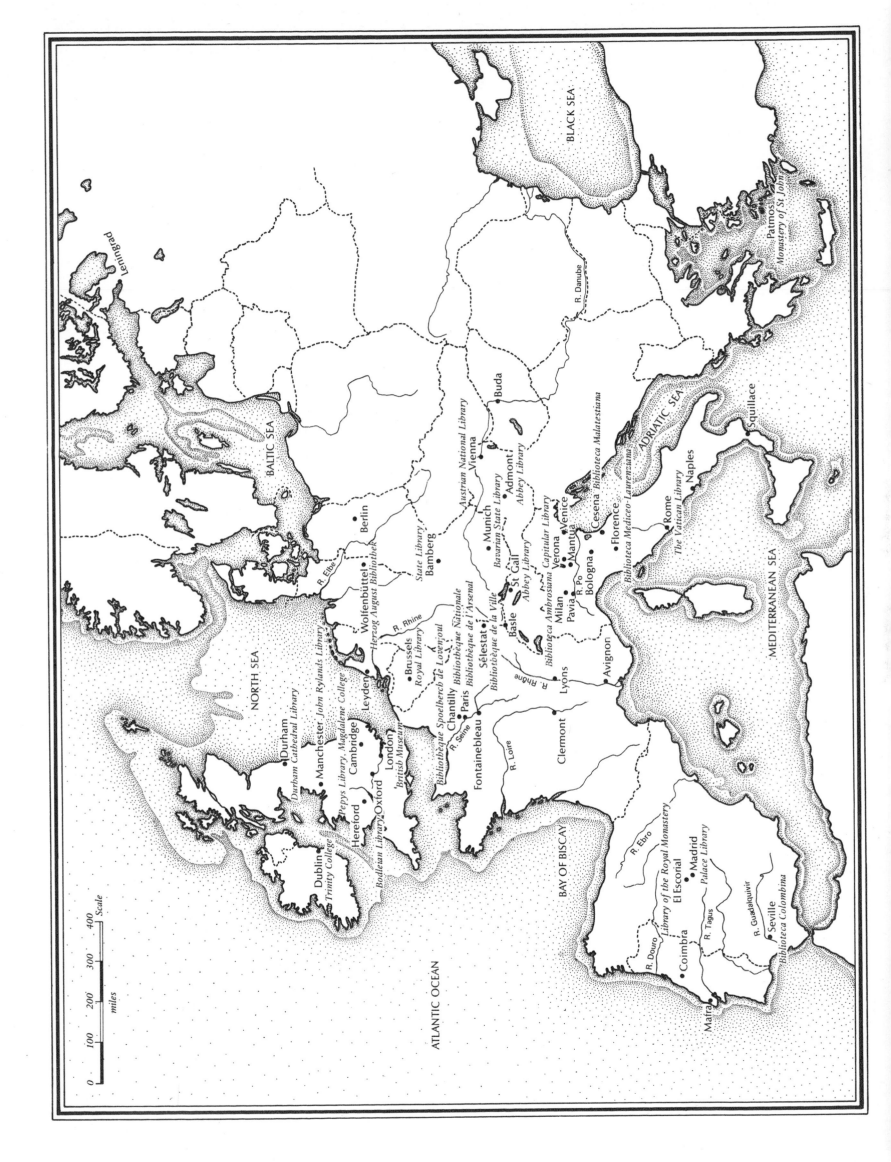

BLACK SEA

BALTIC SEA

Leningrad

Patmos.
Monastery of St John

ADRIATIC SEA

R. Danube

Buda

Austrian National Library
Vienna

Munich
Bavarian State Library

Admont
Abbey Library

Squillace

Berlin

Milan
Bibliotheca Ambrosiana

Capitular Library
Verona

St Gall
Abbey Library

Bamberg
State Library

Wolfenbüttel
Herzog August Bibliothek

R. Elbe

Basle

Pavia

Mantua

Venice

Cesena *Bibliotheca Malatestiana*

Bologna
R. Po

Florence
Bibliotheca Mediceo-Laurenziana

Rome
The Vatican Library

Naples

NORTH SEA

Sélestat

R. Rhine

Brussels
Royal Library

Bibliothèque Nationale

Paris
Bibliothèque de l'Arsenal

Chantilly

Bibliothèque Spoelberch de Lovenjoul

Leyden

Durham
Durham Cathedral Library

Manchester *John Rylands Library*

Cambridge
Pepys Library, Magdalene College

London

British Museum

Oxford
Bodleian Library

Hereford

Dublin
Trinity College

Lyons

Clermont

Avignon

Bibliothèque de la Ville

R. Seine

Fontainebleau

R. Loire

R. Rhône

MEDITERRANEAN SEA

ATLANTIC OCEAN

BAY OF BISCAY

R. Ebro

El Escorial
Library of the Royal Monastery

Madrid
Palace Library

R. Tagus

R. Guadalquivir

Seville
Bibliotheca Colombina

Coimbra

R. Douro

Mafra

Scale

400

300

200

100

0

miles

the most part fell idle. Instead a lay book-trade emerged to copy and distribute a new kind of literature: scholastic theology and philosophy emanating from Paris University, civil and canon law from Bologna. Laymen came to form a significant proportion of the literate public, and the nobility provided a market for illustrated romances and moralising works in the vernacular. Private libraries had been almost unknown in lay ownership in the early Middle Ages – the remains of the 'old imperial library' at Bamberg is an astonishing and unique relic. From the thirteenth century they became increasingly common, not only in the hands of royal collectors such as Charles v, King of France and his son Jean, Duc de Berry, but in those of simple scholars like Hermann Schedel of Nuremberg (1410–85).

To meet the changed conditions new types of library came into being. The first college library belonged to the Sorbonne, founded in Paris in 1257. About the same time Louis ix of France was inspired by accounts of similar establishments in Egypt to set up in the Sainte Chapelle the earliest public library. Its use was restricted to clerics and men of learning, but as these two categories in practice comprised all Latin-speaking readers and all the manuscripts were in that language, presumably no one able to benefit from the contents would have been turned away. In the fifteenth century town libraries, often housed in churches, were founded in many German cities. One of the first, in Brunswick, is said to date from 1413.

Books were too few in the Middle Ages to present a storage problem. They were kept in cupboards placed wherever it was convenient. In England these often stood on the north side of the cloisters, for good light and protection from the weather. Chained libraries, designed to make books available to a larger number of readers, were a creation of the later Middle Ages. Standard works of reference and other books in frequent demand were attached to desks by chains. Some degree of public use seems to have been envisaged, especially in libraries cared for by the new orders, the Franciscans and Dominicans. Malatesta Novello endowed a chained library in the Franciscan convent of Cesena, to serve the needs of the town as well of the friars. In 1443 the Dalmatian Cardinal John Stojković, known as John of Ragusa, gave his Greek and Latin manuscripts to the Dominicans of Basle, directing them to equip a chained library at his expense. Loans from this collection were made with the utmost liberality. Two manuscripts were lent to Erasmus for his edition of the Greek New Testament and returned covered with red pencil marks.

In 1362 Petrarch proposed leaving his books to the Basilica of San Marco in Venice as the nucleus from which might grow 'a great and famous library, equal to the ancient ones'. This offer contained the first suggestion for a state or national library, but nothing came of it at the time; Petrarch changed his mind and left Venice five years later; and it was the Greek Cardinal Bessarion's gift of his manuscripts in 1468 which brought the Biblioteca Marciana into existence. Petrarch's ideas however influenced fifteenth-century thought. Humanist scholars were particularly concerned that early manuscripts of the classics should be collected and preserved somewhere safe but accessible, where they could serve as the bases of reliable texts, and they succeeded in conveying their passionate interest in books to the Italian princes. Many peninsular rulers devoted their energies to assembling libraries of the utmost splendour: the Aragonese kings in Naples, Pope Nicholas V in the Vatican, Federigo da Montefeltre in Urbino, the Medici in Florence. One foreign monarch, Matthias Corvinus of Hungary (1440–90), caught the infection. Less than 200 volumes from his library survived the sack of Buda by the Turks in 1526, but they confirm contemporary accounts that the collection, both for size and richness of decoration, was remarkable even by the standards of its time. The next king to imitate the Italian example was Francis I of France. In design, lay-out, and its emphasis on Greek manuscripts, his library at Fontainebleau closely followed Italian models. Francis was however responsible for one important innovation. He promulgated the first law requiring printers to deposit a free copy of every new book in the royal library. Nearly all governments have since adopted this inexpensive method of stocking their national collections.

In Germany the Reformation, with its attendant theological disputes, led to the formation of several famous princely libraries: among them four founded by Protestants (Julius of Brunswick, the Elector Palatine Ottheinrich, Albrecht of Prussia and August of Saxony) and two by Catholics (Albrecht V of Bavaria and the Emperor Maximilian II). A taste for French romances, German chronicles and genealogy characterises these collections, which have much less of the Renaissance spirit about them than the Fontainebleau Library. Two notable university libraries were founded in northern Europe later in the century: Leyden (1575) and the Bodleian, Oxford (1602); but Queen Elizabeth rejected the pleas of Dr John Dee and other antiquaries to found an English national collection on the Continental model.

Gutenberg's invention of printing by movable type soon after 1450 did not instantaneously transform collecting habits, and it was only towards the end of the century that a new kind of private library appeared. Beatus Rhenanus's books, beautifully preserved in their original collective volumes and bindings by his native town of Sélestat in Alsace, are an example from the first generation of Northern humanists to accept the press as an essential tool of scholarship. Fernando Columbus's library in Seville, the first of many great collections to be financed with American money, is even more modern in spirit. In some respects it reminds one of Samuel Pepys's library, while in its wealth of vernacular works it anticipates collections such as Spoelberch de Lovenjoul's Balzaciana in Chantilly or Texas University's great archive of British and American literature.

Until this time the tide had been running strongly towards secularisation. But at this point a reaction set in. The Spanish royal library, although strongly humanistic in content, was placed by its founder, Philip II, under monastic control in the bleak, inaccessible Sierra de Guadarrama. In the seventeenth century the Jesuit Order, by then the leading force in Catholic education, was active in forming libraries; the Vaticana received vast accessions; many ancient abbeys renewed their collections, and two great public libraries were founded by cardinals, the Mazarine (1643) in Paris, and the Ambrosiana (1609) in Milan.

A chained library was installed in All Saints' Church, Hereford, as late as 1715, but larger collections had long outgrown this system. Fernando Columbus's books in Seville probably stood in wall shelves before 1539, and the French royal library may have adopted this arrangement after its move from Fontainebleau to Paris about 1570. The earliest surviving wall-shelving is to be seen in the Escorial. A library gallery was provided for the first time in the Ambrosiana and immediately copied in Arts End of the Bodleian. Two centuries of baroque and rococo library halls followed, nowhere more gorgeously decorated than in the resurgent abbeys of central Europe. Today these architectural marvels are used for ceremonies or exhibitions but hardly ever for reading in. The modern preference, as in the British Museum, is to pen readers in one area and to stack the books they wish to see out of sight elsewhere.

Few signposts existed to guide early collectors and librarians. In the sixth century Cassiodorus Senator compiled a work known as the *Institutions* for the monks of his monastery of Vivarium at Squillace in southern Italy. It was divided into two books, the first listing writers necessary for an understanding of the Bible, the second mentioning some basic works on the liberal arts. The *Institutions* circulated north of the Alps from the ninth century and were probably decisive in drawing attention to authors whose books might otherwise have perished. In about 1440 a list of books suitable for a convent library was drawn up for Cosimo de' Medici by Tommaso Parentucelli (later Pope Nicholas V, founder of the Vatican Library) and served as a blueprint for the Biblioteca Malatestiana in Cesena and other collections. Sixteenth-century librarians benefited from the first general bibliography, Conrad Gesner of Zurich's *Bibliotheca Universalis*, 1545, listing 12,000 Greek, Hebrew and Latin books, and his *Appendix Bibliothecae*, 1555, adding a further 3,000.

In 1627 Cardinal Mazarin's librarian, Gabriel Naudé, published his *Advis pour dresser une bibliothèque*. He advised collectors to buy books on all subjects, taking pains to seek out the best commentaries and critical editions; the contents were all-important, and nothing was to be bought on account of its antiquity, appearance or associations. This austere treatise, characteristic of an age of massive erudition (satirised in Arcimboldo's painting 'The Librarian') continued to be standard doctrine on the Continent until the end of the century. But although translated by John Evelyn, its influence on English collecting was limited. Nothing could be in greater contrast to Naudé's ideals than Samuel Pepys's Library, with its illustrated books and fine bindings, oddities and curiosities, English literature and travel, all bought for their owner's enjoyment.

One of the ambitions of eighteenth-century Enlightenment was to make knowledge simpler and learning less burdensome. A new concept of the public library gained acceptance: it was to be limited to 'useful books', meaning in practice a number of standard works such as Buffon's natural history or Montfaucon's antiquities of the French monarchy, most of them too expensive for private owners to afford. Books not satisfying these criteria were liable to be discarded. An anecdote from the early years of the Royal Library, Brussels, illustrates how ruthless the choice might be between 'useful' and 'useless'. On the dissolution of the Jesuit Order in 1773, the books from their Brussels house were allotted to the Royal Library. As the Library had no space to accommodate the new accessions, the volumes were left temporarily in the Jesuit church. The building was infested by mice, and the problem of how to protect the books was anxiously debated. The solution was to employ the secretary of the Literary Society to make a selection. 'Useful books' were to be placed on shelves in the middle of the nave, and the remainder left on the floor. In this way, it was calculated, the mice would satisfy their appetite on the latter, leaving the former unharmed.

Meanwhile the same influences were at work to refine private libraries. Books began again to be appreciated for their appearance, and particularly typography (the century was notable for its fine printers – Baskerville in England, Didot in France, Ibarra in Spain, Bodoni in Italy). The importance of owning superior copies was realised, chosen for their size, condition, binding or provenance. Rarity was highly esteemed and copies on vellum or special paper were all the rage. This French type of collecting was popularised in England by the Reverend Thomas Frognall Dibdin (1776–1847). His bibliographical works, infectiously enthusiastic even if sometimes a little absurd, greatly helped to direct the choice of later collectors such as J. Pierpont Morgan.

The French Revolution and the First Empire introduced a new age. Ecclesiastical libraries were secularised, first in France, then in the Low Countries and Germany. The manuscripts were mostly transferred to provincial depôts; the printed books were often sold. Losses were enormous and rare books were thrown onto the market in vast quantities. Napoleon envisaged a universal library to be formed by wholesale requisitioning of books the Bibliothèque Nationale did not already own. The staff was too busy to adopt this scheme, but the Emperor's centralising ideas inspired a huge expansion of national or semi-national libraries in the nineteenth century (Paris, Berlin, Munich, St Petersburg, London, New York Public Library).

A hundred and fifty years of rapid growth have brought some national institutions to the verge of crisis, and technology may soon be called in to solve their problems of space and staff: microfilms in place of books, computers instead of cataloguers. If so, the results will be as revolutionary as the change from roll to codex in the fourth century, or the invention of printing in the fifteenth. Whether it will be agreeable for the readers is another matter.

Capitular Library

VERONA

The Biblioteca Capitolare of Verona is the oldest library in the world. Of the many metropolitan churches which formed collections of books for the use of the clergy in the two hundred years after Constantine's adoption of Christianity in 312, only Verona has a continuous history to the present. In the fifth century it was one of the few important cities of the Western Empire, the favourite residence of the Ostrogoth Theodoric, with a basilica whose grandeur can be reconstructed in imagination from the large surviving areas of mosaic pavement and the fragments (discovered in 1945) in the form of the Chi-Rho (XP) monogram of the many bronze lamps that lit the interior. Almost certainly the cathedral already possessed a library and scriptorium, in which one or more of the five fifth-century codices it still owns were written. Besides two treatises by St Hilary, Bishop of Poitiers, they include the sermons of Maximinus, the Arian bishop of Ravenna, with marginal notes in a gothic script, evidently copied in a centre ruled by the Arian king of the Ostrogoths. The scriptorium's earliest dated product is a little later: the *Life of St Martin of Tours* by his disciple, Sulpicius Severus, transcribed in 517 by Ursicinus, 'Lector' (the second of the orders of priesthood) 'of the church of Verona'.

Literary texts – histories in particular, but also the Younger Pliny's *Letters* and the poems of Tibullus and Catullus, the latter a native of Verona – entered the library at an early date and must have presented later scribes, especially in the seventh and eighth centuries when vellum was scarce and precious, with a constant temptation to wash off the earlier writing and re-use the material. But palimpsests, commonplace in the Bobbio scriptorium, were unusual, though not unknown, at Verona. A first-century legal textbook, the *Institutions of Gaius*, and the Elder Pliny's *Natural History* were both erased to make room for later works, the *Letters* and *Commentary on Ecclesiasticus* of St Jerome. In the eighth century, probably under Bishop Egino, a German from the abbey of Reichenau, new copies in pre-caroline minuscule were made of some uncial manuscripts; Claudian's poems and the anonymous collections of maxims known as the distichs of Cato, still

ABOVE *St Hilary of Poitiers,* Treatise on the Psalms, *copied in Verona in the fifth century; one of the earliest components of the cathedral collection.*
OPPOSITE *Verona: the eighteenth-century library room, a reconstruction after it was destroyed by bombing in 1945. The bust of Homer was a bequest from Monsignor Francesco Bianchini.*

INCIPIUNT ORATIONES

matutinales · seu et vesp(er)
tinales anni circuli ·

In primis de
nat(ivitate) d(omi)ni ·

Largire q(uaesumu)s d(omi)ne famu
lis tuis fidei et
securitatis aug
mentum ut qui de nativitate
d(omi)ni n(ost)ri ih(es)u xp(ist)i gloriantur
& adversa mundi te gubernante
non sentiant & que tem
poraliter celebrare desiderant

in the Capitolare, and Livy's Roman history, now lost. A collection of sermons now in the Berlin Library was illustrated with miniatures – the earliest surviving example of book illustration from Verona – and a few volumes were acquired from abroad. St Gregory the Great's exposition of the Book of Job (*Moralia in Job*) had been copied in the Burgundian monastery of Luxeuil, and a Mozarabic breviary found its way from Spain, via Sardinia and Pisa, to Verona, where a scribe added a couplet in local dialect, 'he divided the oxen, ploughed the white fields, held a white plough and sowed black seed' – an allegory for writing evidently invented in the scriptorium.

In the early years of the ninth century, a time of relative peace and prosperity under Charlemagne's son, King Pippin, the scriptorium was directed by one of those exceptionally able and energetic men whose careers have often been decisive in the transmission of a text or the history of a library, the Archdeacon Pacificus. He was born in 776, probably of a noble landowning family of Verona, and appointed archdeacon in 801. He evidently felt a deep loyalty to the *schola sacerdotum*, the corporation of cathedral clergy of which he was *ex officio* joint head, and obtained from the bishop a grant of property to pay their salaries as well as exemption from episcopal jurisdiction for the canons. When he died in 844, the residue of his substantial estate, after providing for a charitable inn and oratory and for annual gifts to the poor, was left to the *schola*.

Two years later the Canons erected a memorial tablet in the cathedral. This recorded that Pacificus had been 'outstanding in wisdom and of conspicuous appearance; no such man has been known in our time, or we believe ever' – and listed his skills and achievements. Founder or restorer of seven churches; expert worker in gold, silver and other metals, marble and all kinds of wood; author of a commentary on the Old and New Testaments, and of 'many other writings' (among them a manual on the computus and a topographical glossary of Verona); inventor of a night clock and of a poem attached to it (the latter has been tentatively identified: in two manuscripts it is illustrated by a drawing of an instrument shaped like a telescope, no doubt designed to tell the time from the position of the stars). *Bis centenos terque senos codicesque fecerat* – he 'made' two hundred and eighteen manuscripts: the epitaph's claim, formerly regarded as poetic exaggeration, is now accepted as an exact statement of the scriptorium's output under Pacificus. He has been recognised as the scribe of almost a third of the twenty-seven ninth-century manuscripts remaining in Verona; many of the others contain his corrections and notes. They are written in the beautiful minuscule perfected by the Carolingian Renaissance; Pacificus seems to have taken a leading part in its propagation in Italy. He may have been trained at Reichenau and was certainly in touch with Northern scholars, Archbishop Hincmar of Rheims, to whom he sent the sermons of Verona's fourth-century bishop, St Zeno, and Rabanus Maurus, Abbot of Fulda, whose commentary on Judith and Esther was copied at Verona. Other aspects of his

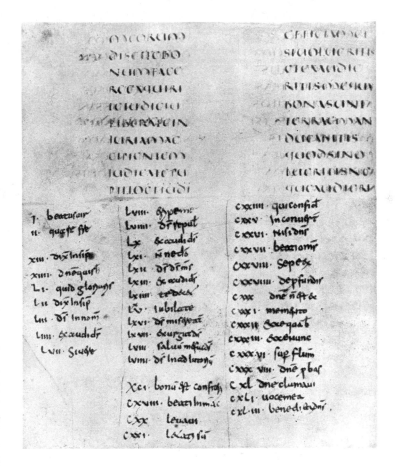

ABOVE *The index to this fifth-century uncial manuscript was added by the Archdeacon Pacificus.* OPPOSITE *One of 218 manuscripts produced by the Verona scriptorium under the Archdeacon Pacificus to restock the cathedral library in the early ninth century. These prayers for morning and evening are in Pacificus's handwriting.* BELOW St Jerome's Commentary on Micah *in the handwriting of the Archdeacon Pacificus, early ninth century.*

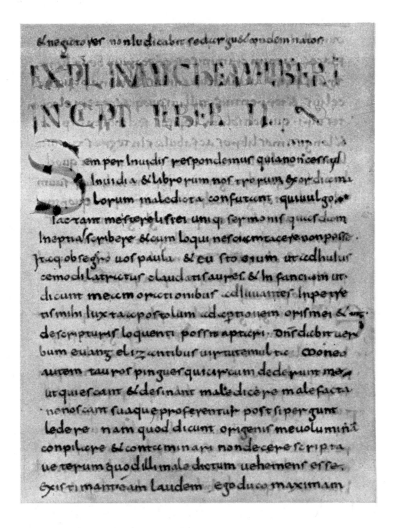

intellectual interests are revealed in an enquiry by a canon of the cathedral, forwarded by Pacificus to a German monk in a Brescian monastery, whether at the Day of Judgement Adam would be among the saved; and in a rather forced comparison of his own composition between the seven grades of the priesthood and episodes in the life of Jesus (e.g., '[Christ] was a *lector* when he opened the book of the Prophet Isaiah'). His favourite light reading, to judge from the frequency of his notes, was the early Christian 'novel', the *Recognitions of Clement*, whose protagonists are St Peter, Clement, the first Pope, and Simon Magus; its stories from Greek mythology, intended to illustrate the immorality of the pagan pantheon, have been attentively studied.

Pacificus's renewal of the Verona Library, designed to provide the clergy and the cathedral school with necessary texts, biblical, liturgical, patristic and conciliar, did not completely exclude secular works. Transcripts were made both of a historical encyclopaedia (now divided between Berlin and Leningrad) and of the collection of biographies of the Roman emperors known as the *Scriptores historiae augustae*. A century after his death the work was continued by Rather, the best scholar of the day, familiar with Plato's *Timaeus*, Horace, Terence and other classical authors. A Fleming, appointed bishop of Verona in 931 by Hugo of Provence, King of Italy, Rather was delighted by the standard of learning in his see, 'another Athens for the multitude of its wise men', and numerous annotations show that he read his way carefully through the library. The anarchic conditions of tenth-century Italy (he was expelled from the diocese three times) prevented any comprehensive modernisation or enlargement of the collection as had been possible in the Carolingian era. But the scriptorium was still at the high level of competence it had attained under Pacificus, and under Rather's direction it completed at least one major enterprise, the preparation of two copies of the pre-caroline Livy. One remained in the cathedral to replace the eighth-century exemplar which in accordance with normal practice was destroyed after being copied. The other was presented to the Emperor and found its way to the cathedral of Worms; rediscovered by Beatus Rhenanus in the sixteenth century, it was used for the edition printed by Froben at Basle in 1535.

Bishop Egino is thought to have taken some Verona books to Reichenau and Rather may have removed others. For the next three hundred years, though the collection continued to be replenished with new works, the early manuscripts were forgotten, until in the late thirteenth and early fourteenth century a school of rhetoric arose in Padua whose exponents started to explore the ancient libraries of the region. Their earliest discoveries were Seneca's *Tragedies* in the abbey of Pomposa and Rather's Livy at Verona. The unique manuscript of Catullus to have survived from antiquity, the source of all modern knowledge of his poems, was the next to attract attention; it was known to Benevenuto Campesani of Vicenza, and probably copied by him before 1323. In 1317 the French Dominican Bernard Gui, on a mission from the Pope to the tyrant of Verona, Can Grande della

The Capitular Library after rebuilding in 1948, with the cathedral and campanile behind it.

St Hilary of Poitiers, On the Trinity, *in fifth-century uncials.*

Scala, came upon the library's rich collection of early councils. Eleven years later a friend of Petrarch's father, ser Simone d'Arezzo, took up residence in the city as canon of the cathedral, and almost immediately occupied himself in transcribing the Livy. Petrarch was shown the transcript and entered its variant readings in his own copy, which in turn was used a century later by Lorenzo Valla for his influential work on the text, *Emendationes in T.Livium*. In 1339–41 Dante's son Pietro used the library to write his commentary on the *Divine Comedy*.

Petrarch himself first visited Verona in 1345, a fugitive from an outbreak of local warfare in Lombardy, and was overjoyed to find in the cathedral, and copy, Cicero's letters *To Atticus, Brutus and Quintus*, on which he modelled his own style in correspondence. In later years through his friendship with Guglielmo da Pastrengo, chancellor to Cansignorio della Scala, he was able to add to his personal library other works derived from the Capitolare: Varro's advice to farmers, the *De re rustica* (the author's only work to survive complete), the *Eclogues* of two minor poets, Calpurnius and Nemesianus, and the *Scriptores historiae augustae*, of which he first obtained a copy, in 1356, and later the ninth-century original.

These early humanists, who seem to have been allowed free access to the library, recovered its ancient texts just in time, as with the crumbling of the della Scala dynasty's authority after 1375 the collection was extensively plundered. The Catullus, Varro and Cicero disappeared; the Livy was appropriated by Antonio da Legnago, one of the four regents for Cansignorio's infant sons; another regent, Giacomo da San Sebastiano, laid hands on an eleventh-century Orosius and an Augustine presented to the cathedral by Pacificus and bearing the archdeacon's solemn malediction on book-thieves. Other volumes passed into the possession of the victorious Visconti rulers of Milan and were eventually removed to Blois by King Louis XII of France with the rest of the Milanese ducal library from the castle of Pavia. The copy of Pliny's *Letters* was last seen by Guarino Veronese in 1419. Probably over four-fifths of the manuscripts present in Rather's day were lost before or soon after 1400.

The chief event in the Capitolare's modern history was the construction of the first library building in 1728, as a consequence of renewed interest in the collection caused by an unlikely sequence of events. In 1630 the librarian, Canon Rezzani, hid the most ancient manuscripts to protect them from foreign troops gathering to attack Mantua. Soon afterwards he and eleven other members of the chapter succumbed to plague, taking the secret of the hiding-place with them to the grave. The early codices were forgotten and their existence denied when the French Maurist scholars, Montfaucon and Mabillon, visited Verona on their Italian journeys. At last in 1713 the historian Scipione Maffei persuaded Canon Carinelli to lay aside temporarily his genealogical studies in order to search for the missing books. They were discovered in the hollow top of a cupboard outside the canons' common-room, concealed under layers of rags and boards. The news, carried instantly to Maffei, so excited him that he ran into

the street dressed in dressing-gown, nightcap and slippers.

Gifts and bequests poured into the library in the aftermath of this sensation: the collections of Monsignor Francesco Bianchini, antiquarian and astronomer, and of Giovanni Morosini, Bishop of Verona; the manuscripts and papers of Scipione Maffei; Matthias Corvinus, King of Hungary's *Livy*, a present from the Bevilacqua family. Since the German historian, Barthold Niebuhr, discovered the submerged *Institutions of Gaius* in 1816 the collection has attracted the leading palaeographers of Europe and America. One of those to visit Verona was Léopold Delisle, the great director of the French National Library. In a letter of 1885 to one of his colleagues in Paris, he wrote of 'a day of debauch among manuscripts, few in number but of such venerable antiquity that I thought I was dreaming when I saw so many treasures assembled on a few shabby shelves.'

War has dealt Verona two hard blows. On 16 May 1797, 'the luckless day' in the words of a former librarian, the French commissioners, in pursuance of the national policy of removing Italian works of art to Paris, appropriated thirty manuscripts and fourteen incunabula, not all of which were recovered after Waterloo. On 4 January 1945, a Liberator bomber out of formation and off course released its bombs on Verona. The library suffered a direct hit and was totally destroyed. The manuscripts, incunabula and archives had been removed to safety but many later printed books were lost. No time was lost in clearing the débris and starting to rebuild: a new library was inaugurated on 28 September 1948, 'much more beautiful', declares Monsignor Giuseppe Turrini, who has been librarian since 1922, 'and more spacious than the old one', and a monument to his own faith and determination in disaster.

Abbey Library

ST GALL

Like explorers searching for relics of civilisation in a continent devastated by nuclear war, a party of Irish missionaries led by St Columban made their way across Europe in the early seventh century. Passing through territory occupied by heathen Alemannic tribes they arrived at the former Roman town of Brigantia (Bregenz) on Lake Constance. Here they halted to proselytise the inhabitants who had relapsed into paganism. Two years later Columban and his companions travelled on to Lombardy to found the monastery of Bobbio, but one of the Irish, Gall, remained, and with two local disciples established a cell in mountainous wooded country south of the lake. There after his death a church containing his relics continued to be tended. About 720, an Alemannic priest, Otmar, became the first abbot of a monastic congregation grouped round the shrine, which under the second abbot adopted the Benedictine Rule. Its early years were harsh, but in the ninth century, through the favour of Louis the Pious and other Carolingian emperors, and under a remarkable series of abbots – Gozbert (816–36), Grimald (841–72), Hartmut (872–83) and Salomo III (890–920) – it grew to be one of the greatest religious houses in central Europe.

Manuscripts began to be copied at St Gall in Otmar's time. From about 760 the dean, Winithar, led the scriptorium in the production of books of the Bible and patristic works. They were hampered by lack of materials; Winithar's colophon to a copy of the Pauline epistles contains a plea: 'If then it seems to you useful that so insignificant a person as I should write something for you, give me your vellum . . .', but the vellum he was obliged to use was dirty yellow in colour and full of tears and holes. In spite of his labours, Ratpert, the ninth-century annalist, records 'a very great shortage of books' before Gozbert's abbacy. During his term well-prepared white vellum became available and the monastery's entire complement seems to have collaborated in the urgent task of enlarging the collection: a hundred scribes' hands have been noted in the St Gall manuscripts of Gozbert's time.

For new works St Gall was mainly dependent on the great religious houses of southern Germany, especially on Reichenau,

ABOVE *A self-portrait by Wendelgarius, the scribe of this collection of German laws in the year 793.*
OPPOSITE *St John the Evangelist, by an Irish artist of the second half of the eighth century; from a Gospels, probably carried to St Gall by an Irish pilgrim in the ninth century.*

the island-abbey in Lake Constance with which there seems to have been a regular exchange of manuscript exemplars. There were close relations with St Boniface's foundation of Fulda, the source of some famous philological documents at St Gall, or of their exemplars: the earliest manuscript of Bede's death-song in Anglo-Saxon; a Latin-German word-list of *c.* 780 known as the *Vocabularius Sancti Galli*; and Tatian's life of Jesus in Latin with an Old High German translation. A second eighth-century word-list, in Bavarian dialect, known from its first word as the *Abrogans*, is perhaps from Freising.

From Italy venerable manuscripts found their way to St Gall along the pilgrim routes: a fifth-century uncial Vergil; the earliest manuscript of the Vulgate Gospels, 'written . . . possibly during the lifetime of Jerome' (Lowe); the seventh-century *Edicts* of the Lombard King Rotharis from Pavia or Bobbio. Palimpsests, perhaps rewritten in Milan or Chur, concealed submerged fragments of Terence's plays and of the fifth-century Roman poet Flavius Merobaudes. From the West the abbey received a seventh-century papyrus codex of Isidore of Seville's *Synonyma* from southern France, and the oldest surviving Bible written in the great scriptorium of Tours.

Under Abbot Grimald the work of the scriptorium was rationalised, with fewer but more expert scribes. A librarian was appointed and the first catalogue of the library compiled. The collection numbered 316 volumes, its contents conforming to the Carolingian Renaissance's ideal of Christian antiquity revived. The Bible, the Church Fathers with Bede and Alcuin, saints' lives and homilies, the Christian poets Juvencus, Sedulius, Prudentius and Alcimus Avitus, Bishop of Vienne, as well as Boethius and Vergil, were the basis of ninth-century St Gall learning. Beside

the familiar titles by Augustine, Ambrose, Jerome and Gregory were less known works rarely present in later foundations – the *Revelations* of St Methodius, Tichonius's lost commentary on the Apocalypse – and some no doubt owed to the abbey's connections with the British Isles: the commentary on the Pauline epistles of the British heresiarch Pelagius (who denied original sin), and the *Letters* of Faustus, the semi-Pelagian Breton Bishop of Riez.

Secular works were limited to a few on the computus, astronomy, law, grammar and spelling, and Gregory of Tours' *History of the Franks*, to which Grimald and Hartmut added the Trojan War and other histories, some medical books, Martianus Capella's *Nuptials of Mercury with Philology* (whose account of the liberal arts influenced all medieval education), Vegetius on military tactics and 'a map of the world of delicate workmanship'.

The catalogue has a unique feature: it starts with thirty volumes headed *Libri scottice scripti*, 'books written in Irish script'. The compiler was mistaken in believing them all to be Irish: at least one text, by the choirmaster in the Northumbrian monastery of Wearmouth, was probably of English origin. That the other books were the remains of Gall's library or were written by Irish monks in the abbey are suggestions now entirely abandoned; it is agreed that they probably reached St Gall as gifts from Irish travellers. Throughout the ninth century the pilgrimage roads through the Low Countries and the Rhineland to Rome were thronged with Irish scholars of striking appearance, with painted eyelids and the front part of the head shaved. To them, remarked the contemporary *Life of Gall*, 'the habit of wandering has become almost a second nature'. The tomb of their saintly fellow-countryman was a recognised stage on the journey. A record has survived of one such visit by pilgrims returning from Rome, an Irish bishop Marcus and his nephew Moengal, the latter 'very learned in sacred and profane knowledge'. The bishop made a prolonged stay, dismissed his retainers and presented his books, gold and ceremonial vestment, the pallium, to the monastery. His nephew joined the community and was given charge of the novices' school.

To the Germanic monks of St Gall the *libri scottice scripti* must have seemed mere curiosities, barely legible and of little practical use. This is the reason for their segregation in the catalogue (which otherwise is arranged by subject and author) and for their almost complete disappearance. Apart from fragments, only three manuscripts written in Ireland survive in the library: an eighth-century Gospels with magnificent miniatures and ornamental pages; a St John's Gospel of about 800; and Priscian's *Grammar* of the ninth century, with Old Irish glosses and marginal verses. One of the quatrains gives an idyllic picture of an Irish scribe's life: 'The clear-voiced cuckoo sings me a lovely chant, in her grey cloak from bush to bush. God's Doom, may the Lord protect me! – happily I write under the greenwood.'

A certain cultivation of Greek studies at St Gall is thought to have been introduced by the Irish. Moengal seems to have had some knowledge of the language, transmitted to his pupil

OVERLEAF *A double-page from the Golden Psalter, written and illuminated at St Gall in the late ninth century, illustrating two verses from Psalm 59:* LEFT *'Thou hast given a banner to them that fear thee, that it may be displayed because of the truth':* RIGHT *'who will lead me into the strong city? who will lead me into Edom?'*

ETSYRIAM SOBAL · ETCONVERTIT
IOAB · ETPERCVSSIT EDOM INVAL
LE SALINARVM · XII MILIA ·

ASCENSIO SCE MARIE

S GALL? PANE PORRIGITUR SO

Notker Balbulus ('the Stammerer') and by the latter to Salomo III. Notker spoke of 'the Hellenic brethren' of the monastery, probably referring to this group of students. An elementary Greek grammar was transcribed in the abbey; Notker borrowed the canonical epistles in Greek from Liutward, the Swabian bishop of Vercelli, and succeeded 'with great travail' in copying them; and the library also possesses a Greek Gospels with Latin interlinear translation written in an Irish colony on the Continent (perhaps at Liège), to which has been added a list of gospel illustrations apparently taken from a Byzantine illuminated model. These Greek traces seem insignificant by Renaissance standards, but were quite exceptional for their period.

The period following Salomo III's death was one of relative eclipse. The abbey was sacked by the Hungarians in 926 and destroyed by fire eleven years afterwards, though on each occasion the books were saved. Notker Labeo ('Large Lips', c. 950–1022) led an intellectual revival in the late tenth century, characterised by a new interest in classical literature. Horace, Lucan, Sallust, Ovid, Juvenal, Quintilian and Statius, Cicero's *Topics* and other works and Seneca's burlesque *Apotheosis of the Emperor Claudius* were copied in the scriptorium. Situated at an international crossroads, St Gall was active in recording and disseminating scarce texts. A letter from Notker Labeo to Bishop Hugo of Sion throws light on this process: the abbot of Reichenau had borrowed the bishop's copy of Cicero's *First Philippic* and deposited instead Cicero's *De inventione* and Victorinus's commentary; if the books the bishop wanted were to be supplied, he must send more vellum and money for the copyists – a clear indication that the scriptorium employed and paid outsiders, presumably secular priests.

St Gall did not only transmit; several notable works were composed by its monks: Notker Balbulus's *Life of Charlemagne*, Ekkehard I's epic poem *Waltharius*, Ratpert's and Ekkehard IV's annals of the monastery, Notker Labeo's treatise on musical theory and his German translations of the Psalter, Boethius, Aristotle, Terence and Vergil. A famous school of illumination flourished in the ninth and eleventh centuries; one of its most celebrated products, the *Evangelium longum*, was bound in carved ivory covers, at least one of which was the work of a St Gall monk.

All these achievements belonged to a remote past when a General Council of the Church met in Constance in 1414. The abbey's intellectual life had long been sunk in torpor, and additions to its library since the eleventh century had amounted to little beyond a handful of legal books and a few works by Bernard, Anselm and later authors (though one manuscript preserved a rare text: the Gaulish Bishop Arculf's account of the Near East in about 670). In the summer of 1416 three Tuscan secretaries employed by the Papal Curia, Poggio Bracciolini, Cencio Rustici and Bartolomeo da Montepulciano, with some unnamed companions, decided to take a holiday from their duties at the Council. They chose to visit St Gall, which was rumoured to have an ancient library. Almost at once they dis-

The hermit Hartker, who was immured in a minute cell in the abbey for thirty-one years, presenting a manuscript he has copied to St Gall, c. AD 1000.

OPPOSITE *An ivory panel by a St Gall monk, Tuotilo, on the lower cover of the* Evangelium longum, *copied in the abbey c. 900 AD. The scenes are of the Assumption of the Virgin, and a bear helping St Gall to build his cell.*

covered a complete copy of Quintilian's *Education of an orator*, which they knew only in a very imperfect form, and three works unknown in Italy: Valerius Flaccus's *Argonautica* and two commentaries on Cicero's orations. They were allowed to borrow them to copy. The Quintilian is still in existence, but the others have vanished. Cencio Rustici noticed the papyrus manuscript of Isidore of Seville, and although deploring its incomplete state and unclassical content, clasped it rapturously to his heart 'on account of its holy and incorrupt antiquity'. But the humanists were roused to anger by the sight of 'innumerable books' in sad condition in Hartmut's tower adjoining the church. Cencio declared that they wept together to see them 'defiled by dust, worms, soot and everything else that destroys books', and vented his indignation against the prince-abbot, Heinrich von Gundelfingen, and the whole community: 'The abbot and monks of that monastery are foreign to any knowledge of letters. O barbarous country hostile to the Latin tongue! O most abandoned scourings of humanity!'

Nearly two generations after Poggio's visit, St Gall experienced an intellectual renewal under an exceptionally talented abbot, Ulrich Rösch (1463–91), who had started life in the monastery as a scullion. Before his election he had already arranged for the books to be recatalogued and many to be rebound; unfortunately, many unwanted early manuscripts were discarded in the process of reorganisation, the uncial Vergil and Gospels among them, and are known only by the chance survival of fragments used as endleaves. He revived the monastic school, sent some of the younger monks to universities and allotted the library a regular annual grant of one hundred guilders for purchases. The money was spent on a wide range of printed books – theology, philosophy, law, travel, Latin classics, humanistic works and popular German romances – thus almost doubling the size of the collection. The library also benefited from bequests, one being from a monk named Gall Kemly. He had taken monastic vows at the age of eleven but later found conventual discipline intolerable and spent most of his adult life outside the abbey walls. As well as a few manuscripts, largely written by himself, he owned two blockbooks; and his habit of pasting single-sheet woodcuts into his books has been the means of preserving many unique examples.

A curious revival of the scriptorium, by then defunct for over three hundred years, took place in the sixteenth century. Abbot Franz von Gaisberg (1504–29) summoned Leonhard Wagner, an Augsburg Benedictine, to train two young monks in calligraphy, and Niklaus Bertschi of Rorschach, a lay illuminator. Under Abbot Diethelm Blarer (1530–64) a number of servicebooks were copied by the monastery's organist, Fridolin Sicher (author of a chronicle), and his pupil, Heinrich Keller, an inmate of St Gall. A gradual and an antiphoner, transcribed by the latter in 1562, with music commissioned by Diethelm Blarer from an Italian, Manfred Barbarini Lupus, and miniatures by a professional artist, Caspar Härtli of Lindau, were the last elaborate manuscripts produced in the abbey.

St Gall: the baroque library room of 1758, designed by the elder and younger Peter Thumb.

An architect's plan of about 830, preserved at St Gall and associated with Abbot Gozbert's rebuilding of the monastery, shows a special room for books above the scriptorium, but it is uncertain to what extent the plan was carried into execution, and the date of the earliest library-room cannot be determined. In the late Middle Ages the books in regular use were kept in the library, while the older manuscripts remained in Hartmut's tower for many years after Poggio's visit. The Swiss historian, Johann Strümpf, described them in 1548 lying 'in a disorderly heap . . . guarded like sacred relics in the vaulted chamber of an old tower'. Rather earlier the Swabian doctor and humanist, Gabriel Hummelberg, had informed Beatus Rhenanus that 'no one, or very few people, and only those who are known and selected, are allowed access [to the library] or to see much.' Abbot Diethelm Blarer laid the foundation stone of a new library in 1551, which Abbot Celestine II Gugger von Staudach replaced in 1758 with the present baroque room, designed by the elder and younger Peter Thumb.

St Gall has suffered losses on many occasions. Its Protestant neighbours of the town occupied the abbey in 1530 and removed the books; several were retained by the humanist burgomaster, Joachim von Watt (Vadianus), when peace was made and the majority given back. A second occupation, by the troops of Zurich and Berne intervening on behalf of the prince-abbot's rebellious subjects in the Toggenburg, took place in 1712. This time the monastery was stripped of all its movable possessions and did not recover its books, again with many deficiencies, for eight years. As replacements Abbot Beda Angehrn bought in 1768 the manuscript collection formed by Gilg Tschudi of Zurich (1506–72) which included a famous thirteenth-century codex of three German epics, Wolfram von Eschenbach's *Parzival* and *Willehalm*, and the *Nibelungenlied*. The abbey was secularised by a decree of the Great Council of St Gall in 1805. Its buildings and books became the property of the Catholic inhabitants of the canton, and the library has since been open to the public.

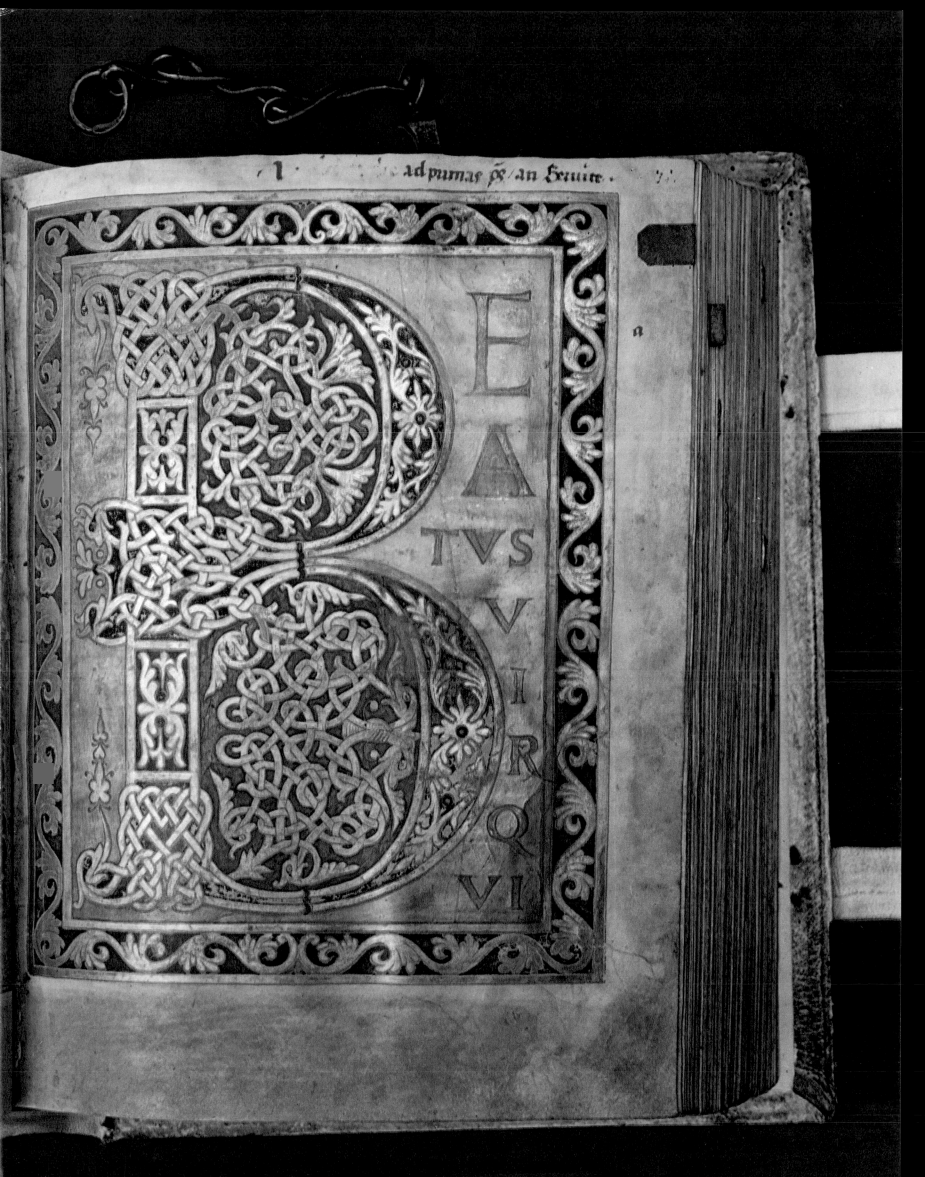

BEATVS VIR QVI

State Library

BAMBERG

ABOVE *Bamberg: the twelfth-century cathedral founded by the Emperor Henry II.* OPPOSITE *The Church leading the blessed, purified by baptism, to the crucified Saviour; a miniature from a Commentary on the Song of Songs, written and illuminated at Reichenau in the late tenth century, which belonged to the earliest stratum of the Bamberg Cathedral Library.*

Between the close of antiquity and the thirteenth century books in the Latin West were largely, though not quite exclusively, in the hands of the clergy. A few laymen who owned private collections are known: Einhard, Charlemagne's biographer, at the close of the eighth century, Count Heccard in Burgundy and the Margrave Eberhard of Friuli in the ninth, and of course Charlemagne himself, whose library was sold and the proceeds given to charity at his death. Only one group of books from a lay foundation of the period survives; they belonged to the library assembled by the Emperor Henry II in Bamberg Cathedral.

Bamberg was Henry II's brain-child. A hill-fortress when he came to the throne in 1002, it had grown nineteen years later into a walled city, the seat of a bishop, with a cathedral which Pope Benedict VIII had travelled from Rome to consecrate, a Benedictine abbey dedicated to St Michael (the Michelsberg) and a collegiate church (St Stephen). The founder intended it to be the leading spiritual and intellectual centre in south Germany; its canons were to 'equal the clergy of Liège in knowledge and those of Hildesheim in the intensity of their religious life'. Several cathedral schools already existed in Germany; they taught a wider range of subjects than the monastic schools and were valuable for training sons of the nobility as potential high officers of Church and State. Henry, who had himself been educated at the Hildesheim school, lost no time in setting one up at Bamberg. A master, Durandus, was brought from Liège, and a dedicatory poem of 1014 by Abbot Gerhard of Seeon provides the information that the school was then already conducting courses in the higher learning, teaching the more advanced *Quadrivium* (Arithmetic, Geometry, Astronomy and Music) as well as the *Trivium* (Grammar, Rhetoric and Dialectics).

The texts provided by the Emperor for the school can be deduced from medieval records, notably a list of 130 books issued to the master in about 1200, and from existing manuscripts. The models for the cultivation of a good Latin style were Horace, Macrobius, Aulus Gellius, Persius's satires, probably Terence's plays, Ovid's *Amores* or *Ars amatoria,* the *Thebaid* of Statius,

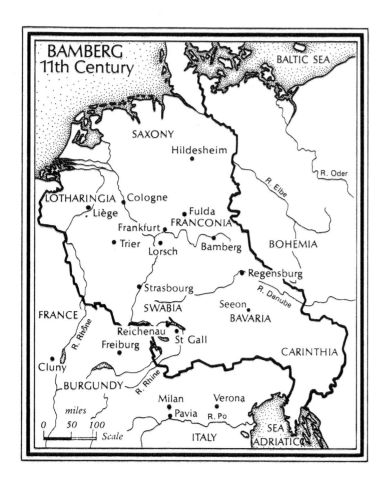

Claudian's poems abusing the eunuch Eutropius, an incomplete copy of Seneca's letters, a fourth-century play (the *Aulularia*, said to have suggested the plot of Molière's *L'Avare*), the *Aeneid* and perhaps the *Bucolics*, which appears in the schoolmaster's list under the odd title 'Translation of Vergil from Greek to Latin'. The school seems to have paid particular attention to dialectics and there was a strong historical section with parts of three decades of Livy, the *Scriptores historiae augustae*, Dares Phrygius on the siege of Troy, Josephus's history of the Jews, a collection of Dark Age chronicles, St Victor of Vita's account of the persecution of the African Church and numerous saints' lives. The pupils could also consult two medical miscellanies, Justinian's *Institutions* (a rare work at this period), two copies of Vegetius's military manual, and 'a book on architecture', probably Vitruvius.

This is an impressive list, amounting to over two hundred volumes, including duplicates, about half of which survive; but the number of books in circulation had greatly declined since the abbey library of Lorsch counted 590 volumes in the ninth century. The quantity of imperfect copies (three of four codices of Pope Gregory's *Moralia in Job* are incomplete) is further evidence of the rigours of collecting in that harsh age.

When it came to providing service-books for the cathedral, no expense was too great, no ornament too lavish. Four are still bound in gold studded with jewels and nearly all are splendidly illuminated, the majority by a school of artists that executed many imperial commissions, believed to have worked in the abbey of Reichenau, on an island in Lake Constance, or, according to a recent suggestion, in the cathedral city of Trier. One miniature represents Henry II's coronation by the hands of Christ: in another, based on a late antique model, he appears enthroned in the full glory of his regalia, receiving tribute from the provinces. A pair of graduals, traditionally known as the Prayer-books of Henry II and the Empress Cunigunde, have bindings of great elegance made from the leaves of two Byzantine ivory diptychs: the manuscripts were written in the monastery of Seeon, possibly for use by the imperial pair at the dedication ceremony of the Michelsberg Abbey.

The schoolbooks had extremely varied origins. The nucleus seems to have been derived from the private library of Henry's two predecessors, Otto II and III. Not all had been acquired in creditable ways. The annalist of St Gall related that in 972 the Emperor Otto I arrived with his son to spend some days in the abbey. During the visit the future Otto II discovered a locked chest in the treasury and asked for it to be opened. Apprehensively, but not daring to refuse, the abbot complied. It was full of books, from which the Crown Prince chose and removed the best. 'He later returned some of them at Ekkehard [the Deacon's] request', the account ruefully concludes. A psalter now at Bamberg, with the Gallican, Roman, Hebrew and Greek versions of the psalms in parallel columns (the first three in Latin, the last in Greek but written in roman characters) copied in 909 for the abbot-bishop of St Gall, Salomo III, seems to have been one of

Byzantine ivory panels of St Paul and Jesus Christ, used on the bindings of the 'Prayer-books of Henry II and the Empress Cunigunde'.

the volumes not returned. The *Heliand*, a ninth-century Christian epic in Old Saxon, is another book that evidently belonged to the Ottonian family.

Many books were provided by south German monasteries: Seeon, Fulda, St Emmeram's at Regensburg, Reichenau (the apparent source of a volume containing Cuthbert's letter on the death of Bede) and probably others. Henry, later canonised, was a favourite with monks. Bebo, possibly the head of the Seeon scriptorium, addressed him as 'sweetest one' and 'dearest Caesar' when presenting a copy of Gregory's *Moralia in Job* which the Emperor had expressed a wish to own, and only asked for his affection to be returned as recompense for his labour; and the anonymous monk-scribe of Gregory's *Commentaries on Ezechiel* called himself 'dear Caesar, your poor friend'.

Even after centuries of anarchy and invasion, Italy had not entirely exhausted its store of late antique manuscripts and its monasteries preserved many rare and surprising texts. Each of the three Ottos visited Rome and Otto II struggled at the head of an army into southern Calabria; Henry II led three expeditions across the Alps and was crowned in Pavia and in Rome. Many manuscripts made the return journey in the imperial baggage, to be rediscovered in the fifteenth century in the recesses of German libraries by Poggio and other humanists. Illuminated service-books were tactfully distributed in exchange, such as the Gospels produced at Regensburg for Henry II, now in the Vatican (Ottoboniano lat. 74). Seventeen manuscripts at Bamberg may have been brought back from these travels. The oldest, a sixth-century collection of works by Jerome and Gennadius of Marseilles, was written in south Italy but possibly acquired in Rome. An eighth-century volume, marked 'Archetype, from whose

ABOVE *The vision of Isaiah; from a glossed Book of Isaiah illuminated at Reichenau c. 1000.* BELOW *The Emperor Henry II holding a jewelled Gospel-book; a miniature from the Bavarian abbey of Seeon, early eleventh century.*

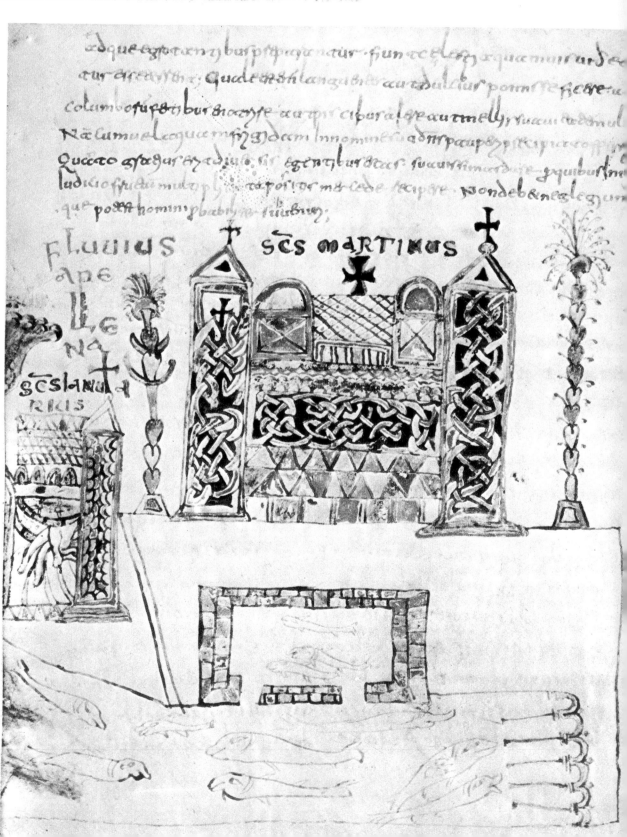

LEFT *The interior of a church, with altar, round window and officiating bishop; from a collection of tracts in defence of Pope Formosus, perhaps from Naples, early tenth century.* BELOW *Cassiodorus's monastery at Squillace in southern Italy; its two churches are shown as well as the fish-ponds (*vivaria*) which gave it its name. From the earliest surviving manuscript of Cassiodorus's* Institutions: *copied, perhaps at Monte Cassino, in the eighth century.*

ABOVE *Job and his wife; from a manuscript of St Gregory's* Moralia in Job *copied in Italy (perhaps in Rome), c. 1000.* BELOW *The monk Bebo presenting another copy of Gregory's* Moralia in Job *to Henry II; the Holy Spirit is seen above, dictating to the author.*

readings other copies are to be corrected', probably belonged to Monte Cassino; it contains the oldest authority for the text of Cassiodorus's *Institutions*, that indispensable guide for the medieval librarian, illustrated with a drawing of the author's monastery at Squillace, together with the only complete copy to survive of Gregory of Tours' *On the courses of the stars*. A unique collection of polemical tracts in defence of Pope Formosus (who died in 896), written, possibly in Naples, soon after the unfortunate pontiff's corpse had been exhumed by his successor, arrayed in papal robes, tried and condemned, may have been presented to Otto III by Bishop Leo of Vercelli. And a third unique manuscript, probably copied in Milan under Archbishop Arnulf II (998–1018), was the means of bringing to northern Europe the Latin translation of the Greek *Life of Alexander the Great*, which, in vernacular versions, became a best-seller in the later Middle Ages.

Several French and Flemish manuscripts seem to represent the response to a broadcast appeal from Henry II. St Odilo of Cluny sent his commentary on St Paul's epistles, Bishop Baldric of Liège a Gregorian sacramentary, Jumièges the lives of its abbots Philibert and Aichadrus and of Archbishop Hugh of Rouen, Rheims Archbishop Hincmar's *Life of St Rémy* and Richer of St Rémy's *History* (though Ludwig Traube, the great palaeographer, believed that the latter had been presented to Pope Sylvester II and by him to Otto III), Stavelot or Malmédy extracts from their archives and the Life of St Remaclus of Stavelot, Lobbes or St Vaast their annals, accompanied by a table of world history to the year 735. Other volumes, from as far away as Brittany, were perhaps brought to Germany by refugees from the Viking invasions. At least three manuscripts are associated with the Carolingian Emperor Charles the Bald and John Eriugena, the Irish master of his palace school in the mid-ninth century: Eriugena's *De divisione naturae* written at Rheims soon after 850, with his autograph notes and corrections; a splendidly illuminated Bible of about 840 from the scriptorium of St Martin's at Tours; and a Boethius, *Arithmetic*, of great elegance, written and decorated at Tours for Charles the Bald. Associated manuscripts, now at Munich, formerly belonged to St Emmeram's, Regensburg, and it is possible that part of Charles the Bald's library was given by the Emperor Arnulf in 893 or shortly afterwards to the Regensburg monks, who were persuaded by Henry II to hand over books to Bamberg a century later.

In about 1615 a Belgian Jesuit, Joseph Horrion, made a systematic examination of the classical texts in the library and was amazed to discover a late tenth-century Livy containing the first seventeen chapters of Book 33, previously unknown. (He published the *editio princeps* in Rome the following year.) In the nineteenth century this volume was associated with a note in another Bamberg manuscript recording a gift of books to Otto III in Piacenza about 996 from the Archbishop, John Philagathos, a Greek protégé of the Empress-mother Theophano, shortly afterwards captured in rebellion and blinded; the list includes

The three Marys at the empty tomb: drawing and miniature of the same subject. Liège work of the early eleventh century.

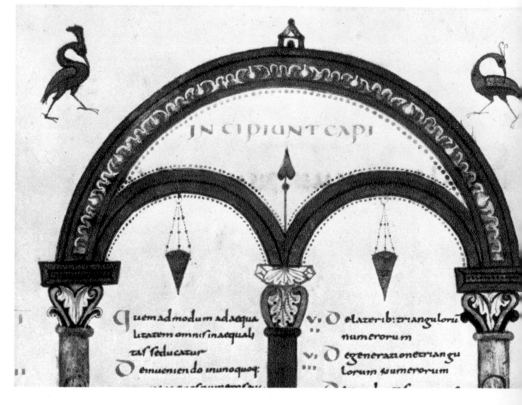

A manuscript of Boethius's Arithmetic written and illuminated at Tours for the Emperor Charles the Bald in the ninth century.
ABOVE *a decorative initial 'S'*. ABOVE RIGHT *architectural decoration of the table of chapters.* RIGHT *Boethius presenting his book to the Roman patrician Symmachus.*

'two books of Titus Livius'. Finally, in 1904, fragments of a fifth-century uncial codex of Livy's fourth decade were noticed in the bindings of two books from the cathedral library and one from the Carmelite convent of Bamberg. It can be concluded that Otto III received the uncial manuscript from John Philagathos in Piacenza and had it copied; Henry II gave both the original and the copy to the canons of Bamberg, whose fifteenth-century successors, finding the characters indecipherable and having forgotten the book's history, sold the former to a bookbinder for the value of the vellum.

There was never a scriptorium in the cathedral, but manuscripts seem to have been readily lent in the eleventh century for copying. Copies of many cathedral exemplars were made for the Michelsberg Abbey, and of at least two, Abbot Salomo's quadripartite psalter and Quintilian's *Institutio oratoria*, for Cologne Cathedral, whose Archbishop Anno, a former master of the Bamberg school, also requested the loan of a Cassiodorus (probably the Monte Cassino 'archetype') in 1064. The Cologne codex of the *Institutio oratoria* (now in the British Museum, Harley 2664) was in turn copied for Strasbourg (now in the Laurenziana) and St Gall, where Poggio transcribed it in 1416. In this way the Bamberg Quintilian was a direct ancestor of the *editio princeps*, printed in Rome in 1470.

With the development of universities in the thirteenth century the school ceased to be of more than local importance. The ancient manuscripts, no longer needed for teaching nor providing the legal and scholastic texts then in demand, were stored in chests in one of the towers and no doubt rarely, if ever, used, though the chapter paid to rebind several in 1454. The only humanist to gain access to the collection was Johann Hess, the Protestant preacher of Breslau, who noted a few patristic works. Dürer's friend, Billibald Pirckheimer, enquired in vain. Ulrich von Hütten removed a book and failed to return it, but as it is described as 'chained', it must have been a service-book from the choir or the printed *Catholicon* that was kept in the church. As late as 1784 Ph. W. Gercken wrote, 'whether there is a library in the cathedral, I could not exactly discover', but by this time other scholars had been admitted and had described some manuscripts. When ecclesiastical property was secularised in 1803 the cathedral library ceased to exist. Four gospel-books in jewelled bindings, the *Heliand* and two others were removed to Munich: the remainder joined the books from the town's religious houses in the State Library. Since 1965 the Library has occupied the former bishop's palace on the cathedral square and Henry II's manuscripts can be consulted within sight of the tower where they were kept for eight centuries.

ABOVE *Monks of the Michelsberg Abbey with their patron, the Archangel Michael, twelfth century. The roundels show stages in the production of a bound codex.* BELOW *Bamberg: the seventeenth-century bishop's palace now housing the State Library. As this photograph shows, it stands in the shadow of the cathedral's towers.*

43

Abbey Library

ADMONT

'And so, most beloved one,' Abbot Gottfried of Admont wrote about 1150 to one of his former monks transferred to another convent,

I wish you to send us something we do not possess from the famous library of your church, either to be copied or copied by you [i.e. either a copy or the exemplar to be transcribed and returned], so that our need may be supplied from your abundance and through it the memory of your love may grow warm among us. The work by Josephus – the destruction of Jerusalem and the famous Roman triumph of Vespasian and Titus – I beg you to make careful and exact enquiries whether your house owns it and in true charity not to delay sending it to us to copy, since long ago I was reliably informed that you owned the work, but I have never been able to see it.

Josephus was not uncommon, so the letter must date from an early stage of Gottfried's campaign to re-equip the Admont Library which had not recovered from the monastery's sack by imperialist partisans in the War of Investitures (the second abbot found it 'almost desolate' in 1090). Standing in the mountainous valley of the Enns in northern Styria (Austria), it had been founded in 1074 by Archbishop Gebhard of Salzburg with monks from the Benedictine abbey of St Peter's in that city, and endowed by the founder with 'precious ornaments of gold and silver, priestly vestments of silk, books, chalices and everything necessary for the divine offices.' The context suggests that the books were liturgical: among existing manuscripts convent tradition identifies only a large two-volume Italian Bible, with impressive initials but no miniatures, as Gebhard's gift. For other essential books the first abbot, Isingrin, would no doubt have applied initially to St Peter's. The mother-house appears to have passed on a mixed lot of duplicates: patristic works a century old, a second Italian Bible, a glossed psalter perhaps from Farfa, near Rome. Only a Gospel-book to lie on the altar was new and splendid, Salzburg work of the finest quality by a scribe and artist whose name, 'Custos Perhtolt', is known from a signed manuscript for St Peter's.

Gottfried, elected abbot in 1137, had literary tastes and has

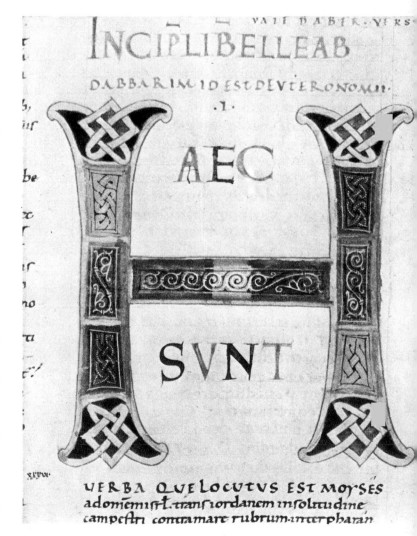

Initial H (the opening of Deuteronomy) from the eleventh-century Italian Bible given to Admont by its founder, Archbishop Gebhard of Salzburg. OPPOSITE *'Death' by Johann Thaddäus Stammel: one of four statues of the 'Four Last Things' in Admont's eighteenth-century Library.*

45

ABOVE *Christ and Zacchaeus, an illustration to a treatise by the abbot of Theres, twelfth century.* BELOW *Abbot Gottfried of Admont dictating under the inspiration of the Holy Spirit; illustration to his Homilies for feast-days, Admont, c. 1160.*

left biblical commentaries and collections of homilies, printed from Admont manuscripts in the eighteenth century. During his twenty-eight-year tenure of office the scriptorium copied numerous manuscripts in bold twelfth-century hands, with decorated initials in the clear tones characteristic of Austrian Romanesque (four scribes and three librarians are named in the annals), and the monastery became known as 'a high school of learning and monastic discipline, a nursery of future abbots.' Thirteen of its monks were chosen as heads of other houses, including St Emmeram's at Regensburg and St Michael's, Bamberg. Gottfried made full use of these contacts in south German abbeys to enlarge the collection: the letter quoted above shows him at work. A copy of Salomo III's quadripartite psalter in Bamberg Cathedral probably came from St Michael's, and a Regensburg manuscript supplied the text of Cuthbert's letter on Bede's death; other texts derive from Salzburg, Tegernsee (Bavaria) and Theres in the diocese of Würzburg. The first works of the Paris school to reach Admont, Peter Lombard's commentaries on the psalms and Pauline epistles, were gifts from Archbishop Eberhard I of Salzburg (d. 1164) – Austrian copies of manuscripts the archbishop had brought back from his studies at Paris University. Before the end of the century monks from Admont had themselves attended the university and returned with Parisian manuscripts of glossed books of the Bible, the standard theological text-books.

From about 1120 until the mid-sixteenth century Admont was a double house, with a convent of nuns beside the monastery: Sophia, daughter of King Bela II of Hungary, being the most illustrious inmate. The sisters had their own books (later incorporated into the main library), some copied by themselves: a *Diemudis scriptrix* is mentioned. Gottfried's brother Irimbert, abbot from 1172 to 1177, whose tall slender figure and expression of mystical detachment is known to us from many historiated initials, was fond of expounding scripture to the nuns. 'Some years ago,' the prologue to his commentary on *Judges* relates, 'as I was discussing the story of the concubine who is cut into twelve pieces [*Judges* XIX] and the story of Ruth with the Admont sisters, two of them devoted diligent study to preserving the record of my interpretation. I have thought fit therefore to add to this work a short explanation of these same histories as it was summarised by the sisters' – whose names are given elsewhere: Regilinde and Irmingarde.

The scriptorium appears to have ceased activity after 1200; no later monk is described as *scriba* or *scriptor* in the abbey records. The two most striking acquisitions of the thirteenth century were made by purchase. The Gebhard Bible, by then considered too plain for a wealthy and important house, was replaced by a richly illuminated 'Giant Bible', bought, perhaps, from a Jew named Farkasch to whom a Hungarian convent had pledged it in 1263. Secondly, to augment the service-books, a Missal was acquired, decorated by one or more Paduan miniaturists. These Italian artists, like many after them, may have sought employ-

cuuidam epi cartula accufationif occulte con
scribitur. Iande accufatoz pedit inpublicu

Illustrations from a German or Austrian thirteenth-
century copy of Gratian's Decretum, the standard
compilation of canon law. ABOVE LEFT *a bishop.*
BELOW LEFT *table of consanguinity.* ABOVE
RIGHT *two canons.* BELOW RIGHT *a father hand-*
ing over his son to become a novice.

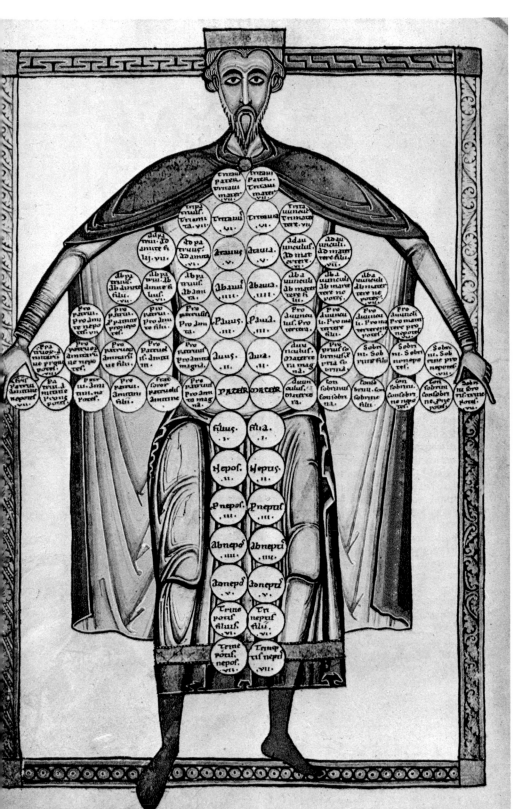

cuuidam eccle questionem mouerunt

PREVIOUS PAGES: LEFT PAGE *Miniatures from three manuscripts written and decorated at Admont in the twelfth century. The fourth* (ABOVE RIGHT) *is Salzburg work of the same period.* ABOVE LEFT *St Augustine teaching pupils.* ABOVE RIGHT *Anselm, Archbishop of Canterbury, presenting a volume of his prayers and meditations to Countess Matilda of Tuscany.* BELOW LEFT *Zacharias and the angel, an illustration to Abbot Irimbert of Admont's* Explanation of books of the Old Testament. BELOW RIGHT *'The Ten Burdens', an illustration to Abbot Gottfried of Admont's* Sermons for Sundays. RIGHT PAGE *The Admont Library, built by Johann Gotthard Hayberger and frescoed by Bartolomeo Altomonte and Johann Georg Dallicher, 1742–76.*

ment in Austria; but the commission could have been negotiated by Engilbert Poetsch, whom Abbot Heinrich sent to study first in Prague, then, from 1276 to 1285, in Padua. Engilbert ruled Admont as abbot for thirty years (1297–1327) and contributed to the library several works composed by himself: *On Christ's sense of pain in the Passion, On the question whether God would have yet been incarnated if the first man had not fallen, On the origin and end of the Roman Empire* (printed at Basle in 1553), *On the cause of the longevity of men before the Flood*, and *On the nature of animals*, which describes giants, cyclops, satyrs, centaurs, dragons, basilisks and griffins, and classes Pegasus among birds.

The first catalogue of the collection, drawn up in 1370 by Peter von Arbon, is preceded by standard instructions for the librarian. 'The first duty of a studious librarian must be to devote his time and labour to increasing the library in his charge.... If he neglects increasing the collection, let him at least take care not to reduce it by losing the books committed to his care or letting them perish in any way. He must therefore particularly suspect and beware of those enemies of books, fire and water.' He is to repair in the same style bindings destroyed by age, remind readers to treat the books decently, keep them in a fixed and safe place, and know the names or authors of individual volumes. 'But if there are too many books for him to remember the numbers and names, he must make a list on a loose leaf or in a notebook [grouping them by authors].'

The 1370 catalogue contains 320 volumes. Six years later seventy volumes were bequeathed by a notary, Fridericus, and 640 volumes are listed in a second catalogue, started in 1380 but recording accessions into the fifteenth century, the increase being partly due to the inclusion of the school-books. Books of the Bible, with or without gloss, patristica, sermons, saints' lives and monastic rules composed the bulk of the collection, with some apocalyptic literature such as the *Prophecies of St Hildegarde* and the *Vision of Tundal*. Medicine (forty-seven volumes) and law (twenty-nine volumes) were important subjects, the latter including some Bolognese lawbooks from Fridericus's bequest, the first class of book produced commercially for an international market. Admont could not match the wealth of classical authors at St Gall or Durham: but in the twelfth century it owned Martianus Capella, Boethius, Seneca's *De ira* and *De beneficiis* and various works by Cicero, with Dares's *Trojan War*, Horace, Ovid and Lucan as later additions. Of medieval Latin poetry Alain de Lille's *Anticlaudianus* and two copies of Gautier de Châtillon's *Alexandreis* were available, but none of the vernacular romances present at St Gall. Oliver of Paderborn's *History of Damietta*, and Burchard of Mount Sion's *Description of the Holy Land* indicate an interest in the Near East, natural to a house one of whose abbots died on the Third Crusade and another on pilgrimage.

Such works of the New Learning as reached Admont before 1500 were introduced by the unfortunate thirty-eighth abbot, Antonio Graziadei. A Venetian Franciscan, professor of theology in Paris and Louvain, he appears to have held a post as tutor at the Hapsburg imperial court, and was imposed by Frederick III on an unwilling abbey in 1483. The appointment proved disastrous. Resented for being neither Austrian nor a Benedictine, Graziadei was accused of harshness to his monks and of squandering the revenues on his Italian relations. What truth there was in these charges now seems impossible to discover, but by 1491 the abbot could stand the snowbound Alpine valley and the atmosphere of hostility no longer. He left Admont surreptitiously for Italy, was intercepted in Carinthia and brought back to the monastery's castle-prison on the Gallenstein, where soon afterwards he died 'of sorrow and wretchedness'. His books, inscribed *antonius abbas*, passed into the library. Beside some modest youthful volumes (a pocket Jerome, and paper manuscripts of Leonardo Bruni's

ABOVE *An Austrian* cuir ciselé *binding of* c. 1457.
BELOW *A master and pupils; Salzburg illumination, thirteenth century.*

51

Letters and Nicholas von Dinkelsbühl's *Sermons*), were a stately series of incunabula from Italian presses, many of classical texts: Galen, Caesar, Apuleius, Macrobius, Lucan, Valerius Maximus, and Lorenzo Valla's translation of Thucydides.

Three successive abbots set on foot a programme of modernisation after the Council of Trent: Johann Hofmann (1581–1614), Mathias Preininger (1615–28) and Urban Weber (1628–59). To replace the fifteenth-century library over the Lady Chapel (apparently Admont's first book room), Abbot Urban built a hall 111 feet long where (as in its predecessor) the books were stored in wooden cupboards. Part of its baroque marbled furniture survives and is used in an anteroom to hold the manuscripts and incunabula. The same abbot introduced an annual grant for purchases and expenses of three hundred guilders, applied in the following two centuries to restock the library on a generous scale. Around a nucleus of the Bible and the Fathers, now symbolically shelved below the central cupola of the rococo hall, excellent collections were formed on the arts and sciences, with many splendid examples of baroque illustration. No narrowly doctrinaire outlook limited the choice, as the presence of the key-work of the French Enlightenment, Diderot and D'Alembert's *Encyclopaedia*, shows. Even some Protestant works are to be seen, mostly acquired by confiscation from Lutheran tenants.

This great work of renewal found complementary expression in the mid-eighteenth century in Johann Gotthard Hayberger's library hall, designed to hold 95,000 volumes. Bartolomeo Altomonte, first approached in 1742 to fresco the ceiling, was granted the contract in 1774 on condition that the work was finished in two summers, and punctually completed the commission at the age of seventy-six. A second artist, Johann Georg Dallicher, was responsible for the architectural surrounds. Standing figures of the 'Four Last Things' (Death, Judgement, Heaven and Hell), eight wall-figures and two bas-reliefs in wood painted to resemble bronze are by Johann Thaddäus Stammel. Apart from Altomonte's sky-blue grounds, the dominant colours are white and gold, and wholesale rebinding (or rebacking) in pigskin was put in hand to adapt the books to this scheme. The library's re-equipment to serve taste and learning, on a scale far beyond the convent's own needs, was a noble achievement: and rococo glamour and grandeur were called in to celebrate it.

'I am once more amongst the kind and hospitable Brothers of Admont,' Sir Humphry Davy, inventor of the safety lamp, wrote to his wife on 2 June 1827. 'The worthy Brothers here make much of the book which I was able to procure for them, and it is worthy of a place in their magnificent library.' His gift was Henry Baber's facsimile of the Codex Alexandrinus (London 1816). From the ex-Empress Marie Louise, who visited Admont in 1820, the abbey received Petrarch's *Trionfi* (Parma 1473).

The library was spared by a disastrous fire which destroyed the church and most of the archives in 1865. The twentieth century was to prove less benign. Between 1935 and 1937, when the collapse of world timber prices had removed its main source of

revenue, the abbey was obliged to sell twenty-one incunabula and seventy-seven manuscripts, among them the two finest: the 'Giant Bible' (now in the National Library, Vienna) and the Paduan Missal (now in the Gulbenkian Foundation, Lisbon). Seven months after the Anschluss, in September 1938, the monks were expelled as 'enemies of the State and People' and their property declared forfeit to the German Reich. Manuscripts and incunabula were sent to Graz, books on coins to Linz, and through one of the bizarre and sinister whims of Nazi rule, over three thousand medical and botanical works to Dachau concentration camp. The Benedictines returned at the end of the war; and by 1955 most of the books had been recovered and reshelved in their old locations, where they continue to be added to and consulted.

Admont after its rebuilding by Abbot Urban Weber, c. 1672, by Georg Matthäus Vischer.

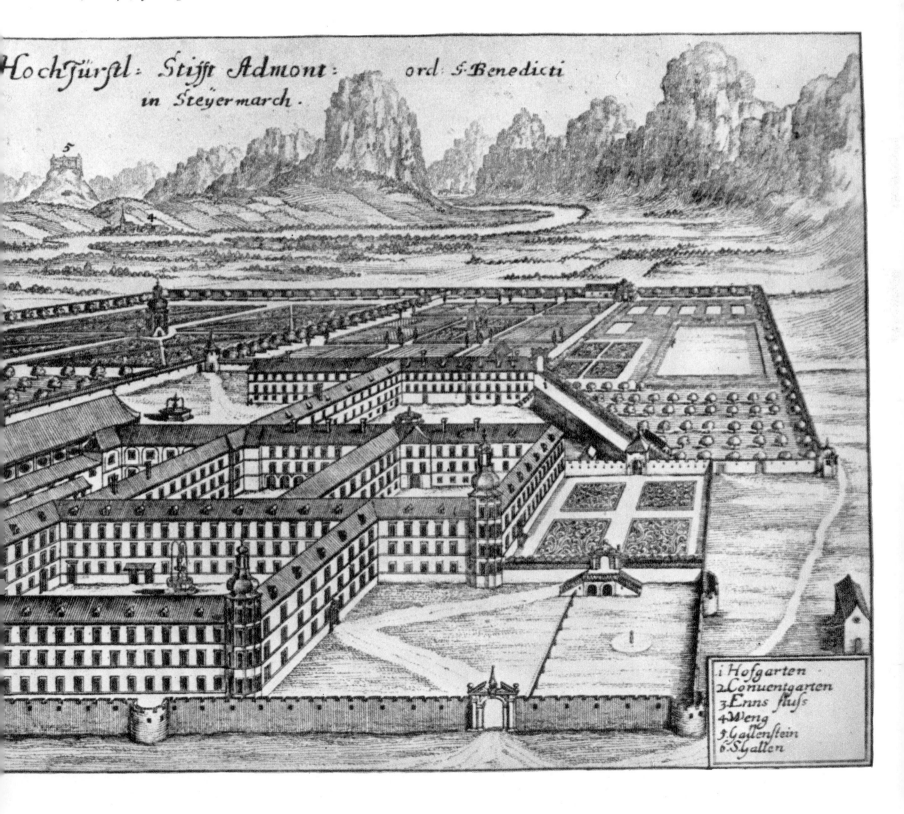

Hochfürstl: Stifft Admont: — ord: S.Benedicti in Steyermarch.

1 Hofgarten
2 Conuentgarten
3 Enns fluß
4 Weng
5 Gallenstein
6 S.Gallen

Durham Cathedral Library

The Benedictine priory of Durham was founded nine years later than Admont, but inherited the traditions and some of the books of a much earlier foundation – the monastery established by St Aidan in 635 on Lindisfarne island, off the Northumberland coast. Lindisfarne was evacuated under the pressure of Danish raids in 875 and the monks took refuge with the body of their seventh-century bishop St Cuthbert and at least part of their library in the swamps and forests of Cumberland before settling at the Roman road station of Chester-le-Street. In the late tenth century new Scandinavian attacks forced the bishop and congregation to abandon Chester-le-Street. They carried the saint's coffin south to Ripon, later returning as far as the dramatic crag surrounded on three sides by the River Wear, where Durham now stands. There miraculous portents guided them to build a new church for the saint.

The monastic organisation of Lindisfarne had given way to an association of secular priests. After the Norman Conquest monasticism had been restored in the north of England by three monks from Evesham who refounded the ancient houses of Jarrow and Wearmouth; and in 1083 William of St Carilef, second Norman bishop of Durham, expelled the English priests from Durham and replaced them with a priory of twenty-three Benedictine monks drawn from Jarrow and Wearmouth. Most of the English priests' books seem to have been appropriated. They received rather mixed treatment, many biblical manuscripts being dismembered in the twelfth century. Only half a leaf survives of a sixth-century uncial Old Testament of Italian origin, perhaps brought back by Benedict Biscop, Abbot of Wearmouth, from one of his journeys to Rome, and only two leaves from an eighth-century Pentateuch, 'fourth in age among our authorities for the text of Leviticus' (Mynors), in each case preserved by chance as fly-leaves in later volumes. On the other hand a Gospel-book, believed in the late Middle Ages to have been written by Bede, was well cared for, as was the Lindisfarne Gospels, the supreme expression of eighth-century Northumbrian art. Non-biblical texts were generally respected; for example, the

Durham Cathedral viewed from the south-west. OPPOSITE *David the Psalmist, by a Northumbrian mid-eighth-century artist, from a manuscript of Cassiodorus's commentary on the psalms belonging to the pre-Conquest collection at Durham.*

ABOVE LEFT *St Augustine, an initial from his* City of God; *Durham, c. 1083–96.* ABOVE RIGHT *David seated in the initial B of the first psalm; from William of St Carilef's Bible, Norman, before 1096.* BELOW *Killing a cockerel; Durham, first half of the twelfth century.*

imposing *Cassiodorus on the Psalms*, carefully restored in the twelfth century, together with certain remains of the early Northumbrian Church, mentioned in medieval inventories as 'the book of St Boisil, master of St Cuthbert', and *Elfledes boc*, in Anglo-Saxon, perhaps a relic of Princess Elfleda, Abbess of Whitby, another figure from the heroic age of Christianity in the north.

To the Norman William of St Carilef the pre-Conquest collection must have seemed inadequate in content, as well as eccentric in script and ornament. He took prompt steps to provide a new library of forty-nine volumes, chosen in accordance with the accepted view of a priory's essential requirements. A complete Bible in two folio volumes heads the list, as it had headed Archbishop Gebhard's benefactions to Admont. Augustine, Jerome, Gregory and Ambrose account for nineteen volumes. One work by Tertullian – perhaps a rare text, the *Apology to Roman governors on behalf of Christians* – was included, and among slightly more recent authors Bede on the Song of Songs and on Mark and Luke, and Rabanus Maurus on Matthew. Besides missals, breviaries and other service-books, sermons and homilies, edifying works

56

on the monastic life were supplied to be read aloud at meals. Law was represented by a volume of papal decrees, Christian literature by the poems of Sidonius Apollinaris, history by Bede's *Ecclesiastical History of the English Nation*, Justin's epitome of Pompeius Trogus, and Eutropius. The books were obtained from Benedictine houses in Normandy and southern England.

The formation of a suitable collection, begun by St Carilef, was energetically pursued during the first half of the twelfth century. An inventory taken in Prior Laurence's time (1149–54), with additions under Prior Thomas (1158–63), records 436 volumes, a large total even allowing for duplicates (each monk had his own psalter and some two or three, all of them counted in the list). The bulk was still of patristic works and only a handful of books by post-Carolingian authors had been admitted. Nine Anglo-Saxon books are separately listed as *libri anglici*, like the *libri scottice scripti* of the St Gall catalogue. An active monastic school is suggested by the astonishing array of over thirty Latin classics, backed by a few translations from Greek – Aesop's *Fables*, Dictys Cretensis, Plato's *Timaeus* and one of two known copies of Homer in twelfth-century England. A group of medical books, seven of which were the gift of a doctor, Master Herebert, included a volume containing 'some of the earliest English drawings of patients and doctors' (N.R.Ker).

The Prior Laurence inventory describes the collection at the peak of its planned expansion. By this time its manuscripts were largely the work of Durham monks and exemplified the merits of English books of the period, 'accurately copied, competently and often beautifully written and decorated, well spaced, fully punctuated and neatly corrected' (Ker). The monastery's needs had by now been largely satisfied and further additions were haphazard, the result more usually of gifts from an individual than of a deliberate policy of acquisition. So in about 1160 a certain Guarinus, perhaps the schoolmaster, gave a group of secular texts. A generation later Robert de Adingtona presented thirty-four volumes collected during his studies in Paris; more than half were glossed books of the Bible, two of them being still in the stamped calf bindings supplied by the university booksellers. Many of the books given by Hugh du Puiset, Bishop of Durham from 1153 to 1195, but by birth a native of the Orléanais, seem also to have been of north French origin. Besides a magnificent four-volume Bible and the usual glossed books of the Old and New Testaments, they included the *Recognitions of Clement*, the description of Christ's trial and descent into Hell known as the Gospel of Nicodemus, and Cicero's *De amicitia*, *Rhetorica* and *De inventione*.

Our next view of the collection is in two catalogues of 1391–5 probably compiled by William de Appleby, the librarian. By then the holdings had grown to nearly nine hundred volumes, the chief increase being in medieval theology. Together with much by Hugh of St Victor, Aquinas and so on, it is surprising to find Wycliffe's heretical denial of transubstantiation, the *De sacramento altaris*. Losses of classical authors outnumbered gains: of

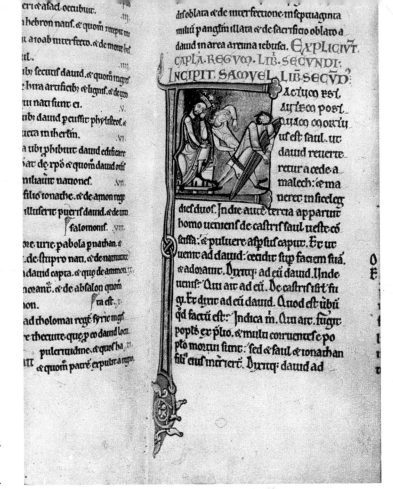

ABOVE *Initial from the twelfth-century Bible given to Durham by Bishop Hugh du Puiset.* BELOW *Cauterising a wound with red-hot instruments – which an assistant is heating in the lower part of the drawing; Durham, c. 1100–28.*

ABOVE *The tree of affinity, illustrating the forbidden degrees of marriage; from* Gregory IX's Decretals, *England, late thirteenth century.* BELOW *Parisian binding of c. 1180, of calf tooled with the Virgin and Child, the elders of the Apocalypse, monsters and abstract tools; part of Robert de Adingtona's gift.*

Ovid's eight works available in 1150, for instance, only an imperfect copy of *De Ponto* survived. Law, limited to Gratian's *Decretum* and Justinian's *Institutions* in Prior Laurence's day, accounted for 114 volumes. Very little of this fourteenth-century intake had been copied in the monastery. Most of it, written in neat professional hands, was obtained from outside by purchase or gift, half a dozen lawbooks from as far away as Bologna.

Until then there had been no library-room in the priory. As usual in English Benedictine houses, reading and writing, to which the middle of the day between dinner and Vespers was devoted, took place in the north cloisters, sheltered by the cathedral from the prevailing weather. A recess on the cloister wall, now filled with masonry, may once have held St Carilef's original donation. By the time of William de Appleby's inventory the collection had been divided. Half the books were in wooden cupboards along the same wall, available for daily consultation. The windows on this side of the cloisters had been glazed and partitions erected in each to form three carrels, narrow panelled boxes where the monks could have some privacy for their studies. The other main book-store was in the Spendiment (or Treasury), two half-underground connecting rooms leading off the west cloisters, where the priory's cartularies and other essential records were kept. The Spendiment books appear to have been treated as a stock for lending; in 1416 several were on loan to the prior of Finchale and single volumes to Bishop Langley and individual monks. A few books of high value to the community were kept in the cathedral; others, for reading aloud at meals, near the refectory door; the schoolbooks for use by the novice-master, in a chest in the west cloister. The system of private carrels – too few in number for every monk to have his own – was apt to lead to disputes, and during the priorate of John Wessyngton (1416–46) the works in most general demand were moved to a new library on the upper floor of the east cloister. It is a small room, well lit by large windows at both ends and originally equipped with ten desks to which the books were chained.

The New Learning reached Durham with the humanist bishop John Shirwood (1483–93). Shirwood's Latin classics, the majority incunable editions printed in Rome or Venice, were given by his successor, Bishop Fox, to Corpus Christi College, Oxford; but a cache of his manuscripts, discovered by Cuthbert Tunstall, may have been the source of the chapter's only Greek texts: Suidas, Aristotle and Plato, copied by Emmanuel of Constantinople, a scribe employed in the 1460s by Shirwood's friend and patron, George Neville, Archbishop of York.

It is sometimes suggested that Benedictine conservatism was slow to accept the invention of printing. Neither Durham nor Admont bear this out. In each case the monks bought the works of medieval learning they needed when the presses made them available. The choice of books by Shirwood's contemporary, Prior John Auckland, to stock a new cupboard in the cloisters is typical in its combination of manuscript with printed, though unusual in including some humanistic texts: a twelfth-century

Suetonius as well as a Nuremberg edition of Duns Scotus, Vincent of Beauvais' *Speculum historiale* transcribed in 1448 and the *De priscorum proprietate verborum* (Treviso 1480) of a contemporary Neapolitan philologist, Giuniano Maggio.

At Henry VIII's dissolution of the monasteries in 1539, the priory was converted into a cathedral chapter without the abrupt break experienced in most English houses. Hugh Whitehead, the last prior, became the first dean and twelve monks remained as canons. The manuscripts suffered for a long period from neglect – a sixteenth-century witness described them as abandoned to the bats and pigeons, and many show marks of the ravages of damp. But they were not destroyed or dispersed wholesale, though groups came into the possession of seventeenth-century antiquaries such as Sir Robert Cotton, or neighbouring land-owners such as Sir Thomas Tempest. In the 1680s Dean Sudbury equipped the medieval refectory as a chapter library with printed books on two rows of open shelves and a cubicle for the manuscripts. Some losses still occurred. Dean Montagu consented to fragments being cut from two pre-Conquest Gospel-books for Samuel Pepys's 'calligraphic collection': an event that possibly encouraged Humfrey Wanley successfully to press the Chapter for Emmanuel of Constantinople's Suidas for the Earl of Oxford's collection in exchange for a printed book, and later to hope for 'Books, Charters, & other things there which will be more useful to the World in my Lords Library, than in that remote corner of the Kingdom.' The Dean and Chapter no doubt thought otherwise. Were they already aware, one wonders, of the activities of Canon Dobson's nursemaid, who cut nearly all the initials from Hugh du Puiset's Bible to amuse her charges? All in all, however, Durham, with 332 of its pre-Dissolution books and manuscripts of a surviving total of 562, escaped the holocaust of monastic libraries exceptionally lightly and has a larger number *in situ* than any other British cathedral.

ABOVE *A marriage: illustration to Gregory* IX's Decretals, *Parisian illumination,* c. *1300.* BELOW *Dean Sudbury's library, installed in the medieval refectory of the priory in the 1680s.*

Monastery of St John

PATMOS

'Alexius, faithful to the Divine Christ, King and Autocrat of the Romans, the Comnene' is the signature in two lines of red ink on the Emperor's bull of 1088 granting the Aegean island of Patmos to the monk Christodoulos to found 'a seminary of virtue'. The island had been uninhabited for two centuries, and was described as 'deserted, uncultivated, covered with an impenetrable tangle of briers and thorns, completely arid owing to the lack of water. ... Barely a quarter of the arable land can be tilled with a plough: the rest must be worked with pick and spade and watered with the sweat and blood of the labourer'. Pirate attacks were a constant threat. Christodoulos, already chased by Turkish raiders from his abbey of St Paul on Mount Latros on the mainland of Asia Minor, then from Halicarnassus and from Cos, was obliged to evacuate Patmos in 1091 and died on Euboea. Nevertheless his foundation prospered and by the late twelfth century the castle-like monastery, built on the highest point of the island, contained 150 monks.

The library was an important feature of every Byzantine religious house, with the *bibliophylax*, or librarian, ranking as one of its high officials. Like Western monastic founders Christodoulos was anxious to establish an active scriptorium. His Rule contains the instruction, 'If anyone is skilled in the art of writing, he must, with the abbot's permission, exercise the talents with which nature has endowed him', but it is doubtful if much was achieved before his death. He did however obtain from the Patriarch of Constantinople a gift of fifty manuscripts from the two hundred he had saved from Latros. These he evacuated to Euboea and solemnly consigned to his successor: 'If ever anyone claims any of the books given me by the most holy Patriarch ... let him draw on himself the curses of the three hundred and eighteen Fathers!' Later abbots built on this nucleus. Joseph the Jasite bequeathed his personal collection of manuscripts, Abbot Arsenios himself copied books, and the island's reputation as the place of exile where St John composed the Apocalypse attracted gifts from a wide area – a richly bound prayerbook from Constantine, Bishop of Leros, for example, and the *Canons of the*

St John dictating his Gospel on the island of Patmos; from a Greek Gospels of 1335 in the monastery's library. OPPOSITE *Patmos: the monastery of St John and village of Chora.*

61

Virgin from the monk Nil of Rhodes.

A catalogue of the year 1201 shows that the library by then contained 330 volumes – 267 on vellum, 63 on paper. Lay libraries had never ceased to exist in the Byzantine Empire; most Greek monasteries had no teaching responsibilities and did not therefore need secular texts, and their collections tended to reflect the monks' specialised interests more narrowly than in the West. Books of the Bible, liturgical and patristic works and lives of saints formed over ninety per cent of the Patmos Library. There was only a handful of profane books, on grammar, medicine and chronology, two lexicons, Josephus's *Jewish History* and a commentary, Aristotle's *Categories*, the world-chronicle to the year 829 of the Patriarch Nicephorus and the *History* of John Scylitzes covering the following three centuries: seventeen volumes in all. Whereas some works of the Greek Fathers were common in Latin translation in the West, Patmos owned nothing of the Latin Fathers, except two volumes of Pope Gregory the Great translated into Greek. Almost the only book other than the Bible common to Admont, Durham and Patmos was the popular account of the Buddha's life which went under the name of *Barlaam and Josaphat*. Many of the manuscripts were described as 'old' or 'very old'. They included an illustrated Job of the seventh or eighth century, a St Gregory Nazianzene with lively decorated initials written at Reggio di Calabria in 941, a St John Chrysostom of 988 and the Gospel commentary of Titus, Bishop of Bostra, of the ninth or tenth century. Manuscripts were lent from the collection with a freedom hardly known in the West until Platina's administration of the Vatican Library (see p. 78). The loans were mostly to Patmos's dependent houses, but books also went to monasteries on the mainland and the islands, to the hermits of Calymnos and the secular priests of Samos, to lay families in Palatia and to the father of one of the monks in Crete. Losses inevitably occurred and a catalogue of 1382 registers a small decline in numbers, to about three hundred volumes.

Although many lay libraries were dispersed after the Turkish capture of Constantinople and several convents on the mainland sold their manuscripts in the sixteenth century, the period does not seem to have been unfavourable to the monasteries on Athos and Patmos. The former were the chief buyers at the sale of Michael Cantacuzene's valuable library in Constantinople in 1578. In 1602 Maximos Margounios, a Cretan scholar in Venice, bequeathed his Latin books to Iviron, one of the Athonite houses. Patmos has several sixteenth-century manuscripts, one of them containing Sophocles's *Ajax* and *Electra*, and must at this time have largely re-equipped its library with printed books (principally from Venetian presses), the earliest being the *Argonautica* of the Alexandrian poet Apollonius Rhodius (Florence 1496). Quattrocento book-hunters in search of Greek classical texts had found most of their prizes in secular collections. It was only after the Council of Trent had created a requirement for patristic works that attention was directed towards monastic libraries in the Aegean. The first Western exploration of Patmos's holdings

ABOVE *Satan, half dragon, half winged human: illustration to a seventh- or eighth-century* Book of Job. BELOW *St Gregory Nazianzene, from a manuscript of his works copied at Reggio di Calabria in 941.*

was instigated by Margounios's boyhood friend, Aloysio Lollino, later Bishop of Belluno, a Venetian born in Crete, who arranged for two Cretan monks to spend three years on the island from about 1583 copying manuscripts. The titles indicate what was then in demand: the biblical commentaries of Basil, Bishop of Neopatras, and of the monk Euthymius Zigabenus, the letters of St Gregory Nazianzene and the Patriarch Nicholas I, the *Panoply of dogma* by the Emperor Alexius Comnenus, his brother Isaac the Sebastocrat's *Ten doubts concerning precognition*, the verse chronicles of Constantine Manasses and the history of George Pachymer. Neither of the two major classical codices in the library, the eleventh-century Diodorus Siculus or the earliest dated manuscript of Plato's *Dialogues*, written in 895 for Arethas of Patras, later Archbishop of Caesarea, was chosen for transcription.

To some extent Patmos withstood the intellectual decline that overtook Greek monasticism during the centuries of Turkish rule. A school which enjoyed a wide reputation was founded on the island in the seventeenth century, although Richard Pococke noted in 1739 that only five books were used for teaching: printed editions of Constantine Lascaris's grammar and Theophilus Corydaleus's logic, and manuscripts of the latter's physics and metaphysics and of George Coressius's divinity. Pococke saw the monastic library, 'furnished with some of the best

The Gospel of St Mark: the Baptism of Christ, and the evangelist writing; from a twelfth-century Greek Gospels.

The Pro-Highoumenos Meletios in the Patmos Library. The long framed document facing him is the Emperor Alexius Comnenus's Golden Bull of 1088, granting the island to Christodoulos.

printed books, mostly the Greek fathers', and was shown a few manuscripts, but subsequent travellers relayed ominous rumours. The Comte de Choiseul-Gouffier, French ambassador to the Porte, was told in 1776 that only three of the monks could read, and Villoison, a classical scholar travelling in his suite, repeated a malicious story that they had recently burned two to three thousand manuscripts.

On 9 October 1801 Edward Daniel Clarke, a Fellow of Jesus College, Cambridge, anchored his caïque in the port of Scalea and climbed the hill to the monastery. With him were an English companion and a Greek interpreter whom he calls 'Riley' – perhaps a member of the Ralli family of Chios.

We entered a small oblong chamber, having a vaulted stone roof, and found it to be nearly filled with books, of all sizes, in a most neglected state; some lying upon the floor, a prey to the damp and to worms; others standing upon shelves, but without any kind of order. The books upon the shelves were all printed volumes; for these, being more modern, were regarded as the more valuable, and had a better station assigned to them than the rest, many of which were considered only as so much rubbish. Some of the printed books were tolerably well bound, and in good condition. The Superior said *they* were his favourites; but when we took down one or two of them to examine their contents, we discovered that neither the Superior nor his colleague were able to read. They had a confused traditionary recollection of the names of some of them, but knew no more of their contents than the Grand Signior. . . .

At the extremity of this chamber, which is opposite to the window, a considerable number of old volumes of parchment, some with covers and some without, were heaped upon the floor in the utmost disorder: and there were evident proofs that these had been cast aside, and condemned to answer any purpose for which the parchment might be required. When we asked the Superior what they were he replied, turning up his nose with an expression of indifference and contempt, 'χειρόγραφα [manuscripts]'! It was indeed a moment in which a literary traveller might be supposed to doubt the evidence of his senses for the whole of this contemned heap consisted entirely of Greek manuscripts, and some of them were of the highest antiquity.

Riley was instructed to open negotiations, while Clarke and his companion fell on the 'contemned heap' and almost immediately discovered Arethas's Plato. They were interrupted by Riley telling them that the monks had agreed to sell five manuscripts provided the islanders did not see the books leave. The price was paid and the travellers retired to their ship to wait.

The whole of Sunday, October the eleventh, was passed in great anxiety. . . . Towards sun-set, being upon the deck of our caïque, and looking towards the mountain, we discerned a person coming down the steep descent from the Monastery towards the port: presently, as he drew near, we perceived that he had a large basket upon his head, and that he was coming towards the quay, opposite to the spot where our vessel was at anchor. . . . As he came along-side, he said aloud that he had brought the bread ordered for us in consequence of our letter from the Capudan Pasha: but coming upon deck, he gave a significant wink, and told us the Superior desired that we would 'empty the basket ourselves, and count the loaves, to see that all was right'. We took the hint, and hurried with the precious charge into our berth, where, having turned the basket bottom upwards, we found, to our great joy, the Manuscript of Plato, the Poems of Gregory, the work of Phile, with the other Tracts, and the volume of Miscellanies containing the Lexicon of St Cyril . . . .

Clarke's account reads like a nineteenth-century pendant to Poggio's exploration of St Gall. The same details of monkish ignorance and indifference are emphasised to justify the rape of the collection. The monastery however soon resumed its traditional care for its possessions. Arethas's Plato and the four other Patmos manuscripts bought by the Bodleian Library from Clarke in 1809 are the only ones the monks are known to have sold, and within a year a notice had been placed over the monastery's library door enjoining the reader to 'guard [the contents] watchfully, more than your life'. The manuscripts were gradually sorted out and rebound. Scholtz saw fifty in 1821, Guérin 240 about 1856, Duchesne 460 in 1874, and 890 are now listed. In the second half of the nineteenth century the island's schoolmaster, Ioannes Sakkelion, spent thirty years cataloguing the collection. The modern visitor is shown thirty-three leaves of a magnificent sixth-century Gospels, in silver uncials on purple vellum, probably written in Asia Minor and dismembered in the same area during the Middle Ages. One hundred and eighty-two leaves were found in a Cappadocian village in 1896 and bought by the Imperial Library of St Petersburg; other leaves are in the Vatican, London, Vienna, New York, Athens and Salonica. Constantin Tischendorf, the German Biblical scholar who came to Patmos fresh from his discovery of the fourth-century Codex Sinaiticus in the monastery of St Catherine on Mount Sinai, did not see this fragment. Ioannes Sakkelion came upon it after his visit, at the bottom of a chest full of old papers.

ABOVE *A Byzantine silver-gilt plaque of the Virgin Mary, used on the binding of a manuscript.* BELOW *This leaf from the Patmos sixth-century purple Gospels belonged to Sir Robert Cotton in about 1600, and is now in the British Museum.*

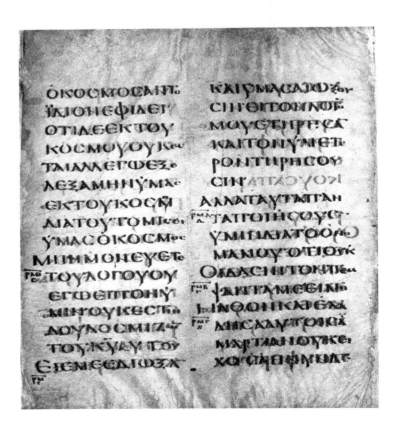

Biblioteca Malatestiana

CESENA

The ends of the desks are decorated with the Malatesta arms. OPPOSITE *The Biblioteca Malatestiana follows Michelozzo's design for the library of San Marco, Florence.*

For two and a half centuries from 1239, when a Malatesta was made Podestà of Rimini, the family ruled parts of the territory on either side of the River Rubicon in northern Italy where the Apennines meet the Adriatic Sea. In 1429 the inheritance was divided between two sons of Pandolfo Malatesta. The elder, Sigismondo Pandolfo, became Lord of Rimini. Although a half-demented tyrant who spent his life in warfare, he has left a noble monument: Alberti's church in Rimini, the Tempio Malatestiano. Along its south wall he placed a line of sarcophagi to hold the bones of a Greek neo-Platonist philosopher, Gemistus Plethon (specially fetched from the Peloponnese), and other scholars. The younger brother, Malatesta Novello, became Lord of Cesena, and founded the only early Renaissance library which preserves its original building, furniture and books.

A *studio*, or miniature university, had existed in the convent of San Francesco in Cesena from the fourteenth century. In 1445, at a period when many religious houses in northern Europe as well as Italy felt the need for a room to hold their books, the friars decided to build a library and were authorised by a papal bull of that year to pay the cost from a charitable bequest intended by the benefactor for other uses. But although the initiative came from the convent, Malatesta Novello seems to have intervened at an early stage. He certainly chose the architect, Matteo Nuti, who had worked for the Malatesti in Fano and Rimini, and his promise to give the library books worth five hundred florins is recorded in a second papal bull of 1450. Building probably started in 1447 and was completed in 1452. It took another two years to furnish the interior and supply the elaborately carved wooden doors.

The new wing of the convent was on two storeys, with a refectory on the ground floor, a dormitory and the library above. The latter follows Michelozzo's design for the library of San Marco in Florence, constructed about 1440 (see p. 88): a rectangular room with a vaulted ceiling carried on two rows of columns. Each aisle is occupied by twenty-nine benches and desks, three to a bay. The light (now partly obscured by new

INCIPIT LIBER BEATI HIERONY
MI CONTRA IOVINIANVM

PAVCI ADMO
DVM DIES
SVNT QD
SANCTI EX

urbe fratres cuiusdā
mihi iouiniani com
tariolos transmiserut
rogantes ut eorum i
neptijs responderem
& epicurum xpianoz
euuangelico atq apos
tolico rigore coterrere.
Quos cum legissem &
omnino non intellige
rem cepi reuoluere cre
brius & non modico
uerba atq sententias
set singulas pene silla
bas discutere uolens
prius scire qd diceret

MALATESTA·NOVELL

buildings) enters by a rosace in the end wall and a line of arched windows on either side, falling conveniently at right angles to the reader's position. In the pediment over the entrance is the family's favourite device of an elephant, with the motto *Elephas Indicus culices non timet* – 'The Indian elephant does not fear mosquitoes'. The Malatesta arms and emblems appear on many capitals and are carved and painted on the end of each desk. Tablets on the entrance wall bear the inscription, MAL. NOV. PAN. F. HOC DEDIT OPUS ('Malatesta Novello, son of Pandolfo, gave this work'), a memorial repeated in a slightly different form at intervals in the floor tiles. The books lie either on the sloping tops of the desks or on a shelf below, and are attached by a chain running from a staple on the lower cover to a ring which moves freely along a metal rod fastened above the shelf.

The convent already owned about fifty books. Besides a splendid thirteenth-century Bible in four volumes and a group of handsomely-illuminated law-books bequeathed by a certain Fredolo Fantini of Cesena, all produced in Bologna, they included several biblical commentaries of north French origin and philosophical works probably acquired by Italian students or professors in Paris. This nucleus was smartened up by being rebound and having missing leaves and tables of contents provided.

If Malatesta Novello had lived in Florence and had been as rich as the Medici, he could have supplemented the collection by buying from booksellers like Vespasiano da Bisticci who were able to secure the services of many copyists, but in a small place like Cesena it was apparently easier to set up his own scrip-

ABOVE *The library is lit by arched windows on either side and a rosace in the end-wall.* OPPOSITE *Johannes de Spinalo, a French notary from Épinal, was the copyist of this manuscript of St Jerome's Letters and Sermons for the Cesena Library, between 1451 and 1465. The name and arms of the library's patron, Malatesta Novello, are painted at the foot of the first page. The initial is imitated from romanesque models.* BELOW *A deathbed scene, by a Bolognese artist, fourteenth century; from a lawbook, probably one of those bequeathed by Fredolo Fantini of Cesena.*

PREVIOUS PAGES *Initials from a three-volume manuscript of Plutarch's* Lives *in Francesco Filelfo's Latin translation, copied in Cesena c. 1450 by Jacopo da Pergola and illuminated in Ferrara by Taddeo Crivelli. From left to right,* UPPER ROW *Demosthenes, Chrysippus, Theseus, the Gracchi;* LOWER ROW *Solon, Lycurgus, Demetrius of Macedon, Mark Antony.*

ABOVE *The Elder Pliny; from a manuscript of his* Natural History *copied by Jacopo da Pergola in 1446.* BELOW *Livy; to illustrate his* Histories, *copied by the same scribe in 1453.* OPPOSITE *St Augustine's* Sermons on the Gospel of St John; *copied in Cesena by Johannes de Spinalo before 1452, illuminated in Ferrara by Taddeo Crivelli.*

torium. This may have started in 1447–8 with a single scribe, Jacopo da Pergola, who had previously been employed in Rimini by Sigismondo Pandolfo Malatesta. By 1465 six scribes were employed and it has been calculated that in the interval at least twenty passed through the scriptorium. Manuscripts begun by one hand and finished by another suggest abrupt changes of personnel; a Venetian, Macario, copied only one volume; on the other hand Andrea Catrinello of Genoa, engaged in 1456 in Ferrara, was still in the prince's service nine years later when he dated a Cicero '20 November 1465, on which day the magnificent lord Malatesta Novello dei Malatesti exchanged life for death.' Four manuscripts are from the hand of one of the friars, Francesco da Figline, the new institution's first librarian. At least three foreigners were employed, the most prolific being a French notary from Épinal who settled in Cesena, married a local wife and Latinised his name as Johannes de Spinalo. Two others were possibly students on their travels: Thomas Blauvart of Utrecht who took seven months to copy Nicholas de Lyra's annotations on the psalms; and a facetious German, Mathias Kuler, who subscribed a commentary on Aristotle 'written by hand and not by foot', and 'All the proceeds have been spent on good wine in the inn and the company of women. *Venite exultemus.*'

These scribes worked in the library, but might accompany the court to the neighbouring castle of Bertinoro in summer or autumn. They wrote in the beautiful roman script evolved by the humanists from the caroline minuscule used at Verona under Pacificus and elsewhere in Charlemagne's empire. The finished volume was corrected in the palace against the exemplar by a court secretary; sometimes the exemplar was imperfect, and then there are gaps and the note *hic deficit*. The next stage was illumination; a few books – Augustine on St John's Gospel, Cicero, and the dedication copy of the Milanese humanist Francesco Filelfo's translation of Plutarch – were sent to Ferrara to be decorated in the workshop of a professional miniaturist, Taddeo Crivelli; but the majority went to a Cesena court artist (probably trained in Ferrara), to be supplied with the prince's arms or emblem and initials, and with an interlaced border or initial imitated from the romanesque models then admired. Finally the volume was given to the court bindery to be bound in brown goatskin, sparingly tooled, and provided with metal bosses, clasps and chain. The binder may have worked close to the scriptorium as he used its rejected sheets as endleaves.

The choice of books was based on the canon drawn up in 1439–40 by Tommaso Parentucelli (afterwards Pope Nicholas v) for Cosimo de' Medici. Malatesta Novello himself wrote to the Medici and to Francesco Sforza of Milan for manuscripts to copy. The scriptorium was chiefly engaged on works by the Church Fathers (Augustine, Jerome, Ambrose and Gregory account for thirty-one volumes) and classical authors, but medieval writers include Bernard of Clairvaux, Thomas Aquinas, Albertus Magnus, Henry of Ghent, Duns Scotus, Richard Fitzralph, Archbishop of Armagh, and William of Occam. Twenty-six

S · AGVSTINVS ·

Decorative initial, from St Cyprian's Letters; *copied by Johannes de Spinalo, Cesena, 1451–65.*

volumes can be classified as history – a special interest of Malatesta Novello's – and there are small groups on cosmography, science and criticism. Care was taken to obtain the latest texts, such as the Younger Pliny's *Panegyric of Trajan* and the commentary on Terence of Donatus (the fourth-century grammarian), which the scholar-bookseller Giovanni Aurispa had recently unearthed in Germany. The library contained no books in Italian, nothing of Dante or Petrarch, and only Latin works of Boccaccio.

Beside the scriptorium's productions, books came from a variety of sources. There are fourteen Greek manuscripts, including the *Odyssey* and Plato's *Dialogues* and *Republic*. Most seem to have been acquired in a single transaction, possibly from an Italian owner – it is tempting to believe that they passed through the hands of Aurispa, the greatest dealer in Greek books of the century. They were supplemented by a Demosthenes written by a Greek scribe in Italy, and another Demosthenes bought in 1431 from a Genoese merchant in Constantinople by Niccolò Martinozzi, later Malatesta Novello's chancellor. Seven Hebrew manuscripts were probably obtained from Cesena's small Jewish colony. A few manuscripts were copied in other towns because the exemplar could not be borrowed; only one was inherited, a work on the care of horses written for the prince's uncle. Valturius's *Res militares* was a present from Sigismondo Pandolfo, and there were gifts from Cardinal Bessarion and Francesco Filelfo. It is doubtful whether Malatesta Novello bought many earlier Latin manuscripts, but he may have owned a Boethius of about 1400 with illumination by Michelino da Besozzo and an unusually handsome Parisian fourteenth-century Bible.

In 1465, when the collection numbered a little over two hundred volumes, its growth was brought to an abrupt halt by Malatesta Novello's death at the age of forty-seven. He had intended to continue enlarging it and the previous year had written of making 'this my library every day more copiously provided with books'. The accident of his early death explains why certain subjects, poetry and humanistic literature, are almost unrepresented. He left no heir and Cesena reverted to the Papal States. The scriptorium and bindery were immediately disbanded, but a legacy from the prince of two hundred ducats a year enabled a few more books to be bought, on which the Malatesta arms were painted in pious memory of the founder. In 1474 the library received its last substantial bequest, the books of Giovanni di Marco of Rimini, who had been doctor to Pope Sixtus IV and to both the Malatesta brothers. After some years' delay about eighty volumes reached Cesena, mostly fourteenth-century manuscripts of medicine and philosophy. It is uncertain whether Giovanni di Marco owned the oldest manuscript in the collection, an Isidore of Seville written in the Verona scriptorium in the ninth century, annotated by Rather and doubtless abstracted from the cathedral library after the fall of the della Scala family (see p. 22).

The Malatestiana is usually claimed as one of the first public

74

libraries, but this function is not mentioned in the only relevant contemporary record, which is solely concerned with the needs of the convent and *studio*. The document in question, a deed of gift of 1455, recites that Malatesta Novello had built a library in the Convent of San Francesco, placed in it 'many volumes of books in the liberal arts' and intended to add many more 'for the use and exercise of the library and *studio* of the friars of the said Order of St Francis wishing to study in the said house and library.' The document goes on to regulate the composition of the *studio*, which was to consist of a reader and ten students, members of the Franciscan Order; only if the Franciscan candidates were too few to fill the vacancies might lay students be accepted, preferably from Cesena, and failing that, from other places under Malatesta rule. In 1461, presumably for greater security, Novello decided to appoint the Commune of Cesena joint guardian of the library with the friars. The Communal Council was instructed to prepare an inventory of the books and to carry out regular inspections.

These duties were conscientiously performed. The inspectors found two books missing in 1496 and the friar-librarian was dismissed for negligence. In 1532 the Bishop of Verona, Gian Matteo Gilberti, asked to borrow the Malatestiana codex of St John Chrysostom for use in a new edition. The Council at first refused, but later yielding to high ecclesiastical pressure authorised the loan against an enormous deposit of a thousand gold ducats. Two councillors, attended by a notary, carried the manuscript to Verona and returned a year later to recover it.

Though it lost its share of control in the seventeenth century, the Commune's supervision saved the library from the neglect and dispersal that were the lot of many other Italian conventual collections. To what extent the secularisation of control made public access to the books easier is not clear, but by the second quarter of the sixteenth century scholars seem to have been admitted, not only the envoys of prelates such as Cardinal Sirleto searching for patristic and philosophical texts, but also laymen like the editor-printer Paulus Manutius. The library survived a crisis during the Napoleonic Wars when the convent was suppressed, the building requisitioned as a barracks and the furniture and books removed to store. Nevertheless in its whole history it has lost only six volumes, one of which was removed by the Inquisition and two by the French Republican commissioners.

ABOVE *Cardinal Bessarion's translation of Aristotle's* Metaphysics; *probably a present from the translator to Malatesta Novello, c. 1460.* BELOW *The conclusion of a Cesena manuscript; the Malatesta arms between Faith and Justice.*

PLATYNAE HISTO
RICI LIBER DE
VITA CHRISTI AC
OMNIVM PONTI
FICVM QVI HAC
TENVS DVCENTI
FVERE ET XX

OBILI
TATIS
MAXI
MAM
PARTE̅

DVCI EX HIS MA
IORIBVS QVI CLA
RI IVSTIQVE FVE
RE QVIQVE OB SIN
GVIAREM ALIQVA

The Vatican Library

Unlike most public libraries, which came into existence to serve some present or past need, the Vatican resembles a family collection whose constituent parts, for reasons no longer clearly remembered, reflect the tastes of different ancestors. It has passed through three contrasting phases: Renaissance public library, citadel of the Counter-Reformation, and modern research collection. In each of the first two phases periods of massive growth alternated with stagnation, depending on the literary interests of the reigning pontiff.

The Papal Library is a creation of the Renaissance. None of the ancient manuscripts for which it is now famous entered its possession before the fifteenth century, and very few before 1600. There are occasional glimpses of earlier collections: liturgical books and Greek manuscripts sent by Paul I to Charlemagne's father Pepin in 761–3, Boniface VIII's library of 443 titles (including thirty-two in Greek, perhaps derived from Frederick II) lost during the fourteenth-century migrations of the Curia round central Italy. A new library of 2,400 works was assembled at Avignon by John XXII and Clement VI, but left behind when the Papacy returned to Rome. By chance two groups of books from the Avignon collection have survived: one was given by Cardinal Pierre de Foix to his college in Toulouse and appropriated by the French Royal Library in 1680; the other, of over three hundred volumes, rediscovered in the Pope's palace at Avignon in the early seventeenth century and presented by Paul V to his nephew, Cardinal Scipione Borghese, reached the Vatican in 1891.

The library's founder was the humanist Tommaso Parentucelli of Sarzana, Pope Nicholas V (1447–55). He had been a great book-hunter in his youth in the monasteries of Lombardy and Emilia, and later Giovanni Aurispa's companion in exploring the German abbeys for unknown texts, as well as the compiler of a bibliographical hand-list for Cosimo de' Medici (see p. 88) – one of many attempts to detail the ideal library. On his election he found a respectable nucleus of about 340 volumes assembled by his predecessor, Eugenius IV; they included several classical authors as Eugenius had fallen under humanist influence during

Pope Sixtus IV, by Bartolomeo Sanvito of Padua, from Sixtus's copy of Bartolomeo Platina's Lives of the Popes; *Rome, 1474–84.* OPPOSITE *The frontispiece of the same manuscript, inspired by an antique memorial.*

ABOVE *Lorenzo Valla offering his Latin translation of Thucydides to Pope Nicholas V; illustrations in the dedication manuscript of the work, Rome 1452.* BELOW *Bartolomeo Platina kneeling before Pope Sixtus IV; a detail from Melozzo da Forlì's fresco for Sixtus IV's Vatican Library.*

the Council of Florence (1439–40), but only two Greek books, bilingual copies of Boethius and the Psalms, perhaps from southern Italy. During his short pontificate, by purchase (a Bible that had belonged to the Anti-pope Clement VII and to the Duc de Berry was one acquisition), by employing scribes, commissioning translations or original works from humanists, and dispatching Enoch d'Ascoli on buying expeditions to Greece, Germany and Denmark, Nicholas increased the total to over 1,200 books, a third of which were Greek. A tenth-century Augustine, *City of God*, seems to have been the oldest manuscript, but in early codices the Papal collection was less rich than the capitular library of St Peter's, then recently enlarged by a handsome bequest from Cardinal Giordano Orsini. The revenues from pilgrims in the jubilee year of 1450 were used to finance this rapid expansion, to the disgust of Nicholas's successor Calixtus III, a Spanish canonist, who is said to have exclaimed on being shown the library, 'Just see what the property of God's church has been wasted on!'

Nicholas's books were kept in presses in one, or possibly two rooms. Under Sixtus IV (1471–84) a chained library of the normal Renaissance type, accessible to the public, was built on the ground floor beside the Sistine Chapel. It was divided into four rooms, an arrangement containing the germ of all future Rare Book Rooms and *Réserves*: the Latin library, with sixteen desks; Greek, with eight; Secret, where most of the Papal registers were kept, with six desks, five cupboards and twelve chests; and Pontifical, with twelve desks. Readers were apparently admitted only to the first two. All were decorated with painted windows, portraits of authors and savants, and frescoes by Melozzo da Forlì, Antoniazzo Romano, Ghirlandaio and others. Only one of the latter survives, Melozzo's fresco (in the Vatican Museum) of the Pope's appointment of Bartolomeo Platina, the Cremonese humanist, as librarian in 1475

Platina held office for six years at a monthly salary of ten ducats with free food for himself, three assistants and a horse, and free wood, salt, vinegar, candles, oil and brooms. (The assistants, who were employed as copyists, *scriptores*, as well as on general duties, seem to have been poorly paid; one is spoken of as 'half naked and suffering from cold'.) During his librarianship the library became the most advanced in Europe, heated in winter and supplied with both author and subject catalogues. The holdings, 2,500 manuscripts at the beginning of the reign, increased to over 3,600 by the end. The choice was entirely humanistic, with large sections of classical authors, Greek manuscripts, medicine and science, and one venerable relic of antiquity, the fifth-century illustrated Codex Vaticanus of Vergil, which had belonged to the great French abbey of St Denis. Although the volumes were chained to the desks on which they rested, an astonishingly liberal lending system was also in operation. Besides loans to cardinals, bishops and humanists, we find a simple friar borrowing a service-book for the Mass and a certain Cola di Giovanni, who worked in the Roman depot of a Milanese merchant, being lent a treatise on precious stones. Sixtus IV's library, the greatest of the Renaissance, sumptuously housed and equipped and opened to scholars with the utmost generosity, acted as a powerful inspiration to later founders of libraries, especially Albrecht V of Bavaria and Philip II of Spain.

In Raphael's famous portrait in the Uffizi, Pope Leo X is shown seated at a table on which a manuscript Bible lies open, but he has not sent for it to read the scriptures; he holds a magnifying-glass and is preparing to examine the illumination. The painting was evidently intended to commemorate the Pope's passionate interest in fine books. Shelves of presentation copies, printed on vellum and bound in silk or textile, survive from his pontificate. Among them are Cardinal Ximénez's Polyglot Bible (Alcalá de Henares, 1514–7), whose editors were lent two Greek manuscripts from the Vatican collection, and four copies, as well as the manuscript, of Henry VIII's anti-Lutheran tract, *Assertio septem sacramentorum*, 1521.

The Renaissance library reached its peak under Leo X; its further development was violently checked by the Imperial army's sack of Rome in 1527. The extent of the disaster is uncertain: a contemporary letter described a scene of devastation, manuscripts 'with the covers and clasps wrenched off, mutilated, torn, cut in pieces and thrown among the rubbish'. By some accident Leo X's additions escaped almost intact, but the older parts of the collection dating from Nicholas V and Sixtus IV suffered considerable loss.

The latter part of the century was uneventful. Intervals of growth under energetic librarians – Cervini (the first Cardinal-Protector, later Pope for twenty-one days as Marcellus II), Sirleto and Caraffa – were succeeded by longer periods of stagnation when the office of Cardinal-Librarian was purely honorary. Paul IV first appointed a boy of fourteen to the post, then his nephew, aged nineteen. The chief novelty was architectural: the construction under Sixtus V (1585–90) of Domenico Fontana's great library hall on an upper floor, frescoed by Cesare Nebbia of Orvieto, Giovanni Guerra of Modena and assistants, with views of Roman monuments and ancient libraries, œcumenical councils and portraits of the supposed inventors of alphabets.

The Renaissance conception of the library as a storehouse of knowledge which would attract international scholarship to Rome was gradually giving place to a view of it as an arsenal of intellectual weapons against heresy. Both attitudes were in evidence in the sixteenth century; in deference to the second there was a shift of emphasis from the classics to the most ancient manuscripts, especially of the Greek Fathers, the lack of which was noticed during the Council of Trent (1545–63). The desks from the old library were installed in the new *Salone Sistino* and readers continued to be admitted freely, though Sixtus V decreed an absolute ban on loans. But the liberal Renaissance policy was at its last gasp. Paul V had the desks removed in 1613 and an adequate reading room was not provided again until 1890. For

ABOVE *A detail from Raphael's* Portrait of Leo X. *The Bible is open at the beginning of Genesis; the miniatures represent the days of Creation.*
BELOW *Dido offering a sacrifice to the gods; an illustration in the fifth-century Codex Vaticanus of Vergil.*

the next three centuries the manuscripts were shelved in wooden presses along the walls and round the piers. 'No books or MSS. are visible,' Augustus Hare complained, '. . . and it is only disappointing to be told that in one cupboard are the MSS. of the Greek Testament of the fifth century . . . and that another contains a Dante, with miniatures by Giulio Clovio.' A selection of curiosities was kept at hand to amuse visitors; English Grand Tourists were always shown the manuscript of Henry VIII's *Assertio septem sacramentorum*; Montaigne saw a Chinese book, a papyrus leaf with writing and a breviary said to have belonged to St Gregory. But access to the main collections was difficult to obtain, and they were normally closed to Protestants.

A new spirit of determination was brought to bear in two notable transactions. The collection of Fulvio Orsini (1529–1600), librarian to Cardinal Alessandro Farnese, was believed by contemporaries to surpass the Vatican and may still be thought the finest of its size ever formed. It consisted of 495 manuscripts and 229 printed books, the latter all annotated by humanists. Many of the former had belonged to the celebrated humanist Cardinal Pietro Bembo and were wheedled from his heir by a mixture of perseverance and guile. They included uncial manuscripts of Terence and Vergil (the Codex Romanus), a fragment of another fourth-century Vergil (the Codex Augusteus) obtained from a French antiquary, Claude Dupuy, by ceaseless importunity, two collections of Provençal poetry, Boethius's *De consolatione philosophiae* in the handwriting of Boccaccio, a *Canzoniere* and other works in Petrarch's hand, and Michelangelo's autograph *Rime*. Orsini proposed to offer the collection to Philip II for the Escorial, but Sirleto and Caraffa intervened. The owner received an annual pension of two hundred ducats and retained possession of the books for his lifetime, undertaking in return to bequeath them to the Holy See. They reached the Vatican in 1600.

Ninety-five years after the sack of Rome by Lutheran landsknechts a Catholic army marched into the Palatinate to punish its Calvinist Elector. To Pope Gregory XV a glorious prize suddenly appeared within reach: the famous public library of Heidelberg, founded in the mid-sixteenth century by the Elector Ottheinrich, celebrated for its ancient manuscripts sequestered from the abbey of Lorsch (including another Vergil of great antiquity). The nuncio in Cologne was instructed discreetly to make known in Germany the Pope's willingness to accept an offer of the collection, and his wish was granted by Maximilian of Bavaria within five days of the town's capture. Three thousand, five hundred manuscripts and five thousand printed books from the Elector's private collection and the university as well as from the public library were removed to Rome. Thus the Palatina ceased to exist; its shelves were chopped up to make packing-cases, and Bavarian soldiers helped themselves to the books that remained behind. Two centuries later consciences were still troubled and in 1815–6 Pius VII returned all the German manuscripts, 842 in number, and forty-two in Latin to the Duchy of Baden.

The other accessions of the seventeenth century, momentous though they were, can only be briefly mentioned. Paul V obtained twenty-nine manuscripts from Bobbio, whose monks after giving a larger group to Cardinal Federigo Borromeo for the Ambrosiana (see p. 189) could hardly refuse the Pope. One of them contained as the lower text of a palimpsest, undetected until the nineteenth century, the unique copy of Cicero's lost *Republic*. Alexander VII bought the library of the Dukes of Urbino, founded by Federigo da Montefeltre, in 1657; its 1,900 manuscripts entered the Vatican and the printed books were given to Rome University. Alexander VIII (1689–91) acquired the 'Reginenses', Queen Christina of Sweden's collection of over two thousand manuscripts, some of which had been looted from the Imperial Library in Prague in the last weeks of the Thirty Years War. Under Clement XI (1700–21) two Lebanese Christians, Elia and Giuseppe Simone Assemanni, were sent to hunt for books in the Coptic monasteries of the Wadi Natrun in the Nile delta, Cairo, Syria and Lebanon. Under Benedict XIV (1740–58), Marchese Capponi's library was bequeathed and the Ottoboni collection of 3,300 manuscripts purchased.

These riches attracted the acquisitiveness of the French Directory and the Treaty of Tolentino of 1797 required Pius VI to surrender five hundred manuscripts. The Republican commissioners were ill-equipped for the responsibility of making a selection, and the advice of a French librarian to take all the Reginenses, most of which had been bought in France, never reached them. Their eventual choice, which included the Codex Vaticanus of Vergil and the Bembo-Orsini Terence, arrived in Paris via Leghorn and Marseilles in 1798. After Waterloo Pius VII attached more importance to French goodwill than to the manuscripts' return. Two collections of Provençal poetry were presented to the Royal Library and the loss of two Reginenses politely overlooked. The Pope was ready to give up the Vergil Vaticanus as well, which Dacier, the Royal Library's director, particularly wanted to keep in Paris; but the papal envoy, Marino Marini, disregarded Pius's instructions and secured its restitution with the remainder.

In the nineteenth century during the long librarianship of Cardinal Mai restriction of access reached extreme limits. Readers were not allowed to consult indexes or catalogues and had only a small and ill-lit room to work in. The Vaticana's third phase as a modern research collection was delayed till the reign of Leo XIII (1878–1903), who opened both library and archives and built the present reading-room, well supplied with works of reference, below the Salone Sistino. It was an 'awakening . . . after a long sleep – almost a resurrection' (Tisserand). Massive additions – notably the Chigi collection of manuscripts annotated by the bibliophile Pope Alexander VII – were made by Pius XI, a former Doctor of the Ambrosiana. Present holdings are sixty thousand manuscripts and seven hundred thousand printed books, of which seven thousand are incunabula.

ABOVE *Federigo da Montefeltre, Duke of Urbino, the great* condottiere *and book-collector; Florentine illumination of* c. 1472. BELOW *Terence's* Comedies, *a ninth-century copy of a late classical original. One of the volumes removed to Paris in 1798.* OVERLEAF *The Salone Sistino of the Vatican, Sixtus V's library built by Domenico Fontana in 1587–9 and frescoed by Cesare Nebbia, Giovanni Guerra and their assistants. This view by Francesco Pannini dates from the late eighteenth century, when the books were kept in cupboards built round the bases of the piers.*

Biblioteca Mediceo-Laurenziana

FLORENCE

The Laurentian Library is the collection formed by successive generations of the Medici family, with eighteenth-century and later additions from other sources. The first bibliophile in the family, and the founder of its fortunes, was Cosimo 'il vecchio' (1389–1464). His father, Giovanni di Bicci de' Medici, had owned only three books, all in Italian, the Gospels, the Legend of St Margaret and a volume of sermons. Cosimo however spent three formative adolescent years attending lectures in Latin and Greek and discussing philosophy in the 'academy' of Roberto de' Rossi and emerged with fully developed humanist tastes. With the collector Niccolo Niccoli and a Venetian friend, Francesco Barbaro, he planned a journey to search for Greek manuscripts in Palestine; with Poggio Bracciolini he explored Grottaferrata, Ostia and the Alban Hills for Roman inscriptions; with his brother Lorenzo, the historian and philosopher Giannozzo Manetti and others, he attended readings of Xenophon's *Cyropaedia* supervised by Ambrogio Traversari at the convent of Santa Maria degli Angeli. He built and equipped at least three conventual libraries: San Giorgio Maggiore in Venice, San Marco in Florence and the Badia at Fiesole. For the last Vespasiano da Bisticci boasted of having performed a *tour de force* of organisation, the employment of forty-five scribes to write two hundred manuscripts in twenty-two months.

Cosimo's library consisted of sixty-three titles in 1418, with a long series of classical authors as its chief component. There were also a Bible and school-books, a few devotional works (they included a life of his patrons, SS. Cosmas and Damian), Dante's *Canzoni* (but not the *Divine Comedy*), Petrarch's *Sonnets*, Boccaccio's *Teseide*, *Fiammetta* and *Decameron*, and two copies of Francesco Barbaro's *On marriage*, composed in 1415 for the wedding of Cosimo's brother Lorenzo. The inventory mentions one early manuscript, an eleventh-century Justinus from Monte Cassino, and many others 'di lettera antica', written, that is, in the roman script revived a few years earlier by Poggio from twelfth-century models. (Cosimo was its first influential patron.) He took books with him even on commercial journeys. 'I sent a

Cicero's Orations, *copied by Giovanni Aretino for Cosimo de' Medici in 1416. An early example of the* lettera antica *or humanistic script of which Cosimo was one of the first patrons; the initial is imitated from romanesque models.* OPPOSITE *The Laurentian Library, built by Michelangelo. The pavement is decorated with devices of the Medici family.*

Suetonius to Cosimo in Pisa,' runs a note in the 1418 inventory 'wrapped in a towel and in oilskin, by the coach, with the carter who carried the Pisan cloth.'

An older friend, Niccolo Niccoli, played an important part in the formation of Cosimo's collection. Niccoli had brought together 'with great industry and study, avoiding no labour from youth and sparing no expense' (as his own will declared) the largest library in Florence, of between six and eight hundred volumes, with unrivalled wealth in classical texts. He was a generous lender; five extant manuscripts were copied from his Tertullian, six from his Ammianus Marcellinus and eight derive from his Lucretius. According to Vespasiano (whose statistics however are usually exaggerated) two hundred of the books were out on loan at the time of his death. In the true spirit of the Renaissance Niccoli made a principle of helping other collectors. Poggio depended on him for supplies of vellum as well as for exemplars, Cosimo for advice and the supervision of practical details. We find him recommending Cosimo to accept a Sicilian friar's offer for his Boethius (in gothic script) as the price will pay for two new copies 'di lettera all' antiqua'; arranging for a transcript of Seneca's *Letters* in a roman hand; and reporting the discovery in a Dominican convent in Lübeck of a manuscript of the Elder Pliny's *Natural History* which Cosimo succeeded in buying, the first complete copy to reach Florence.

In return for these services Niccoli was allowed a sizeable overdraft at the Medici bank and died (in 1437) heavily in debt, leaving his books to sixteen trustees, including Cosimo, his brother Lorenzo, Poggio, Leonardo Bruni, Chancellor of the Florentine Republic, Ambrogio Traversari, prior of Santa Maria degli Angeli, and Giannozzo Manetti. He had earlier intended them to go to Traversari's convent 'for the use both of the monks serving God there and of all citizens devoted to learning,' and after his death the Merchants' Guild made an attempt to obtain them for the church of Santa Croce. But Cosimo, as the estate's largest

Interior of the Laurenziana in the eighteenth century; engraving by F. Bartolozzi after G. Zocchi. BELOW *Decorative initial in a twelfth-century manuscript of Pliny's* Natural History, *discovered by Niccolo Niccoli in Lübeck.*

OPPOSITE *Medallion portraits of Cosimo de' Medici (ABOVE) and his son Piero, by Francesco d'Antonio del Cherico c. 1465. From a Latin translation of Aristotle's* Physics *by John Argyropoulos.*

87

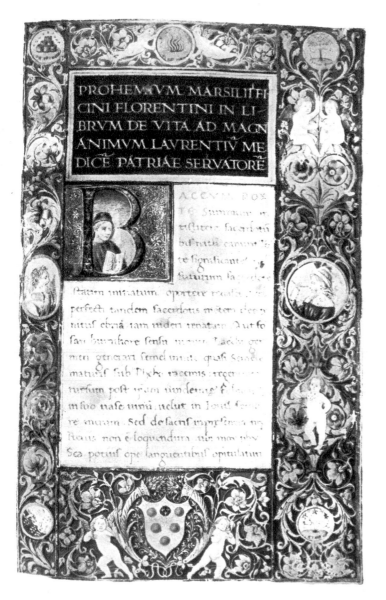

ABOVE *The Elder Pliny writing his* Natural History. *This initial in the first complete Pliny to reach Florence is by a Danish artist, Petrus de Slaglosia (Slagelse).* BELOW *Marsiglio Ficino,* De triplici vita, *Florence, 1489–92; the dedication copy to Lorenzo the Magnificent, illuminated by Attavante degli Attavanti, with the author's portrait in the initial and Lorenzo's arms in the lower margin.*

creditor, was in a position to block other claims. He had recently started rebuilding the convent of San Marco for the Dominican observants, and was evidently anxious to secure the collection for his protegés. Tommaso Parentucelli (later Pope Nicholas v), in Florence for the Council of 1439–40, was asked for his advice and drew up a list of works suitable for a convent library. Armed with this authoritative document, Cosimo succeeded in persuading the trustees to consign the books to him, some for his own collection (though the record of this part of the transaction has disappeared), the remainder for the projected library in San Marco. In return he accepted responsibility for Niccoli's debts to a limit of seven hundred florins, and undertook to supply bosses and chains for the volumes and to erect a commemorative tablet. The library, designed by Michelozzo, was opened to the public in 1444, but damaged by an earthquake in 1457. A new building, probably a replica of the original, was at once erected. It has lost its books and furniture but survives otherwise unchanged, the most beautiful library-room of the early Renaissance.

Both Cosimo's sons were book-collectors. Giovanni, who died before his father, circulated a 'wants list' to ecclesiastical relatives in the hope of extracting treasures from unappreciative churches. Piero, the elder brother, matched the colour of his bindings to their contents: theology was bound in blue, grammar in yellow, poetry in purple and so on. Both patronised the miniaturist Francesco d'Antonio del Cherico, their taste in this respect contrasting with their father's austere simplicity, but Piero was a keen connoisseur of earlier illumination as well and owned remarkable twelfth- and thirteenth-century work. Illuminated books and a collection of portraits in rare or precious materials were his main distraction from the gout that killed him at an early age. 'He would look at his books as if they were a pile of gold,' Nicodemi, the Florentine ambassador to Milan, reported.

The 'Medicean private library' (as it came to be known to distinguish it from the San Marco collection, the 'Medicea pubblica') was already large and important as it entered the third generation of family ownership. Vespasiano thought that it deserved a special building and pressed this view on Lorenzo ('The Magnificent'), the new owner, in a notably incoherent letter of 1472: 'That site for that library, which I discussed with Your Magnificence once, the more I think of it, the more it seems to me a labour worthy of you; because, without blaming any of your forebears, I hope that it will be in no way inferior to theirs. And I shall go on saying, it's a long time in Florence since a more worthy enterprise was conceived. . . .' Possibly a library building was in fact begun, though no trace of it now exists, but Lorenzo was more poet than scholar, and seems to have lacked his father's and grandfather's passion for collecting. The books he kept to hand in his country villa and town study were the ones he presumably most often read: gospels, psalters, Hours of the Virgin, the *Revelations* of St Bridget and other devotional works, Dante, Petrarch, Boccaccio, Villani's chronicles, Luigi Pulci's burlesque epic, the *Morgante Maggiore*, works on medicine (for ill-health had long troubled him), but of classical literature, besides Valla's translation of Thucydides, only Augustine and Seneca. The Greek manuscripts he bought from Francesco Filelfo's heirs or sent the learned Greek Janos Lascaris to search for in the Levant were not for his own diversion but for scholarly use, and particularly for his enthusiastic young friends Poliziano and Pico della Mirandola. This surely is the meaning of the exquisitely polite remark he addressed to Poliziano on his deathbed: 'I wish that death had at least waited until I had finished *your* library.' Certainly the collection was opened with wonderful liberality. Marsiglio Ficino, the neo-Platonist philosopher, Lascaris, Demetrius Chalcondylas, professor of Greek in Florence, Vespasiano, Giorgio Antonio Vespucci (the navigator's uncle) and many others made constant use of it. Books were out on loan for three years, seven years or even more. Poliziano borrowed as many as thirty-five volumes at a time.

By now the collection incorporated the fruits of more than a century of Florentine humanistic initiative. It had only a single uncial codex, a sixth-century Orosius from southern Italy, but Carolingian and early romanesque manuscripts were numerous, some of them unique. Besides Cosimo's Justinus and Pliny already mentioned, they included Seneca's *Tragedies* from the abbey of Pomposa, Ammianus Marcellinus's history of the later Roman Empire from Fulda, Apuleius's *Metamorphoses*, Tacitus's *Histories*, books 1–5, and *Annals*, books 11–16, and Varro's *On the Latin language*, all brought from Monte Cassino by Boccaccio, Celsus's *On medicine* from Sant' Ambrogio in Milan, Horace's poems annotated by Petrarch, Rather's Livy from Verona, Cicero's orations, found by Poggio in France, and *Familiar Epistles* from Vercelli Cathedral, and Quintilian's *Institutio oratoria* from Strasbourg. There were the earliest Renaissance copies of Tibullus, in the hand of the fourteenth-century Chancellor of Florence, Coluccio Salutati, and of the anonymous *Priapea* – comic verses addressed to the god of fertility – in the hand of their discoverer, Boccaccio. The Greek holdings were equally remarkable and included the oldest manuscripts of Herodotus and of Aristotle's *Nicomachean Ethics*, and a volume sent from Constantinople by Aurispa to Niccoli about 1423 which constitutes a basic source for the text of Aeschylus and Sophocles.

The year of Lorenzo's death, 1492, marked the culmination of the original library. Two years later the Medici had been expelled, their palace sacked, an unknown number of books lost. The remainder, 1,019 volumes, were transferred to San Marco. Here they were again in danger when a lynching mob broke in searching for Savonarola, but were saved by the promptness of volunteers who held the library doors until the guard hastily dispatched by the authorities arrived. Subsequently one-third of the collection was bought by the Salviati family of Florence and two-thirds by the Dominicans of San Marco, who resold their share in 1508 to Lorenzo's younger son, Cardinal Giovanni de' Medici, later Pope Leo x. Cardinal Giovanni removed the collection to Rome, where the chief accession was the unique

Cicero, De natura deorum *and other works; a ninth-century manuscript obtained by Poggio from Strasbourg Cathedral for Niccolo Niccoli.*

manuscript of books 1–6 of Tacitus's *Annals*. A visitor has left a description of the library in its temporary Roman quarters. The room was decorated with 'a very beautiful satyr' and other statues. Students were admitted by order of the Cardinal, himself 'most learned in Greek and Latin and expert in music.'

Leo's nephew, Pope Clement VII, returned the books to Florence and commissioned Michelangelo to design a chained library on the model of San Marco in the cloisters of San Lorenzo, a church associated with the Medici since Cosimo's time. When Clement died in 1534, the structure had been completed but the interior was undecorated and unfurnished. Work was resumed by Cosimo I, Grand-Duke of Tuscany, fifteen years later. Ammanati, with Michelangelo's advice, built the staircase; ceiling, pavement, stained glass windows and desks were supplied; and in 1571, with holdings increased to three thousand manuscripts, the library opened its doors to readers.

The Laurenziana was founded as a monument to the Medici family rather than as a working collection, and no arrangement was made for regular accessions. Initially Piero Vettori and other scholars were encouraged to edit its early texts, and a few gifts were made by the Grand-Dukes, among them the fifth-century Codex Mediceus of Vergil, from the monastery of Bobbio, given by Duke Francis I. But in the seventeenth and early eighteenth century it stagnated until A. M. Bandini was appointed librarian in 1757 and published the first printed catalogues. Great acquisitions followed, from the Gaddi and Strozzi families, Santa Croce, San Marco and other suppressed convents. Among them were two famous manuscripts: the Codex Amiatinus, a Bible written and illuminated in Northumbria about AD 700 as a gift to the Pope from Ceolfrith, abbot of Wearmouth and Jarrow; and the *Pandects* of Justinian, part of his great code of Roman Law. The latter, probably transcribed in Constantinople soon after its promulgation in the sixth century, was removed as war booty from Pisa in 1406 and preserved in the Palazzo Vecchio until 1783. In the nineteenth century Count Angelo Maria d'Elci gave his classical first editions, for which a circular tribuna was constructed adjoining the library; and the Italian government bought and deposited in 1884 the Ashburnham-Libri collection, formed by Guglielmo Libri (1803–69), the book-thief, and sold by him to Bertram, fourth Earl of Ashburnham (1797–1878). The manuscripts continued to be attached to the desks in Michelangelo's *Sala* until the 1920s. Now they are stored out of sight, but still have chains to remind us of their Renaissance origins, and haunt the reading-room with sudden crashes and spectral clanking.

The cloisters of San Lorenzo with Michelangelo's Laurentian Library.

Royal Library

BRUSSELS

Contemporary with Malatesta Novello and Pope Nicholas V, but very different from their libraries, was the greatest lay collection of northern Europe, the Librairie de Bourgogne of Philip the Good, third Duke of Burgundy of the Valois line and ruler of the Netherlands (1419–67). A taste for jewels, gold and silver plate, and books had become hereditary in the French princes descended from his great-grandfather, John II of France. At the death of his father, John the Fearless, in 1419, there were 245 volumes in the Ducal palace in Dijon: sixty-seven service-books, kept in the chapel, the remainder forming a representative selection of French works then in circulation. They included some celebrated manuscripts: the dedication copies to Charles V of France of Nicolas Oresme, Dean of Rouen's translations of Aristotle's *Ethics*, *Politics* and *Economics*; the Duc de Berry's *Belles Heures* with his portrait by André Beauneveu; and the *Laws* of King James II of Majorca, one of the few surviving examples of medieval illumination in the island.

Philip added to these from many sources: the *Grandes Chroniques de France* from the Governor of Lille; Latin classics from Jean de Wilde, a magistrate of Bruges; Humphrey, Duke of Gloucester's copy of *La Queste del Saint Graal*. An English Psalter magnificently illuminated for Peterborough Abbey was one of several books from the library of the Louvre, perhaps bought from its purchaser, Philip's brother-in-law, John, Duke of Bedford. A good cross-section of contemporary literature and learning was acquired in this way, though all in inherited, second-hand or ready-made copies.

About 1445 there was a complete change. For the next twenty years Philip was mainly interested in new books, sometimes original compositions but more often translations from Latin or adaptations into modern prose of earlier verse epics or romances whose language no longer satisfied current taste. The suggestion for a new work might come from the Duke himself, from a courtier or from one of the professional editors and heads of scriptoria in the Low Countries, who (like Caxton at Westminster) combined book production with providing fresh reading

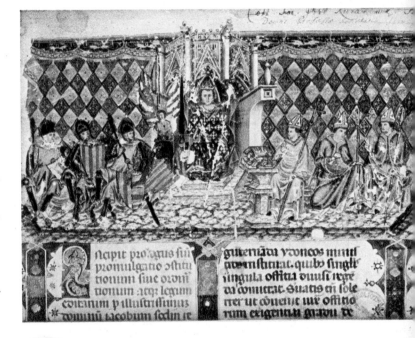

ABOVE *King James II of Majorca with his knights and bishops: from a manuscript of his code of laws, fourteenth century.* [*Copyright, Bibliothèque Royale, Brussels; Section des Manuscrits.*]
OPPOSITE *Two presentation scenes.*
ABOVE *Jean Miélot presents his translation of a treatise on the Lord's Prayer to Philip the Good, c. 1457.* BELOW *Jean Wauquelin presents his translation of the Chronicles of Hainault to the Duke, 1448. On Philip's left is his son, the Count of Charolais, later Charles the Bold, Duke of Burgundy; on his right is the Chancellor, Nicolas Rollin.* [*Copyright, Bibliothèque Royale, Brussels, Section des Manuscrits.*]

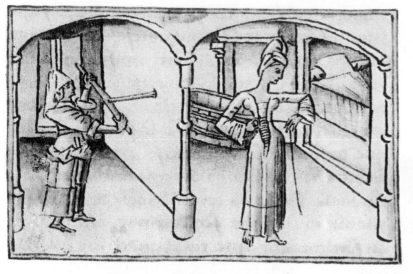

Illustrations to The Romance of Girart de Nevers, *a paper manuscript of* c. *1460.* (*1*) *An old woman surreptitiously boring a hole in the wall,* (*2*) *so that Liziart, Comte de Forest, can spy the mark on La Belle Euriant's breast when she is in the bath.* (*3*) *He boasts untruthfully at court of having slept with her.* (*4*) *Euriant's fiancé, Girart de Nevers, takes her to the Forest of Orléans and is about to behead her.* (*5*) *They are interrupted by a dragon; Girart thanks God for the distraction.* (*6*) *Nevertheless he abandons Euriant and visits Liziart's castle incognito; while warming himself by the fire, he overhears the old woman describing how he had been tricked.* [Copyright, Bibliothèque Royale, Brussels, Section des Manuscrits.]

matter. One of the latter, David Aubert, the copyist of a *Legend of St Hubert* of 1463 (now in The Hague), described how the manuscript was chosen. A citizen of Bruges (a certain Hubert le Prévost) compiled a 'little book' of St Hubert's life and miracles which he made bold to present to the Duke, knowing the pleasure he took in 'seeing the deeds of the ancients written – especially those to do with devotion – and hearing them related.' The Duke had the book read in his presence, was pleased with it and instructed David Aubert to prepare a copy on vellum.

The author, in fact, having written his book on paper (often with miniatures sketched in watercolours), had to face an alarming ordeal: its public reading to the ducal court. The scene is portrayed in a manuscript of Jean Wauquelin's translation of the Latin *Annals of Hainault*; on either side of Philip enthroned stand a group of courtiers and his son, Charles, Count of Charolais (whose reign was to prove the dangers of an unrestricted diet of romances of chivalry in youth); Wauquelin, kneeling, reads from a volume resting on a stool. Reading aloud was a common medieval practice – still surviving, after all, in church: Justus of Ghent's picture at Hampton Court records an occasion of this kind at the court of Urbino, and we learn from David Aubert's prologue to a chronicle of 1462 that Philip the Good listened to 'ancient histories' for an hour every day – but the reading of Hubert le Prévost's *Legend* was more like the submission of a modern author's manuscript to a publisher. On its reception depended whether it would pass on to the next stage of production.

Vasco Mada de Villalobos, one of the Portuguese attracted to the Burgundian court by Philip's marriage to Isabella of Portugal, had a similar experience. He decided to offer a French translation of Juan Rodríguez de la Cámera's Spanish work, *The triumph of the ladies*, to the Duke, of whose interest in the opposite sex the seventeen ducal bastards were incontrovertible proof. As his own French was uncertain, his compatriot Fernando de Lucena undertook the work. The manuscript was presented to Philip who asked the advice of a literary panel consisting of four courtiers: Philippe Pot, Seigneur de la Roche-Nolay, *grand maître d'hôtel* and seneschal of Burgundy, the Grand Bastard Antoine (who had a fine library of his own), the Bailiff of Hainault and the Bastard of Comminges. Their verdict was favourable and the book was sent to be elegantly transcribed and illustrated. Many works however, translations of Anselm's *Cur Deus homo* ('Why God became man') and of the German mystic Henry Suso's *Horologium sapientiae* ('The clock of wisdom'), for example, failed to pass the test and stuck at the paper manuscript stage.

In the prologue to an imaginary debate between Alexander the Great, Hannibal and Scipio, another of the Duke's editor-copyists, Jean Miélot, described the three ways a book could give pleasure: 'Everyone,' he wrote, 'enjoys reading [stories of these three heroes], hearing them related or seeing them in pictures.' Once a book's contents had been accepted, its appearance had to be suitably transformed. As there was no court scriptorium this

The death of King Alberic of Norway: illustration to Guillebert de Lannoy's Instruction of a young prince. [*Copyright, Bibliothèque Royale, Brussels, Section des Manuscrits.*]

Commet saturne eut response des dieux qui

Saturn and his children: miniature from the workshop of Loyset Liédet of Bruges in Raoul Lefèvre's History of Troy, *completed after Philip the Good's death, between 1467 and 1487. [Copyright, Bibliothèque Royale, Brussels, Section des Manuscrits.]*

meant sending it to a professional copyist's office to be written out on vellum in the large rounded gothic script characteristic of Flemish manuscripts. From there, protected by an oilskin envelope (like Cosimo de' Medici's Suetonius), it might go to Bruges (Loyset Liédet, Guillaume Vrelant, Jean Le Tavernier) or Brussels (Jean Dreux) to be illustrated. Miniatures in shades of grey, like landscapes seen by moonlight, were popular; and both guests and attendants at the Banquet of the Pheasant in 1454 wore the blacks, whites and greys of this genre. The whole process was long and expensive. Wauquelin began his translation of the *Annals of Hainault* in 1446; the vellum copy of the second volume reached the Duke's library in 1455; the illumination of all three volumes was completed before Philip's death in 1467 but not paid for until the following year.

The Librairie de Bourgogne had no educational purpose and although no doubt available to courtiers to a limited extent (one book was on loan to Louis de Luxembourg, Count of Saint-Pol, at the time of the Duke's death), it was in no sense public. Philip chose the books for his own amusement or, very occasionally, instruction. Apart from a breviary and book of hours (the first requirement of a princely bibliophile), his commissions were mostly for his favourite subject of 'ancient histories'. They were taken from the Bible or from Voragine's *Golden Legend* (Ludolphus of Saxony's *Life of Christ*, the *Miracles of the Virgin*, lives of St Helena, St Catherine and St Josse), from antiquity (Jean Mansel's *Histoires romaines* and the ducal chaplain Raoul Lefèvre's *Jason et Médée* and *Recueil des histoires de Troie*), from history (chronicles of Hainault, and of France, England and Flanders) or from epics or the literature of chivalry (*Histoire de Charles Martel*, the conquests of Charlemagne, the *Roman de Girart de Roussillon*, legendary first Duke of Burgundy). There were a few treatises: Gilles de Rome on the art of government, the Duke of Milan's doctor on keeping fit, Christine de Pisan on the qualities of the perfect knight, Honoré Bonet on the laws of warfare, Miélot on the *Ave Maria* and the Lord's Prayer. The only manuscript of a classic in direct translation that Philip the Good may have commissioned was of Ovid's *Art of Love*.

Although a 'library tower' is mentioned at Dijon, there seems to have been no library room in any of the ducal residences in the Netherlands. The books were in the custody of the keeper of the jewels, probably in chests. With the exception of the servicebooks and a few others (a *Tristan*, for instance, in cloth of gold and a *Lancelot* in black figured satin), they were plainly bound in calf or boards (intended, perhaps, to be enclosed in an embroidered wrapper when the Duke sent for a volume) – hardly suitable for display on desks in the Italian manner. Philip owned palaces in Brussels, Ghent, Bruges and Hesdin; it is not known whether the library was divided, or whether part or the whole travelled round with him.

The inventory taken after Philip the Good's death listed 876 volumes, a map of the world and an elephant's tusk; but the figure is rather misleading. It includes ninety-seven service books from the chapel, and over two hundred paper manuscripts, mostly works subsequently engrossed on vellum, or rejects, though some – like the charming *Roman de Girart de Nevers* – were perhaps waiting their turn for luxurious treatment. Philip himself seems to have commissioned fewer than three hundred volumes, and possibly no more than two hundred: it was their sumptuous execution, rather than their number, that was the basis of the collection's celebrity.

Philip's son Charles the Bold, who succeeded in 1467, made some additions and paid for unfinished manuscripts to be completed with miniatures. At his death in battle in 1477 leaving no son, the Netherlands became part of the Hapsburg Empire as the result of the marriage of Charles's daughter, Mary of Burgundy, to Maximilian, King of the Romans (the future Emperor Maximilian I). The library's existence became precarious and a partial dispersal occurred before 1500, when manuscripts were acquired by several private owners. In Charles v's division of the Hapsburg dominions, the Netherlands fell to the share of Philip II of Spain. The latter issued letters patent in 1559 ordering the

The marriage of Charles V, King of France, and Jeanne de Bourbon in Rheims Cathedral: illustration by Simon Marmion to Jean Mansel's La fleur des histoires, *c. 1450–60. [Copyright, Bibliothèque Royale, Brussels, Section des Manuscrits.]*

books in royal residences in the Low Countries to be brought together in Brussels to form a royal library 'in order that he and his successors may find a pastime in reading these books'. Besides the Librairie de Bourgogne two collections were involved, formed by successive Governesses of the Low Countries: Margaret of Austria (1507–30), who owned twenty manuscripts from the ducal library of Savoy through her first marriage and bought seventy-eight 'covered with velvet of various colours' from Charles de Croy, Prince of Chimay; and Mary (1531–55), widow of the last King of Hungary, to whom Belgium owes the Missal of Matthias Corvinus, used for the oath of governors-general of the Netherlands for over two centuries. Viglius de Zwichem, President of the Privy Council, was appointed keeper of the new royal library, which numbered 960 manuscripts and 666 printed books.

Ordinances of 1594 and 1595 required two copies of every new book, 'well bound in black, red or yellow leather' and stamped with the royal arms, to be deposited, one for the Royal Library, the other for the Escorial. Booksellers however ignored the obligation and in spite of the devoted librarianship of Aubert Le Mire, chaplain of the Archdukes Albert and Isabella, from 1617 to 1640, the collection in 1683 contained 128 fewer items than a century earlier. On the night of 3–4 February 1731, fire broke out in the palace. The books, kept in a tower room, were hastily thrown out of the window, one thick folio allegedly causing the death of an onlooker. The majority of the manuscripts, now reduced to 526, were saved and stored in the crypt of the court chapel. Here, fifteen years later, they were discovered by the French occupying troops and 188 removed to Paris, the majority for the Royal Library, others for the Minister of War, whose books later passed into his nephew's collection in the Arsenal (see p. 260).

At this lowest point in the library's fortunes, its second real founder, Charles, Count of Cobenzl, the Empress Maria Theresa's minister plenipotentiary to the Netherlands, reached Brussels. For months he enquired in vain for news of the Librairie de Bourgogne before discovering the books in the crypt and arranging for them to be installed in a building vacated by the Crossbowmen's Company. He was responsible for the institution of a Literary Society of the Low Countries, ancestor of the Académie Belge, and his final service was to recover eighty of the looted manuscripts from Paris in 1770.

In 1772 the Literary Society petitioned Maria Theresa to open the library to the public; the Austrian Chancellor, Prince Kaunitz, gave his cautious approval ('There is no question of forming one of those libraries celebrated for the great number or the rarity of the works preserved in it; it is to be limited simply to what is useful'); and on 26 June of that year the decree was promulgated. It inspired much patriotic enthusiasm and attracted gifts of useful works from the nobility and religious houses, recorded in the Library's Golden Book: Diderot and d'Alembert's *Encyclopaedia* from the thirty-ninth abbot of St Martin at

OPPOSITE *The editor-copyist Jean Miélot, by Jean Le Tavernier of Bruges, c. 1450. All the details of this portrait are admirably observed: the holes in the desk for inkwell and pens, the clamp to hold open the manuscript that is being copied, the square of matting on the floor, the trunk with a roll as well as bound volumes. The fire is out; the rewards of a literary career are precarious. [Copyright Bibliothèque Royale, Brussels, Section des Manuscrits.]*

Ozologue du translateur
sur la xclamacion ou

IMMORTALITATI.

...semper honos, Nomenque tuum, laudesque manebunt.

Virg. Æneid. Lib. I.

Tournai, celestial and terrestrial globes by Vincenzo Coronelli from the Duke of Arenberg, Willughby's *Ornithology*, 1678, from the prior of the English Carthusians of Nieuwpoort, the *Philosophical Transactions* of the Royal Society from the delegates of Brabant, Flamsteed's *Atlas Coelestis*, 1753, from the city of Antwerp. The resulting collection would have pleased Sir Thomas Bodley: folios predominated, Latin was the commonest language: there was only one French literary work: Molière's *Oeuvres*, 1734, with Boucher's illustrations. In succeeding years the emphasis continued to be on utility and protests were uttered at the folly of buying incunabula ('These precious but useless objects honour the cabinet of a bibliomane more than a public library, where everything, even magnificence, must be wise and reasonable'): but important accessions came from the suppressed Order of Jesus, among them the autograph manuscript of Thomas à Kempis's *Imitation of Christ* from the Jesuit house at Antwerp.

This promising period of growth was cut short by a second French occupation. Seven cartloads of books were removed to Paris in 1794, followed by a further 171 manuscripts and 159 printed books. The library fell victim to the revolutionary zest for reorganisation and was at one stage attached to the central school of the department of the Dyle (the French revolutionary authorities divided Belgium into nine departments, each called after a river: Brussels was in the department of the Dyle). Finally the printed books were given to the city of Brussels, while the manuscripts formed a separate Bibliothèque de Bourgogne. This division persisted after the peace, when over a thousand volumes were recovered from Paris, although the same librarian, Charles Van Hulthem, directed both institutions.

Van Hulthem's taste for books, nourished on the riches of secularised abbeys and distressed aristocracy, had reached the stage of mania. His personal collection of 32,000 volumes, all excellent copies and including many great rarities, filled to overflowing one house in Brussels and another in Ghent. Books were heaped on every table, so that there was never room to spread a tablecloth, and stood in piles in the alcove where he slept. He allowed no fire in the house and in cold weather kept himself warm in bed by putting folios on his feet, his favourite for this purpose being Barlaeus's account of Maurice of Nassau's expedition to Brazil. His contemporary, Voisin, records that he

LEFT *Fame proclaiming the names of donors to the Royal Library, by Durondeau, 1772: the frontispiece of the donors' book.* [Copyright, Bibliothèque Royale, Brussels, Section des Manuscrits.]
RIGHT *Celestial globe by Vincenzo Coronelli, presented to the Royal Library by the Duke of Arenberg.*

pzince qui viue sil ne me conquiert. ¶ Et
quant ad ce quil maintient que say vers luy
offense autre amende nen aura se non ce quil
en prendra a lespee. Et de ma part le vueil de
tant aduertir que sil refuse ceste parçon ie pze
dzay Incontinent vengence des Inuzicieuses me
naces quil ma fait sauoir par le conte de mons
en harmau qui cy est present .

Comment langele du ciel pacifia lempereur
charlemaine / et doon / et deuindzent bons amis

Istoire tesmoigne que tantost que
charlemaine vit entrer doon en sale
Il fu tant naure de courroux comme
chun aultre sans auoir sentement de parler

would sometimes be found contemplating with infantile pleasure an engraving of a 'fine female torso'; this was his sole contact with the opposite sex. 'Carried away by a sudden apoplectic fit, he died on a pile of books like a warrior on the battlefield.'

Van Hulthem's collection was bought for the state and in 1837 a decree of Leopold I established the Royal Library, in which the manuscripts of the Bibliothèque de Bourgogne and the printed books of Van Hulthem and of the city of Brussels were amalgamated. The library, now installed in the modern Bibliothèque Albertine after more than a century in the adjacent Palais de l'Industrie, owns 231 manuscripts of Philip the Good (of a surviving total of about 350) and can trace its direct descent from the Librairie de Bourgogne in spite of greater vicissitudes than any other national collection.

OPPOSITE *An angel intervening to halt a combat in champ clos between the Emperor Charlemagne and the knight Doon. This illustration by Jean Le Tavernier, 1458–60, to David Aubert's* Chronicles and conquests of Charlemagne *is en grisaille, a popular style at Philip the Good's court.* [*Copyright Bibliothèque Royale, Brussels, Section des Manuscrits.*]
BELOW *The former Royal Library, Brussels, in course of demolition.*

Biblioteca Colombina

SEVILLE

The Biblioteca Colombina was formed and endowed by Fernando, natural son of Christopher Columbus and of Beatriz Enríquez, whose brother, Pedro de Arana, commanded one of the ships on the explorer's third voyage. Fernando was brought up by his father, whom he accompanied at the age of fourteen on his fourth voyage across the Atlantic. After Columbus's death in 1506 and the family's long but ultimately successful lawsuit to claim their inheritance, Fernando found himself one of the richest men in Spain with an income estimated at 2·5 million *maravedis* a year, mostly from property and slaves in the West Indies. He undertook an official mission in 1509 with his half-brother Diego to found churches and monasteries in Santo Domingo, and on his return settled in Seville, the centre of the American trade.

Fernando Columbus never married; his only portrait is lost but he is described as rather tall, most amiable and very fat. He was a close friend of the Emperor Charles V, whom he accompanied on three journeys and from whom he received many favours. Jurist, cosmographer and amateur poet, he was the author of a dictionary of Latin definitions, a treatise on colonising the Indies and a geographical lexicon of Spain. He served on a mixed arbitration commission with the Portuguese to decide sovereignty over the Moluccas, headed a group of experts charged with correcting sea-charts and constructing an accurate globe of the new discoveries, and founded a school of mathematics and navigation in Seville.

He was a devoted book collector, invariably visiting the book-sellers on his numerous journeys in Spain and abroad. His habit of writing in each volume the date and place of purchase has made it possible to reconstruct his travels: to Rome in 1512–3, Italy in 1515–6, Flanders, Germany, Italy and England in 1520–2, Italy again in 1529 and 1530–1, and Montpellier and Lyons in 1535. These inscriptions record, for example, that he bought Vespucci's account of his voyages, the *Delle isole novamente trovate* (Florence 1505–6) and the 1502 Seville edition of the popular Spanish novel, *La Celestina*, in Rome, in Venice Waldseemüller's *Cosmographiae Introductio* (Strasbourg 1509; the 1507 edition had

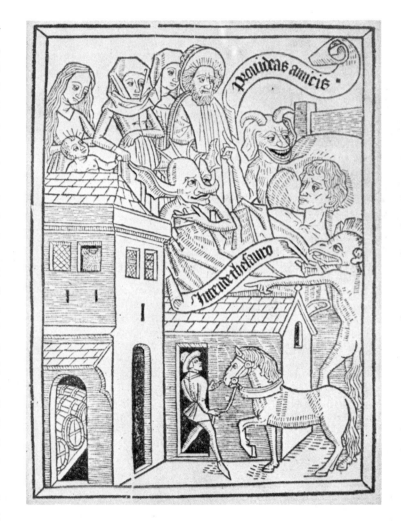

A dying man tempted by Avarice; from a blockbook Ars Moriendi, *a treatise on holy dying, bought by Fernando Columbus in Nuremberg in 1521 for 2 kreutzer (about 1½d.).* OPPOSITE *The Biblioteca Colombina; the late gothic cathedral of Seville is seen behind the library.*

first suggested the name 'America' for the new continent), an *Ars moriendi* in Nuremberg, the *Facetiae* of Alfonso of Aragon in London for fourpence, and *Palmerin de Oliva* and other romances in northern Spain in 1525. Erasmus gave him his latest book, the *Antibarbarorum*, in Louvain in 1520, and in 1522 he sent to Alcalá de Henares to buy Cardinal Ximénez's Polyglot Bible (1514–7) for three ducats. The book trade, much of it in the hands of expatriate Germans and Flemings, was still thoroughly international. When Fernando arrived in London in June 1522 his ignorance of English was no hindrance to buying books, as a wide range of Latin works were available in the shops. His purchases included Alexander of Hales's commentary on Aristotle printed in 1481 by the first Oxford printer, Theodoric Rood; but nearly all the others were from Continental presses, the most recent a Cologne imprint of the same year, the earliest a Venetian incunable of 1476. Prices varied from a halfpenny for a slim unbound volume to sixty-four pence for a substantial bound folio.

Fernando Columbus bought in Pavia in 1521 a tenth-century *Commentaries on Donatus*, which had once belonged to the monastery of Bobbio, but on the whole he did not share the Italian humanists' keen interest in early codices or feel to the same degree their enthusiasm for manuscripts and printed editions of ancient authors. He owned a few fourteenth- or fifteenth-century manuscripts, mostly of literary texts (the *Roman de Brut,* the *Voyage of St Brandan* in Italian and an account of the Passion in Catalan verse, for example), as well as a collection of his father's papers, but the vast majority of works in the library were printed and a high proportion was in modern languages: Castilian, Catalan, French and Italian. He was unique among early library founders in placing the emphasis of his collection on the contemporary and the ephemeral. He bought romances of chivalry and *chansons de geste,* ballads, carols and poetry of all kinds, moral tales and love stories, saints' lives, accounts of miracles, prodigies and funerals, relations of current events, mystery plays, prognostications, chapbooks and jestbooks, and works by Villon, Olivier de la Marche, Margaret of Navarre, Aretino, Clément Marot, Alain Chartier, Poliziano and Luigi Pulci. He bought his books to read – and indeed his capabilities in this direction now seem prodigious: in Valladolid in February 1523, for example, he finished an alphabetical vocabulary of Canon Law and immediately started Hugo de Prato Florido's *Sermons for saints' days* which occupied him until May.

A small but precious group of books had come to Fernando by inheritance and contained his father's notes, as well as some by his uncle, Bartolomé Columbus: Pliny's *Natural History* (Venice 1489), Pope Pius II's description of Asia (*Historia rerum ubique gestarum,* Venice 1477), a treatise on cosmography by Cardinal Pierre d'Ailly printed in Louvain by John of Westphalia (which greatly influenced the Discoverer) and Marco Polo's account of the East (Gouda *c.* 1484) annotated by Christopher Columbus with lists of the Oriental riches which he hoped to find on his expedition. If the Discoverer heard any rumour of Norse voyages

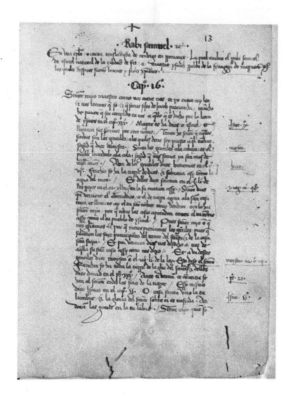

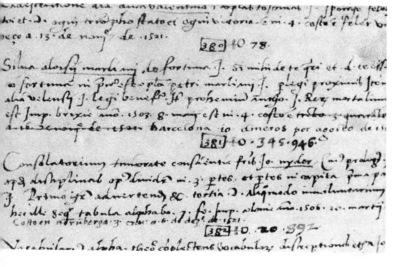

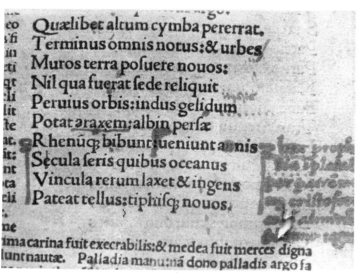

ABOVE *Christopher Columbus's* Book of Prophecies: *this page has a letter from Rabbi Samuel of Fez to another rabbi.* CENTRE *Entries in Fernando Columbus's register of purchases, recording books bought in Nuremberg and Barcelona.* BELOW *The prophetic passage in Seneca's* Medea (Venice 1510) *annotated by Fernando Columbus.*

to Vinland, no record of it has survived in the library and it is not mentioned in the *Book of Prophecies*, a manuscript collection compiled by him in 1502 with the help of a Carthusian monk, of quotations from the Bible, the Fathers and other sources, which, he considered, foretold his discoveries. Most of these 'prophecies' are tenuous in the extreme; but Seneca scored a hit with the famous lines in the *Medea*:

> The age will come in the late years
> When ocean will unlock its chains
> And a great land lie open;
> Typhis shall reveal new worlds,
> And Thule will no longer be
> Earth's boundary.

In his copy of Seneca's *Tragedies* (Venice 1510) Fernando noted against this passage, 'This prophecy was fulfilled by my father, the Admiral Christopher Columbus, in 1492.'

At its maximum the library numbered over fifteen thousand titles and occupied a large room in a house built by Fernando in Seville in 1526, standing in a park planted with American trees on the banks of the Guadalquivir. The books stood in wall-cases, arranged by subject and 'every one with its title by name and number', and were probably placed with the fore-edges outwards. This was the earliest library shelved in the modern manner, half a century before the Escorial, which is usually considered the first. Two catalogues were produced: a register of purchases started about 1525 but left incomplete after some four thousand entries, and an alphabetical index of authors and titles. Some progress was also made with a subject index, a resumé of every book in the collection and a universal common-place book, recording what different authors had written on every subject. Fernando wanted the collection to be of use to men of letters and offered it to Charles v as a national library, but the Emperor felt unable to accept the financial responsibility. Not only the collection's future as a public institution, but its security preoccupied the founder. He had no doubt visited the Vatican and other Italian chained libraries and learned that 'it is impossible to protect books even if they are secured by a hundred chains'. His solution was original: readers were to be separated from the books by a metal screen; they would be seated on one side and might put their hands through the screen to turn the pages of the volumes, which would lie on desks on the other side. If anyone objected to this arrangement he should realise, Fernando remarked, that the object of the library was not so much to facilitate study as to preserve the books.

Fernando Columbus died in 1539 leaving a will of forty-four pages. After a few trifling legacies the whole estate was to pass to his nephew Luís Colón on certain onerous conditions; in case of his refusal it would go to the Chapter of Seville Cathedral, or failing that to the Dominican priory of San Pablo in Seville. The entire annual income was to be spent on the library. Careful instructions were given for obtaining new publications from the six chief printing centres – Rome, Venice, Nuremberg, Antwerp, Paris and Lyons – and for the sale of duplicates; every sixth year the librarian was to be sent all over Italy to hunt for fresh acquisitions. The librarian was to be a graduate of Salamanca; he was allowed a room near the library with a 'country bed', two mattresses, four sheets, four white pillows, a quilt and a blanket, a chest, an armchair, a wooden bench to sit on and a large cupboard for books. He was to be fined for non-attendance and kept in order by a monthly visitation from 'a learned person'. Don Luís must undertake to spend one hundred thousand *maravedis* a year of his own on the library; if he failed to do so, or lost ten books and did not replace them within a reasonable time, he was to forfeit the estate to the next in line.

Don Luís declined the inheritance, and after a long lawsuit the Chapter established its claim. In 1552 the books were installed in a room adjoining the cathedral, built in the courtyard wall of the former Moorish mosque. The canons were at first delighted with their new possession; a librarian was appointed and the library room decorated with frescoes, inscriptions and gilt ornament. From the beginning however it is unlikely that the clauses of the will were strictly observed, and losses soon occurred. In 1577 Philip II ordered the early manuscripts to be transferred to the Escorial. Fourteen years later the collection came under the scrutiny of the Inquisition; the German Protestant Oecolampadius's edition of St Cyril's *Works* (Basle 1528) had most of its second volume and the whole of the third removed, and an unknown number of other books were condemned. The seventeenth century was a period of prolonged neglect, with brief intervals of solicitude, as in 1683 when the fabric was repaired and many books rebound in vellum. Rafael Tabares, who was under-librarian a hundred years later, described how in his youth he and other children were allowed to play in the room and run their fingers over the illuminated manuscripts and books of prints. 'The neglect . . . was such that some volumes were drenched by leaking gutters and reduced to dust.' Even as late as 1884 several hundred pamphlets were surreptitiously sold. Only about 5,500 titles of Fernando Columbus's bequest now survive in the Colombina.

Another book collector with naval connections, Samuel Pepys, was in Seville during the winter of 1683–4. He had announced his intention of seeing Spanish libraries before he left England, and cannot have neglected to visit the Colombina, which a new and conscientious curator, Juan de Loaisa, was engaged in putting in order. The experience was perhaps in some way unsatisfactory; it may have prompted his observation years afterwards to Humphrey Wanley that Spain is 'a Country where I experimentally know there is nothing for a Scholler to hope to learne, but what hee carrys Notices along with him to enquire after.' Did he, one wonders, learn the terms of Fernando Columbus's will, whose provision that the beneficiary should forfeit the whole collection if he lost more than ten books so curiously anticipates Pepys's arrangements for his own library?

ABOVE *St Jerome writing a letter; from an edition of his letters (Valencia, Juan Joffre, 1520).* BELOW *View of the library. Fernando Columbus's books are shelved through the arched door in the background.*

QVATVOR EVANGELIA, AD VETVSTISSIMORVM
EXEMPLARIVM LATINORVM FIDEM, ET AD
GRAECAM VERITATEM AB ERASMO ROTE
RODAMO SACRAE THEOLOGIAE PROFES
SORE DILIGENTER RECOGNITA.

ΕΥΑΓΓΕΛΙΟΝ ΚΑΤΑ ΜΑΤΘΑΙΟΝ.

EVANGELIVM SECVNDVM MATTHAEVM.

ΙΒΛΟΣ γενέ
σεως ΙΗΣΥ ΧΡΙ
ΣΤΟΥ, ἱοῦ Δα/
βίδ, ἱοῦ ἀβρα/
άμ. Ἀβραὰμ ἐ/
γέννησεν τ' ἰσα
άκ. ἰσαὰκ δ, ἐγέννησεν τὸν ἰακώβ. ἰακὼβ
δε, ἐγέννησεν τὸν ἰούδαν, καὶ τὺς ἀδελ
φοὺς αὐτω. ἰούδας δε, ἐγέννησεν τὸν φα/
ρὲς, τ τὸν ζαρὰ, ἐκ τῆ θάμαρ. φαρὲς δε,
ἐγέννησεν τ' ἐσρώμ. ἐσρὼμ δε, ἐγέννησεν
τὸν ἀράμ. ἀράμ δε ἐγέννησεν τὸν ἀμί
ναδάβ. ἀμιναδὰβ δ, ἐγέννησεν τ' ναασ
σόν. νααασὸν δε, ἐγέννησεν τ' σαλμών.
σαλμὼν δ, ἐγέννησεν τὸν βοὸζ ἐκ τῆ ῥα
χάβ. βοὸζ δ, ἐγέννησεν τὸν ὠβήδ, ἐκ τῆ
ῥύθ. ὠβήδ δ, ἐγέννησεν τὸν ἰεσσαί. ἰεσσαὶ
δε, ἐγέννησεν τὸν δαβίδ τὸν βασιλέα.
Δαβίδ δ ὁ βασιλεὺς ἐγέννησεν τὸν σο/
λομῶνα ἐκ τῆ τῷ οὐρίου. σολομὼν δε,
ἐγέννησεν τ' ῥοβοάμ. ῥοβοὰμ δ, ἐγέννησεν
τὸν ἀβιά. ἀβιὰ δε, ἐγέννησεν τ' ἀσά. ἀσὰ
δ, ἐγέννησεν τὸν ἰωσαφάτ. ἰωσαφὰτ δ,
ἐγέννησεν τὸν ἰωράμ. ἰωρὰμ δ, ἐγέν ησ
σεν τὸν

Iber generatio
nis Iesu Christi
filij Dauid, Filij
Abrahã, Abra
ham genuit Isa
ac. Isaac aũt, ge
nuit Iacob. Ia
cob aũt, genuit Iudã, & fratres eius.
Iudas aũt, genuit Phares, & Zarã,
e Thamar. Phares autẽ, genuit Es
rom. Esrom aũt, genuit Aram. Arã
autem, genuit Aminadab. Amina
dab aũt, genuit Naasson. Naasson
aũt, genuit Salmon. Salmon autẽ,
genuit Boos, e Rhachab. Boos aũt,
genuit Obed, e Ruth. Obed autẽ,
genuit Iesse, Iesse aũt, genuit Dauid
regem. Dauid autẽ rex, genuit So/
lomonem, ex ea q̃ fuerat uxor Vrie.
Solomon autem, genuit Roboam.
Roboam aũt, genuit Abiam. Abia
autem, genuit Asa. Asa autem, ge
nuit Iosaphat. Iosaphat autem, ge
nuit Ioram. Ioram autem, genu

A   it Oziã.

IOANNES,
FROBENI
VS SVIS
TYPIS
EXCV
DE,
BAT

Bibliothèque de la Ville

SÉLESTAT

Beatus Rhenanus, whose books are at Sélestat, was born in that prosperous Alsatian town in 1485, the son of the Master Butcher, and christened Beat Bild, though even as a schoolboy he preferred to Latinise the territorial name Rheinauer, from the neighbouring village of Rheinau where the family had once lived. He was educated in the parish school and at Paris University where he studied Aristotle under Jacques Lefèvre of Étaples and worked for two years as corrector in the printing house of Henri Estienne. His name first appeared in print as a collaborator in Lefèvre's edition of the Catalan mystic Ramon Lull's *Contemplations*, 1505.

He was again employed as corrector by Matthias Schürer in Strasbourg from 1507 to 1511, and later by the Amerbach and Froben partnership of printers in Basle. He had learned in Paris the importance of working from manuscripts and while at Strasbourg had collected material for Lefèvre's edition of Cardinal Nicholas of Cues: but before embarking on a career as a book-hunter and editor, he first had to perfect his knowledge of Greek by taking lessons from a German Dominican in Basle, Johannes Cono. He was still in Basle when Erasmus set up house there in 1514. A close friendship sprang up between them, and Erasmus trusted the younger man to see many of his works through the press.

Beatus had already edited a series of books for Schürer in Strasbourg – contemporary Latin poetry, a revised edition of Erasmus's *Adagiae* (1509) and Geiler von Kaisersperg's *Ship of Fools* (1510) to which he contributed a life of the author: in Basle he supervised the publication of the standard medieval compilation of canon law, Gratian's *Decretum* (1512), for a consortium of three booksellers. But his main literary work was concentrated in the two decades after his meeting with Erasmus and consisted in a series of critical editions printed in Basle by Froben. The most notable were of two selections of Erasmus's letters, chosen at his own discretion from the author's rough drafts (1518, 1519 and 1521), Velleius Paterculus (1520), Tertullian (1521), Eusebius (1523), the Elder Pliny's *Natural History* (1526), Procopius, Jordanes and other Dark Age histories

Theodore de Bry. Portrait of Beatus Rhenanus, *after a lost original once in the Sélestat archives.* OPPOSITE *Erasmus's edition of the New Testament (Basle, Froben, 1516), the first publication of the Greek text.*

Prelū Ascensianū·

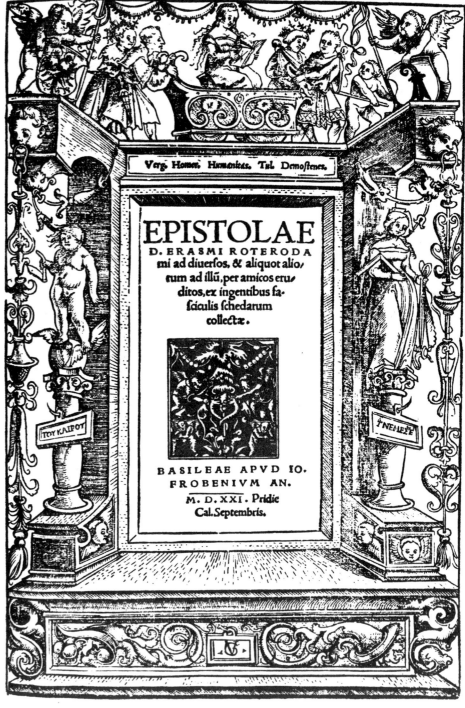

Verg. Homer. Humanitas. Tul. Demostenes.

EPISTOLAE
D. ERASMI ROTERODA
mi ad diuerſos, & aliquot alio/
rum ad illū, per amicos eru/
ditos, ex ingentibus fa/
ſciculis ſchedarum
collectæ.

BASILEAE APVD IO.
FROBENIVM AN.
M·D·XXI· Pridie
Cal. Septembris.

ABOVE *The Paris printing-press of Josse Bade of
Asch; the corrector – a post held by Beatus at various
times, though never in Josse Bade's shop – is seated
on the right.* RIGHT *Erasmus's correspondence, edited
by Beatus Rhenanus (Basle, Froben, 1521);
woodcut border by Urs Graf.*

(1531), Tacitus (1533), and Livy, in collaboration with Sigismund Gelenius (1535).

Beatus was not above using an earlier printed source without acknowledgement on occasion; his Seneca, *Apotheosis of the Emperor Claudius* (1515), although derived from the St Gall manuscript of Notker Labeo's period and described on the title page as 'recently found in Germany', was taken from the Rome *editio princeps* of 1513. But most of his editions were based on new manuscripts. Until then, with the conspicuous exception of Nicholas of Cues, literary discoveries north of the Alps had mostly been made by Italians such as Poggio and Aurispa. Beatus now set about investigating the ancient libraries of Alsace and the Upper Rhine at the same time as the Augsburg antiquary Conrad Peutinger and his circle were exploring Franconia and Bavaria. His greatest discovery was the unique manuscript of the Greek and Roman history of Velleius Paterculus in the Alsatian abbey of Murbach, an eighth-century foundation from Reichenau. At Worms he came upon Rather's Livy in the cathedral library. Speyer Cathedral proved to own a second Livy and the list of imperial office-holders in late antiquity, known as the *Notitia dignitatum*, which had received attention a century earlier during the Council of Basle (1431–7). He used one Tertullian lent by the Benedictines of Hirsau (Wurtemberg), collating it with a second manuscript – originally from Payerne, near Lausanne – which he found in a private collection at Colmar. For his edition of Tacitus he was sent Matthias Corvinus's copy from Vienna by Jacob Spiegel, a Sélestat friend employed in the imperial secretariat. Another friend of Erasmus, Simon Grynaeus, brought him a tenth-century Vitruvius and a Pliny from the library formed by Johann von Dahlberg, Bishop of Worms (d. 1502). Nearer at hand he could consult the collection of Greek manuscripts given by Cardinal John of Ragusa to the Basle Dominicans, the source of two codices used by Erasmus for his Greek New Testament (1516).

Although Beatus constantly attacked the monks for their ignorance and hostility to learning, he seems to have gained

Beatus Rhenanus's edition of Seneca, Apotheosis of the Emperor Claudius *(Basle, Froben, 1515); woodcut border by Urs Graf. 'Selati Tribunorum' is Latin for Sélestat.*

ABOVE *The beard a manly adornment: illustration to a poem by Beatus's Sélestat friend Johann Witz.*
BELOW *Erasmus's* Antibarbarorum (Basle, Froben, 1520); *woodcut border by Hans Holbein.*

access to these collections quite easily, often with the help of a fifth column of humanist sympathisers. His correspondence at Sélestat preserves some details of these transactions. Otto Brunfels, later the author of a popular *Herbal*, but at the time of writing (1520) an inmate of the Strasbourg Charterhouse, provided an extreme example of surreptitious methods: 'I send the letters of the Emperor Frederick, once called Barbarossa. I cut them from a manuscript in our library. If anyone did this openly he would be declared anathema. I don't consider this thunderbolt is to be feared, as I do not give but only communicate.... When you have read it through, return it cautiously and I will sew it in the volume again.' The dean of Worms sent the cathedral's Livy unconditionally, but the abbot of Hirsau would only lend their Tertullian for six months (the normal time needed for a scribal copy) against a deposit and an agreement to pay compensation if the volume was stained or damaged. (Beatus later succeeded in obtaining two eleventh-century manuscripts from Hirsau for his own collection.)

Beatus's only major original work was a history of Germany which appeared in 1531 under the title *Rerum Germanicarum libri tres.* It was the first to be based on research among archives, including those of the priory of Sainte Foy at Sélestat, and had involved a journey to Augsburg in 1530 to consult Conrad Peutinger's unique plan of the Roman road system, the *Tabulae Peutingerianae.* The visit was fruitful in other ways: he borrowed his host's codex of Ammianus Marcellinus and discovered at Freising a ninth-century paraphrase of the Gospels in German verse by Otfrid of Weissenburg. His last compositions were a short biographical sketch of Erasmus prefaced to the latter's posthumous edition of *Origen* (1536), subsequently expanded for the 1540 edition of Erasmus's works. He died in 1547, bequeathing his books to his birthplace.

Beatus belonged to the first generation to grow up with the printing press as a commonplace of their lives, and his library is accordingly different in kind from earlier ones. There is no trace of a belief (such as princely collectors like Federigo da Montefeltre of Urbino may have felt) that manuscript is superior to print: on the contrary, the handful of post-Caroline manuscripts, the thirteenth-century Ovid bought in Paris, and the Greek lexicon bequeathed by Cono are quite incidental. The most obvious symptom of change is the size of the collection, 671 volumes containing 1,159 works, of an original total perhaps of about 1,300, or six times what would have been considered large a century earlier. A significant novelty is the high proportion of contemporary authors, reflecting the literature explosion produced by printing. Five-sixths of Coluccio Salutati's books at the beginning of the Quattrocento had been of classical or early medieval writers. In Beatus's library the same texts, in revised editions by living scholars, lay beside travel books like Damian à Goes's description of the Ethiopians (Louvain 1540), topography such as Tschudi's account of Switzerland (Basle 1538), controversial pamphlets and political news-letters. Two examples will illustrate this mixture of subjects and periods. A typical collective volume bound in 1510 contains François Tissard's editions of *Hesiod* and Homer's *Batrachyomachia,* both used by Beatus for his Greek studies, together with a report on the Portuguese in India (*Gesta proxime per Portugalenses in India,* Nuremberg 1507) and an anti-Jewish tract by Johann Pfefferkorn (Cologne 1508). In 1512, when his tastes were more antiquarian than in later life, his purchases included one of his few Italian illustrated books (Bergomensis, *De claris mulieribus,* 1497), Arrian's biography of Alexander the Great, Celsus's *De medicina,* St John Chrysostom, Pietro del Monte on the powers of the Pope and of a general council, the French humanist Guillaume Budé on Justinian's *Pandects,* Eusebius and other histories, Gaffori on music (Brescia 1502), Hippocrates translated by Dr Wilhelm Cop of Basle, Varthema on the Red Sea route to India (Milan 1511), the Aldine Ovid and the first illustrated edition of Vitruvius (1511).

We can trace the development of the owner's interests through the collection, guided by his frequent habit of noting the date and place of a purchase, with the added formula *nec muto dominum* for favourites: 'I belong to Beatus Rhenanus and won't change.' Venetian editions of the classics and a volume of works by the grammarian Antonio Mancinelli, bought when he was fifteen, record his youthful determination to write good Latin prose. Annotated copies of Marsiglio Ficino and Pico della Mirandola remain from his introduction by Lefèvre to neo-Platonist

ABOVE *A young man of fashion; the architecture is characteristically Alsatian: illustration to Jacob Wimpfeling's* Adolescentia *(Strasbourg 1500).*
BELOW *Beatus Rhenanus's edition of Aeneas of Gaza,* De immortalitate animae *(Basle, Froben, 1516): woodcut border by Hans Holbein depicting the fortitude of Mucius Scaevola.*

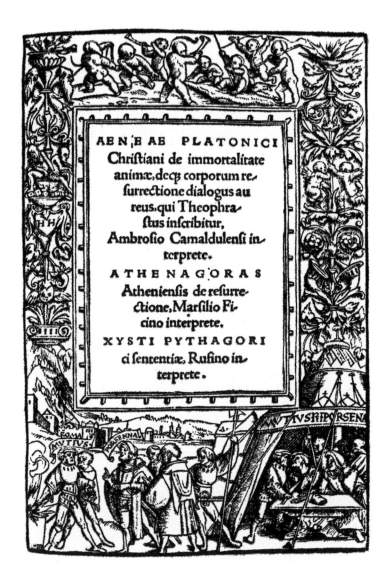

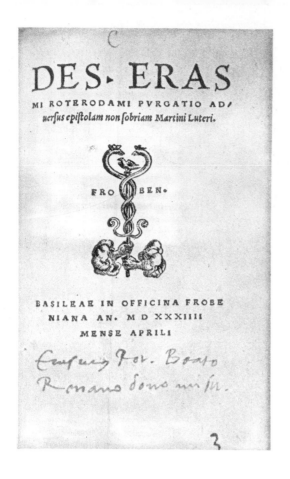

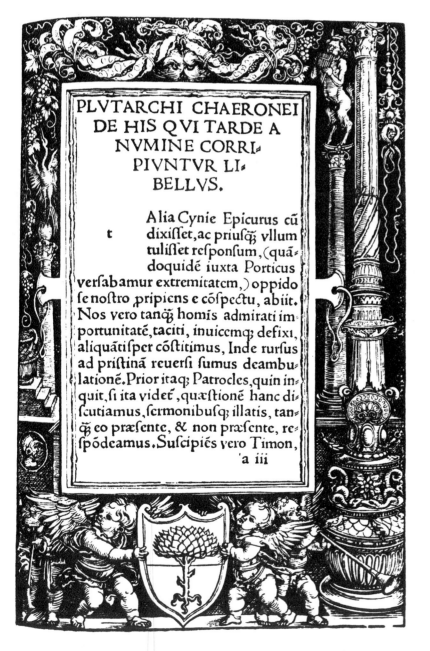

ABOVE LEFT *This answer to a letter of Luther's (Basle, Froben, 1534) has been inscribed by Erasmus, the author, to Beatus.* ABOVE RIGHT *Cardinal Nicholas of Cues's Works, edited by Jacques Lefèvre of Étaples (Paris, Josse Bade, 1514); a present from the editor to Beatus, who had helped him to find material for the book, inscribed by the recipient.* LEFT *Billibald Pirckheimer's edition of Plutarch (Nuremberg 1513). This copy was given to Beatus by Pirckheimer, whose arms appear in the lower margin. The woodcut border is attributed to Dürer or Hans Springinklee.*

philosophy, an interest later expressed in his editions of Aeneas of Gaza (1516) and Maximus Tyrius (1519) – the latter dedicated to the most celebrated of all bibliophiles, the French Treasurer Jean Grolier, whose letter of thanks is at Sélestat. The library reflects a sober and serious taste. His only light reading seems to have been contemporary Latin verse. Baptista Mantuanus's *Georgius* – a Vergilian poem on St George. Zambechari's *Loves of Chryseas and Philochrysus* and similar forgotten works take the place of the vernacular romances that most contemporary laymen would have owned.

Fifty-three of the books were presents. Billibald Pirckheimer sent his edition of Plutarch (Nuremberg 1513) with its woodcut border attributed to Dürer; Lefèvre the collected works of Nicholas of Cues (Paris 1514), received in Basle the following year. Cono's Gregory of Nyssa is the dedication copy to Beatus who arranged for Schürer to print it in Strasbourg in 1512. Numerous annotations, even when used only to mark Poggio's *Facetiae* 'not to be read to the young' or to record that the owner first came across Julius Polydeuces's lexicon when visiting '*humanissimus vir*', the Hellenist and Hebrew scholar Dr Johann Reuchlin, enhance the collection's interest and invite a new form of literary treatment, a bio-bibliography. Other notable components are the long series of first editions of Erasmus, starting with his *Lucubratiunculae,* containing the first printing of the *Enchiridion militis Christiani* ('The Handbook of a Christian Knight'), published at Antwerp in 1503 and bought in Paris the same year – one of four complete copies known: the productions of French, German and Swiss humanist presses (Froben is better represented than in the British Museum), with their handsome founts of roman type and title page borders by Holbein and Urs Graf: and the Reformation pamphlets acquired on publication. The last were close to Beatus's experience, as he knew Zwingli, Bucer and Ulrich von Hutten and sympathised with their aims, though he did not follow them into schism when they left the Roman Church. The first edition of Luther's *De libertate Christiana* ('The Freedom of a Christian Man', Wittenberg 1520) was inscribed by the author to Pirckheimer's friend, Bernhard Adelmann, Canon of Tübingen, and by him to Beatus, who has marked it up for the press. Luther's circle was anxious to disseminate this important statement of his principles; Beatus seems to have been the channel by which the pamphlet reached the press of Adam Petri of Basle who reissued it twice in 1521 without printer's name or place.

Beatus has been accused by a modern scholar of deliberately destroying manuscript exemplars in order to enhance the value of his printed editions. His own library makes this charge hard to believe: he was one of those collectors who could throw nothing away – a school notebook, Paris lecture notes, Greek exercises, Janus Pannonius's poems copied from a manuscript belonging to Jacob Sturm's uncle have all been kept. Periodically he had his books bound in substantial stamped calf over wooden boards, the smaller works grouped several to a volume. A few

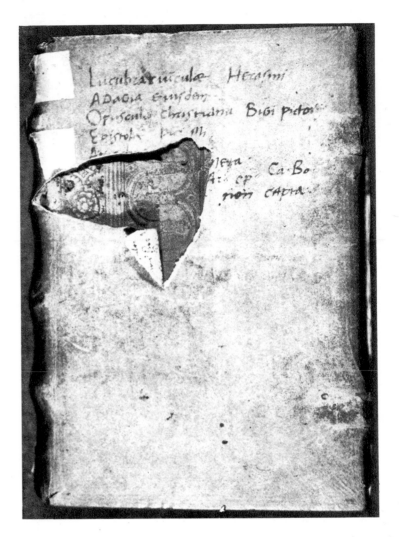

ABOVE *An early dustwrapper. A vellum document used to protect the binding of a collection of pamphlets, including Erasmus's* Lucubratiunculae (Antwerp 1503). BELOW *Martin Luther's* De Libertate Christiana (Wittenberg 1520), *inscribed by the author to Bernhard Adelmann and by him to Beatus.*

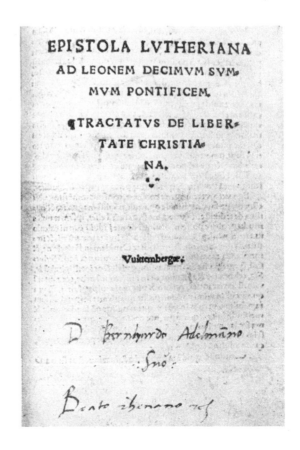

books were singled out for special treatment. In Lefèvre's
edition of Aristotle's *Politics* and *Economics* (Paris 1506), in which
Beatus collaborated, a Parisian illuminator has painted the
latter's arms between kneeling angels at the foot of the preface.
His arms have also been added, probably by a Swiss hand, in
Erasmus's editions of Jerome (1516), Ambrose (1527) and Chrysostom (1530), and tooled on the bindings of his own Tertullian,
Guillaume Budé's work on Roman coinage *De Asse* (Paris 1514)
and a composite volume containing Erasmus's editions of
Origen (1527) and of five works of Chrysostom (1525–7). The
choice bears the characteristic stamp of Northern humanism:
the rediscovery of the Church Fathers and the eclipse of the
medieval schoolmen by the heroes of the new learning with
Erasmus at their head.

A chained library had been established by the magistrates in
the church of St George at Sélestat about 1450 and had received
gifts from several natives of the town, among them Jacob
Wimpfeling, the 'Preceptor of Germany'. This library was the
beneficiary of Beatus's will, though his books were placed not in
the church but in the storeroom of the municipal archives. Losses
inevitably occurred. The royal library in Paris requisitioned forty
incunabula: Matthias Corvinus's Tacitus was removed, apparently by an artillery officer of Napoleon's army, and has found
its way to Yale University. In spite of these lacunae, the collection
is surprisingly complete and in admirable original condition,
more so perhaps than that of any other Northern humanist.

BEATI 1534 RHENANI.

26

Bibliothèque Nationale

PARIS

When Columbus first sighted the American continent the new learning of the Renaissance was concentrated in Italian libraries, with one notable outpost of peninsular culture at Matthias Corvinus's court in Hungary. A hundred years later the pattern had completely changed. Only the Vaticana retained its impetus: Budapest had fallen to the Turks, two other famous Quattrocento collections had disappeared, and the remainder were eclipsed by new foundations beyond the Alps and in Spain. France was the chief heir to the humanist tradition, and, by right of conquest, the largest foreign owner of its manuscripts.

A taste for letters had been traditional in the French royal house since the reign of St Louis (1226–70). King Charles V in 1373 assembled on three storeys of one of the towers of the Louvre a library that totalled 917 volumes. The walls of one room were panelled with Irish bog-timber; brass window grilles were installed as protection against 'birds and other beasts': and the furniture included lecterns with revolving tops, ancestors of the sixteenth-century and later 'book-wheels'. But in 1424 the books were bought by John, Duke of Bedford, brother of Henry V, and dispersed in England after his death.

The next nucleus of a royal collection dated from Charles VIII's expedition to Naples in 1495. Among the spoils of the Aragonese kingdom, tapestries, paintings, marble and porphyry transported to Anne of Brittany's residence at Amboise 'for the decoration and use of the said castle' was a *librairie* of over a thousand volumes, printed and manuscript. They even included some in Greek, confiscated by Ferrante I of Naples from his disgraced favourite, Antonello Petrucci. Charles VIII, although ignorant of Greek and Latin, had humanistic leanings and employed Paulus Aemilius, a Lombard man of letters, and Janos Lascaris, who attached himself to the rising star of France after the Medicis' expulsion from Florence.

Leopold Delisle considered that the idea of the royal library as a national possession originated in the reign of Charles's cousin and successor, Louis XII (1499–1515). Certainly Louis was a great collector. He had inherited over two hundred manuscripts

ABOVE *The Harrowing of Hell, from the Duc de Berry's 'Grandes Heures', 1409. One of the manuscripts seen by Antonio de Beatis in the Blois library in 1517.* OPPOSITE *Death, natural and violent; Reason is enthroned on the right, Fortune in the background. From Petrarch,* Des remèdes de l'une et de l'autre fortune, *Rouen 1503, the dedication manuscript from the translator to Louis XII.*

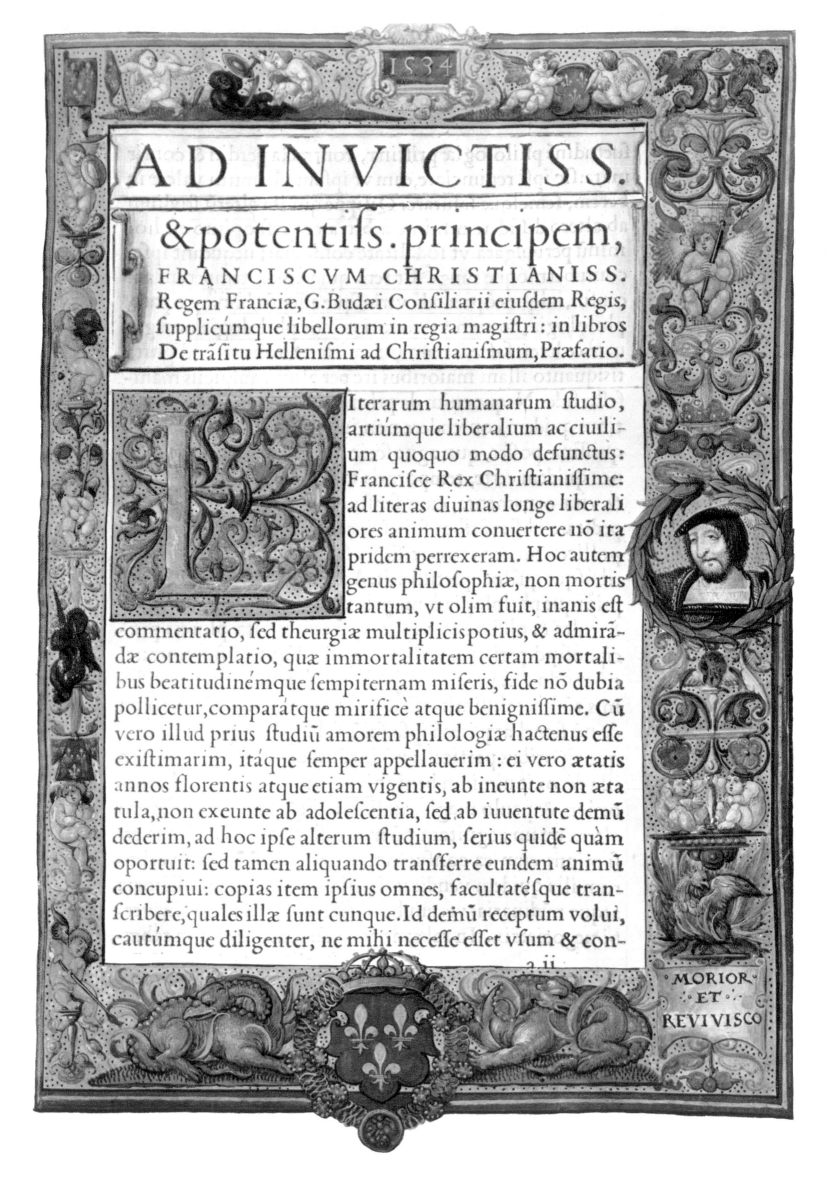

AD INVICTISS.

& potentiſſ. principem,

FRANCISCVM CHRISTIANISS.
Regem Franciæ, G. Budæi Conſiliarii eiuſdem Regis,
ſupplicúmque libellorum in regia magiſtri : in libros
De trãſitu Helleniſmi ad Chriſtianiſmum, Præfatio.

Literarum humanarum ſtudio,
artiúmque liberalium ac ciuili-
um quoquo modo defunctus:
Franciſce Rex Chriſtianiſſime:
ad literas diuinas longe liberali
ores animum conuertere nõ ita
pridem perrexeram. Hoc autem
genus philoſophiæ, non mortis
tantum, vt olim fuit, inanis eſt
commentatio, ſed theurgiæ multiplicis potius, & admirã-
dæ contemplatio, quæ immortalitatem certam mortalibus beatitudinémque ſempiternam miſeris, fide nõ dubia
pollicetur, comparátque mirificè atque benigniſſime. Cũ
vero illud prius ſtudiũ amorem philologiæ hactenus eſſe
exiſtimarim, itáque ſemper appellauerim : ei vero ætatis
annos florentis atque etiam vigentis, ab ineunte non æta
tula, non exeunte ab adoleſcentia, ſed ab iuuentute demũ
dederim, ad hoc ipſe alterum ſtudium, ſerius quidẽ quàm
oportuit: ſed tamen aliquando transferre eundem animũ
concupiui: copias item ipſius omnes, facultatéſque tran-
ſcribere, quales illæ ſunt cunque. Id demũ receptum volui,
cautúmque diligenter, ne mihi neceſſe eſſet vſum & con-

a. ii

MORIOR
ET
REVIVISCO

in the château of Blois from his father, Charles d'Orléans, the poet. To these he added the Aragonese books from Amboise, a large part of the defeated Duke of Milan's library from his castle at Pavia, and manuscripts bought from Ferrante of Naples's widow, and from a Flemish gentleman, Louis de Bruges, who had secured some of Charles v's books from England: the whole forming an impressive but unsystematic array of gothic and Renaissance texts and ornament. The earliest documentary evidence of loans, however, belongs to the next reign, and if a date is to be chosen for the origin of a French national collection, maintained and augmented for the benefit of scholarship from one generation to the next, then 1544, the year of the definitive constitution of the Fontainebleau Library, probably has the best claim.

An inventory of the books at Blois drawn up in 1518 by Guillaume Parvy, the king's Dominican confessor and keeper of the collection, listed 1,626 volumes, of which forty-one were Greek, four Hebrew and two Arabic. A Neapolitan visitor, Antonio de Beatis, the secretary of Cardinal Luigi d'Aragona, has left a description of the library in the previous year:

> In the said castle or palace we saw a fair-sized library, arranged both with desks from head to foot, and with shelves around [the walls] from ground to ceiling, and all full of books. Besides these, others are in chests in a small back-room. The said books are all written by hand in the finest lettering, covered with silk of different colours and with ornate clasps and catches of silver gilt . . .

In other words the books were placed partly on two rows of free-standing desks in the Italian manner (distinguished in surviving pressmarks as 'on the courtyard side' and 'on the moat side'), partly on sloping shelves (*tabulae*) attached to the walls, on which they seem to have lain with the lower cover upwards bearing the title-label. The two chests were used as a reserve for books of special value, some of which were shown to the Neapolitan visitors: Petrarch's *Trionfi* and *De remediis utriusque fortunae*, a large Hours of the Virgin, a Mysteries of the Passion 'with Greek painting' and Ovid's *Metamorphoses* in French and Latin. The choice is significant. The Passion miniatures *di pictura greca* have defied identification, but the others are all gothic works, evidently more highly regarded than the humanistic manuscripts which the library owned in profusion: the Duc de Berry's *Grandes Heures* with large miniatures (since removed) by Jacquemart de Hesdin, and two French translations of Petrarch presented to Louis xii, weakly illuminated by artists of the Loire school.

Meanwhile a new reign had started, more favourable to humanistic influence. Francis i, although not a classical linguist, was steeped in Roman history and the heroic exploits of antiquity, as can be seen from the books he kept to hand: French translations of Justinus, Thucydides, Appian and Diodorus Siculus, besides the *Destruction de Troie la Grant*, the *Roman de la Rose* and a few other medieval romances. The humanist Guillaume Budé's proposition, in a *Collection of Apophthegms* presented to the king in 1519, that a prince's glory depends on his patronage of letters

ABOVE *Minstrel and lady, from* Le livre des eschecs amoureux *(early sixteenth century), written for Francis I before he became king.* OPPOSITE *Guillaume Budé,* De transitu Hellenismi ad Christianismum *(Paris, Robert Estienne, 1535): the dedication copy to Francis I, printed on vellum and illuminated with his arms, motto and portrait.*

was sympathetically received and the author rewarded with an official appointment and the newly created title of Master of the Royal Library. There is little evidence that Budé treated the latter post as anything but a sinecure, and successive keepers – Jacques Lefèvre of Étaples (Beatus Rhenanus's tutor), Jean de la Barre and the poet Mellin de Saint-Gelais – continued to administer the collection as before; but Budé was anxious to promote Greek studies independently of the intensely conservative Sorbonne and persuaded the king to set up a royal college for this purpose, ancestor of the present Collège de France. Readers for Greek, mathematics and Hebrew were appointed in 1530 and for Latin in 1533, and Greek manuscripts began to be collected for their use. The Dauphin's tutor, Girolamo Fondulo of Cremona, bought fifty manuscripts on a special expedition to Italy: twenty were obtained from the estate of Jean de Pins, Bishop of Rieux; and other purchases were made by the French ambassadors to Venice and Rome. The most numerous accessions came through Guillaume Pélicier, Bishop of Montpellier and ambassador in Venice from 1539 to 1542, and included thirty-eight manuscripts from a Corfiote refugee, Antonios Eparchos, and the Greek and Latin collection of Giovanni Francesco d'Asola, the printer Aldus's brother-in-law.

As late as 1540 Pélicier informed the French envoy in Constantinople that the books were intended for the king's college in Paris, but an alternative proposal, namely their addition to the Royal Library to form a focus of national scholarship, must have been suggested at about this time. The new emphasis on the library was perhaps due to Pierre Du Châtel, appointed *lecteur du Roy* from 1537 with the task of reading Greek and Roman authors aloud to the king and *Maître de la Librairie* on Budé's death in 1540. Its earliest consequence was the famous royal edict of 28 December 1537 known as the *Ordonnance de Montpellier,* the first law of legal deposit in any country. Printers and booksellers were required to deliver a copy of every new book to the keeper of the library at Blois; foreign books imported for sale were to be deposited for examination and purchase if considered suitable. In this way (the edict explained) contemporary works would be assembled at Blois as a monument to the literary glory of the reign, the king's successors would acquire a taste for study and be more inclined to continue their patronage of letters, and posterity would find texts in their original purity which might otherwise become corrupt or disappear.

The next reference to Francis's intentions comes from Robert Estienne, who had been granted the royal brevet as Printer and Bookseller in Hebrew and Latin in 1539 and as Greek Printer three years later. In his edition of Cicero's *Tusculanae disputationes* (1542) he related that the king 'has at great cost furnished and is daily furnishing a noble library of every kind of book, Hebrew, Greek and Latin. . . . Far from grudging to anyone the records of ancient writers which he at great and truly royal cost has procured from Italy and Greece, he intends to put them at the disposal and service of all men.' The library thus described came

NTEREA CVM ROMA GOTTHORVM IRRVP
tione agentium sub rege Alarico atq; impetu magne cladis euersa
est : eius euersionem deorum falsorum mutorúq; cultores quos
usitato nomine paganos uocamus: in christianā religionē referre
conantes: solito acerbius & amarius deū uex blasphemare cœperūt
Vnde ego exardescens zelo domus dei: aduersus eorū blasphe
mias uel errores: libros de ciuitate dei scribere istitui. Quod opus
per aliquot annos me tenuit. eo qp alia multa intercurrebāt quę
differri nó oporter& & me prius ad soluendum occupabāt. Hoc
autē de ciuitate dei grande opus tandem. xxii. libris est termiatū
quorū quinque primi eos refellunt qui res humanas ita prospari
uolunt: ut ad hoc mutorum deorum cultum quos pagani colere
consueuerūt: necessariū esse arbitrēt. et quia prohibētur: mala ista
exoriri atq; abundare contendunt. Sequētes autem quiq; aduersus
eos loquuntur: qui fatētur hęc mala nec defuisse ūq nec defutura mortalibus
& ea nunc magna nunc parua: locis: tēporibus: personisq; uariari. Sed deorū
mutorum cultum quo eis sacrificatur: propter uitam post mortem futuram
esse utilem disputant. His ergo. x. libris duę istę uanę opiniones christianę
religioni aduersarię refelluntur. Sed ne quisq; nos aliena tantum redarguisse
non autem nostra asseruisse reprehender&: id agit pars altera operis huius:
quę. xii. libris continetur. Quanq ubi opus est: & in prioribus. x. quę nostra
sunt asseramus: & in. xii. posterioribus redarguamus aduersa. Duodeci ergo
librorum sequentium primi quatuor continent exortum duarum ciuitatum
quarum est una dei altera huius mundi. Secundi quatuor excursum earum
seu procursum. Tertii uero qui & postremi: debitos fines. Ita omnes. xxii.
libri cum sint de utraque ciuitate conscripti: titulum tamen a meliore acce
perunt ut de ciuitate dei potius uocarentur. In quorum decimo libro non
debuit pro miraculo poni: in Abrae sacrificio flammam cęlitus factam inter
diuisas uictimas cucurrisse: quoniam hoc illi in uisione monstratum est. In
xii. libro quod dictum est de Samuele non erat de filiis Aaron: dicendum
potius fuit: non erat filius sacerdotis. Filios quippe sacerdotum defunctis
sacerdotibus succedere magis legitimi moris fuit. Nam in filiis Aarō repiē
pater Samuelis: sed sacerdos non fuit: nec ita i filiis ut eū ipse genuerit Aarō:
sed sicut omnes illius populi dicuntur filii israel DE ADVERSARIIS NO
MINIS CHRISTI QVIBVS IN VASTATIONE VRBIS PROP
TER CHRISTVM BARBARI PEPERCERVNT VICTIS CAPRI

LORIOSISSIMAM CIVITATEM DEI siue
in hoc tempoz cursu cū inter impios peregrinatur ex
fide uiuens: siue i illa stabilitate sedis eternę quā nunc
expectat per patientiam: quoadusq; iustitia conuertat
in iudiciū: deinceps adeptura per excellētiam uictoria
ultima et pace perfecta: hoc opere ad te instituto et mea
promissione debito: defendere aduersus eos q condi
tori eius deos suos pręferūt fili carissime Marcelline
suscepi magnum opus et arduum: sed deus adiutor noster. Nam scio quibus
uiribus opus sit: ut persuadeatur superbis ąta sit uirtus humilitatis. qua sit
ut oīa terrena cacúina temporali mobilitate nutantia: non humano usurpata
fastu: sed diuina gratia donata celsitudo transcendat. Rex enim & conditor

ABOVE *Daniel in the lions' den, attributed to Jean Cousin; miniature in Henri II's Book of Hours, c. 1550.* OPPOSITE *Polybius's* Histories *(the first six books); copied by Angelos Vergecios for Francis I or Henri II in 1547. The headpiece contains the royal arms.*

into being in 1544 when the books from Blois, by then increased to 1,894 volumes, together with a globe and a crocodile's head in a leather case, were transported to a gallery in the palace of Fontainebleau and amalgamated with the king's 268 Greek manuscripts (increased to 540 in the next few years) and the Bourbon family collection, confiscated after the Constable de Bourbon's defection. The library was not very accessible at Fontainebleau, but from Estienne's account it is clear that an integral part of the programme was to print its unpublished texts, so making them generally available. Three special founts of Greek type, the 'grecs du roi', cut by Claude Garamond and modelled on the writing and ornament in manuscripts copied by Angelos Vergecios, a Cretan employed on the library staff, were financed by royal grants. The *editio princeps* of the Greek text of Eusebius's *Ecclesiastical History,* 1544, was the first work to appear: the Greek New Testament, published in 1550 and based on nine royal manuscripts, the most influential. Francis I is said to have chosen the Roman history of Dionysius of Halicarnassus for publication (1546–7) and to have suggested the small Greek type used for a pocket New Testament in 1546.

A programme of rebinding the Greek books and the shabbier volumes from Blois, inaugurated by Francis I, was continued on a lavish scale by his successor, Henri II. Over nine hundred bindings from his reign (1547–59) survive. Designers of genius, the ready availability of morocco skins from the Levant and the stimulus of Islamic models brought the bookbinder's art to a culmination at this period, and the Fontainebleau series, the most splendid in existence, must have been unforgettably impressive when displayed in a single room on desks or sloping shelves. It was perhaps in imitation of the French royal collection that the Grand-Duke Francis I of Tuscany had the Laurenziana manuscripts uniformly rebound in red morocco in 1585.

In 1567 a Regius Professor, Pierre Ramus, petitioned the Queen-Dowager Catherine de Médicis for the books to be brought to Paris, where they would be accessible to men of letters and close to the University, citing the example of Cosimo and Lorenzo de' Medici 'who did not place their library in their delightful villas in the Tuscan countryside but in the limelight of their fatherland'. These arguments prevailed and a few years later the collection, by then amounting to 3,650 titles, was installed on two floors of an unidentified building in Paris, where they may have been for the first time shelved in the modern manner. This was a momentous decision. At Fontainebleau the library might have atrophied when later kings preferred other residences: in the capital it was to grow and develop in response to national needs.

Under Henri IV (*r.* 1589–1610) the books were placed in the Collège de Clermont, left empty by the Jesuits, then moved by the Master, Jacques-Auguste de Thou, to the convent of the Cordeliers, later to a dependency of the convent in the Rue de la Harpe. The first catalogue, of 1622, listed nearly six thousand works, increased one and a half times by the bequest

ΠΟΛΥΒΙΟΥ ΜΕΓΑΛΟΠΟ
ΛΙΤΟΥ · ΙΣΤΟΡΙΩΝ
ΠΡΩΤΗ

Εἰ μὲν τοῖς πρὸ ἡμῶν ἀναγράφουσι τὰς
πράξεις παραλελεῖφθαι συνέβαινε
τὸν ὑπὲρ αὐτῆς τῆς ἱστορίας ἔπαινον, ἴσως
ἀναγκαῖον ἦν δὲ προτρέπεσθαι πάν-
τας πρὸς τὴν αἵρεσιν ἐπὶ παραδοχὴν τῶν τοι-
ούτων ὑπομνημάτων, διὰ τὸ μηδεμίαν ἑτοιμοτέραν εἶναι τοῖς ἀνθρώποις
διόρθωσιν, τῆς τῶν προγεγενημένων πράξεων ἐπιστήμης.
Ἐπεὶ δ' οὐ τινὲς οὐδ' ἐπὶ ποσὸν, ἀλλὰ πάντες ὡς ἔπος εἰπεῖν,
ἀρχῇ καὶ τέλει κέχρηνται τούτῳ, φάσκοντες ἀληθινωτάτην μὲν εἶναι παιδείαν καὶ γυμνασίαν πρὸς τὰς πολιτικὰς πράξεις, τὴν ἐκ
τῆς ἱστορίας μάθησιν, ἐναργεστάτην δὲ καὶ μόνην διδάσκαλον,
τοῦ δύνασθαι τὰς τῆς τύχης μεταβολὰς γενναίως ὑποφέρειν τὴν τῶν
ἀλλοτρίων περιπετειῶν ὑπόμνησιν, δῆλον ὡς οὐδενὶ μὲν ἂν δό-
ξαι καθήκειν περὶ τῶν καλῶς καὶ πολλοῖς εἰρημένων ταυτολογεῖν.
ἥκιστα δ' ἡμῖν. αὐτὸ γὰρ τὸ παράδοξον τῶν πράξεων, ὑπὲρ
ὧν προῃρήμεθα γράφειν, ἱκανόν ἐστι προκαλέσασθαι καὶ πα-
ρορμῆσαι πάντα καὶ νέον καὶ πρεσβύτερον, πρὸς τὴν ἔντευξιν

αʹ

of Jacques Dupuy's collection in 1656: among the latter was a fifth-century codex of Livy's *Third Decade*, 'one of the oldest classical manuscripts in existence' (E.A.Lowe). J.-B.Colbert's direction of the library from 1661 to 1683, exercised through the titular keepership of his brother, was a period of lively activity; collections were bought, ambassadors instructed to send current foreign books, travellers dispatched to the East in search of manuscripts. Gaston d'Orléans' medals formed the nucleus of the present *Cabinet des Médailles*, the Abbé de Marolles' prints of the *Cabinet des Estampes*. For his own convenience Colbert installed the library in the Rue Vivienne, at the end of his garden. In 1724 a final move was made, into the Duke de Nevers' house across the street.

All this time the library was not open to the public and even a scholar of the eminence of Isaac Vossius could only gain admittance through influence at court. It was therefore a great event, celebrated by 'a magnificent repast', when the Abbé de Louvois (a precocious savant whose father had bought him the office of Royal Librarian as a ninth-birthday present) opened the collection twice weekly in 1692. This régime was in operation six years later when Dr Lister found the books occupying twenty-two rooms on two floors in bookcases protected by grilles, but it again lapsed and the library was not permanently opened to readers until 1735 and even then only on two days a week.

The French Revolution brought a harsh introduction to the disagreeable realities of political control. Lefèvre d'Ormesson, the last Royal Librarian, and his two successors, nominees of the Gironde, Carra and Chamfort, were arrested; Chamfort died in prison, the two others under the guillotine. The Abbé Barthélemy and his nephew were released from jail just in time to prevent the *Cabinet des Médailles* being melted down. A deputy proposed burning the library on the grounds that it had been defiled by the name of 'Bibliothèque du Roi' – a threat which only lack of time and shortage of incendiary materials prevented the Communards of 1871 from carrying into execution. Another proposal, that 'the books of the Public Libraries of Paris, and of the Departments, could no longer be permitted to offend the eyes of the Republicans by shameful marks of servitude, and that all such must be immediately effaced: Fleurs-de-lis, for example, and armorial bearings, whether on the bindings, or in other parts of books, together with all prefaces and dedications addressed to kings and nobles must disappear', was drafted as a decree, but fortunately quashed by a newspaper campaign conducted by two booksellers and a printer, Renouard, Chardin and Didot.

The Revolution plunged the French library system into turmoil: in the twenty years after the fall of the Bastille over ninety-five per cent of books in the country changed ownership. One and a half million volumes confiscated from emigrés, religious houses and the condemned were assembled in eight stores in Paris alone: officials of the Bibliothèque Nationale selected, as best they could, a hundred thousand printed books and about seventy thousand manuscripts. On top of this the major literary monu-

ments of western Europe started to reach the library from the commissioners appointed to remove cultural trophies from the conquered territories. These had to be restored after Waterloo, and Joseph Van Praet, Keeper of printed books for forty-three years, succeeded in imposing a façade of order on his department by 1818, when the high priest of British bibliomania, the Rev. Thomas Frognall Dibdin, found him 'mild and pleasant' and flatteringly attentive in plying his English visitor with uncut classics and vellum Aldines. But a high proportion of the flood of accessions was still uncatalogued and even unarranged forty years later, and arrears of cataloguing were only made good during the administration of the great Léopold Delisle (1874–1905). To its right of legal deposit the Bibliothèque Nationale has added in this century the right to pre-empt at auction sales. It has equal claim with the British Museum to be considered the world's greatest library.

Manuel Phile, On the properties of animals, copied by Angelos Vergecios for Henri II in 1554. The illustrations are of a dog and a mantechora.
BELOW *The Bibliothèque Nationale: the main entrance in the Place Louvois.*

Bavarian State Library

MUNICH

ABOVE *St Ambrose baptising St Augustine: from the Missal of Bernhard von Rohr, Archbishop of Salzburg, 1481–c.1490.* OPPOSITE *Marginal drawings by Dürer, 1515, in the Prayerbook of the Emperor Maximilian I. The book was printed on vellum in a specially cut type.*

Duke Albrecht v of Bavaria's purchase of Johann Albrecht Widmanstetter's books in 1558 is considered the founding date of the Munich Library. The Duke (r. 1550–72) had inherited a quantity of manuscripts, works such as Ulrich Fuetrer's *Adventures of the Knights of the Round Table* in German, but the new acquisition was intended not for his personal entertainment but as a 'princely library' for the use of savants and court officials. He himself was fond of music and became a considerable collector of works of art and curiosities; he enjoyed browsing in chronicles of Bavarian history, but otherwise was no reader. 'He exercises his body in honest hunting and refreshes his soul with musical instruments,' wrote a panegyrist. The purchase was an act of policy due to the advice of various counsellors: Johann Jakob Fugger of the Augsburg banking family, a retired diplomat Georg Seld, and the Jesuit Order, newly established in Bavaria, whose concern with education gave them a special need for a readily accessible library. The tortuous course of the negotiations throws some light on the combination of motives involved.

Widmanstetter's was a philologist's library (he had studied Hebrew and the Cabbala with Jewish teachers in Italy, edited the first Syriac New Testament and explained the Copernican system to an audience composed of Pope Clement VII, two cardinals, an archbishop and the Pope's doctor), rich in Hebrew, Arabic and other Oriental manuscripts, the Gospels in Hungarian, printed books in Czech, Polish, Croat and the romance languages, but containing only a single book in English, *A Glasse of the Truthe*, 1531 (classified in the Ducal Library as a sub-division of French). He died in 1557, leaving three daughters. A letter of Georg Seld's of February 1558 reported that the Duke was negotiating with the heirs, anxious to equal the Pope, the King of France, the Venetian Republic, the Medici and the Elector Palatine – all owners of famous libraries – in this form of princely display. But a discouraging report on the collection reached him – it was nearly all printed, there were few manuscripts and of these almost nothing worth publishing, the whole bought indiscriminately from dealers and convents and containing many sophistic works

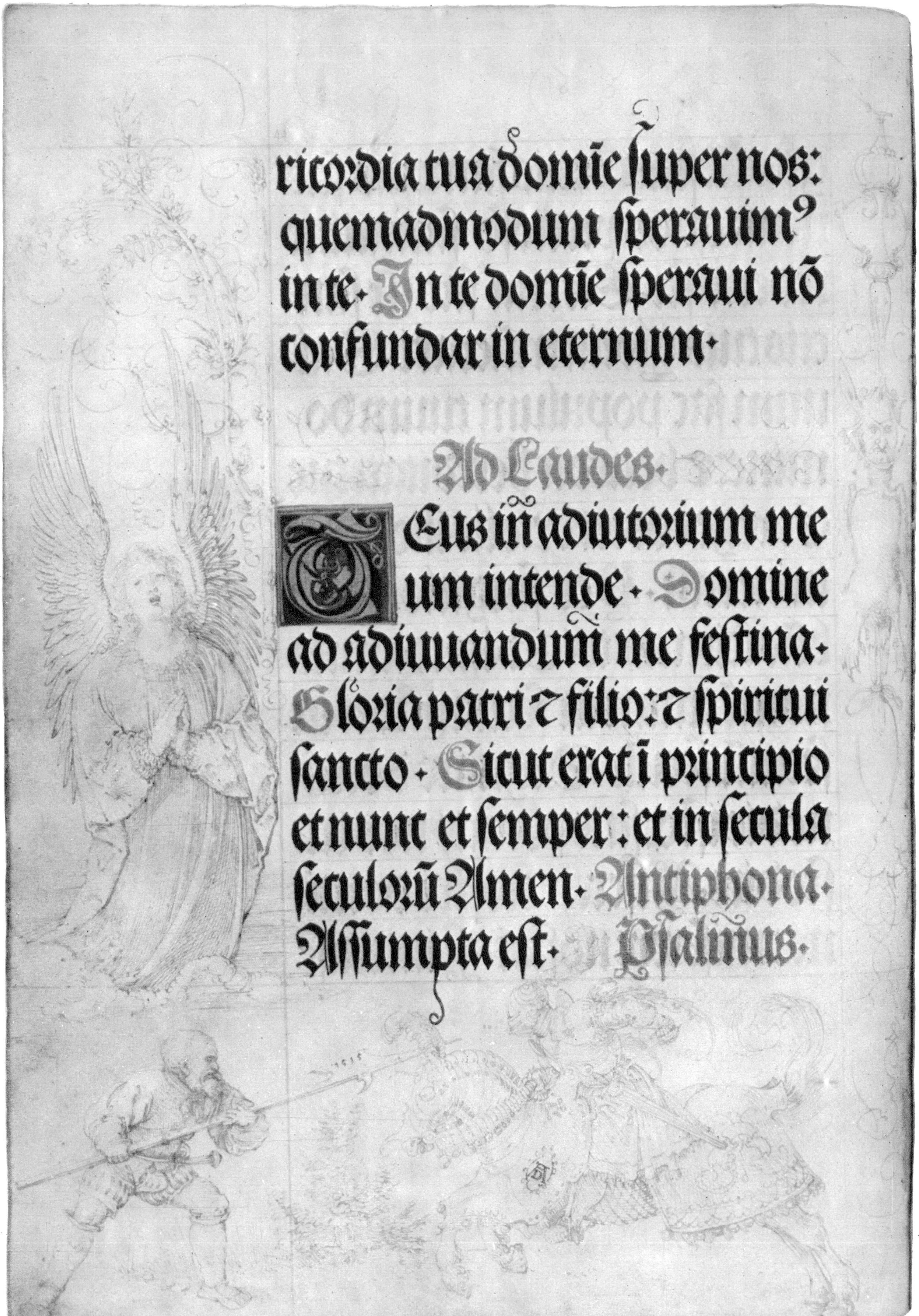

ricordia tua domie super nos:
quemadmodum sperauim⁹
in te. In te domie speraui no
confundar in eternum.

Ad Laudes.

Eus in adiutorium me
um intende. Domine
ad adiuuandum me festina.
Gloria patri ⁊ filio: ⁊ spiritui
sancto. Sicut erat i principio
et nunc et semper: et in secula
seculorū Amen. Antiphona.
Assumpta est. Psalmus.

Vidam vir cū nō
haberet vxorem
quandā meretri
cem sibi cōiugio
copulauit q̄ erat
sterilis neptis in

Vidam eps ages in ex
tremis succeſſorē sibi ex
teſtamēto inſtituit·indo
suorū amicorū patroci
mo in eūdē epatū elig
tur poſt electōnez p in
cōmitate eccie canomcis iuramentū pre
buit·accuſatur de ſimonia tanq̄ munu

Vidā clericī a pa
relinquē nolunt.
de suis z eccie re
bus teſtāta cō
ficiūt·de rebs ec
cleſie nōnulla lar
giūtur·Odo primū queriť·utrū

Vidam laicus
baſilicam a ſe fa
ctā a dyoceſana
lege ſegregare
queit·Eps eccie

PREVIOUS PAGES: LEFT *Miniatures from a copy of Gratian's* Decretum *(Mainz, Peter Schoeffer, 1472) printed on vellum and illuminated for Bertold von Henneberg, later Archbishop of Mainz.* RIGHT *Hans Mülich. Duke Albrecht V of Bavaria, with his sons and councillors: an illustration in Orlando di Lasso's setting of the penitential psalms written and illuminated for the Duke in 1565.*

LEFT *Duke Albrecht V playing chess with his wife, Anna, by Hans Mülich: frontispiece to an illustrated catalogue of the Duchess's jewels, 1552–5.* RIGHT *Portrait of Albrecht V after Peter Weinher, from a binding by Heinrich Peisenberg, c. 1574.* BELOW *Duke William IV of Bavaria jousting with Duke Leonhart of Lichtenstein, by Hans Ostendorfer; from William IV's tournament book, 1541.*

of the previous century, legendaries and suchlike. Albrecht's
enthusiasm cooled. Then came a fresh incentive; the news was
leaked by the Imperial ambassador that the King of Bohemia
was interested in its acquisition. King Maximilian (later Emperor
as Maximilian II), although outwardly a conforming Catholic,
was notorious for his Lutheran sympathies; the books could not be
allowed to fall into dubiously orthodox hands, and Albrecht
quickly clinched the deal at a thousand florins, so combining a
show of princely magnificence with a denial of potential ammuni-
tion to the Protestants.

At first uncertain what to do with his purchase (a few volumes
were given away to the Jesuits), the Duke was persuaded by Seld
to bring the books to Munich as the basis of a court library
(Hofbibliothek): the Prince would find it convenient when he
wanted an old history; it could be cared for properly in the
capital; its value would be greatest where affairs of state were

decided: it would be an ornament of the court, to be shown to foreign savants. Not long after the books were installed in the Alter Hof they were joined by a legacy from Albrecht's uncle, the Archbishop of Salzburg, a bequest conditional on the nephew's accepting responsibility for the Archbishop's two natural sons.

The other great accession of the reign was Johann Jakob Fugger's library. Fugger had deliberately set out to rival the Aragonese kings of Naples and made full use of his banking house's international network for information and supply. In Italy, where he earned something of the reputation Pierpont Morgan later enjoyed ('*il primo ricco di Germania*'), Fugger was served by three main agents: Jacopo Strada of Mantua, who in the intervals of shipping complete collections to Germany himself copied 'eighteen great volumes on coins'; and two Flemings in Venice, Arnoldus Arlenius and Nicholas Stoppio, who supplied Greek and Hebrew manuscripts, the former chiefly Byzantine theology, the majority of the latter contemporary transcripts but including some that may have belonged to Pico della Mirandola, the first Italian humanist to read Hebrew. Manuscripts from Matthias Corvinus's collection were provided by two cultivated managers of mines, in Tyrol and Slovakia. But the most interesting component was the thousand manuscripts and 670 printed books of Hartmann Schedel, one of the first generation of German humanists and editor of the *Nuremberg Chronicle* (1493), bought from his grandson for five hundred florins. A codex long considered one of the chief treasures of the Hofbibliothek, the tenth-century papyrus *Traditions of the Church of Ravenna,* was brought back from Italy by young Dr Samuel Quiccelberg, who succeeded Hieronymus Wolf, an eminent scholar but indifferent librarian, as curator.

The Fugger collections were arranged in the specially built Antiquarium, designed by Jacopo Strada, in the Residenz. The library occupied the first floor, the bookcases apparently standing in the middle of the room, their line broken by a table under which volumes of special value were kept in a wooden chest. The room was decorated with two globes by Peter Apian of Ingoldstadt and maps above the cases and the windows, but a proposal of Strada's to paint the ceiling with the story of Psyche, in imitation of the Palazzo del Tè in Mantua, seems to have come to nothing. There were two catalogues, of printed books and of manuscripts; a small group of rarities, mostly illuminated manuscripts, was distinguished. Protestant theology, on the Papal legate's advice, was separately shelved and in theory available only in exceptional circumstances. The art collection on the ground floor included 109 of Albrecht's favourite picture-books, the Strada volumes, his father Duke William IV's tournament-book, volumes of drawings of arms and armour, fireworks, jewels, architecture, fish, horse-bits, coats of arms, costumes of all nations, armed and unarmed combat, and a palmleaf manuscript from Burma or Ceylon.

Albrecht's successors, William V (1579–97), and the first Elector of Bavaria, Maximilian I (1597–1651), made large

ABOVE *A duel with sickles, by Jörg Breu the younger, c. 1560. From Paul Hektor Mair's* Fechtbuch, *bought by Albrecht V in 1567.*
BELOW *Book of Gospel-lessons given to Bamberg Cathedral by the Emperor Henry II (early eleventh century): the Ascension, facing the appropriate chapter of St Mark's Gospel.*

additions to the library, which by 1586 was estimated to comprise eleven thousand volumes. A catalogue of the Greek manuscripts was published in 1602, the first printed catalogue of any German princely collection. The outstanding acquisition of these years, which (rather than the Yates Thompson Aristotle: see p. 294) may be claimed as 'the most beautiful book in the world', was bought in 1609 from the heirs of Cardinal Granvelle, the Emperor Charles v's minister: the Emperor Maximilian i's copy of a specially printed prayerbook of 1513, its margins decorated with drawings by Dürer and Cranach.

Bavaria was involved in the Thirty Years War from the outset: it was a Bavarian army which captured Heidelberg, and Maximilian i of Bavaria (to whom the Emperor transferred the defeated prince's Electoral title) who offered the Palatina, the only German library to rival his own, as a gift to the Pope. Retribution came nine years later with the sack of Munich in 1632 by Gustavus Adolphus's Swedes. Albrecht's *Kunstkammer* on the ground floor of the Antiquarium was systematically looted and his picture-books were destroyed or dispersed. Most of the Strada volumes and many German manuscripts found their way through William of Weimar to Gotha; four Strada volumes were bought by the Earl of Arundel while on an embassy from Charles i of England to the Imperial Diet in Regensburg and are in the British Museum: a Greek manuscript reached Archbishop Laud and was given to the Bodleian; Peter Wiener's manuscript atlas of Bavaria is in Stockholm. The library suffered less severely; about two thousand volumes disappeared, less than a tenth of the total, and the loss in numbers was made good when Electoral troops appropriated most of Duke Christoph of Wurtemberg's books two years later.

The eighteenth century was uneventful, the only addition of note being the library of Pietro Vettori, the humanist editor of Cicero. Then came the massive upheavals of the Napoleonic Wars, from which Munich emerged a gainer on a vast scale. In 1803 all ecclesiastical property in Germany was secularised to compensate lay rulers dispossessed from the left bank of the Rhine. One hundred and fifty Bavarian religious houses were affected, sixty-five of which had large libraries. Descriptions of the sequestration by one of the commissioners, Johann Christian von Aretin, still make painful reading. At Tegernsee, for example, an eighth-century foundation with sixty thousand volumes and its own printing-press, the monks tried to save the abbey's most venerable treasures by hiding them in their cells or in the village, and were bullied and threatened until they confessed. Manuscripts and incunabula went to Munich, later books to Landshut University, the schools or for sale. Not much was spared. The Gospels of Charles the Bald were taken from Regensburg after more than nine hundred years; Bamberg lost books which the Emperor Henry ii had given the cathedral in the early eleventh century. On the pretext that Salzburg had been annexed to Bavaria during these years, King Maximilian's representative secured for Munich 150 volumes confiscated by the French from

Liber antiquitatum, *a collection of inscriptions, humanist poetry, etc., written and decorated by Hartmann Schedel, with his arms at the foot of the page (Nuremberg 1504–5).*

the prince-archbishop. On the other hand much of value came to light in the process: the sixth-century *Breviarium Alarici* from Würzburg Cathedral, the *Türken-Calendar* from the Augsburg Jesuits – the unique copy of the first book printed with movable type, and some of the earliest German philological documents, such as the *Muspilli* from St Emmeram in Regensburg, a ninth-century poem on the Last Judgement.

Thomas Frognall Dibdin was in Munich in 1819 and admired 'the apparently interminable succession of apartments . . . it should seem as if every monastery throughout Bavaria had emptied itself of its book-treasures . . . to be poured into this enormous reservoir.' But behind the bold face put on for visitors, conditions were chaotic. The books were in sixty rooms and passages in the Academy of Sciences; a report of 1832 speaks of 'two hundred thousand volumes, partly of highly important works, lying in the stores under the roof, in danger of becoming unusable through mould and mildew, exposed to a very high fire risk . . . endangering the whole building with the weight of a giant load for which it was not designed.' Five hundred thousand volumes were 'arranged in threefold or fourfold rows, in dark, or on dull days totally black, rooms.'

This state of crisis was resolved in three ways: by the construction of a new library building on the Ludwigstrasse, opened in 1843; by the prodigious labours of Johann Andreas Schmeller, who catalogued eighteen thousand manuscripts between 1829 and 1837 as well as completing his Bavarian Dictionary, in itself the work of a lifetime; and by the sale of innumerable duplicates. Dibdin succeeded in buying a blockbook guide to the sights of Rome (*Mirabilia Romae*) in German, and the first German Bible for Lord Spencer, and a copy of Bernhard von Breidenbach's *Reise in das gelobte Land* ('Journey to the Holy Land'), 1486, was thrown in free; but he failed to come to terms over another blockbook: 'the value fixed upon it was too high; indeed a little extravagant'. Over fifty years later this huge dispersal was still going on; the British Museum's incunabula to a considerable extent are duplicates from Munich.

In the Second World War the library was bombed on four occasions and its buildings almost totally destroyed. The manuscripts and incunabula had been evacuated and were saved, but five hundred thousand volumes perished, among them much that is irreplaceable, copies that had belonged to Widmanstetter or Fugger, the collection of Bibles, large sections on European travel and geography. It is pleasant to be able to record that restoration of the library is nearly complete, a new reading-room seems able to hold as many students as the British Museum, and the four Greeks, replicas of the statues by Schwanthaler, are again in position contemplating the Ludwigstrasse.

zu hercnia Die des keisers vō cōstātinopel
was Also ist ym begegent gar ein grof
ser has Vñ ist dē turckē vil folkes midd
gelegē Almechtig got du wollest diner
cristēheit plegē Vñ gnedeclich gebē crafft
fridē vñ einikeit Vñ das sie sich mit ir
grossen macht bereide Den ubeln turken
vñ sin folck zuurribē Vñ dz sie ir keinen
lebendig lasse blybē · wedd in turky gre
cie alye noch eropa Des helff uns die kō
nigin maria Die do ist ein mut dʼ heilgē
cristēheit Der ein swert yrees mielidens ir
hertz ūsneit Do ir son in dodelichem unge
mach Virwont hāgē an dē crutz sprach
Ich befelen dich dem iungern min Also
laß dir die cristenheit befolen sin Vñd
bidde gnedeclich vor sie in aller not Das
zij nuwe am himmel stat Off dinstag
noch nicolai des milden herren Vor mit
tage so sechs stunde her zu keren ···:·····

Eyn gut selig nuwe Jar

LEFT Eyn manung der cristenheit widder die
durken *(Mainz 1454): the unique copy of the
earliest printed book, consisting of nine leaves. It
belonged to Conrad Peutinger, the Augsburg humanist, was bequeathed by a descendant to the Jesuit
College of Augsburg and came to Munich at the
secularisation.* BELOW *The 'Four Greeks' outside
the Munich State Library are post-war replicas of
Schwanthaler's statues, destroyed by bombing.*

Austrian National Library

VIENNA

In July 1575 a Dutch Calvinist, Hugo Blotz (or Blotius) was disagreeably startled by the sight of the library which had just been placed in his charge:

> How neglected and desolate everything looked! There was mouldiness and rot everywhere, the débris of moths and bookworms, and a thick covering of cobwebs. . . . The windows had not been opened for months and not a ray of sunshine had penetrated through them to brighten the unfortunate books, which were slowly pining away; and when they were opened, what a cloud of noxious air streamed out!

The library was the Emperor's Hofbibliothek in Vienna: it was situated in a room on the first floor of the Minorites' convent and Blotius was its first curator.

There was no immediate way of correcting the building's disadvantages as a repository of books: the absence of windows from all sides but one so that the air could not circulate, the damp seeping up from the convent's well directly below, or the layout of the rooms which involved passing through a corn store and the monks' dormitory in order to reach the library. Two tasks were of overriding urgency: to arrange the books in order and to prepare a catalogue, as the collection had become so disorganised that the existing index was useless. Blotius toiled away through the autumn and winter with intermittent help from Helfrich Guett, President of the Privy Council, Dr Wolfgang Pudler, Government Councillor of Lower Austria, Dr Georg Tanner, professor of Greek at the University, Pudler's son and Tanner's sons' tutor. By 24 April 1576 two copies had been engrossed of a rather summary alphabetical catalogue; one copy was forwarded to the Emperor Maximilian II in Prague, the other retained in the library. The books had been consecutively numbered and arranged in twenty-eight presses (plus, in all probability, a few chests). With the exception of some Greek and Hebrew books they seem to have stood spines outwards and were identified by a paper label bearing their number and press letter at the foot of the spine. There were altogether 7,379 volumes.

Fifty years earlier the Emperor Maximilian I (1493–1519),

The Emperor Maximilian I dictating a romance to his secretary, Marcus Treitzsaurwein. OPPOSITE *Vienna: the National Library, designed by the elder and younger Fischer von Erlach. The frescoes are by Daniel Gran.*

ABOVE *Kundalbrecht, King of Hungary and Bohemia, a design for Maximilian I's monument; Innsbruck, studio of Jörg Kölderer, 1522–3.*
OPPOSITE Bouquet d'anemones *by Nicolas Robert; from a collection of flower-drawings by Robert and his pupils executed for Louis XIV's minister, J.-B. Colbert. They entered the Vienna Library with Prince Eugene of Savoy's collection.*

himself a poet and the author of autobiographical romances, *Freydal, Tewrdannck* and *Der Weisskunig*, had owned a magnificent library, inherited in part from his father Frederick III and including some splendid examples of Bohemian illumination derived from King Wenceslas I (1378–1400). In its accent on romances of chivalry and heroic sagas the collection resembled the Librairie de Bourgogne; indeed Maximilian had married Philip the Good's granddaughter and been deeply impressed by the knightly conventions of the Burgundian court. But in his library these gothic influences were diversified by a current from the Italian Renaissance. Conrad Celtes, the Nuremberg humanist who acted as Imperial librarian for some years before his death in 1508, described the collection in the dedication of his *Rhapsodia* (1505) as 'small but adorned by Greek, Latin and exotic [*i.e.,* Hebrew and Arabic] authors'; and some of the books he was referring to can be tentatively identified, manuscripts of Terence and of Latin translations of Aesop and Aristotle's *Politics*, and printed editions of Cicero, Crescentius and Ptolemy.

Like Philip the Good, Maximilian I seems to have kept his books in chests, divided among various residences. The major part was in Innsbruck at his death, with another substantial group at Wiener Neustadt. A few of Maximilian's manuscripts were certainly among the books Blotius saw in 1575: and to this extent the authors of the Austrian National Library's official history are justified in insisting on its continuous existence since the fourteenth century. But the link between Maximilian's library and the new Hofbibliothek was tenuous and accidental. Maximilian's grandson Ferdinand I may have let the latter have some inherited manuscripts, but he gave the Innsbruck Library with the Lordship of Tyrol to his younger son, Archduke Ferdinand, and never bothered to transfer the Wiener Neustadt books to Vienna. Essentially, as a contemporary, Angelo Rocca, founder of the Biblioteca Angelica in Rome, remarked, the Hofbibliothek was a mid-sixteenth-century creation; and the Emperor Maximilian II, great-grandson of the first Maximilian, was its creator.

Behind its founding, or re-founding, can be discovered the familiar collaboration of prince and humanist: Maximilian II, King of Bohemia from 1549 and Holy Roman Emperor from 1564, and a young diplomat who entered his service in 1550 and died seven years later, aged not much more than thirty, Caspar von Niedbruck. Their common interest was not in Greek letters but in religion: both were Lutheran sympathisers and actively concerned to help the Protestant controversialist Matthias Flaccius Illyricus, who was the sponsor of an audacious attempt to prove from historical sources that only the Lutheran Church was apostolic. Details of Niedbruck's activities are almost wholly lacking: we catch sight of him buying books at Frankfurt (among them, characteristically, a collection of Franciscan documents printed in Salamanca in 1511), borrowing works by Wycliffe and Huss from the Collegium Caroli III in Prague and acquiring manuscripts in the Rhineland which, although intended for Vienna, were first sent to be copied for Flaccius Illyricus in

Fasciculus Anemonum.

Bouquet d'Anemones doubles

Regensburg. A decree of 1551, suggested no doubt by the *Ordonnance de Montpellier*, required printers to deposit three copies of every book published with the Imperial privilege; of these the Hofbibliothek was to receive one. In 1558 Maximilian was forestalled by Duke Albrecht of Bavaria in an attempt to buy the Syriac scholar Johann Albrecht Widmanstetter's books; but by this time the library was already large enough to require a team of students to put it in order and a member of Maximilian's household compiled two 'huge indexes' of its holdings.

The 1560s were marked by two important accessions. In 1546 Wolfgang Lazius, professor of Medicine at Vienna University, had attracted Ferdinand I's attention by an account of the city and had been rewarded with the title of Court Historian. Between 1548 and 1551 he carried out three bibliographical tours in Austria, south Germany, Alsace and Switzerland in search of material in monastic libraries. He equipped himself with royal letters of recommendation and drew a sum of money from the Treasury for expenses; his technique seems to have been to 'borrow' anything he thought of interest, remove it to Vienna and forget to return it. Here is his description of finding the *Historiae apostolicae* of Pseudo-Abdias in Ossiach:

It happened that about two years ago, on my second journey to the southern provinces of Austria, when I was in Carinthia, I visited Ossiach, by far the oldest monastery in that region, founded by Carloman. There was no library there, as the result of repeated devastations by fire and savages; but with my inborn love, or rather passion for antiquity I explored their cellars. There, by luck, in the middle of tattered archives and foul-smelling dirt, I hit on a vellum manuscript written in ancient and very faded characters. As I was in a hurry to continue my journey, I only examined it superficially, as the title was written at the end and the beginning was defective. When I had read half a page and found it pleasing, I threw it into my luggage and took it with me to Vienna, perhaps only on account of the age of the vellum and the script. And here, when I had leisure to inspect the basket-full of books I'd brought back, I discovered it was an account of the apostles' history.

Although Ferdinand I's name had been invoked to obtain possession of these manuscripts, they appear not to have reached the Hofbibliothek until after Lazius's death in 1565. Towards the end of the decade they were joined by about 1,500 works in 618 volumes collected by Hans Dernschwam, whose life had been spent managing mines in Slovakia.

These, then, were the chief sources of the books committed to Blotius's care. Apart from Lazius's manuscripts and a few earlier books presumably bought by Niedbruck, the great majority had been printed in the Empire after 1540 and dealt with a variety of subjects — law, history, politics, religious controversy, warfare, medicine and so on. As light literature there were Margaret of Navarre's *Les marguerites*, 1552, Rabelais's *Oeuvres*, 1553, his fourth book of *Pantagruel* (1548) and a spurious sixth book (1549). One press was reserved for books in French, Italian and Spanish, another for large folios — mostly albums of drawings or maps. Dernschwam's collection, by contrast, had been formed

by a humanist with international contacts and was rich in editions of the classics and of the Italian scholars of the Renaissance, in books printed by Aldus, Froben, Robert Estienne and Josse Bade, and in mathematics, astronomy and chemistry.

The Hofbibliothek had developed to satisfy three main requirements: for political intelligence, Austrian and Hapsburg historical records, and 'prestige' books to impress foreigners. The first was mostly supplied by manuscripts of the kind described by Henry Wotton in 1591: 'I found one [manuscript discourse] of all the Pope's revenues and expenses: another of all the ports and fortresses in England, and the Queen's uttermost strength: a third, the revenues of the State of Venice. . . . .' Of the books intended to astonish visiting scholars the chief, when Blotius took over, were the sixth-century illustrated Dioscorides, discovered in Constantinople by the Imperial ambassador, Augerius Busbeck, in the possession of the son of Suleyman the Magnificent's Jewish doctor, and the Syriac Gospels written out for Ferdinand I by a travelling envoy of the patriarch of Antioch. The list was considerably extended in the course of time. Edward Browne was shown numerous curiosities in 1668, from 'a Letter of the present Emperor of China' to 'a Magical Glass, obtained by the Emperor Rudolphus, whereby to see Apparitions, and converse with Spirits'.

There was no space to consult books on the premises and Blotius instituted, with Imperial sanction, a liberal system of loans. A century later the attitude had changed; copying and publication of unpublished texts were deprecated as tending to impair the collection's uniqueness, and the philosopher Leibniz was refused permission to borrow two manuscripts. These restrictions were fortunately short-lived. In 1726 Charles VI declared the library open to all, except 'idiots, servants, idlers, chatterboxes and casual strollers'.

Blotius's views on his own office were coloured by the fact that he had married a rich widow. He considered that the Emperor's librarian, besides being a master of several languages, honest, reliable and industrious, should not be poor (or he might be tempted to misappropriate the books) nor superstitious (meaning that he must not be shocked by the quantity of Protestant theology on the shelves). He believed that the librarian must make every effort to increase the collection and should not be ashamed of soliciting bequests; but paradoxically the chief augmentations during his period of office were due not to himself but to Augerius Busbeck and Johannes Sambucus, a Hungarian scholar-dilettante who spent most of his life in the university cities of Germany, France and Italy. Busbeck had bought 274 Greek manuscripts during his Turkish embassy; Sambucus had assembled 565 Greek and Latin manuscripts, some of them in the hands of Pontano, Sannazaro, Filelfo and other humanists, others deriving from the Aragonese kings of Naples, Cardinal Bessarion, Guarino Veronese and Giorgio Antonio Vespucci. Both collections were acquired after protracted negotations (for which Blotius was not responsible) and delays in payment extending over decades.

From these uncertain beginnings the library progressed, gathering rarities and reputation. The fruitful collaboration of the bibliophile Leopold I (1658–1705) and his north German librarian, Peter Lambeck; the magnificent baroque hall, built by the younger Fischer von Erlach to his father's plans and frescoed by Daniel Gran; Prince Eugene of Savoy's collection, bought in 1738, with its first editions of the classics, its unique Roman road map, the *Tabulae Peutingerianae*, its French manuscript romances, its Blaeu's *Atlas Major* extended to forty-six volumes with extra maps and views, and its albums of flower and bird drawings by Nicolas Robert and his pupils – these were the main stages in its rise to a pinnacle of fame in the mideighteenth century. 'Imperial and Royal Hofbibliothek' until 1918, 'Austrian National Library' since, it has 1·6 million volumes – not a large number by modern international standards. But manuscripts of textual or artistic importance and rare early printed books form a higher proportion of this total than in any comparable library except the Vatican.

View of Acapulco, by A. Boot; first half of the seventeenth century. From Prince Eugene's copy of Blaeu's Atlas Major.

Library of the Royal Monastery

EL ESCORIAL

ABOVE *The royal monastery of El Escorial, built by Philip II of Spain.* OPPOSITE *The Emperor Conrad and Empress Gisela adoring Christ in Glory; illuminated page from a Gospels written in Echternach (Luxembourg) between 1043 and 1046 for the Emperor Henry III.*

Soon after he ascended the throne in 1556 Philip II of Spain was presented by his chaplain, the Hellenist Juan Páez de Castro, with a memorial urging him to set up a public library: 'It is no small advantage to have a possession which ennobles the Nation and persuades the principal scholars of the world to visit us.' Specific recommendations followed: Valladolid, a favourite royal residence and university city, on the road to France, was suggested as the most suitable site. The library should be housed in a solid fire-proof building with good light and should consist of three rooms: the first to contain the Bible, the Church Fathers, Civil and Canon Law, Medicine and History, accompanied by portraits and sculpture; the second for maps, globes, views of cities, genealogical trees, curious watches, natural marvels and antiquities; the third for archives and documents.

Páez de Castro's proposal was for a library on the lines of Fontainebleau, Florence and Venice. Philip II accepted the need for a national book collection, but since he valued learning chiefly as the means of confuting heresy and confirming the truth of revelation, these secular Renaissance establishments held no attraction for him. He preferred to find inspiration in the early Middle Ages when the great abbeys were the centres of culture and education, and by a deliberate anachronism consigned the custody and administration of the library to monks – and not even to an order with a tradition of scholarship, but to the Hieronymites whose principal expertise was in singing the offices in the choir. The life of meditation requires solitude and isolation; therefore the new monastery-palace of San Lorenzo and the books with it, were placed not in a large and easily accessible city as Páez had advised, but beside the hamlet of El Escorial in the foothills of the wild Guadarramas. The books were to be of service to the monks and 'for the public benefit of all men of letters who may wish to come and read them', but more inconvenient arrangements could scarcely have been devised. 'At San Lorenzo', Luis de León, the poet, observed to Gonzalo Pérez, 'those books will be treasures buried underground.' This

St Theresa of Avila's autobiography, Libro de la Vida, *the saint's autograph manuscript written in Avila in 1565–6.*

proved an accurate prediction, and for nearly three centuries after Philip's death little use was made of the collection.

The manuscripts Philip considered his most precious were the Golden Gospels written for the Emperor Henry III, an early seventh-century St Augustine *On the baptism of infants* (which he believed to be autograph) and a Greek Evangelary thought to have belonged to St John Chrysostom. The only manuscripts he commissioned were breviaries, missals and choir-books produced by a flourishing school of illuminators in the Escorial, and the only acquisition which he initiated as king was of the autograph texts of four works of St Theresa of Avila (1515–82), the reformer of the Carmelite Order. He obtained her autobiography, the *Libro de la Vida,* from the Inquisition of Toledo to which it had been denounced by the Princess of Eboli: the first redaction of the *Camino de Perfección,* written as a spiritual guide for her nuns, from a private owner; and applied to the vicar-general of the Carmelites for the *Fundaciones* (describing the convents she had founded) and *Modo de visitar los conventos.* They were kept first in

St Lawrence, patron of the Escorial, with his grid-iron; a double-page opening from Philip II's book of Hours, illuminated in the Escorial in 1568.

a locked desk behind a grating, later in a special reliquary; privileged visitors were allowed to touch them.

In the choice of other acquisitions Philip was content to be guided by Spanish scholars who were agreed that a library's distinction depended on its holdings of ancient manuscript texts, particularly of Greek authors. The king however was always short of funds, and the beginnings were cautious and tentative. Forty-two theological works for use in composing sermons reached the monastery in 1565, two years after the foundation-stone had been laid. The next year they were followed by many of the greatest treasures of the royal house, among them the Golden Gospels, Augustine and Chrysostom already mentioned, and a magnificently illuminated Apocalypse that had belonged to Charles v's sister, Mary of Hungary. Some setbacks now occurred; the valuable library of a leading humanist, Francisco de Mendoza y Bobadilla, Cardinal of Burgos, was available for purchase on his death in 1566, but the price fixed by Juan Páez de Castro (acting as an independent expert)

aginuus·de illo ē non de nobis·Ꝑ aspe
ritatem uero ordei opa sanctoꝛ designia
tur·que aspera quidem uidentur ꝑ opa

tati doctoꝛibʒ ecclesie tribuit
ecce equus pallidus. Equus ꝑ
prophetas sigt. Pallor uero

ABOVE *The opening of the fourth seal, from an apocalypse illuminated between 1428 and 1435 for Margaret of Austria, wife of Filiberto, Duke of Savoy. The manuscript was given to the library in 1566, stolen during the Civil War and returned anonymously in 1963.*

OPPOSITE *The Woman on the Beast, from a manuscript of Beatus of Liebana's* Commentary on the Apocalypse, *written in northern Spain in the tenth or eleventh century.*

OVERLEAF LEFT *Adam and Eve, from the* Codice Vigilano, *a history of Church Councils, written in the monastery of Albelda (north Spain) in 976 AD.* RIGHT *A miracle of the Virgin. The story is of a villein who stole the consecrated Host in his mouth and hid it in a beehive. The Virgin and Child materialised in the hive and did not disappear until Mass had been celebrated with the hive on the altar. Illustration to Alfonso the Wise of Castile's* Hymns to the Virgin, *written in Galician, the masterpiece of thirteenth-century Castilian illumination.*

alarmed the king and the opportunity was lost. From the rich collection of Honorato Juan, Bishop of Osma, only ninety-six printed books and three manuscripts were obtained in 1567, and in the same year from the collection of Martin Pérez de Ayala, Archbishop of Valencia, only sixty-nine volumes. The library of Gerónimo Zurita, the historian of Aragon, was missed altogether. He had given his books to the Carthusians of Saragossa, whose prior was willing to sell them to the king for 35,000 ducats, but again the price seems to have been an obstacle and the affair dragged on for years without reaching a successful conclusion.

After these early hesitations the library grew swiftly in the five years from 1570. A large part of the library formed by the Aragonese kings of Naples had been brought to Spain earlier in the century by the last member of the dynasty, Ferdinand, Duke of Calabria. Manuscripts from it now reached the Escorial from three sources; in a group of classical texts bought from the Conde de Luna, in two cases of books from Francisco de Rojas, and among 169 volumes (which also included Pope Alexander VI's *Ptolemy* and many Greek codices from Basilian monasteries in Calabria) collected by Gonzalo Pérez. One hundred and fifty manuscripts, including sixty-one in Arabic, and the same number of printed books, one of them an interleaved and copiously annotated Bible which represented the owner's chief literary legacy, were acquired from the estate of Juan Páez de Castro. Visigothic manuscripts were bequeathed by the Inquisitor General, Pedro de Ponce de León, Bishop of Plasencia. The royal historian, Ambrosio de Morales, searched the dioceses of northern Spain; manuscripts of Isidore of Seville were collected from monasteries and churches for use in a critical edition; Greek manuscripts were bought by the Spanish ambassador in

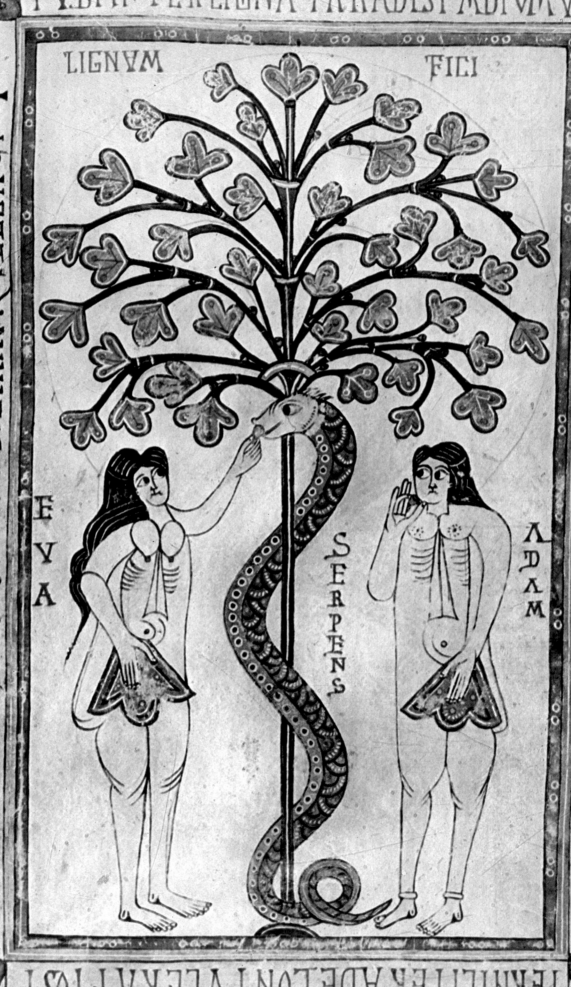

† VBI INTER LIGNA PARADISI ADPOMV̅ Q̅MODO̅ ISTA̅ VI̅IT VT

EVA MANVM PORREXERAT SVMENS̅ Q̅ D DESERPENTIS ORE

FOLA FICI COSVERVNTS IBIQ̅ PERIZOMATANAOQ̅ FECERVNT

TERNILIT̅ R ADELONTV̅ ERA Q̅ POST

LIGNVM

FICI

EVA

SERPENS

ADAM

Cun mlão furtou o corpo xpist na boca p cõstillo dũa uella.

Couulio meteu o corpo x na colmẽa e pois achou e sca cõ seu fillo

Couulão foy chamar un clerigo e lli mostrou sca oõ na colmẽa.

C uceẽ todos cõ prisõ e acharõ sca oõ cõ seu fillo na colmẽa

C trouxerõ a colmẽa e a poserõ sobelo altar e disserõ missa.

C outro dia u dizian missa nõ acharõ na colmẽa en aostia sagrada

tanto por su grande fermosura/ como
por su riqueza:ℸ astucia:entre las na=
ciones estremeras/ℸ del cabo del mũ=
do/touo muy gran renombre. ℸentre
los otros/llego su fama alos griegos
entre los quales : perseo en aꝗl tiẽpo
el mas garrido mãcebo delos griegos
oydo la fama por muchos:ℸ la relaci=
on/que de ella se fazia / cayo en desseo
de ver vna tan fermosa dama/ℸ de to=
mar le su thesoro. E assi luego subio
en vna naue que leuaua por estandar=
te el cauallo pegaso/ℸ nauego cõ ma=
rauilloso/ℸ presto viaje a poniente. y
ende vsando de seso/ℸ de armas/ pren
dio la reyna/ℸ apaño su thesoro. ℸ car
gado de presa tan abundosa : ℸ de vn
tan rico despojo/ boluio a su patria: ℸ
alos suyos. E dende houo su inuẽcio
aꝗlla fabula : ℸ fiction delos poetas.

los hombres que miraua en piedras:
ℸ ꝗ por yra de minerua:sus cabellos:
se le tornaron sirpiẽtes / porꝗ echãdo
se con neptuno/ le ensuzio su templo.
del qual ayũtamiẽto pario a pegaso:ℸ
perseo/el qual caualgãdo en vn caua=
llo/ꝗ tenia alas/volo asu reyno. Bes
uenturada cosa es por cierto posseer
oro/ℸ riquezas:porꝗ si estan ascondi=
das/ℸ secretas/ ninguna pro trahẽ al
ꝗ las possee Si se discubrẽ/ℸ estan ma
nifiestas/ nascẽ assechanças infinitas
delos ꝗ las codician:ℸ ahũ ꝗ no ha=
ya quiẽ las ose robar/no cessan ya por
esso/ los ansiosos cuydados del ꝗ las
possee/ ca ni tiene reposo/ ni sossiego
en su coraçõ/ℸ pierde el sueño. ℸ siem
pre esta con temor:ℸ pocos le guardã
fe/ ni lealdad/ℸ acrescienta se la sospe
cha : ℸ al desuẽturado se le abreuiã los

Venice, the chief entrepôt for trade with the Levant, and scribes were employed to copy others when the original texts could not be purchased; while in northern Europe the eminent Hebraist Arias Montano, editor of the Plantin Polyglot Bible (Antwerp 1569 72), ransacked the abbeys of the Netherlands, bought at the Frankfurt Fair as well as in Paris and Lyons, and intercepted booksellers on their way from Italy to England. When the collection, until then provisionally stored nearby, was formally handed over to the monks in 1575, it numbered 2,820 manuscripts and 1,700 printed books in Hebrew, Greek, Latin, Castilian, Portuguese, Italian and Catalan.

OPPOSITE *Perseus, Neptune and Medusa, from* Boccaccio's Famous Women, *in Spanish (Saragossa, Pablo Hurus, 1495).* ABOVE *The man who took the thorn from the lion's paw, from Aesop's* Life and Fables *in Spanish (Saragosse, Juan Hurus, 1489).*

Two major accessions followed. Diego Hurtado de Mendoza, a distinguished Aristotelian and mathematician and former Spanish ambassador to Venice and Rome, bequeathed his collection to the King in 1575. It was rich in publications of the Aldine Press and contained four hundred Arabic, two hundred Latin and three hundred Greek manuscripts, many obtained from Mount Athos, one at least a present from the Sultan, all bound in the owner's heraldic tinctures, the upper cover red, the lower green. Antonio Agustín, Archbishop of Tarragona, was another of the humanists whose advice had shaped the formation of the library. On his death in 1586 all his Greek manuscripts were bought for the Escorial and a choice of his printed books (among them the Mainz *Cicero* of 1465) and Latin manuscripts. The removal to the monastery from the Chapel Royal of Granada of Queen Isabella's manuscripts (1591) marked the apogee of the collection in its founder's lifetime. Subsequent negotiations to buy Fulvio Orsini's and Cardinal Sirleto's libraries from Rome were not pursued energetically; the former was acquired instead by the Vatican and the latter by Cardinal Ascanio Colonna.

In 1577 Arias Montano, the first librarian, arranged the books according to a self-invented system of extreme complexity. They

OPPOSITE *The apocalyptic vision; an illustration to* Beatus of Liebana's *Commentary on the Apocalypse; north Spain, tenth/eleventh century.* ABOVE LEFT *Ferdinand of Aragon praying to St Saturninus, from the Breviary of Isabella the Catholic; written in Castille c. 1480.* ABOVE RIGHT *St Elizabeth, from the Breviary of Isabella the Catholic. The device of the Catholic kings, a sheaf of arrows, appears in the borders.*

were divided by language, subdivided into printed and manuscript, and subdivided again into sixty-four subject classifications. Handwritten labels overlapped each other on the shelves and the effect was 'very confused and ugly' according to an eye-witness, while the king's secretary, Antonio Gracián, complained to Antonio Agustín that the disorder was worse than the antique chaos described by Hesiod. Arias Montano was however, like Schmeller, a cataloguer of prodigious energy and succeeded in keeping pace with accessions, as well as giving the monks some elementary instruction in Greek and Hebrew. The decoration of the *Biblioteca Principal* was not completed until 1593; cases designed by the architect Juan de Herrera lined the walls below a ceiling exuberantly painted by Pellegrino Tibaldi and Bartolomé Carducho. The second librarian, Fr José de Sigüenza, followed a much simplified subject arrangement when filling the shelves with books in Latin, Greek and Hebrew. Printed books in other languages were placed in a second room, manuscripts in a third, all three libraries being decorated with portraits, globes, astrolabes and mathematical instruments. The books stood with the fore-edges outwards. This practice was common in the sixteenth century, but the Escorial is the only library in which, through respect for the founder, it has never been altered.

Two more collections were added under Philip II's successors: the library of Mulay Zeidan, King of Fez, captured at sea off the Algerian coast and said to have numbered over three thousand Arabic manuscripts; and a thousand manuscripts from the libraries formed by Philip IV's minister, the Conde-Duque de Olivares, and his son-in-law, the Duke of Medina de Las Torres, presented by the latter. An effort was made to secure a regular influx of printed books by a royal order of 1616 (widely disregarded in the event) requiring a copy of every new publication to be deposited in the Escorial. But in other ways a decline had set in. For long periods the Hieronymite Order was unable to supply librarians who could read Greek, let alone Hebrew or Arabic. The silver mounts and clasps which had been removed to avoid scratching adjacent bindings were sold by weight. In 1671 a disastrous fire broke out while the monks were in church. The flames were beaten back by heroic efforts from the door of the *Biblioteca Principal* (where charred panels can still be seen), but the monks seeing all three library rooms threatened had thrown out as many volumes as they could into the courtyard. Here a spark caught the dry fabric of a Turkish banner, captured at Lepanto, which collapsed setting fire to the heap. About a third of the library's total holdings of eighteen thousand books and manuscripts were destroyed, some of them unique texts.

Philip V (1700–46), the first king of the Bourbon dynasty, set up a new Royal Public Library in Madrid and no accessions came to the Escorial after 1700. Losses occurred in the nineteenth century, when Joseph Bonaparte had the books moved to the capital, and later, during the Carlist Wars. In 1837 the Hieronymites were expelled and a single brother remained in charge of the collections. The state of the library in 1855 is described in a letter from Sir Frederick Madden, Keeper of Manuscripts in the British Museum, to Sir Thomas Phillipps:

They must have some splendid MSS in this Escorial Library, but it is difficult to get into it. It is 40 miles from Madrid and only a daily coach there Spanish pace. When you get there it is open only three hours a day, and not on Saints days – therefore shut two thirds of the week. An ignorant monk is the librarian, and will let nothing be copied without an Order from the Queen [Isabella II], which is very seldom granted! Here is a royal library for you!

In 1885 the library was handed over to the Augustinian Order and its modern history began. The Augustinians began immediately to reorganise and catalogue the holdings. A card index of printed books was completed by 1903. By 1936 catalogues had been published of all the manuscripts except the Greek catalogue of which only one volume had appeared. This devoted work gave the monks no protection at the outbreak of the Civil War. In Madrid, where they had taken refuge, the majority were systematically executed by Communist or Anarchist murder gangs; both the director of the library, P. Julián Zarco, author of the catalogue of Castilian manuscripts, and his predecessor, P. Melchor Martínez Antuña, perished. The contents were

The Escorial Library. The bookcases were designed by the architect, Juan de Herrera. The frescoes are by Pellegrino Tibaldi and Bartolomé Carducho.

better cared for, the most precious being evacuated to Catalonia. They were recovered after the war, though Mary of Hungary's Apocalypse reached the library from France in an anonymous parcel only in 1963. The Augustinians returned in 1939 and the Escorial again has the benefit of their expert curatorship.

Bodleian Library

OXFORD

Sir Thomas Bodley's monument in Merton College Chapel. The books are piled on either side of the bust with their fore-edges outwards. OPPOSITE *The Divinity School with Duke Humphrey's Library above.*

The earliest university library in Oxford was a collection of books kept in chests in St Mary's Church in the thirteenth century, to be lent out to scholars against adequate security. About 1320 Thomas Cobham, Bishop of Worcester, proposed to replace it with a chained library on an upper floor of the church, but owing to a dispute with Oriel College the room was not completed until 1367, and the double-sided desks to which the books were fastened were only installed in 1410.

In 1439 the University received the first of a series of generous gifts from King Henry VI's uncle, Humphrey, Duke of Gloucester, amounting in all to 280 volumes. The effect was to direct the authorities' attention to the library. They decided to move it to new premises, larger than the old, as was appropriate to its enhanced prestige, and centrally placed, 'more remote' (in the words of their letter to the Duke) 'from secular noise'. (Anyone now exposed to the savage roar of traffic in Oxford's High Street has cause to bless this act of foresight.) In 1444 the University wrote to inform Duke Humphrey of their plans to add a second storey as a library-room above the Divinity School, then in course of construction, and offered him the title of Founder. His death three years later deprived them of his expected support. Nevertheless in gratitude for his benevolent interest the new library, although not completed until 1488, was called after him. It was larger than its predecessor, but arranged on the same principle with two rows of double-sided lectern desks projecting from the walls.

The collection of books would have been of exceptional interest if it had survived. Duke Humphrey was the first important English patron of the new learning; his choice of books had been guided by the Milanese humanist, Pier Candido Decembrio, and his gifts included many rediscovered classics, Latin translations of Plato, Aristotle and Plutarch, and works by Dante, Petrarch and Boccaccio. Unfortunately, though the individual Oxford colleges were rich in the sixteenth century, the University had virtually no central funds and was unable either to maintain the fabric of the library or to equip it with printed books to meet

Duke Humphrey's Library from Selden End. The roof and beams are decorated with the arms of Sir Thomas Bodley and the University.

contemporary requirements. The room became increasingly neglected and derelict; the books were abstracted and sold for the value of the vellum to bookbinders and tailors; and in 1556 Christ Church College bought the furniture. For the next forty-two years there was a Fellows' library in each college but the University had none.

On 23 February 1598 Thomas Bodley wrote to the Vice-Chancellor:

Where there hath bin heretofore a publike library in Oxford: which you know is apparent, by the rome it self remayning, and by your statute records[,] I will take the charge and cost vpon me, to reduce it again to his former vse: and to make it fitte, and handsome with seates, and shelfes, and Deskes, and all that may be needfull, to stirre vp other mens benevolence, to helpe to furnish it with bookes.

Bodley had been born in 1545 and brought up by parents of strong Protestant convictions who found it prudent to emigrate to Geneva during Queen Mary's reign. After taking his degree and spending twelve years as a Fellow of Merton College, he had left Oxford to travel in Germany, France and Italy and make a career in diplomacy. He had lately retired from public service after eight years as English Resident to the Netherlands, where he most certainly would have visited Leiden University Library, opened in 1594 (see endpapers). Leiden's example influenced many of his own library arrangements and perhaps helped to inspire his offer to the Vice-Chancellor. If the Dutch university, founded only twenty years before, already boasted a public library, Thomas Bodley must have thought it unworthy of so ancient a foundation as Oxford to have none.

The legislative assembly of the University met on 2 March 1598 to accept his proposal. Work was put in hand at once. By 1600 the restoration of the room was finished but the search for books continued. Bodley appreciated the importance of making a good first impression on donors, and postponed the formal opening until 8 November 1602 when the shelves were well stocked with weighty folios and holdings amounted to 299 manuscripts and over 1,700 printed volumes. Two years later he was knighted by James I and letters patent were issued naming the library after him. By 1605, when the first printed catalogue was published, there were about six thousand volumes and the collection was regarded as substantially complete.

The existing windows in Duke Humphrey's Library obliged Bodley to follow the medieval arrangement of desks projecting from the walls, but instead of lecterns he adopted the new stalls system, first used it is believed, at Merton in 1590, which provided room for many more books. Each double-sided desk supported three shelves of chained folios, placed with fore-edges outwards and fastened with strings which the reader was required to tie on replacing the volume. The books were arranged alphabetically, by authors, in four faculties: Theology, occupying all the shelves on the south side; Medicine, Law, and Arts, comprising mathematics, history, philosophy and everything else, on the north. Manuscripts and printed books were shelved together, with the happy result that both can still be consulted in the same reading room. Access to the folios was free and readers were guided by a shelf-list or 'Table' fixed to the end of each case. For octavos and quartos application had to be made to the Keeper or his deputy; they were kept initially in the 'Closets' at the east end (now the librarians' studies), later – as they became more numerous – in a gallery at the opposite end. Books of special value stood in two locked cupboards known as 'the Archives', 'the Grated Places' or 'the hutche', and could only be issued to readers by the Keeper in person. The ceiling was gaily painted with Bodley's coat at the intersections of the beams and the University's arms in every panel: *Dominus illuminatio mea*, apt expression of the founder's belief in the power scholarship could draw from godliness and faith from learning.

The statutes required the librarian to be 'a graduat . . . and a Linguist, not encombred with mariage,' adding by way of explanation, 'mariage is too full of domestical impeachements' to leave him time to perform his duties. However Thomas James, librarian from 1600 to 1620, threatened to resign unless the obligation of celibacy was relaxed in his favour, and Bodley reluctantly consented. They shared the same strong Protestant views and suited each other well; although the founder freely criticised James's cataloguing, his slowness in answering letters

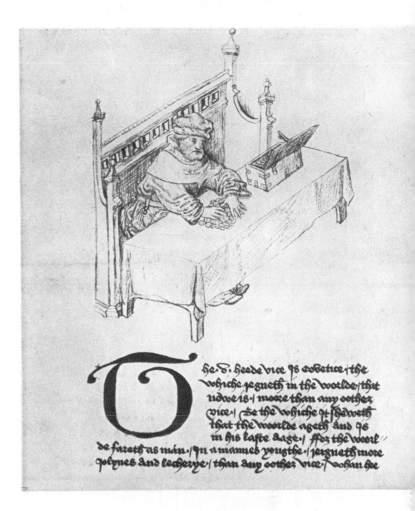

Covetousness, from The Mirroure of the Worlde, *(England, fifteenth century); given to the Library by Robert Barker, the King's printer, in 1604.*

and even his handwriting, he treated him courteously and with affection. At first on his own, from 1610 James had the assistance of an under-keeper 'to affourd some Leasure to the Keeper for his priuat studie and contemplation' and a janitor 'to wipe, sweepe and keepe cleane' the books and furniture.

Sir Thomas Bodley relied largely on private donors for his supply of books. Though he received considerable groups of manuscripts from St George's Chapel, Windsor, and from Exeter Cathedral, his main appeal was to the English country families. They were wooed as assiduously as any modern alumnus of Harvard or Yale, with letters of thanks from the University and entries in a Benefactors' Register, and responded nobly. Among the founder's learned friends William Camden, Sir Henry Savile, Sir Walter Raleigh, Lord Lumley and Sir Robert Cotton made contributions. Gifts were supplemented by purchases from two London booksellers, John Norton and John Bill, financed partly from Bodley's purse, partly from presents in cash and the sale of duplicates. Many books were obtained from the Frankfurt Fair, others on expeditions by John Bill to Paris, Seville and through north Italy as far as Rome, Venice proving especially productive.

Bodley made his own choice of books. One of the few titles to be found both in his library and in those of twentieth-century enthusiasts for Elizabethan and Stuart literature like Henry Clay Folger and Henry E. Huntington was Chaucer's *Workes*, 1561. His preference was for folios printed on the Continent, particularly in Basle, Venice, Paris and Antwerp. Ninety-five per cent were in Latin, by obscure and learned authors such as

Views of the Bodleian Library, from David Loggan's Oxonia illustrata, *1675.* ABOVE Arts End *with globes given by Sir Thomas Bodley standing on either side of the entrance to Duke Humphrey's Library.* BELOW Selden End *with Selden's books on the lower shelves and the manuscripts of Barocci, Digby and Laud in the gallery.* OPPOSITE *Majnun making friends with the wild animals, by Dhanun. This copy of Nizami's Persian poem on the two lovers, Laila and Majnun, was illustrated in India in the late sixteenth century. It was bought by the Bodleian Library in 1952.*

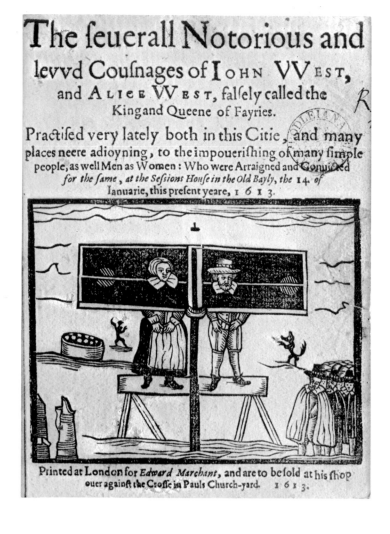

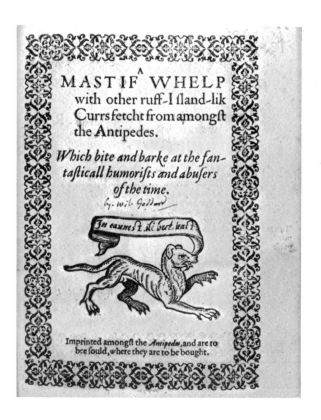

Pamphlets bequeathed by Robert Burton in 1640.
ABOVE The seuerall notorious and lewd cousnages of John West and Alice West, *1613.*
BELOW *William Goddard,* A mastif whelp with other ruff-Island-lik currs, *1599(?)* OPPOSITE ABOVE Looke up and see wonders, *1628.*
BELOW *Thomas Dekker,* O per se O, *1612.*

Borrhaeus, Mollerus, Farinaceus, Menochius, Velosillus, on whom Folger and Huntington would have turned a cold eye. The next most popular language was Italian, followed by French, Spanish, Greek, Hebrew and English, in that order. Science and geography were well represented with works by Copernicus, Tycho Brahe, Ortelius and Mercator. When it came to literature the continuing prestige of the Florentine Renaissance and the influence of his own Italian travels were apparent. There were four copies of Dante's *Comedy* as against two each of Homer and Euripides; Boccaccio's *Decameron* and *Filocolo*, but no Spenser or Skelton; Guarini's *Pastor Fido* and Juan de Mena's *Obras*, but no Ronsard or Villon. There was no Shakespeare or other English dramatist and in a celebrated letter to Thomas James the founder expressed his determination to banish such 'riffe raffe bookes':

> I can see no reason to alter my opinion, for excluding suche bookes, as almanackes, plaies, & an infinit number, that are daily printed, of very vnworthy maters & handling ... Happely some plaies may be worthy the keeping: but hardly one in fortie ... Were it so againe, that some litle profit might be reaped (which God knowes is very litle) out of some of our playbookes, the benefit thereof will nothing neere counteruaile the harme that the scandal will bring vnto the Librarie, when it shal be giuen out, that we stuffe it full of baggage bookes.

Efforts were made to buy works in Oriental languages: there was talk of sending a scholar to Turkey to find Hebrew and Arabic books, and in 1606 purchases included some in Chinese. But unlike his Continental predecessors and contemporaries, Bodley was relatively indifferent to Greek manuscripts. Again the reason is perhaps to be sought in his Dutch experiences and in the example of the great Orientalist, Joseph Scaliger of Leiden.

The library was considered by its founder primarily as a collection of Protestant theology, but the works of doctrinal opponents were not excluded, although permission to read them (at any rate in 1620) had to be sought from the Vice-Chancellor and the Regius Professor of Divinity. Nevertheless the theological collection of Fernão Martins Mascarenhas, Bishop of Faro and later Grand Inquisitor of Portugal, stood on the shelves, a present from the Earl of Essex who had captured it on his expedition against Cadiz; and James I shook his head over a copy of Robert Gaguin's defence of the dogma of the Immaculate Conception (*De puritate conceptionis Virginis Mariae*, Paris 1498) and wished such objectionable works could be entirely suppressed.

'The Publique Librarie in the Vniversitie of Oxford' was Bodley's term for his foundation, and it was intended from the beginning to be generally accessible. Graduates entered by right, as did also (by a very English provision) 'the sonnes of Lordes', but any 'gentleman stranger' might obtain permission to study by making due application. The first 'Extraneus', admitted on 15 February 1603, was a Frenchman, and other readers before 1620 included Spaniards, Italians, Jews and one Ethiopian: but it was to students from the Protestant North, Germany and Scandinavia, that the Bodleian's resources proved particularly attractive. While one of these, a young native of Bergen named Ludvig Holberg, was in Duke Humphrey's Room between 1706 and 1708, the thought first occurred to him 'how splendid and glorious a thing it would be to take a place among the authors'. He lived to become 'the father of Danish and Norwegian literature' and to have it said that he found Denmark bookless and left it a library.

Sir Thomas Bodley endowed his foundation with property near Maidenhead and in London, the income from which was optimistically expected to pay staff salaries and other expenses and to buy new foreign books. In the last three years of his life he made further provisions for the library's growth. In 1610 the Stationers Company agreed to give a copy of every book printed by its members, an arrangement confirmed by successive Copyright Acts, the Bodleian being one of the six libraries of legal deposit in the British Isles. Between 1610 and 1612 an addition was built across the east end of Duke Humphrey's Room, which in consequence assumed the form of a T. Known as 'Arts End', it was designed to accommodate the growing numbers of books in that faculty, and of all octavos and quartos. Once again Bodley showed himself an innovator by adopting the latest Continental fashion of wall shelving in the new room, with access to the upper shelves from a gallery – a feature used previously only in the Ambrosiana.

Sir Thomas Bodley died in 1613 and was given a public funeral in Merton College Chapel. Two anthologies of mourning verse celebrated the deceased knight's virtues, mostly in Latin. Robert Burton was one of the contributors:

> Where erstwhile Chaos and thick darkness reigned,
> And moth and wood-worm barbarous sway maintained;
> Where far aloft their webs the spiders threw,
> And all was foul and filthy to the view,
> Now from gilt beam and painted roof there falls
> New fretted light on Bodley's noble halls:
> The well-bound volumes shine in goodly rows;
> Each Muse her own appointed alcove knows,
> And is herself again, through Bodley's care,
> While what belonged to one now all may share.

The library underwent many changes in the century after Bodley's death. A second addition was made to Duke Humphrey's Room corresponding to Arts End and converting its T-shape into H. Although called Selden End, it contained, besides the folios of the lawyer and Orientalist John Selden, the Greek manuscripts assembled by Giacomo Barocci of Venice and presented to the University by its Chancellor, the Earl of Pembroke, and Archbishop Laud's large donation of early manuscripts, many of them looted from Würzburg Cathedral and other spiritual owners during the Swedish army's triumphant progress through south Germany in 1631. Galleries were erected above the stalls in the original part of the Reading Room to hold a bequest from Bishop Barlow and the extra weight imposed so great a strain on the fabric that in 1700 no

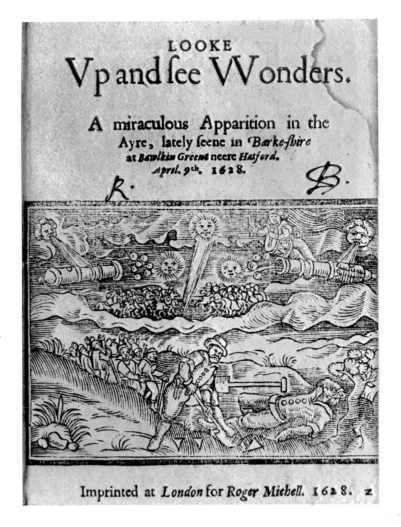

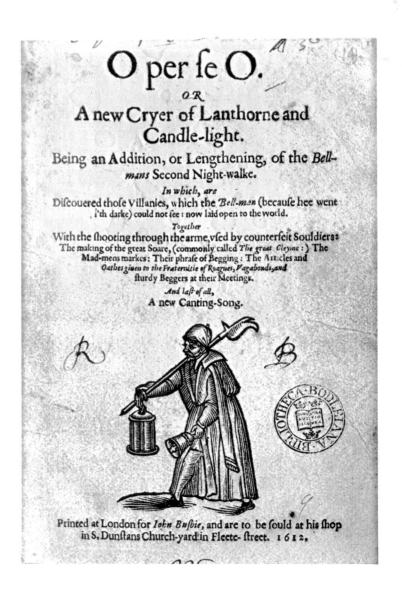

Memorie de saint george. ã.
eorgi martir inclite te decet laus
et gloria. pre dotatum milicia. p̃ quẽ

less an architect than Sir Christopher Wren had to be called in to prevent the whole structure collapsing. To 'Arts End' were added the bound volumes of plays bequeathed by Robert Burton. But the record was not only of gains. In accordance with Sir Thomas Bodley's instructions to dispose of duplicates, by which he meant not only second copies of the same edition but inferior editions of the same work, the First Folio of Shakespeare, rendered superfluous by the Third Folio's arrival in 1664, was discarded (and was not recovered till 1906). On top of the Schools Quadrangle, on one side of which Duke Humphrey's Library stands, a third floor was built with funds bequeathed by the Founder for the purpose and decorated with a frieze of scholars' and authors' heads chosen by Thomas James. Intended as a reserve of space for the library's further expansion, it remained empty of books throughout the century and held the Bodleian collections of coins and portraits. The principal curiosities were displayed in the Anatomy School and could be visited on paying a fee to the janitor: the Tsar of Russia's lambskin coat, a crocodile from Jamaica, an Irish skull, a whale caught in the Severn, a mummy and the dried body of a negro boy.

Here we must leave the Bodleian's history, pausing only to note that great purchases and bequests of incunabula, first editions of the classics and illuminated manuscripts (sometimes regarded as the yardsticks of a collection's status) entered the library between 1780 and 1860; that the whole Schools Quadrangle has been engulfed, the Radcliffe Camera (erected by the architect James Gibbs in 1737–47) absorbed and a vast new annexe thrown up; and that the present holdings are four million printed books, over forty thousand manuscripts and 18,500 charters and deeds. To a uniquely successful degree, the library manages to combine regard for its history and traditions with the work of a rapidly growing modern research collection.

Trinity College

DUBLIN

The Library, completed in 1732, with the statue of W.E.H. Lecky, the historian. OPPOSITE *The interior of the library. The coved roof is nineteenth century: the busts originally stood on the balustrade of the gallery.*

Trinity College was established in Dublin in 1592 by royal charter of Queen Elizabeth I to be 'a college and nourceserye [nursery] of good letters in this rude desolate and ignorant country', or in other words, as a centre of the Protestant religion and English manners in Ireland. Students were admitted in 1594, but there were at first no funds for books and six years later the library contained only forty-two works. Then a sum of £600 – equivalent to the College's income for a year – came to hand, subscribed, according to an early tradition, by officers of the English army in Ireland, and in June 1601 Dr Luke Chaloner, prebendary of St Patrick's Cathedral and one of three original Fellows, was shopping for books in London. Further buying expeditions to London followed: in 1603 by Chaloner with James Ussher, one of the College's foundation scholars, in 1608 by Provost Alvey, and the year after by Chaloner and Ussher again. Four years later Ussher, once more in London, was reporting the dispatch of a consignment worth £20 and enquiring whether a benefactor could be found to pay for Sir Henry Savile's edition of St John Chrysostom (Eton 1610–12), which at £9 was beyond Trinity's means.

The next person to take an interest in the collection was Provost William Bedell (1627–9). He found much in the College in need of reform: 'the abandoning the hall and chapel, and newfangledness in apparel, and long hair, and ruffles . . .'. The post of librarian, first held by James Ussher's brother Ambrose, a distinguished Hebrew and Arabic scholar, had degenerated into an annual chore for a junior fellow. Bedell required the incumbent to be 'Frugal, a Keeper at Home, given to Study, and a lover of Books' and persuaded a Senior Fellow to take on the job for a stipend of £6 a year. He codified the statutes, until then 'consisting of a few papers tacked together, part English, part Latin, and all out of order', and issued library regulations. It was to be open for four hours a day; Senior Fellows were allowed a key but must take a public oath to enter every book they borrowed and return it within a fortnight; reference books in constant use might not be taken out; if a volume was missed, a stringent

search should be made of the undergraduates' studies and dormitories (a procedure possibly invoked only once, in 1793, against a BA caught selling library books on the Quays).

It was perhaps at Bedell's initiative that a fair copy was drawn up of the library catalogue started by Ambrose Ussher and used to record subsequent accessions. The policy at Dublin, as Bedell lamented to James Ussher, had been 'to neglect the Faculties of Law and Physick, and attend only to the ordering of one poor Colledg of Divines,' and the choice of books was heavily weighted towards theology, which occupied twelve presses against ten for all other subjects. As at Oxford Latin works printed abroad were in the majority. Hardly a book, apart from grammars and dictionaries, was in any modern language other than English, and there was no post-classical literature, with the single exception of Chaucer's *Workes*, 1598. The total amounted to over seven thousand volumes.

The library consisted of two rooms, apparently connected by steps (as an 'upper' and a 'lower library' are mentioned) and separated by a 'partition door' normally kept locked. (In 1611 a Mr Frith, who had offered violence to it in an impatient moment, was punished with a week's exclusion from hall.) In the inner library behind the door the books stood fore-edges outwards in twenty-two presses with desks attached. They were not chained and could be borrowed: a system that led to many losses and complaints, as in 1643 when the prebend of St Owen's found eight volumes in the convent of the Dublin Franciscans and demanded that 'the Provost and Fellowes would hereafter take order and see that no Papist Priest or Jesuite be admitted into the College Library hereafter'. Only the Provost and Fellows and Bachelors of Divinity were allowed access to the shelves. Books were brought to other readers in an outer room, which was furnished with four Dutch tables, a quantity of maps, a pair of globes and a skeleton 'with taffety hangings'. As no more than thirteen students graduated in medicine before 1700, the latter was presumably more of a *Memento mori* than a tool of instruction. Before the end of the century it had been replaced by an even greater curiosity, 'the skin of one Ridley, a notorious Tory . . . tann'd, and stuff'd with Straw'.

In 1661 the College received its most important accession, the library of its former professor of divinity, James Ussher (1581– 1656), Archbishop of Armagh, Primate of the Church of Ireland and a scholar of extraordinary erudition and intellectual power. His collection contained nearly seven hundred manuscripts, mostly relating to his special subjects of Biblical criticism, ecclesiastical antiquities, history and chronology. Many had belonged to English monasteries before the Dissolution (1539) – Fountains, Rievaulx, St Albans, St Augustine's Canterbury, and others. Syriac and Arabic versions of scripture, valued for their textual evidence, had been obtained from the Levant through an English merchant in Aleppo and a professor of Upsala with contacts in Constantinople. Manuscripts of the Waldenses – the heretic peasants of the western Alps who had

LEFT *Illustrations from Matthew Paris's* Life of St Alban, *partly written and illustrated by the author in the abbey of St Albans, before 1240.* ABOVE *Offa, King of Mercia, setting off to make war on the West Saxons.* BELOW *Clearing the site for St Albans Abbey.* ABOVE *St Mark writing his Gospel; from a New Testament and Psalter of the twelfth century. This belonged in the fifteenth century to Winchcombe Abbey, Gloucestershire, and later to Henry VIII.*

adopted the reformed religion – reflected the Archbishop's concern with dissident movements in the Roman Church, works by Galileo and Kepler and the papers of John Bainbridge, Savilian Professor at Oxford, his interest in mathematics and astronomy. He kept himself informed of newly discovered peoples and territories as described in Richard Hakluyt's *Voyages*, Samuel Purchas's *Purchas his pilgrimes*, Lopes's *Report of the Kingdom of Congo*, 1597, and John Smith's *A Map of Virginia* (Oxford 1612); and owned, more or less by accident, a handful of English literary works: two manuscripts of *Piers Plowman*, a

poetical miscellany by the Tudor poets, Wyatt and Surrey, and
the 1492 Antwerp editions of Caxton's *History of Jason* and
Hystorye of Paris and of the fayre Vyenne.

Ussher's library had a European reputation and its disposal
became a matter of high politics after his death. Both Cardinal
Mazarin and Frederick III of Denmark were reported to be
anxious to acquire it, but Cromwell intervened to prevent the
sale. Some obscure transactions followed and were succeeded by
an implausible announcement that the army had subscribed the
purchase price of £2,200 from its arrears of pay. The books were
shipped to Ireland to stock a proposed public library in Dublin.
At this stage the weak flame of governmental interest flickered
and died away. In 1661 the Irish House of Commons, learning
that the collection was still stored in Dublin Castle, ordered its
transfer to Trinity College.

The library may have moved to new premises in 1651: or if
not, it was altered (perhaps to accommodate an influx of books
confiscated from Catholic religious houses) and embellished with
two oak staircases, the gift of Henry Jones, Vice-Provost and
later Bishop of Meath. Further changes were made to house the
Ussher collection, and a room added for accessions, known as 'the

The veray trew history of the val iaūt knight Jasõ

How he conqueryd, or wan the golden fles.by the Counsel of Medea. and of many othre victoryouse and wondrefull actis and dedys that he dyde by his prowesse and cheualrye in his tyme . : . .

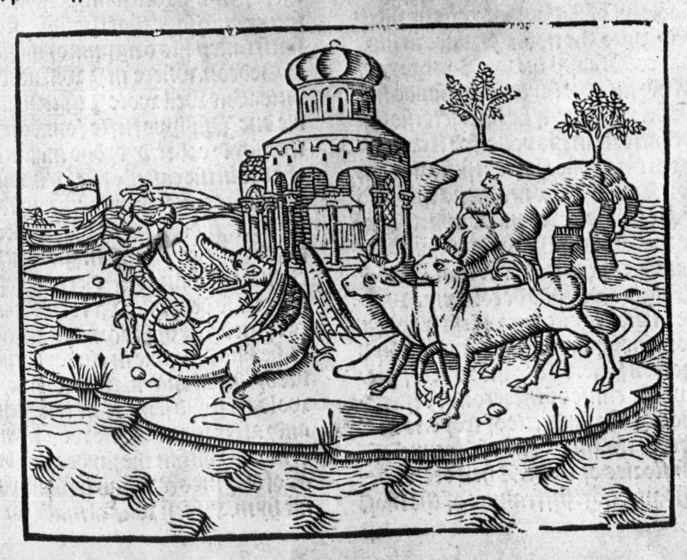

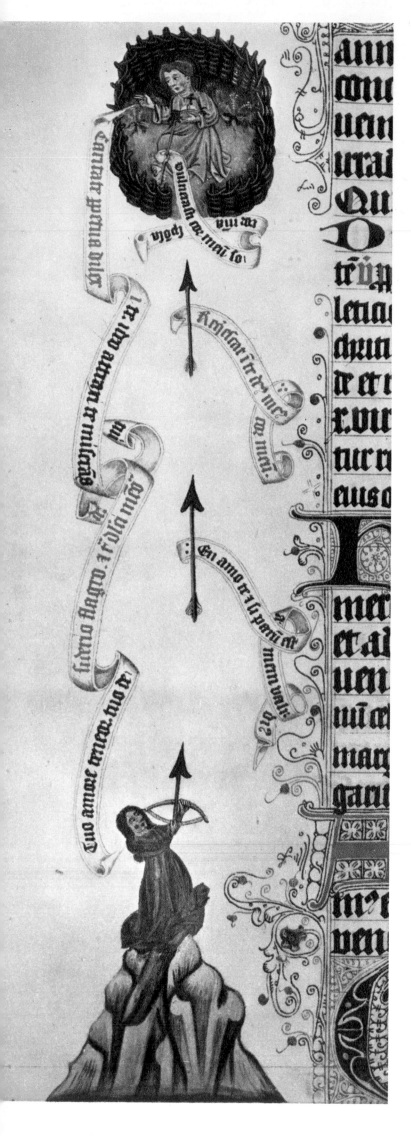

Countess of Bath's Library' since the nucleus had been bought in 1671 with her donation of £200. By the early eighteenth century these premises were hopelessly overcrowded and the bold decision was taken to construct a new library on a grand scale. Thomas Burgh, Chief Engineer and Surveyor-General of Fortifications, 'the first indisputably and unmistakably Irish architect' (Craig), designed the building. It cost £20,000 and took twenty years to complete (1712–32). Constructed of a warm sandstone (hidden behind the present facing of Portland stone) it was originally carried on a row of open arcades intended to insulate the books from the damp ground, a feature imitated from its model, Wren's Library of Trinity College, Cambridge, and shared with Gibbs's Radcliffe Camera. The Long Room and gallery, occupying the two upper storeys and lit by eighty-two windows, had space for one hundred thousand volumes and were not filled for over a hundred years.

Three great accessions were received in the century after the new library's completion: the collection of thirteen thousand volumes given in 1736 by the Vice-Provost, Dr Claudius Gilbert: the library of Greffier Fagel, chief minister of the Netherlands, bought for £20,000 in 1802 before its auction sale at Christie's: and the fastidiously selected Bibliotheca Quiniana bequeathed by Henry George Quin in 1805.

Gilbert was interested in sixteenth-century printing (especially by Aldus and the Estiennes) and owned incunable editions of the classics, presentation copies from the Danzig astronomer Hevelius to Ismael Boulliau of Laon, and many books from the Colbert and Loménie de Brienne sales. But his principal strength was not in rarities but in the collected editions and erudite compilations which then cost far more than Caxtons or *editiones principes*: such works as Montfaucon's *L'Antiquité expliquée* (1719) in ten volumes, and De la Bigne's *Maxima bibliotheca veterum patrum* (Lyons 1677) in twenty-seven. His record of purchases shows that he paid the highest price, £67 5s., for Rymer's *Foedera*, 1701–17, and bought his two Grolier bindings for seventeen shillings and sixpence, and fifteen shillings.

The Fagel library was the product of a century of rich Amsterdam taste, remarkable for its large collection of maps and of European topography and views, though its ten thousand political pamphlets may have been the principal attraction for the College. Traditional Dutch interest in gardens was represented by

LEFT *St Mary Magdalene piercing Christ's heart with the arrows of her love: from a Missal written and illustrated by the Augustinian canonesses of the convent of St Agnes at Delft, 1459–60. From the Fagel collection.* RIGHT *An astronomer and his assistant; from Johannes Hevelius,* Machina coelestis, *Danzig 1673, presentation copy from the author to Ismael Boulliau of Laon.*

R. Steel Delin.   J. Saal Sculpsit

de luxe copies of botanical works with the plates illuminated and the titles lettered in gold, and by volumes of drawings of flowers by Nicolas Robert and of tulips by a native artist, the latter annotated with the prices paid for Semper Augustus and other varieties during the tulip mania.

Henry George Quin's bequest was different from anything Trinity had received before. His books – only 108 titles in all – had been bought not as aids to knowledge, but to be admired and enjoyed. Nearly all were of literary texts (more than two-thirds

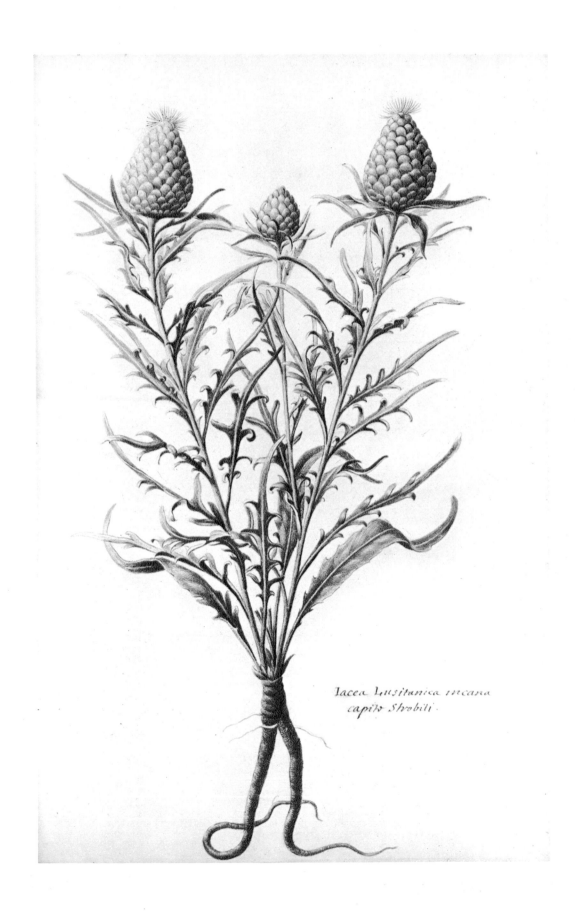

Jacea Lusitanica incana
capite Strobili.

in Latin or Italian, only four in English) and every one was remarkable for its typography, illustration or binding. He owned the 1472 Foligno Dante, Aldines on vellum and on blue paper, a vellum copy of the Emperor Maximilian's *Tewrdannck*, 1517, Renaissance bindings for Jean Grolier and Thomas Mahieu, and contemporary bindings by Roger Payne and Derome. His and the Fagel books introduced a lighter element into a library previously devoted to the austere requirements of scholarship.

Most of the Irish manuscripts for which Trinity College Library is celebrated reached it independently of these large gifts and purchases. Ussher was not greatly interested in Irish and owned only five manuscripts in the language; two of these, the Books of Lecan and Ballymote, were lost in the seventeenth century and now belong to the Royal Irish Academy. The most famous of all, the ninth-century Book of Kells, was long believed to have been his, but fresh research has identified the real donor – Henry Jones, Bishop of Meath, whose gift of oak staircases in 1651 has already been noticed. Jones also presented the seventh-century Book of Durrow, which, although now thought to have been written in England at Wearmouth or Jarrow, belonged at an early date to the Irish monastery of that name. In 1786 the statesman Edmund Burke, who was educated at Trinity, persuaded Sir John Sebright to give twenty-one Irish manuscripts collected by the Celtic philologist, Edward Lhuyd. The most valuable were a volume of Brehon (or Irish customary) Law tracts and the twelfth-century Book of Leinster, containing the 'Cattle-Raid of Cooley', *Táin Bó Cualgne*, and other tales of the heroic age. The eighth-century Book of Dimma and the Book of Armagh of the year 807 entered the library in 1836 and 1858 respectively; each had previously been offered at public auction and failed to reach its reserve. Until twenty years ago the College was in the peculiar position of owning more literary manuscripts in Icelandic than in English. Its greatest literary archive, the papers of the Irish poet and playwright J. M. Synge (1871–1909) was acquired as recently as 1968.

By the Copyright Act of 1801 the library became entitled to receive a free copy of every book printed in the United Kingdom. No provision was made for public access and until the middle of the century only graduates entered by right; undergraduates were excluded and strangers had to be guaranteed by the Provost or one of the Fellows. A century and a half's intake of books has exacted its toll of architectural change. The roof of Thomas Burgh's Long Room has been raised and the ground-floor arcades enclosed. A reading room was added in 1937, and in 1967 a new library building. The manuscripts, like a flight of swallows, have migrated across the Fellows' Garden to a small temple overlooking an abandoned croquet-lawn. In this rural retreat the conditions of study in ancient Ireland are agreeably reproduced: 'A hedge of trees surrounds me, a blackbird's lay makes music for me. . . . Above my lined book the birds trill.'

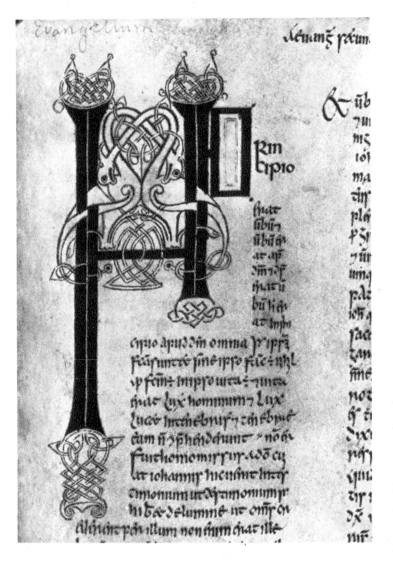

ABOVE *Beginning of St John's Gospel from the Book of Armagh (Ireland, AD 807).* OPPOSITE *Four bindings from the collection of Henry George Quin.* ABOVE: LEFT *by Edwards of Halifax, 1789;* RIGHT *for Jean Grolier, Paris, c. 1545.* BELOW: LEFT *by Roger Payne, 1793;* RIGHT *attributed to Derome, Paris, mid-eighteenth century.*

185

Biblioteca Ambrosiana

MILAN

ABOVE *Cardinal Federigo Borromeo, by an anonymous artist.* OPPOSITE Vitae archiepiscoporum Mediolanensium, *written in Milan c. 1500. The miniature of the baptism of the Apostle Barnabas, claimed as the first bishop of Milan, is by a Lombard artist.*

'Let us pray God,' Cardinal Federigo Borromeo wrote to a friend, shortly before leaving Rome in 1595 to become Archbishop of Milan, 'that such crude centuries may not return, the ancient barbarism that our grandfathers or great-grandfathers saw, towards which Italy seems to be declining, although she has been the nurse and mother of all the graces and all civilised customs. In this corner of Italy, on her frontiers, at the foot of the Alps and of mountains once hard to cross, we shall try to keep the fine arts with us, however much they want to escape over the mountains or beyond the sea.' The passage illustrates the complex motives of the Ambrosian Library's founder. Besides the paramount aim – already noted in Germany and Spain – of establishing a centre of Catholic learning as a firm base from which to refute heresy and propagate the Faith overseas, there was a specifically Italian anxiety lest the brilliant achievements of the Renaissance should succumb to a new Dark Age. One of his foundations was a college to teach Tuscan, with Dante, Petrarch, Boccaccio and the philosopher and critic Speroni as models, and a member of his staff recorded the Cardinal's pleasure that the famous Vergil with a frontispiece by Simone Martini – an early purchase – was 'annotated throughout with most beautiful notes by the hand of Petrarch himself'. All this suggests that he felt the need of a focus of *Italianità* in a peninsula mainly subject to foreign rule. Even the characteristically modest decision to name the library not 'Fredericiana' after himself, but 'Ambrosiana' after the Church Father who had been the city's greatest bishop, was in some degree an expression of Milanese patriotism.

Federigo Borromeo was born in 1564, scion of an illustrious Milanese patrician family and cousin of St Charles Borromeo. After studying rhetoric, philosophy and mathematics at Bologna and theology at Pavia, he spent ten years in Rome. He was created Cardinal at the age of twenty-three and Archbishop of Milan in 1595, where his acts of charity, particularly during the famine of 1627–8, and his devoted heroism in the plague of 1630 are well known from the account in Alessandro Manzoni's novel *The Betrothed*. He is said to have become interested in books as a

Arnabas apostolus Jhesu Christi
natione Cipzus. mediolani Epus
pzimus. venit ad sedes Anno do.
xli. sedit annis vij. hic pzimus.
Rome & Anthioche pzedicaue
rat annis iiij. postea de Roma se
cessit. et ad ciuitates mediolaneses se transtulit. & inea
pzedicans ciues asti ad Christus conuertit. fide et mo
ribus informauit. Pzisenses Crucis per Anathelones ei
discipulus similiter ad Christus conuertit.

IL SAGGIATORE
Nel quale
Con bilancia esquisita e giusta
si ponderano le cose contenute
nella
LIBRA·ASTRONOMICA·E·FILOSOFICA
DI·LOTARIO·SARSI·SIGENSANO
Scritto in forma di lettera
All'Ill.mo et Rever.mo Mons. D.
VIRGINIO·CESARINI
Acc.o Linceo M.o di Camera di N.S.
Dal Sig.r
GALILEO·GALILEI
Acc.o Linceo Nobile Fiorentino
Filosofo e Matematico Primario
del
Ser.mo Gran Duca di Toscana.

FILOSOFIA NATVRALE

MATEMATICA

IN ROMA·M·D·C·XX III·
Appresso Giacomo Mascardi

F. Villamœna Fecit.

The title-page of Galileo Galilei's Il Saggiatore, *printed in Rome in 1623. This copy was sent by the author to Cardinal Borromeo.*

boy on finding an old work on cosmography in the family palace at Arona. He trained himself to read and write when lying down, and saved time by reading while being shaved or when on a journey, always travelling by litter for this reason. His writings – nearly all unpublished – are inspired by a widely ranging intellectual curiosity. Besides the classics, the Church Fathers and humanist authors, he quotes from contemporary travel-books, discusses why birds sing, the speech of angels and the pronunciation of demons, whether angels have proper names and why some animals live longer than others, and speculates about the food in Iceland, Egyptian hieroglyphics, the customs and beliefs of the Africans of Guinea and the origin and antiquity of writing. On the other hand he had little of the bibliophile's concern with a book's physical appearance and commented to a collector who had shown him a well printed and handsomely bound Cicero, 'I should like it more if it were a little less clean and a little more used.' He was keenly interested in science, knew

Galileo and tried to enrol the latter's friend, Bonaventura Cavalieri, as a Doctor of his new foundation. The Ambrosiana contains the copy of *Il Saggiatore*, 1623, which Galileo presented with a covering letter to the Cardinal, 'not because I think it worthy to be read by you, but for my own esteem and to procure life and reputation for the work, in itself low and frail, in your most Illustrious and Reverend Lordship's heroic and immortal library.'

The library was opened in 1609. Its contents had been assembled in the six preceding years by a team of purchasing agents, members of the Cardinal's establishment or ecclesiastical *hommes de confiance*. These emissaries, who travelled over much of the Mediterranean, were kept under strict financial control from Milan and worked to a master plan devised by the Cardinal. In this scheme Greek manuscripts, of which there were more than a thousand, held the position of honour that had become normal since the Renaissance, but Oriental languages were given greater prominence than in earlier public collections. There was only one large block purchase; attempts to buy the library of Cardinal Ascanio Colonna in Rome and those of Giacomo Barocci and Pietro Bembo in Venice were unsuccessful, though Lucrezia Borgia's love-letters presumably came from the last. Otherwise the books were acquired singly or in small groups.

An important source of supply was the churches and monasteries of northern Italy to whom the Cardinal-Archbishop was clearly well placed to appeal. The most valuable codex obtained in this way was perhaps the sixth-century papyrus Josephus from Sant' Ambrogio in Milan, and the greatest coup, the acquisition of part of Bobbio's ancient library in exchange for 'more useful' modern books. Bobbio had been founded in the early seventh century by a party of Irish monks under St Columban, and still owned the only substantial group of Italian pre-Caroline manuscripts outside Verona Cathedral. Cardinal Federigo chose a suitable envoy, Gian Giacomo Valeri, of an old Milanese family, Canon of Santa Maria della Scala and an antiquarian collector on his own account. Negotiations were opened in 1605 and had immediate success. The following year about seventy-four manuscripts reached the Ambrosiana, among them at least two written in Ireland (one at Bangor in County Downe), and several palimpsests, one of the submerged texts being of three lost orations of Cicero.

Antonio Olgiati, the Cardinal's librarian and first Prefect of the Ambrosiana, was sent on a buying mission to south Germany, the southern Netherlands and France. Francesco Bernardino Ferrari, later Olgiati's successor as Prefect, made a similar journey to Spain. An Ambrosian Doctor, Antonio Salmazia, spent a year from 1607–8 in Corfu hunting for Greek manuscripts. Harrassed by delays in the transfer of funds and by the Corfiotes' hostility, tantalised by travellers' tales from the mainland of 'a very numerous and good library which once belonged to an Emperor in Constantinople' or of a Gospels with the words of Christ written in gold and those of 'the Jewish hordes' in black, he

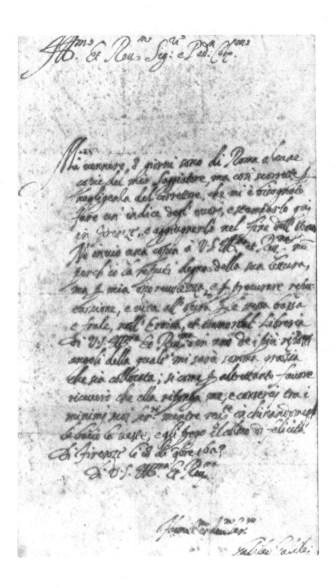

Galileo Galilei's letter to Cardinal Borromeo, accompanying a copy of Il Saggiatore *in 1623; 'to procure life and reputation for the work in your most Illustrious and Reverend Lordship's heroic and immortal library'.*

وزعموا أن ولد الذئب من الكلبة الديسم ورووا البشار من بود ورديسم الغيرك

ثم رجع فيه من غير مباينة له لكان في ذلك أحق ما النظافة من الانعام في حبرتها وجسمها وآسها
والسيتها وإن الارنب لتيض خضا بينا فما عاف لحم اصحاب النقرز

لشاركتها الانعام في الجرة و قال صاحب الكلب اثما ما عبتموه به من

nevertheless succeeded in buying 113 manuscripts by weight (one Corfiote pound weight of manuscript cost five Milanese lire). A group of Greek manuscripts was purchased in Venice from the titular archbishop of Philadelphia, and others were received in a consignment from Chios, and discovered in the monasteries of the Abruzzi. Hebrew manuscripts and some rare printed books were obtained from the Jewish communities of Bologna and other Italian towns by Domenico Gerosolimitano, a converted rabbi in the Cardinal's service.

Works in Oriental languages have been a feature of the Ambrosiana's holdings since its foundation, but little is known of how or where the 340 Arabic, Persian and Turkish manuscripts of the *vecchio fondo* were acquired. A Lebanese Christian was dispatched to the Levant from 1610 to 1617, but with what result, other than a gift of 'Chaldaean books' from the Maronite patriarch, is not recorded. Probably the advice of Diego de Urea, a Spanish Arabist living in Naples, was followed; he recommended asking the Grand Duke of Tuscany and the Grand Master of Malta to instruct their ships to buy Arabic manuscripts in quantity when they visited Cairo and 'those parts'. Even so the founder's appetite for the exotic was not satisfied. He owned works in Glagolitic (the medieval alphabet of Croatia) and a Japanese *Contemptus mundi* printed in Amakusa in 1596, and begged Cardinal Bandini's secretary to find him hieroglyphic books.

In 1601 Cardinal Federigo's correspondent and friend, Gian Vincenzo Pinelli, died in Padua. Two hundred volumes of transcripts of state papers were impounded by the Venetian Republic and more books were lost when pirates attacked the galleys carrying the consignment down the Adriatic to the collector's Neapolitan heirs. The remainder of the library was offered at auction in Naples in 1608 (the earliest recorded book auction sale in Italy) and bought for the Ambrosiana for 3,050 *scudi*. There were further delays – Pinelli's niece was disappointed by the price and refused to give up the collection, the printed books would not have paid the cost of shipping and had to be left behind, for safe transport it was necessary to wait for the Genoese fleet returning from escorting a new archbishop to Sicily. Eventually in the middle of 1609 five hundred and fifty

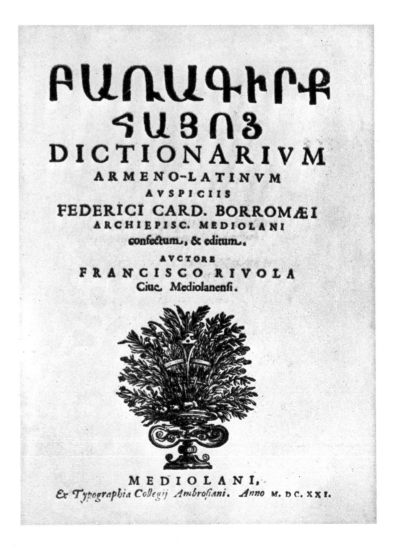

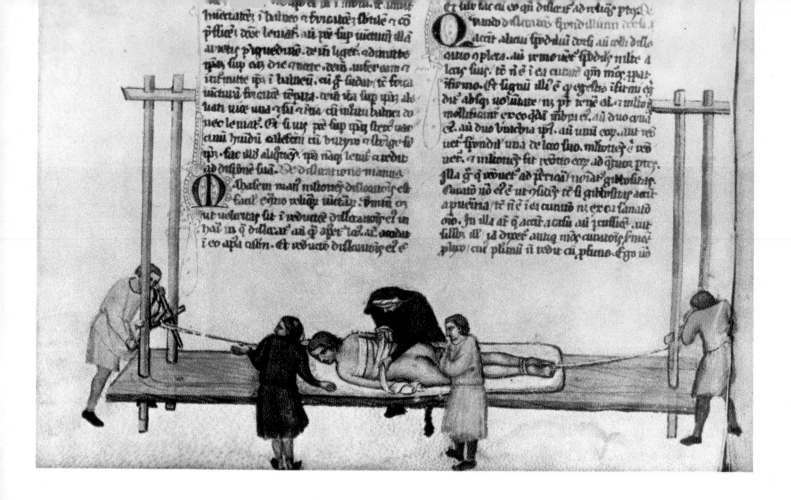

ABOVE *A surgical operation illustrated in Rhazes,* Opera chirurgiae, *written in Bologna in the fourteenth century.* OPPOSITE *Two miniatures from the 'Ambrosian Iliad' of the fourth/fifth century: part of G. V. Pinelli's library, bought at auction in Naples in 1608.* ABOVE *Ares complaining to Zeus.* BELOW *Battle between Greeks and Trojans.*

manuscripts, nearly half of which were Greek, arrived in Milan. They included the fragments of a fourth- or fifth-century illustrated Homer known as 'the Ambrosian Iliad', a tenth- or eleventh-century Horace, Dante's *Divine Comedy* written in Padua about 1355, Boccaccio's *La Fiammetta* annotated by Pietro Bembo, and many antiquarian, humanistic and topical miscellanies.

The Ambrosiana was given what is now its most famous possession in 1637, six years after Cardinal Federigo's death, by the Marquis Arconati, who had refused a tempting offer from Thomas Howard, Earl of Arundel. It was the album of drawings by Leonardo da Vinci, formed by the sculptor Pompeo Leoni and known as the *Codice Atlantico* from its large size, incorporating three dismembered notebooks and many single sheets.

The library – fifteen thousand manuscripts and thirty thousand printed books – was shelved behind brass grilles round the walls of a single room with a high coved ceiling, designed by Francesco Maria Richino and Lelio Buzzi and completed by 1609. Two friezes of authors' and artists' portraits, mostly copied from Paolo Giovio's famous series at Como, ran along the gallery and above the bookcases. Rooms to hold collections of pictures and casts of antique statues, to which was later added accommodation for schools of painting and sculpture, occupied the remainder of a long narrow building adjoining the churches of San Sepolcro and Santa Maria della Rosa in the centre of Milan.

The most original feature of the library's constitutions was to separate responsibility for administration from that for the scholarly use of the collections. The former was entrusted to seven *conservatori,* to include the senior member of the Borromeo family. For the latter purpose a College of Doctors was instituted.

They were encouraged to specialise in different subjects and released from all routine duties, but required to publish a learned work within three years of appointment. The librarian was given onerous responsibilities, among them the purchase of new books and advice to the Doctors on subjects for research; but (by a provision now obsolete) he remained a functionary, without the dignity of a Doctorate. Separate alphabetical catalogues of books and manuscripts were to be prepared, but must not be shown freely to readers or 'for certain reasons well known to us' ever printed. It has been suggested that the motive for this veto was to prevent knowledge of condemned books spreading, but as books on the Index were anyhow banned from the library and doubtful titles could easily have been omitted, the explanation is unconvincing. Possibly Cardinal Federigo feared the acquisitiveness of the king of Spain or his Milanese viceroy if the collection's riches became too well known; massive Spanish buying for the Escorial was still fresh in the memory. Unfortunately the veto, although now interpreted as applying only to Doctors of the Ambrosiana, has hampered the systematic publication of catalogues of the library's holdings. A handful of clauses in the constitutions reflect the Ambrosiana's ecclesiastical origin: at least four of the Doctors should profess theology, communication with foreigners 'of depraved religion' was forbidden, each Doctor within ten years of his appointment must publish a work on the Virgin Mary to whom the college and library were dedicated.

That the library was from the beginning genuinely open to the public (for four hours a day – now increased to five) is confirmed by early travellers. 'The Bibliotheca Ambrosiana is one of the best Libraries in Italy, because it is not so coy as the others, which scarce let themselves be seen; whereas this opens its dores publikly to all comers and goers, and suffers Them to read what book they please' (Richard Lassels, *The Voyage of Italy*, 1670).

The later history of the library is of eminent scholars among the Doctors – the historian Ludovico Antonio Muratori (1695–1700), Angelo Mai, decipherer and editor of the Bobbio palimpsests and later cardinal-prefect of the Vaticana (1810–19), Achille Ratti (Pope Pius XI) and Cardinal Giovanni Mercati – increased holdings (at present five hundred thousand books and thirty thousand manuscripts), enlarged premises (now almost three times the original site) and war-time disasters similar to those suffered by Verona. Of the thirty-three books carried off by the French commissioners in 1796 (among them every famous showpiece the library owned), twelve notebooks of Leonardo were not recovered in 1815 and are now in the Institut de France. On the night of 15–16 August 1943 the oldest part of the building was severely damaged by an Allied air-raid. Manuscripts and incunabula had been removed and escaped intact, and the damage to the fabric was made good after the war (the paintings are now particularly well displayed), but fifty thousand volumes perished, and – an even sadder loss – Cardinal Federigo's original library room was totally destroyed.

ABOVE *The interior of the Ambrosiana before its destruction by bombing in 1943.* OPPOSITE *The frontispiece, by Simone Martini, to Petrarch's manuscript of Vergil. Vergil is seated at the foot of a tree in the act of composition; Servius, the author of a famous commentary on the poet, points him out to the spectator. Aeneas, beside Servius, and two men pruning vines and tending sheep, are references to Vergil's three major poems.*

Ytala felaros tellus alis alma poetas!
Sz tibi grecou redir hic attangere metus.

Scimus alulloqui tegens archana maromis.
ve pareant ruralis pastorib; atop colonis.

Harvard University Library

CAMBRIDGE
MASSACHUSETTS

ABOVE *Harvard: the Widener Library.* OPPOSITE
*S.S. Adalbert, Vitus and Wenceslas, from a wood-
cut attributed to Matthias Grünewald in a* Prague
Missal *printed in Leipzig in 1522.*

'Here I am,' Henry James wrote from Cambridge, Massachusetts, in May 1870, 'here I have been for the last ten days – the last ten years. It's very hot! the window is open before me: opposite thro' the thin trees I see the scarlet walls of the president's *palazzo*. Beyond, the noble grey mass – the lovely outlines, of the library: and above this the soaring *campanile* of the wooden church on the *piazza*.'

The institution named in this masterly evocation of Harvard Yard was already two and a third centuries old, contained close on 134,000 volumes and was housed, in rather cramped conditions, in an awkward, though architecturally harmonious, building in flamboyant gothic style. It dated from the bequest in 1638 to 'the little school for clergymen in New England', founded two years before, of the books of John Harvard, MA, of Emmanuel College, Cambridge, who had been less than a year in America before his death at the age of thirty. Of the four hundred books in the bequest – three-quarters theological, but including Bacon's *Essays*, Chapman's *Homer* and Francis Quarles's *Divine Poems* – only one survives: John Downham's *The Christian Warfare against the Devill World and Flesh*, 1634. Englishmen were active in helping the young college. Sir Kenelm Digby (1603–65) – surprisingly, as he was a Royalist and a Catholic – gave twenty-seven volumes of Greek and Latin Fathers. John Lightfoot, Vice-Chancellor of Cambridge University, bequeathed a collection of Oriental literature in 1675. But the greatest benefactors of the library were three generations of the London merchant family of Hollis. The youngest, Thomas Hollis (1720–74), an eccentric devotee of freedom commonly known as 'The Republican', presented many hundred volumes in bindings decorated with specially designed emblematic tools, followed by a bequest of £500, the income from which is still used for purchases. The eldest, though he never visited New England, gave advice as well as books, as in a letter of 1725:

Your library is reckond here to be ill managed, by the account I have of some that know it, you want seats to sett and read, and chains to your valuable books like our Bodleian library, or Sion College in London,

S. Adalbertus. S. Sigismund. S. Vitus. S. wencesla.

ABOVE *Some of the books presented to Harvard by Thomas Hollis, 'the Republican' (1720–74), in emblematic bindings.* BELOW *A page from a sketchbook of Giuseppe Galli Bibiena (1696–1756).*

you know their methods, wch are approved, but do not imitate them, you let your books be taken at pleasure home to Mens houses, and many are lost, your (boyish) Students take them to their chambers, and teare out pictures & maps to adorne their walls . . .

Whether these strictures were justified cannot now be determined, as almost the entire original library perished on a stormy January night in 1764 when Harvard Hall was burned to the ground, only 404 volumes being saved. In the new Hall completed two years later the library shared the upper floor with the lecture room, the books being arranged according to their donors. 'Over the Chapel, on the second floor, is the Library, containing thirteen thousand books, disposed in ten alcoves, in each of which is a window, and over the windows inscriptions to perpetuate the names of the benefactors. . . . The floor of the library is covered with a rich carpet, and the walls are ornamented with various paintings and prints.' This description of 1790 records a quick recovery from the disaster and suggests a lay-out resembling that of some Oxford colleges, for instance the late seventeenth-century library of the Queen's College.

British troops occupied the College buildings during the War of Independence and the books were evacuated; but the Battle of Bunker's Hill (1775) was so little alarming to those not directly involved that Samuel Phillipps Jr wrote in his diary: 'Amid all the terrors of battle I was so busily engaged in Harvard Library that I never even heard of the engagement until it was completed.'

The library continued to grow: from 4,350 volumes in 1766,

to 30,000 in 1830, to 334,000 in 1895, to 675,000 in 1915. Donors included Benjamin Franklin (the Baskerville Press *Vergil*, 1757, with the remark that many thought it 'the most curiously printed of any book hitherto done in the world'); Goethe (a thirty-nine volume set of his works); Carlyle (the books he had used in writing *Cromwell* and *Frederick the Great*, many heavily annotated); and – to anticipate – Amy Lowell, the New England poetess, who bequeathed her collection of English literature, particularly rich in Keats, with the manuscript of *The Eve of St Agnes* and the copy of *Lamia* given to Fanny Brawne; and the curators of the Bodleian Library, who commemorated Harvard's tercentenary in 1936 by presenting their duplicate copy (one of only two known) of the seventh edition of Columbus's letter to Raphael Sanchez announcing his discovery of the Indies (Paris, Guiot Marchant, *c.* 1493). The last went to augment a notable collection on American history based on the library of Professor Christoph Daniel Ebeling of Hamburg, purchased for $6,500 in 1815 and presented by a Boston merchant.

The first special library building, Gore Hall, whose grey outline delighted Henry James, was erected in 1841, but soon proved inadequate to house a steady flow of accessions. Every expedient was tried: it was enlarged in 1877, remodelled in 1895, added to in 1907; nevertheless, by 1912 lack of space had become critical. In the late winter of that year a twenty-seven-year-old Harvard graduate, Harry Elkins Widener, a promising book-collector and member of the richest family in Philadelphia, was in London with his parents. The dispersal of the Huth library had begun and Widener succeeded in picking up many rare works in English literature, among them the octavo Bacon's *Essayes*, 1598. 'I think I'll take that little Bacon with me,' he said to Quaritch, 'if I'm shipwrecked it will go down with me.' The words were tragically prophetic: the family sailed on the *Titanic* and both father and son were drowned. His mother established in his memory the Harry E. Widener Library at Harvard. This colossal edifice, inaugurated in 1915, was not a happy addition to the Yard; its massive classicism dwarfs the discreet symmetry of its earlier neighbours, while its thick columns and rhetorical flight of steps make any human activity, short of the coronation scene in *Boris Godunov*, appear inadequate.

For the time being the library's problems were solved, but as the rate of accession quickened, the claims of book-space again became urgent. By 1940 the Widener Library was packed full: moreover, air-conditioning was needed to satisfy modern standards of conservation and could not easily be installed in the old building. Two years earlier William A. Jackson had been appointed Assistant Librarian in charge of the Treasure Room (the rare book collection), with the rank of Professor. At the same time Philip Hofer, a Harvard graduate and notable private collector, who had worked in the Pierpont Morgan and New York Public Libraries, inaugurated a new Department of Printing and Graphic Arts devoted to 'the study of the history of the development of the arts of the book'.

Hercules with the dead hydra; frontispiece by Giorgio Ghisi to the architect Vitruvius's Gli oscuri et dificili passi, *Mantua 1558.*

RIGHT *The King of Aragon in council:* Usatges de Barcelona e Constitucions de Cataluña; *printed in Barcelona by Père Miquel in 1495.* BELOW *Edward Lear's autograph manuscript,* The Owl and the Pussycat, *with the author's drawings.*

This was the most formidable combination in the annals of librarianship. Jackson was a librarian of the calibre of Panizzi and Gabriel Naudé, a scholar of the most exacting standards, untiring industry and prodigious memory, with a range that seemed to encompass the whole of European and American literature and history, so that he was equally at ease discussing French gothic *plaquettes*, the first editions of Alfieri or variant issues of English books printed before 1640. He was on familiar terms with the chief collectors and booksellers of both continents, and his enthusiasm, combined with the transparent uprightness of his character, were as successful in charming gifts from a wide circle of alumni as in persuading dealers that to sell a book to Harvard was more rewarding than to make a large profit. It was characteristic of his soundly-based scholarship that the second language in which he was most proficient was Latin, and of his professional absorption that his own collection was of library catalogues annotated by past bibliophiles.

Philip Hofer was, and is, no less remarkable a character. When he founded his department (the first of its kind in any university library) few connoisseurs thought of 'fine illustrated books' as meaning anything beyond woodcut incunabula, the French engraved work of the eighteenth century, and perhaps books illustrated by Rowlandson, Cruikshank and the English aquatinters. Hofer, however, always more interested (as Jackson observed) 'in choice copies of the unusual than in the rare but well known', has enormously extended the frontiers of taste. Books, essays, catalogues and exhibitions, on *Baroque Book Illustration, The Artist and the Book 1860–1960,* Japanese scrolls and albums, the French sixteenth, English seventeenth and Italian eighteenth century, have charted successive explorations of new aesthetic territories.

To relieve the pressure on the Widener Library, a Harvard graduate and distinguished collector, Arthur Amory Houghton Jr, President of the Steuben Glass Company, offered a new rare book building. The Houghton Library was inaugurated in 1942 (Jackson had led the staff in a hectic mouse-hunt through the premises the previous night). Of modest size, with the stacks discreetly hidden below ground, bow-fronted and of brick, it is in polite and elegant contrast to Widener towering behind. The stacks were designed to hold 250,000 volumes and were half full, from the old Treasure Room, when the library opened. The accommodation has since been doubled but is again approaching saturation and more underground burrowing will soon be needed.

The growth of the rare book collection was recorded in a series of annual reports. In 1944, the Gutenberg Bible on paper; 1947, two tons of Thomas Wolfe's archives; 1951, William K. Richardson's collection of illuminated manuscripts, fine bindings and first editions of the classics, chosen with discriminating taste: 1954, the first book printed in Africa; 1956, the Gabrow collection of early Russian maps; 1958, the Friedman Judaica. In 1952 Jackson reported, 'Over ten per cent of the 1,645 books printed in England before 1640 which have been added to the Library during this decade are either unique or unrecorded. In later periods it is possible to say of many authors, including some who may be described as prolific, that all their printed works known to bibliographers are now on Harvard's shelves.' Ten years later he announced with particular satisfaction that the use made of the rare book room had increased more than threefold.

Harvard has the papers of Emerson and Longfellow, Emily Dickinson and Trotsky; it has 3,600 incunabula; it has collections of Luther, Erasmus, Machiavelli and Ronsard, Keats, Lewis Carroll, Edward Lear, Henry James and e.e.cummings, Heine, Rilke and Hugo von Hofmannsthal, Corneille, Racine, Molière and Bossuet, Dante, Tasso and Goldoni, Camões and Cervantes, of calligraphy and type-specimens, the best collection of Russian literary first editions in the West, and far more besides than can possibly be mentioned. When Jackson died in 1964, at the tragically early age of fifty-nine, he had achieved for Harvard much of what Panizzi did for the British Museum. Harvard can never hope to rival the great European foundations in its holdings of medieval manuscripts, but it is already in the front rank as a collection of first editions of European and American literature.

ABOVE Le cheval, *from Pablo Picasso's* Eaux-fortes originales pour des textes de Buffon, [© by s.p.a.d.e.m. Paris.] *Paris, Martin Fabiani, 1942.* BELOW *The Houghton Library at Harvard.*

Herzog August Bibliothek

WOLFENBÜTTEL

Duke Julius of Brunswick-Wolfenbüttel (*r.* 1568–86) is considered the founder of the library. A younger son, born in 1528 and originally intended for the Church, he was sent to study at Cologne and Louvain. A journey to Paris, Orléans and Bourges followed, where he bought *Tristan* and other romances, evidence of a taste for French light literature leading to the later purchase, in a collection from Nuremberg, of the only complete copy known of Jean d'Arras's *Histoire de Melusine* (Geneva 1478). On his succession Lutheranism became the state religion. The monasteries were not immediately suppressed but officials were encouraged to remove suitable volumes for the ducal collection, and five nunneries lost all their manuscripts; from four the total was only 148 (though including two handsome illuminated Psalters), but from the fifth, Marienberg, 292 books and manuscripts were 'taken by Paul von Cleve with some soldiers and brought to Wolfenbüttel by Cosmas, the Duke's waggoner'. A collection of Luther's writings, brought from the widow of the editor of his works, Johann Aurifaber, and a few presents, notably an illuminated Gospels of 1194 from the abbey of Helmarshausen in Westphalia, given by the Landgrave William of Hesse, were other accessions of the reign.

Frugal and sober (delicacies sent by his wife were returned with the message, 'Bacon and sausages are good enough for the Illustrissimo'), and extremely mean, Duke Julius was not an easy man to serve. His instructions to his librarian provided that he was to be busy in 'Our Bibliotheca' daily, summer and winter, early and late, and always available; he must wipe and clean the books once a week, lend no book without written permission and allow no one to enter armed, or in a gown or overcoat. Leonhard Schröter, the first holder of the office, was to double his work in the library with tutoring the Duke's son and singing in the choir, for all of which he would be paid fifty *thalers* a year, with free board and lodging and two suits of clothes. He did not last long enough to receive the summer suit but fled to Leipzig to complain of the Duke's 'unfriendly harsh words' (accompanied on one terrible occasion by blows of the ducal fist) whenever he found

Woodcuts from a Totentanz, *printed in Ulm by Johann Zainer, c. 1488.* ABOVE *Dance of Death.* BELOW, UPPER ROW *Death and the Thief; Death and the Doctor;* LOWER ROW *Death and the Burgher; Death and the Maiden.* OPPOSITE *A manuscript from the most celebrated Renaissance library outside Italy, that of Matthias Corvinus, King of Hungary. The gold medal bears the king's portrait. The work is a humanist Latin poem, the* Laudes Bellicae *by Alexander Cortesius, and the magnificent calligraphy is by Bartolomeo Sanvito of Padua, c. 1480–90.*

Schröter away from his post. Lucas Weischner, a bookbinder, succeeded him for three years. Then came a long interval. When in 1600 a full-time librarian again entered the library he found the books in utter confusion, 'so much disturbance in the cases, everything disarranged, twisted, ravaged, decayed and neglected', while the newly opened room released so fearful a stench that the master of the adjacent choir school feared for the health of his charges.

A librarian was needed to look after a major purchase by the new Duke, Heinrich Julius (*r.* 1589–1613): the collection of 165 vellum manuscripts (priced 1½ *thalers* each) left by the Protestant historian, Matthias Flaccius Illyricus. Many were of very early date, among them a sixth-century Greek St John Chrysostom in uncials, an eighth-century code of laws of the Alamanni and two capitularies of Charlemagne. Flaccius's agent had travelled as far as Scotland in search of rare texts, which is why Wolfenbüttel now owns a hymnal with musical notation from St Andrew's (extracts have recently been recorded) and a thirteenth-century Claudian from Arbroath in Fifeshire. At Heinrich Julius's death in 1613 there were over ten thousand volumes, many containing several works bound together, all of which were given by his successor, Friedrich Ulrich, to the university of Helmstedt. They were not reunited to the ducal collection until 1814.

The next Duke, Augustus of Brunswick-Luneburg (1579–1666), a member of a collateral branch of the ruling family of Brunswick, found himself heir in 1634 to a duchy ravaged by war and occupied by an Imperial army; nine years passed before he secured possession of his own castle at Wolfenbüttel. A model ruler, equally successful in negotiating the withdrawal of the occupation troops and in rehabilitating his country, he was also one of the most able and assiduous of all book-collectors. After studying at Rostock and Tübingen, a grand tour to the Netherlands, England, France and Italy, and an appointment as canon of Strasbourg Cathedral, he settled in a 'princely residence' at Hitzacker. Here he spent his time in scholarly pursuits, publishing works on cryptography and chess, and in forming a library, to which he devoted the major part of his income, fifteen or sixteen thousand *thalers* a year. In 1627 he owned about ten thousand works. After his accession the pace quickened: in 1649 there were sixty thousand; in 1661, 116,357 works in 28,415 volumes. Most of the books were in Latin or German, relatively few in Italian, French or Greek; among a handful of English books was the 1637 quarto *Hamlet*. The majority were contemporary editions, but the number of important incunabula and especially of early illustrated books was evidence of a taste far in advance of the period. Augustus's tolerance of original condition caused him to preserve gothic bindings and to accept damaged or imperfect copies of many woodcut books which might otherwise have been lost. The best known example is the volume containing three of the notoriously rare books printed by Albrecht Pfister at Bamberg, one of them being the unique copy of Ulrich Boner's *Der Edelstein*, 1461, the first illustrated and the

LAVDES BELLICAE

ILIACAS ALII
FLAMMAS THE
BANAQVE FRA
TRVM ARMA
ET IASONIIS
INSIGNEM HEROIBVS ARGO

A strox cursus & dilis inania regna:
F id taq; pierio referant miracula cantu:
N os proprijs spectanda oculis nos inclyta dextre
F acta tue canimus quibus aurea sydera viuus
T angis & aetherias fama petis arduus arces:
S ed sine te nunq tenues ad carmina tanto
S ubsistant uires oneri tu numine toto
D exter ades: da maeoniam tua facta canenti
M atthia coruine chelyn: si delphica parent
T empla tibi: sentitq frequens tua nomina cyrrha
S i musae si phoebus amant: hoc tempore solus
C arminibus si digna facis: quae nulla uetustas

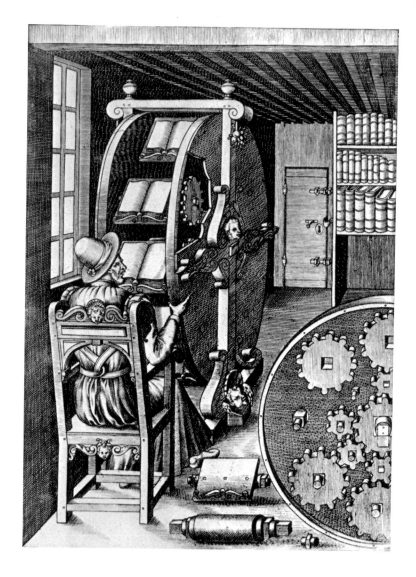

ABOVE *A book-wheel, from Agostino Ramelli's* Le diverse et artificiose machine, *printed in Paris in 1588.* RIGHT *The book-wheel ordered by Duke Augustus from Augsburg, now holding three volumes of his library catalogue.*

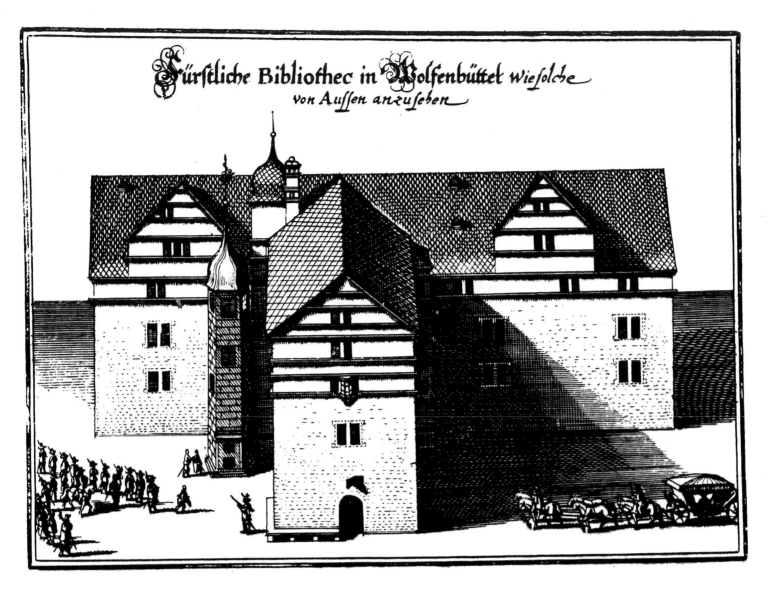

first dated German book printed with movable type.

Augustus himself wrote the title with characteristic pen flourishes on the spine of each volume, either directly on the vellum of new bindings or on labels stuck to the older ones. He also compiled and wrote his own catalogue, four folio volumes of several hundred pages each, only delegating the writing to a secretary when he had completed page 5,900. These catalogues are astonishing for the fulness of their entries, which list detailed titles with places and dates of printing, and the wealth of cross-references to other editions of the same work. For the convenient use of these large volumes Augustus ordered a 'book-wheel' from Augsburg; this invention was first illustrated in the Italian engineer Ramelli's *Le diverse et artificiose machine* (Paris 1588) as an aid for the gouty in handling folios, but the few surviving examples are all of Northern manufacture. The books were kept above the stables on the first floor of a substantial rectangular building adjacent to Wolfenbüttel Castle. They were arranged according to size in high cases against the walls, classified in twenty categories. Theology, History and Law were by far the largest. Manuscripts were classed separately. Philosophy was divided into Ethics and Logic; arts and sciences into Poetry, Rhetoric, Grammar, Music, Politics, Economics, War, Arithmetic, Geometry, Astronomy, Geography, Physics and Medicine. Miscellaneous subjects were grouped under *Quodlibetica*, a category that tended to grow disproportionately large.

The exterior of the library at Wolfenbüttel in the seventeenth century.

207

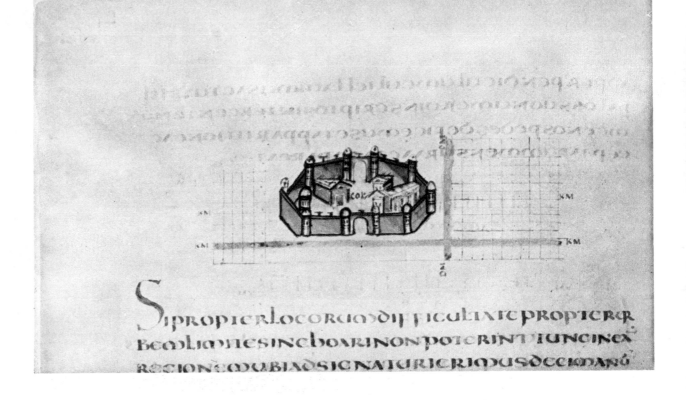

Books and manuscripts were obtained through an international network of agents. These were not booksellers but gentlemen dealers like Philipp Hainhofer of Augsburg (who also bought Maximilian's prayer-book for the Munich Library), Heinrich Julius von Blum, a diplomat in the Imperial service, or Abraham Wicquefort, the Brandenburg resident at the French court, or scholarly correspondents such as the Jesuit polymath Athanasius Kircher who gave the Duke a Syriac Gospels of the year 634 'in gratitude for much kindness'. Augustus confiscated manuscripts from the monasteries of St Blasien in Brunswick and Marienthal near Helmstedt, and he received many gifts, including a hundred volumes from Mazarin with the Cardinal's arms and two Hebrew manuscripts from a Jew of Halberstadt. With these exceptions his books were acquired by the civilised method of purchase, even in the case of those whose earlier history was irregular, such as the Bavarian Missal taken by the Swedes from Munich, or the three Greek manuscripts belonging to Guarino Veronese looted at the capture of Mantua by the Emperor's forces in 1630. Germany was naturally the chief source of supply but the earliest manuscript, the Codex Arcerianus, a sixth-century collection of Roman authors on land survey which had belonged in the Middle Ages to the monastery of Bobbio and in the Renaissance to the Amerbachs in Basle, was bought in the Netherlands; the medieval Icelandic *Eyrbyggia Saga* had passed through Denmark and Holstein; an Aquitaine cartulary was obtained from the archives of Bordeaux, one of the few documents to escape their destruction in the Revolution, and from England came an unusually handsome Wycliffite Bible which had belonged to Lord Lumley. The Duke's correspondence with his agents is bound in thirty volumes in the library, the bills are in the state archives – a unique unpublished hoard awaiting the enterprising writer of a doctoral thesis.

Augustus opened the library to ecclesiastical and lay councillors and 'others worthy': the rules, composed in Latin verse and written over the door in gold letters, were as amiable as every-

34 Es ist võ rechter natur · Das meiste teil alle cre=
natur · Mit fleis nerē ire kint · Die von in gepo=
ren sint · Eine mÿner die andere mee · Ir kind schäde
tut in wee · Ein maus mit grosē fleise zoch · Ir kint
traut die zeit kã doch · Sie sprach ir sult mich eben
verstã · Do sie an ir erbeit wolt gã · Nu horet mein
vil liebē kint · welch freunt oder veint sint · Das mu=
get ir gewissē wol · Das lant ist veint vol · Volget
ir dē rate mein · Vnd laset ewr laufen sein · Vnd be=
leibt in dem haus · Also schied võ in die alt maus ·
Die iũgen tanzē huben an · Vnd wolten freude hã
Sie liefen ein sie liefen aus · Ein han geloffen kam
in das haus · Geflogen mit den hennen schir · Vil
schon was seins kämes zir · Sein sporn stũden ym

thing about him. 'If [the reader] finds anything not entirely to his taste, or something in his view too strongly to be approved, let him contain himself calmly and reflect on it in silence . . .'. His will bequeathed the collection to the eldest prince of the Wolfenbüttel line (it became the property of the province of Lower Saxony only in 1954 after the death of the last reigning Duke) and directed that every opportunity should be taken of adding to it. This instruction was taken seriously; in 1689, 105 manuscripts from Weissenberg Abbey in Alsace were acquired, more than half dating from before the year 900; in 1710, 467 manuscripts from a Danish statesman, Marquard Gude; in 1753 the private collection of Duke Ludwig Rudolph. The philosopher Leibniz, the greatest figure in the learned world of his period, was chief librarian from 1690 to 1716 and produced an alphabetical author catalogue that is still in use. From 1770 to 1781 the post was held by Lessing who was delighted by the discoveries he made in the collection. 'This treasure,' he wrote of one of them, 'belongs not to Vienna but to Wolfenbüttel; the savant must come here to find it' – a sentiment still familiar, though not often expressed. Between 1705 and 1710 Augustus's *Marstall* was replaced by a circular library with a single gallery designed by Hermann Korb, which may have influenced Gibbs's Radcliffe Camera in Oxford (1747) and ultimately the British Museum Reading Room. Built entirely of wood, too small and too risky to last, it gave way to a more solid but less decorative building in 1886.

Wolfenbüttel was occupied twice by a French army. In the Seven Years War the Duc de Richelieu placed the books under his special protection; nothing was taken except three current maps for which the library still holds a receipt. Half a century later Brunswick, as an early member of the hostile coalition, was singled out by Napoleon for harsh treatment. About four hundred volumes were 'found worthy to augment the collection of the Imperial Library' and removed to Paris; among them were the three Pfister imprints, which were expensively rebound in red morocco by Bozérian. Later Jerome Bonaparte's Westphalian government proposed to abolish the library altogether and assign the major part of its contents to Göttingen. Nearly everything was recovered after Waterloo, though Van Praet succeeded in substituting an inferior copy of the thirty-six-line Bible, lacking one leaf, for the immaculate Wolfenbüttel copy which has remained in Paris. George IV's brother, the Duke of Clarence, on a visit four years later to his German cousins (whose father had fallen at Quatre Bras), was shown *Der Edelstein*. A feeling of satisfaction with the workings of Providence assailed him; he called for pen and ink, and addressed posterity on the flyleaf: 'This most remarkable work was restored to the Legitimate Family of Brunswick after the capture of Paris in 1815. This anecdote is wrote by William Duke of Clarence . . . in Commemoration of the happy restitution of the Illustrious House of Brunswick and of his particular regard and friendship for these two young promising Princes.' He was right to be pleased, for the Wolfenbüttel Library had survived its gravest trial.

ABOVE *View by Louis Jacke of the old library at Wolfenbüttel, built by Herman Korb, 1705–10.* OPPOSITE *The mice and the hens; from Ulrich Boner's* Der Edelstein, *printed by Albrecht Pfister at Bamberg in 1461; the unique copy of the first illustrated book printed with movable type.*

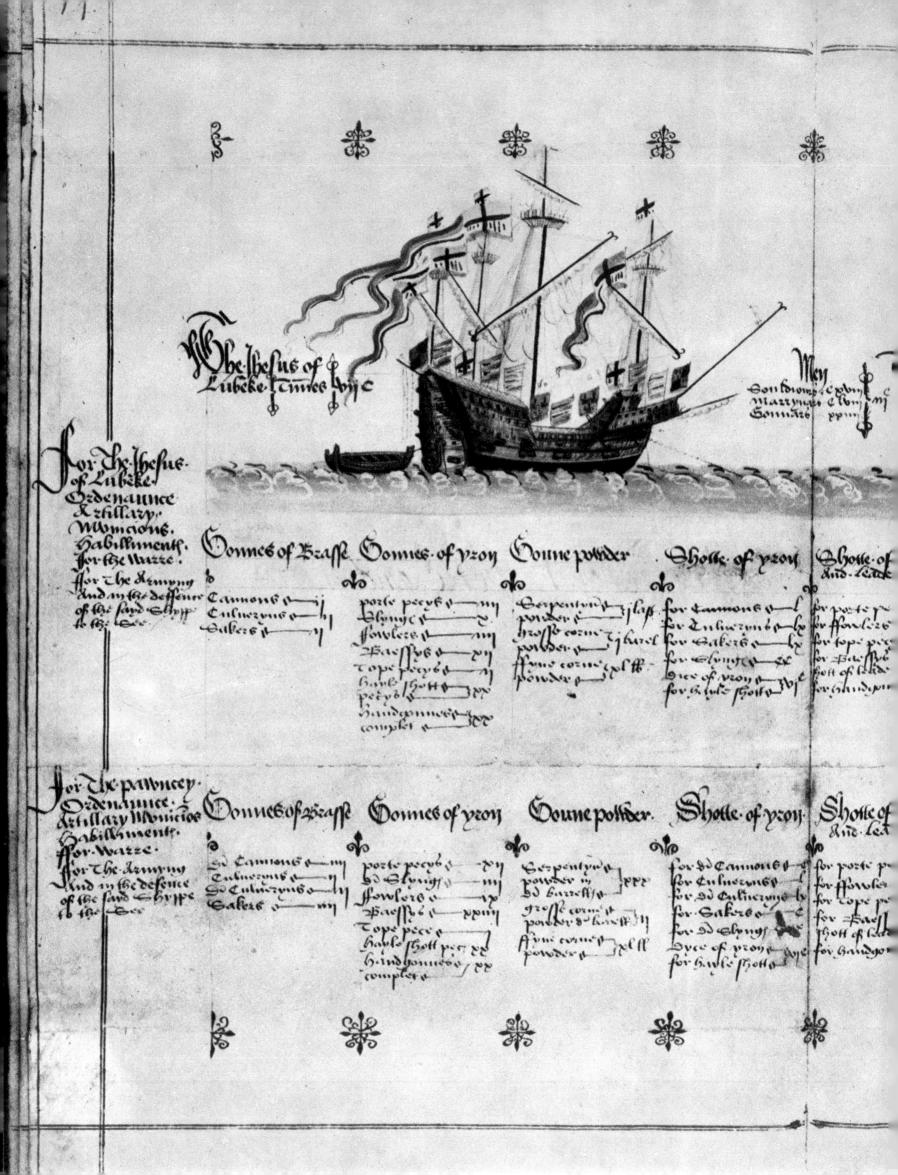

The Jhesus of
Lubeke tunnes vij C

Men
Souldiours
Marynars
Gonners

For the Jhesus of Lubeke Ordenaunce Artillary Municons Habillments for the Warre.

For the Armyng and in the defence of the said Shipp to the Sea

Gonnes of Brasse	Gonnes of yron	Gonne powder	Shotte of yron	Shotte of Stone and Lead
Cannons	Porte peces	Serpentyne powder	for Cannons	for porte peces
Culveryns	Slynges	Grosse corne powder	for Culveryns	for fowlers
Sakers	Fowlers	Fyne corne powder	for Sakers	for tops peces
	Basses		for Slynges	for Basses
	Tope peces		Dyce of yron	Shott of Lead
	Hayle Shott peces		for Hayle Shott	for handgonnes
	Handgonnes complet			

For the Pawncey Ordenaunce Artillary Municons Habillments for Warre.

For the Armyng and in the defence of the said Shipp to the Sea

Gonnes of Brasse	Gonnes of yron	Gonne powder	Shotte of yron	Shotte of Stone and Lead
Cannons	Porte peces	Serpentyne powder	for Cannons	for porte peces
Culveryns	Slynges	barrells	for Culveryns	for fowlers
Culveryns	Fowlers	Grosse corne powder	for Culveryns	for tops peces
Sakers	Basses	Fyne corne powder	for Sakers	for Basses
	Tope pece		for Slynges	Shott of Lead
	Hayle Shott peces		Dyce of yron	for handgonnes
	Handgonnes complet		for Hayle Shott	

Pepys Library Magdalene College

CAMBRIDGE

'So to piper and Duck Lane, and there kissed bookseller's wife and bought Legend.' Samuel Pepys's brisk account of buying Voragine's *Golden Legend* (Wynkyn de Worde, 1521) on 10 April 1668 is one of numerous records in the *Diary* of shopping expeditions by this inveterate book-hunter, reader and browser. Like all educated men of his day he was a competent Latinist, able to carry on a conversation in that language with an otherwise monoglot Dutch admiral, and rising at four in the morning to read his 1582 Venetian edition of Cicero, whom he thought 'as good a writer as ever I read in my life'. He was also a devout believer and a keen judge of a sermon. But here any resemblance between his library and Sir Thomas Bodley's Latin theology ceases. From today's viewpoint Bodley seems one of the last in a tradition stretching back to Cassiodorus; Pepys, with his taste for English literature, voyages and navigation, and science, is a recognisably modern collector.

By 1668 Pepys had more books than would fit into his two presses, over five hundred altogether, and was thinking of giving some away. During the next twenty years, for most of which he held the influential post of Secretary to the Admiralty, the 'Tumult of Business' (as he afterwards expressed it) greatly reduced his opportunities of visiting bookshops. Nevertheless the collection grew and many desirable rarities were acquired, among them two of the three rolls containing Anthony Anthony's illustrated record of Henry VIII's navy, given to Pepys by Charles II, and a manuscript life of Mary, Queen of Scots, a present from his other royal master, James, Duke of York.

In 1689 in the aftermath of the Whigs' 'Glorious Revolution' Pepys retired from the public service. As he settled down to a life of unaccustomed leisure his collections came to occupy the chief part of his attention, the first sign of the new order being a journey by chair in November 1690 to attend a print auction in Covent Garden. Foremost in his bookish circle was his old friend John Evelyn, whose translation of Gabriel Naudé's *Instructions concerning Erecting of a Library*, presented as long ago as 1665 with the misprints corrected and a polite inscription, 'Be pleasd to

ABOVE *Samuel Pepys by Geoffrey Kneller. This portrait hangs in the library at Cambridge.*
OPPOSITE *Anthony Anthony's illustrated roll of Henry VIII's navy, given to Pepys by Charles II.*

Pepys's books on wooden bases designed to make them all the same height on the shelves.

accept this trifle from your most humble servant J E,' he had then found 'above my reach'. Since that time the two *Virtuosi* had frequently sent each other gifts, Pepys emerging as a clear winner; for while his library still possesses a valuable collection of historical papers officially on loan from Evelyn but which the latter 'afterwards never asked of him', the best piece Pepys offered in return was 'a map of Caxton's', whatever that may have been. Other correspondents included Dr Arthur Charlett, Master of University College, Oxford, where his nephew John Jackson was *in statu pupillari*; a brilliant young palaeographer, Humfrey Wanley, assistant in the Bodleian Library; Dr Hans Sloane, then at the start of his career as a collector; and John Bagford, cobbler, book-breaker and commission agent; while his fellow savants of the Royal Society were entertained at his house in York Buildings, London, every Saturday evening. At least half the library was acquired in the last thirteen years of his life.

In 1692 he decided that the time had come to review and re-organise his holdings. The first step was to withdraw to the country for three months to put his papers in order (they were not placed in the library and are not at Magdalene, but formed part of Richard Rawlinson's bequest to the Bodleian Library). Other preparations included sending his copy of the first book in English on navigation, Pierre Garcia's *The Rutter of the Sea* (printed *c.* 1555 and too optimistically dated 'about 1490' by the owner) to Oxford to be collated with Selden's copy. Some time in 1693 all was ready for the complicated operation which Pepys called an 'Adjustment'. This involved marshalling all the books in strict order of size and numbering them from the smallest upwards. Any volume not matching its neighbours exactly in height was liable to summary ejection, but, if a favourite, was made up to size with a wooden plinth disguised with gilt leather. After the volumes, now nicely graded, had been arranged in the presses, two catalogues, one by number, the other alphabetical, and a subject index, termed 'Appendix Classica', were drawn up. The catalogue was grandly titled 'Supellex Literaria' (literary furniture), as Pepys had a weakness for Latin names: 'Consutilia' for bound volumes of pamphlets, and 'Repertorium Chiro-Typicum' for a collection of facsimile signatures of famous people.

The Library's appearance in York Buildings after the 1693 Adjustment is known from drawings. It was a long room panelled and uncarpeted, with windows looking onto the Thames at one end. Seven oak presses with glass doors stood on the other sides, the earliest extant glazed bookcases, from a design contrived by Pepys with 'Sympson the joyner' in 1666. They held about 1,600 volumes, with room for more. Above them hung portraits of Evelyn, Robert Boyle and other celebrated contemporaries; James II, three-quarter length, was over the fireplace. A draped table of almost Oriental lowness (concealing, one suspects, the folios too large to fit into the cases) stood in the middle of the room, with two volumes open on top – probably the catalogue. The final piece of essential furniture was a pair of steps, to allow the owner, a short man, to reach the top shelf.

The contents of the presses after the next Adjustment, in 1700 – by then increased to 2,474 volumes – are recorded in the existing catalogue. In 1694, when invited to contribute a list of his manuscripts to the *Catalogi librorum manuscriptorum Angliae et Hiberniae* in course of preparation at Oxford, Pepys replied that he had had no time for 'lookeing-out for Curiositys' on any subject except the sea. This part of his collection had been commenced at least as early as 1664 when he contemplated writing an account of the Dutch War, 'it being a thing I much desire, and sorts mightily with my genius' – later expanded into a projected history of the navy. He owned manuscript voyages of Clement Adams to Russia (presented to Philip II and Queen Mary), of Frobisher's second-in-command, Edward Fenton (a gift from Evelyn) and of Bartholomew Sharpe, the buccaneer, and among other official papers seventeen volumes of Admiralty letter-books, for whose return his successor as Secretary to the Admiralty appealed in vain. An important group on navigation contained two fine Elizabethan works, bound together: Robert Recorde's *Castle of Knowledge*, 1556, and William Cuningham's *The Cosmographical Glasse*, 1559. And the section on shipbuilding started engagingly with Athanasius Kircher's *De Arca Noe*, Amsterdam 1675 (a topic on which Pepys felt qualified to express a professional judgement: 'Mr Shere computes from its dimensions that six months would have sufficed to have built what Moses assigns an hundred years for') and included Sir Anthony Deane's *Doctrine of Naval Architecture*, over whose neat scale drawings Evelyn displayed en-

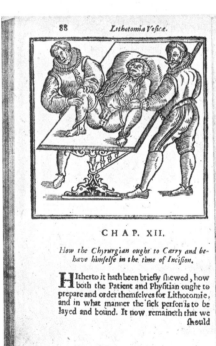

ABOVE *Pepys's Library in York Buildings, London, c. 1693. The Thames can be seen through the windows; portraits of celebrated contemporaries line the walls.* BELOW *Preparing a patient to be cut for the stone, an operation which Pepys himself underwent in 1658.*

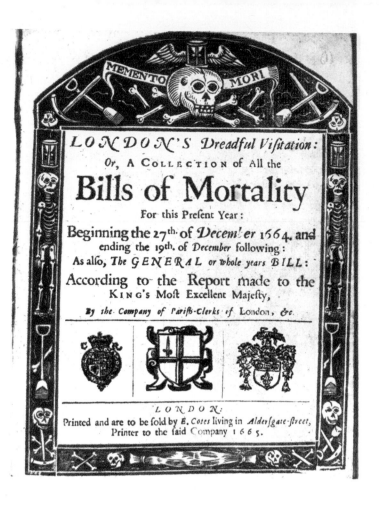

ABOVE *London's Dreadful Visitation, 1665: a record of deaths in the Great Plague.* BELOW '*The Hercules Leape' from Will Stokes,* The Vaulting-Master, *Oxford 1652. The origin of the vaulting horse?*

thusiasm on 28 January 1682: 'I do not think the world can show the like. I esteem this book an extraordinary jewel.'

The collection was strong on the heroic period of the Elizabethan navy, and even Henry VIII's pocket calendar was discarded in favour of Francis Drake's. Augustine Ryther's plates illustrating the movements of the Armada were present; so was the book of charts used by the English ships in the action – Waghenaer's *Speculum Nauticum*, the Dutch, Latin and English editions (the 'Waggoners' whose supposed loss was one of Pepys's chief anxieties during the Great Fire of 1666). At some time in the 1690s he obtained – perhaps through an English merchant in Seville – a volume that must have given him particular pleasure: the contractor's list of stores supplied to the Spanish fleet in 1587. The near-coincidence of date proved irresistible, and the accession was entered as 'The Original Libro de Cargos . . . of the Proveedor of the Spanish Armada 1588'.

Certain categories are set out in chronological tables in the 1700 library catalogue. One of these surveys his holdings of English literature from Bede's *Ecclesiastical History* in Anglo-Saxon and Latin to 'the Attempt last made towards its Refinement by Sir Philip Sidney in his Arcadia'. It is an impressive list, containing Chaucerian poems in manuscript 'wherof some never printed', six Caxtons, among them the only known copy of *Reynard the Fox*, and a fragment of a seventh, and the unique manuscript of books 10–15 of Caxton's translation of the *Metamorphoses* of Ovid – the first volume of which was discovered as recently as 1965 among

the waste paper piled up by that insatiable bibliomane, Sir Thomas Phillipps. Scottish literature was listed separately, the chief feature being two collections of verse by Sir Richard Maitland, Gavin Douglas and William Dunbar, bought at the Duke of Lauderdale's sale in 1692.

Of the Origine & Growth of Printing in England is the title of another table, bound at the end of Joseph Moxon's *Mechanick Exercises*, 1677: a reasonably accurate survey (although misled by the legend of Corsellis's Oxford press), based on information from Moxon, Bagford and his own observation. This was an interest that led him to buy examples of Machlinia's and the St Albans presses, seventeen Wynkyn de Wordes and sixteen Pynsons. The fathers of the craft were preferred to their successors; thus a later printing of St John Fisher's *Fruitful sayings of David* (probably Thomas Marsh's of 1555) was discarded in favour of Wynkyn de Worde's edition of 1509. When it came to modern times, which Pepys seems to have envisaged as starting about 1590, the contrary principle applied: the later edition replaced the earlier. So the Third Shakespeare Folio, bought on 7 July 1664, was ejected to make room for the Fourth, of 1685.

Other components of the library reflect the range of his interests: science, chiefly by his colleagues of the Royal Society, notably forty-two works by Robert Boyle and Newton's *Principia*, printed in 1687 with Pepys's *imprimatur* as President; music; books on shorthand; grammars and dictionaries; the first collected edition of Racine, 1676, and works by Molière, Pascal, Descartes and Boileau; Spanish plays and chap-books, bought on a visit to Seville in 1684; parliamentary papers, newsletters and tracts on the 'Popish Plot'; broadside ballads; popular romances, jest-books and moral tales, with titles like *The Famous and Remarkable History of Sir Richard Whittington* and *An Allarum from Heaven: or, a warning to Rash Wishers*, grouped as 'Vulgaria', 'Penny Merriments' and 'Penny Godlinesses'; and curiosities – the *Divan* of Anwari in Persian; a Slavonic book of Hours; two specimens of Chinese block-printing and an empty Turkish notebook, of black paper inside lacquered covers.

Summoned before the House of Commons in 1674, Pepys boldly challenged the whole world to prove that he had ever had a 'Popish' book in his house. It was as well that the challenge was not taken up, as he had never ceased to be interested in the liturgy of the 'old Catholique days' and the discipline of the modern Roman Church. In later years he owned the *Index librorum prohibitorum* (1624) of Mascarenhas (the Portuguese Inquisitor-General whose books found their way to Bodley), an illustrated relation of the *auto da fé* celebrated in Madrid in 1680, and the second part of a *Praeparatio ad Confessionem* consisting of an index of sins on detachable slips, perhaps for the convenience of penitents mute with embarrassment. Catholic homiletic and transcendental works are more unexpected, such as the three-volume *Mystica ciudad de Dios* (Lisbon 1681) of the Spanish nun, María de Jesus.

Pepys probably bought his illuminated manuscripts for anti-

ABOVE *The narrator, accompanied by 'Discretion', meeting 'a ladye olde and amyable/Syttinge in a castell both fressh and gay/On an olyphauntes backe in strength so stable'. The unique copy of Stephen Hawes,* The example of Virtue, *printed by Wynkyn de Worde in 1510.* BELOW *Poems by Sir Richard Maitland, copied for his daughter Mary in 1586.*

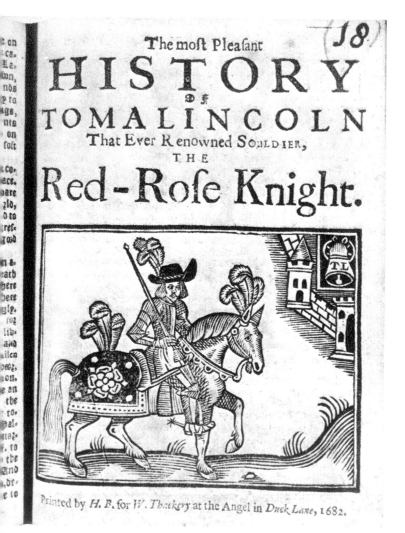

ABOVE *One of the Spanish chap-books bought in Seville in 1694; Francisco de Quevedo's* Satiras graciosas. BELOW The most Pleasant History of Tom a Lincoln, *London 1682. This is one of the popular romances which Pepys called his 'Vulgaria'.*

quarian reasons; his beautiful fourteenth-century English artist's sketch book was modestly described as 'an ancient book of Monkish drawings and Designes for Church use'. Of contemporary illustration, however, he was an ardent connoisseur, spending an hour at Joseph Kirton's shop in St Paul's Churchyard admiring the 'excellent cuts' of Braun and Hogenberg's *Theatrum Urbium* and Sanders's *Flandria illustrata*, and owning not only English works like Francis Barlow's Aesop (a book he had sumptuously bound), but uncommon Continental ones such as La Torre Farfan's *Fiestas de Sevilla* (1675) with plates after Murillo, Valdes Leal and the younger Herrera.

'My delight is in the neatness of everything': this guiding principle of the library had been decided as early as 1663. The books were ruled in red ink and supplied with manuscript indexes where required. In The Hague in 1660 Pepys had made three purchases 'for the love of the binding' (they seem to have been in rather plain vellum) and he never lost his taste for a well-bound book. The music was mostly in decorated wrappers, the others in calf with gilt spines; apart from a few presents, morocco was reserved for his Wycliffite New Testament and other highly prized rarities. He owned bindings with the royal arms of Charles I (for which he had given Silvanus Morgan, 'the Herald Painter', a guinea), and books that had belonged to Henry VII, Lord Burghley, Lord Chief Justice Coke, Sir Robert Cotton, Dr John Dee, Robert Burton, Ben Jonson and Henri, Duc de Rohan. As the century drew to an end Pepys could survey his library with satisfaction.

But he was not finished yet. He must take his *Workes of King Charles the Martyr* to collate with the copy at Lambeth which had been censored by the Inquisition in Lisbon. John Jackson had set off on a Grand Tour; he knew his uncle's *gusto* by now and could be relied on to bring back something of interest from Italy – guide-books, views of Roman monuments, Corelli's sonatas, the characters of the twenty-two most *papabile* cardinals; perhaps he could secure a more accurate copy of Henry VIII's letters to Anne Boleyn in the Vatican Library than Dr Fall, precentor of York, had obtained seventeen years before. Then there were the albums to complete and bind, the collection of views of Paris started in the 'Taille-Douce shops', to which Evelyn had directed him thirty years earlier, the views of London, his 'Miscellany of Prints General' which must be carefully ordered by subject: 'Scripture Story, Devotion Pieces, Solemnity & Pastimes', and so on; his collection of Heads and Figures. But both his latest collections, frontispieces and calligraphy, were running into difficulties. It was true that Dr Shadwell was sending frontispieces from Paris and his cousin Gale from Amsterdam, but Jackson had found disappointingly few in Rome. For the calligraphic collection, which was to start with manuscript specimens and end with the latest writing-books, he must depend on Bagford for the contents and Humfrey Wanley for identifications and descriptions. He wanted it to span a thousand years (a neat number), but Wanley could produce no example of the seventh

Dame se promenant a la Campaigne

Ce vend à Paris proche les Grands Augustins aux deux Globes a la seconde Chambre Avec Privil du Roy.

ABOVE *Three bindings from Pepys's collection.*
LEFT *London binding, perhaps by Nott.* CENTRE
White and gold wrappers. RIGHT *by Samuel
Mearne, c. 1685.* BELOW '*Dame se promenant a
la Campaigne*', *after I.D. de St Jean, 1670:
from a collection of French costume prints.*

century – and even the Isidore of Seville he sent as a consolation proved to lack half a dozen leaves. Then a provoking letter had arrived from Durham about the fragments his old friend the Dean, Dr John Montagu, had obligingly cut from two manuscripts for him to contemplate their 'Character and Antiquity'; it seemed that now the Chapter wanted them back. How could they refuse them to 'the Curiosity of One of my Gusto in these matters'? The future of the library must also be carefully considered; it had taken such infinite pains and time and cost to collect and methodise. . . .

Like Fernando Columbus, Pepys was concerned that his books should be well looked after; but he wanted them to be of benefit to posterity as well. Two codicils to his will signed on 12 and 13 May 1703, a fortnight before he died, attempted to reconcile these principles. John Jackson was to have the books for his lifetime and was instructed to 'complete' the library by adding missing volumes and sets, binding up the unbound pamphlets, stamping Pepys's arms on the covers of every volume and carrying out a final Adjustment. After Jackson's death the testator expressed a preference that the library should go to Magdalene, his own and his nephew's college at Cambridge. The books must be accommodated there in a separate room, to be called Bibliotheca Pepysiana, and must remain unchanged in perpetuity, without addition or subtraction; the library was to be forfeit to Trinity College if these conditions were disregarded.

John Jackson died in 1723. The following year the books, amounting in theory to three thousand volumes – another neat number – though in fact a few short owing to gaps in the enumeration, were transported to Cambridge, together with twelve presses and a writing-table designed to hold large folios, and installed on the first floor of a seventeenth-century addition to the college. Here a German traveller, Nathanael Jacob Gerlach, took a gloomy view of their prospects in 1728: 'This library has no *supplementa* [additions] and may not be moved from the spot but remains preserved *in honorem familiae*. I look upon it as a *monumentum vanitatis*. After some time the whole lumber may grow out of date, the little gold blackened, and the use of the library [will] vanish.' The exact reverse occurred. At first little known or visited, the collection concealed a time-bomb with a hundred-year fuse: the six volumes of Pepys's *Diary*, written in Thomas Shelton's system of shorthand. When Lord Braybrooke's partial publication appeared in 1825 from the Reverend John Smith's transcript, Pepys – until then a forgotten naval administrator – became suddenly famous. Interest in his books has steadily increased since that date. The collection has indeed a powerful attraction, perhaps from having been formed for enjoyment by a naturally happy man. 'O Fortunate Mr Pepys!' (Evelyn once addressed him) 'who knows, possesses, and injoyes all that's worth the seeking after.'

RIGHT *Interior of the Library.* BELOW *The Pepys Library occupies the first floor of this seventeenth-century building in Magdalene College.*

Yale University Library

NEW HAVEN CONNECTICUT

In the year 1700 there was general agreement in Connecticut that the colony needed a college. Ten ministers appointed to give effect to the decision held their first meeting in Branford Parsonage. 'Each member brought a Number of Books and presented them to the Body; and laying them on a Table, said these words, or to this effect, "I give these books for the founding a College in this Colony".' Though historians are inclined to doubt the truth of this story, which is taken from President Clap's *Annals of Yale-College*, 1766, at least it shows an early appreciation of the library's central rôle in what became Yale University.

The new foundation migrated several times before settling in 1718 into a three-storey building in New Haven, with the library on the second floor, grown by then, with the help of numerous gifts solicited by the colony's London agent, Jeremiah Drummer, to a thousand volumes. Steele had given complete runs of the *Tatler* and *Spectator*; Newton gave his *Optics*, the second edition (1713) of his *Principia*, Estienne's Greek *Thesaurus* and another Greek book; Halley, the astronomer, his edition of Apollonius; and a consignment from the most distinguished native of Connecticut in England, Elihu Yale, a former governor of Fort St George (Madras), included what seems to have been the first medieval illustrated manuscript to reach North America, a fourteenth-century *Speculum humanae salvationis*. In addition to the usual theology there were the works of Chaucer, Spenser, Milton, Ben Jonson, Bacon's *Essays*, Butler's *Hudibras*, Temple and Cowley. In 1733 Yale received nine hundred volumes from Bishop Berkeley, 'the finest that ever came to America together'. Ten years later the first printed catalogue listed 2,600 volumes, with Shakespeare, Dryden and Pope added to the English authors already mentioned.

In 1763 the library underwent the first of many moves, to a classical building shared with the chapel, and in the same year received from Jared Eliot its first endowment for purchases, £10. As at Harvard the War of Independence brought British occupation; the library books were hurriedly evacuated and many lost. There were two more moves to fresh premises. Then, in 1843,

ABOVE *Map of Utopia from the first edition of Sir Thomas More's* Utopia, *printed in 1516. This copy belonged to Cuthbert Tunstall, Bishop of Durham.* OPPOSITE *The binding of Matthias Corvinus's* Tacitus (Buda, c. 1480). *The manuscript belonged to Beatus Rhenanus and was abstracted from Sélestat by an artillery officer of Napoleon's army.*

ABOVE *Speculum humanae salvationis, written in England in the fourteenth century. Given to the library by Elihu Yale in 1714. This is possibly the first medieval illustrated manuscript to reach North America. The drawings are of Daniel and the dragon Bel, and David cutting off Goliath's head.* BELOW *View of Yale College, c. 1745; by T. Johnson after J. Greenwood.* RIGHT *Interior of the Beinecke Library, Yale University, opened in 1964; the architect was Gordon Bunshaft.*

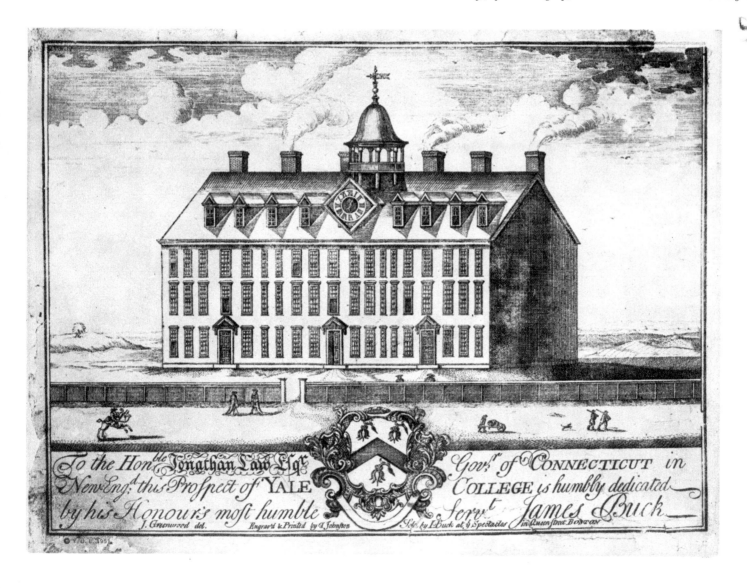

To the Honᵇˡᵉ Jonathan Law Esqᵣ Govᵣ of CONNECTICUT in New:Engᵈ; this Profpect of YALE COLLEGE is humbly dedicated by his Honour's moſt humble Servᵗ JAMES BUCK

J. Greenwood del.   Engrav'd & Printed by T. Johnston   Sold by I. Buck at ÿ Spectacles in Queen ſtreet Boſton

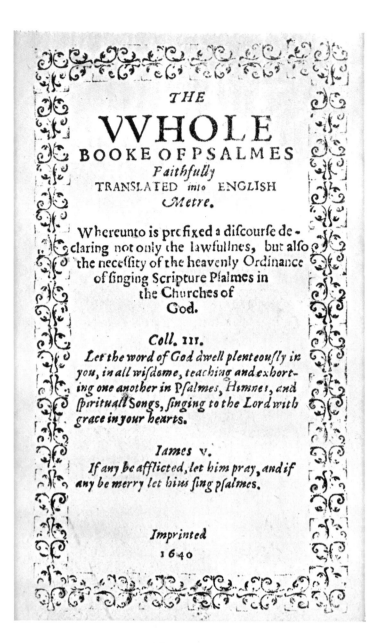

THE
VVHOLE
BOOKE OF PSALMES
Faithfully
TRANSLATED *into* ENGLISH
Metre.

Whereunto is prefixed a difcourfe de-
claring not only the lawfullnes, but alfo
the necefsity of the heavenly Ordinance
of finging Scripture Pfalmes in
the Churches of
God.

Coll. III.

*Let the word of God dwell plenteoufly in
you, in all wifdome, teaching and exhort-
ing one another in Pfalmes, Hımnes, and
fpirituall Songs, finging to the Lord with
grace in your hearts.*

Iames v.

*If any be afflicted, let him pray, and if
any be merry let him fing pfalmes.*

Imprinted
1640

ABOVE *The 'Bay Psalm Book', printed in Cambridge, Mass., in 1640. One of three complete
copies known of the earliest surviving book printed
in North America*

OPPOSITE *The Gutenberg or 42-line Bible, printed
in Mainz 1454–5. This copy belonged to the abbey
of Melk on the Danube: the initials were added by a
contemporary German or Austrian illuminator.*
OVERLEAF LEFT *Drawings by Alfred Jacob Miller on the William Drummond Steward expedition to
the Far West in 1837–8.* ABOVE LEFT *two Sho-
shone Indian girls.* RIGHT *Snake Indian girl swing-
ing.* BELOW *wounded buffalo.* OVERLEAF RIGHT
J. J. Audubon. Snowy Owl, *from his* The Birds
of America, *1831–4.*

the first separate library building was completed. This was a flight of the wildest architectural fantasy, quite small but ambitiously modelled on King's College Chapel, Cambridge, and marvellously bepinnacled. A romanesque hall was added in 1889 and a gothic one in 1905, but all were outgrown and eventually replaced in 1930 by the Sterling Memorial Library (financed by funds bequeathed by John W. Sterling); on a monumental scale, it vaguely recalls Albi, part fortress, part cathedral, impressive, if a little unexpected on a university campus, but in keeping with Yale's tendency to surround itself with a landscape from the *Très Riches Heures.*

When the decision to erect the Sterling Library had been made, but six years before it opened, the Professor of English Literature, Chauncy Brewster Tinker, addressed a meeting of alumni. He reminded them that the new building would not be the Yale Library; *that* would be inside; and of the probable contents he drew a depressing picture. 'Harvard . . . has been perpetually in the lead. It is a little galling for a Yale graduate to reconcile himself to Yale's being always second in the race; but even that is better than being fifth or sixth . . . already we rank sixth in current expenditure.' One cannot now read these words without amazement; forty years have passed and Yale's position in the first rank of American libraries is unquestioned. But it is true that in the nineteenth century the value to a university of a rare book collection was not perceived. The library was open only a few hours a day; the trustees begrudged money for books or maintenance, and in the winter the only heat came from a single stove in a corridor. When the librarian, Daniel Gilman, resigned his appointment in 1864 in protest at this neglect, he was surprised to receive a letter of warm congratulation from President Woolsey: 'The place does not possess the importance which a man of active mind would naturally seek; and the college cannot, now or hereafter, while its circumstances remain as they are, give it greater prominence.'

Nevertheless, at the time of Tinker's speech Yale already owned, in three collections, a firm basis for future eminence. These were the American literature presented by Owen F. Aldis in 1911, the Goethe collection deposited in 1913 by William Alfred Speck, who became its first curator (his interest in the poet had first been aroused at the age of eight on hearing an upper class discussing *Goetz von Berlichingen*), and the books in the Elizabethan Club given by Alexander Smith Cochran. The latter had made little stir during his time at college (indeed his letter announcing the gift was so unexpected that Professor Phelps 'almost fell off' his chair), but had nursed a silent regret at the unintellectual, the almost invariably athletic, tenor of conversation. His club was to change all that. There, in an eighteenth-century clapboard house, its walls hung with portraits and documents of Queen Elizabeth and James I, the student members would meet daily at teatime to discuss the literature of the two reigns, verifying their quotations from the Huth library's four Shakespeare folios and twenty-four quartos, and the first edition of

226

Incipit plogus scti Jeronimi in libros palippine

i septuaginta inter-
pretum pura · et ut
ab eis in grecu versa
e editio pmaneret:
superflue mi chroma-
ti episcoporum sanctis-
sime atq; doctissime impelleres: ut he-
brea volumina latino sermone trans-
ferrem. Quod enim semel aures homi-
num occupauerat · et nascentis ecclesie
roborauerat fidem: iustum erit etiam
nostro silentio comprobari . Nunc
uero cum pro varietate regionum di-
uersa ferantur exemplaria z germana
illa antiquaq; translatio corrupta sit
atq; violata: nri arbitrij putas · aut e
pluribz iudicare quid uerum sit aut
nouum opus in ueteri opere condere:
illudentibusq; iudeis · cornicum ut di-
citur oculos configere. Alexandria et
egiptus in septuaginta suis esichium
laudat auctorem: constantinopolis
usq; antiochiam luciani martiris exemplaria probat. Medie int has prouincie palestinos codices legunt: qs
ab origene elaboratos eusebi⁹ z pam-
philus vulgauerunt . Totusq; orbis
hac inter se trifaria varietate compu-
gnat. Et certe origenes non solum ex-
empla composuit quatuor editionu
e regione singula verba describens · ut
unus dissentiens statim reteris inter
se consentientibus arguatur: sed qd
maioris audacie est in editione septuaginta theodocionis editione miscu-
it: asteriscis designas que minus fue-
rint · et virgulis que ex superfluo vide-
bantur apposita . Si igitur alijs licu-
it non tenere quod semel susceperant ·
et post septuaginta cellulas q vulgo

sine auctore iactantur singulas cellulas apruere. Nunc; in ecclesiis legitur
quod septuaginta nescierunt: cur me
non suscipiant latini mei qui inuio-
lata editione veteri ita nouam condidi ·
ut laborem meu hebreis et quod hijs
maius est apostolis auctoribus com-
probem; Scripsi nuper librum de o-
ptimo genere interpretandi · ostendes
illa de euangelio · ex egipto uocaui fi-
lium meum · et quoniam nazareus
vocabitur · et videbunt in que cumpun-
xerunt · z illud apostoli quod oculus
no vidit nec auris audiuit et in cor ho-
minis non ascenderunt que sparauit
deus diligentibz se · ceteraq; hijs simi-
lia in hebreoz libris inueniri . Certe a-
postoli et euangeliste · septuagita inter-
pretes nouerat: et unde eis hec dicere q
in septuaginta no habent; Xps dominus noster vtriusq; testameti conditor
in euangelio secundu iohanne q credit inquit in me sicut dicit scriptura:
flumina de uentre eius fluent aque viue. Vtiq; scriptum est: qd saluator scriptum esse testat . Vbi scriptum e; Septuaginta no habent: apocrifa nescit
ecclesia. Ad hebreos igit reuertendu e:
unde z dns loquitur · et discipuli exem-
pla psumunt. Hec pace veteru loquor:
et obtrectatoribz meis tantu respondeo
qui canino dente me rodunt: in publi-
co detrahentes z legentes in angulis
id est accusatores et defensores : cum
in alijs probet quod in me reprobat:
quasi virtus et vicium non in rebus
sit · sed cum auctore mutetur. Ceterum
memini editionem septuaginta trans-
latorum olim de greco emendatam
tribuisse me nris: nec inimicum debe-
re estimari eor quos in conuentu fra-
trum semper edissero . Et quod nunc

Snowy Owl

Bacon's *Essayes*, 1597 (bought for $10,000 from Quaritch) – though to protect these small and precious objects a strong-room door was installed, so thick and heavy that an athlete was needed to open it.

The first notable result of Tinker's appeal was the copy of the Gutenberg Bible from the abbey of Melk on the Danube, presented in 1926 by the wife of one of Yale's most generous benefactors, Mrs Edward S. Harkness. Dr Rosenbach had bought it for her at auction in New York, exceeding his commission by $31,000. Twenty-one years later the opportunity occurred of securing, again at auction, a complete copy of the other typographical monument which a great American library must own, the 'Bay Psalm Book' of 1640, the first book printed in North America. Again Rosenbach bid for Yale and bought it for the world record price of $151,000, $61,000 over his commission. But this time his action was not condoned. Mrs Harkness, who had promised $30,000 towards the cost, withdrew her offer in outrage, and when after agonised negotiations the book reached Yale, it was subsidised by an involuntary contribution of $45,900 from the Rosenbach brothers.

Apart from donors, the two men most responsible for the library's present distinction have been Tinker himself, a greatly beloved teacher who inspired more than one generation of collectors with his enthusiasm for English literature, and James T. Babb, librarian from 1945 to 1965. Both men specialised in the English eighteenth century, and it is no accident that this is a field in which Yale excels, though by a lucky chance it was already exceptionally strong in newspapers of the period. It has the best collection of William Beckford (Babb's particular interest), while an elder statesman of the library, Wilmarth S. Lewis, has recreated – spiritually, if not architecturally – Strawberry Hill in his house in Connecticut, where three thousand letters to and from Horace Walpole and two-fifths of the books from Walpole's library are destined for New Haven.

Mr Lewis has written a witty and delightful account of his collection (*Collector's Progress*, Constable), but even he would admit that its history had not been as extraordinary as that of the Malahide Papers. In the early 1920s Tinker followed the appearance of his *Young Boswell* by inserting an advertisement for Boswell letters in Irish newspapers. He had two replies; one, anonymous, read, 'Try Malahide Castle'; the other, illegibly signed, 'The last representative of Boswell and owner of Auchinleck is Honble James Talbot, Malahide Castle, Co. Dublin. He has lately imported here an escritoire of Boswell's which is full of letters, so far uncatalogued.' Tinker passed on these clues to Ralph Isham, a Yale man and former colonel in the British Army, who finally succeeded through assiduity, charm and diplomacy of a high order in buying from the Talbots not only the papers in the desk, but six other caches discovered later in attics, an old croquet-box, an outhouse, and at Fettercairn House in Scotland (where they had been taken by Boswell's executor). It was appropriate that most of these papers should eventually

Dedication

To Sir Joshua Reynolds.

My Dear Sir,

Every liberal motive that canactuate an Author in the dedication of his labours concurs in directing me to you as the person to whom the following Work should be inscribed.

If there be a pleasure in celebrating the distinguished merit of a Contemporary mixed with a certain degree of vanity not altogether excusable, in appearing fully sensible of it, where can I find one in complimenting whom I can with more general propriety gratify those feelings. Your excellence not only in the art over which you have long presided with unrivalled fame, but also in elegant philosophy and literature are well known to the present

(1949) have been acquired by Yale. They included Boswell's unpublished journals, the manuscripts of his *Account of Corsica* and the *Journal of a Tour to the Hebrides*, a long unbroken fragment of the *Life of Johnson*, and letters of Goldsmith, Burke, Chatham, Burns and Voltaire.

Other holdings can only be mentioned briefly: a papyrus fragment of Genesis that is said to be the earliest piece of a codex and the earliest of any Christian biblical manuscript; Western Americana, including the best Texas collection; sporting books and manuscripts; ornithology, with two copies of the cornerstone of any such collection, Audubon's four-volume *The Birds of America*, 1831–4; the Vinland map, considered by some experts the earliest representation of the American continent. In adjacent areas of the basement, rows of old whiskey cartons contain Professor James M. Osborn's amazing array of English literary manuscripts, mostly of the seventeenth and eighteenth century, and Charles Dickens's pet raven broods over Colonel Richard Gimbel's collections of aeronautica, Thomas Paine and Dickens himself. The Yale Historical Medical Library, separately housed, is only rivalled by the Wellcome Historical Medical Library in London. Recently Mr Paul Mellon has announced the gift of his English colour-plate books, his thirteen Caxtons and his collection of Blake, which includes the unique coloured copy of *Jerusalem*.

Accessions require shelf-space; thirty years after it was finished, the Sterling Library's storage facilities were *in extremis*. Three brothers of the Beinecke family came forward at this moment with an offer of a new building to hold the rare books collection. All three were, naturally, Yale alumni and collectors – Frederick W. Beinecke of Western Americana, Edwin J. of Robert Louis Stevenson, Walter of James Barrie. The Beinecke Library, designed by Gordon Bunshaft of Skidmore, Owings and Merrill, and formally opened in April 1964, is the most imaginative construction of its kind for at least two centuries. The exterior is of squares of Vermont marble framed in Woodbury granite, and nothing in its severely horizontal lines prepares the visitor for the shock of pleasure as he enters. The main decoration comes from the books themselves, ranged spines outwards on six floors of stacks round the centre of the building, but the whole interior glows with a rich and varied light transmuted by the veined marble panels. The curators' offices are placed round a sunken courtyard, furnished with an abstract landscape of white marble sculpture by Noguchi. This is a library of all the virtues, luxurious for readers, administratively convenient and with an exhibition hall of a brilliance that has had no parallel since central European baroque.

The Beinecke Library, by Gordon Bunshaft, opened in 1964. The Sterling Library is in the left background.

Coimbra and Mafra

John v of Portugal was a cultivated and pacific monarch, with a taste for mathematics and a passion for music. His love of books and mania for building made his reign (1706–50) a golden age for Portuguese libraries. His two major constructions, the monastery-palace of Mafra (inspired by the Escorial) and Coimbra University Library were started in the same year, 1717.

The University, the oldest in Portugal, had of course owned a collection of books long before. Founded in Lisbon in 1290, it had moved between the capital and Coimbra until finally settled in the latter in 1537 by King John III. A royal order of 1541 directed that its books should be transferred from Lisbon. In 1548 the library was described as being open for two hours in the morning and two in the afternoon. The University statutes of 1597 increased the hours of opening to six a day and prescribed an expenditure on new books of a hundred *cruzados* every three years. Shortly afterwards – at much the same time as similar expeditions were undertaken on behalf of the universities of Oxford and Dublin – the librarian was dispatched with five hundred thousand *reis* (4,000 *reis* = one *cruzado*) to spend on a buying tour to Venice and Flanders.

As elsewhere in the Peninsula, the seventeenth century was an era of decay. By 1705 the library building was in ruins and the books were stored in the registry. Eleven years later the collection of books of Dr Francisco Barreto was offered for sale and an able and energetic rector, Nuno de Silva Telles, obtained the king's consent to buy it for 14,000 *cruzados*. Authority for a new building, by then urgently needed, was granted on 31 October of the same year. The contract for the fabric was given on 14 August 1717 to João Carvalho Ferreira, and to João Rodrigues d'Almeida for the woodwork. The bookcases were ready by August 1723 when a painter from Lisbon, Manuel da Silva, received the contract to decorate them with gilt *chinoiseries*, the first use of this style in Portugal. At the same time two other Lisbon artists, Antonio Simões Ribeiro and Vicente Nunes, were commissioned to paint the ceilings with allegorical figures of virtues and the continents. Work was completed in 1728.

ABOVE *King John V of Portugal by Debrie; from Antonio Caetano Sousa de Castro's* Series of the Kings of Portugal, *Lisbon 1743.* OPPOSITE *Coimbra University Library.*

ABOVE *St Jerome and his lion: a woodcut from* Antonio de Beja's Against the prophecies of astrologers, *attacking the prediction of a disastrous flood in February 1524.* BELOW LEFT *A Portuguese 'fan-binding' with the arms of King John V; Lisbon 1708.* BELOW RIGHT *King John III and Queen Eleanor of Portugal adoring Christ on the Cross; a woodcut illustration to Ludolphus of Saxony's* Vita Christi, *printed in Lisbon in 1495. It was financed by the royal family and is the handsomest Portuguese publication before 1500.*

The library stands at one end of the three-sided University square. An imposing portico is surmounted by the royal arms and six arched windows decorate the south side facing the Mondego valley. The interior is of the utmost sumptuousness. It consists of three rooms of equal size joined by arches, the impression of height being accentuated by the *trompe l'œil* perspective of the ceiling paintings. Each room is lined with bookcases decorated to simulate Oriental lacquer, the first and third rooms green (now much darkened), the centre one red. At the far end, facing the door, a full-length portrait of John v, probably by his Italian court artist, Giorgio Domenico Duprà, is framed behind painted wooden curtains held aside by *putti* below trumpeting angels. The original furniture is present, six tables of Brazilian ebony inlaid with yellow jacaranda, two to a room, with a silver-gilt inkstand on each. Ladders ingeniously concealed in the uprights of the case in the gallery pull out to give access to the upper shelves. The first room is devoted to history and literature, the second to law and natural sciences, the last to theology and canon law. Eleven recesses behind curtained doors were available for professors or other privileged readers; a larger recess, labelled *Cimelios* (Treasures), contained both the reserve of rare books and the librarian's office.

Coimbra is, with the sole exception of the Vienna Hofbibliothek, the most beautiful library building of the eighteenth century, and it is tantalising that its architect is unknown. Both Claude de Laprade, a French sculptor employed by the Univer-

sity from 1700 to 1702, and John v's German protégé, Johann Friedrich Ludwig (known in Portugal as Ludovice), have been proposed, but neither suggestion is entirely convincing. The source of the design is equally obscure. It was the first library since the Renaissance to abandon the single hall pattern popularised by the Salone Sistino of the Vatican. John v was the Hapsburg Emperor Charles vi's brother-in-law, and it is tempting to speculate that the lay-out of three intercommunicating rooms with wall-shelving was based on a Viennese model, Prince Eugene's library in the Upper Belvedere. This too was divided between three rooms, each probably with a different colour scheme as the books were bound in red, yellow or green according to subject. But the dates make this hypothesis untenable: the plans for Coimbra must have been in existence by 1717, while Lucas von Hildebrandt only started the Upper Belvedere in 1721. It is an equally serious objection that the *Bibliothec* illustrated in Salomon Kleiner's engraved views of the Belvedere (1731) bears no resemblance at all to the Coimbra Library.

That this ornate baroque interior derives from England may seem a surprising suggestion, but there are grounds for believing it to be possible. John v was interested in Northern library arrangements and many of his books were procured through the Portuguese envoys in Paris, The Hague and London. The two former bought works on commerce and navigation and bid at the sale of Cardinal Dubois' collection in 1725; the latter secured six cases of the Earl of Sunderland's manuscripts, as well as Rymer's *Foedera* and the Astronomer Royal, John Flamsteed's *Historia coelestis Britannica* (1725). In 1726–7, when work was

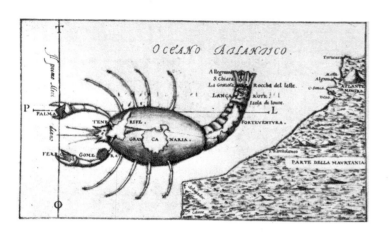

nearly at an end at Coimbra and about to begin at Mafra, a royal emissary, Luis da Cunha, was sent to report on the libraries of England and the Low Countries. He visited Oxford, investigated the Cotton library and saw the Jesuit houses of Antwerp and Ghent and the university of Louvain. Of all European university libraries in the early eighteenth century the Bodleian was by far the most celebrated, and its general appearance must have been known to the king from Loggan's *Oxonia illustrata*, 1675. The galleries at Coimbra with their fragile pillar supports and balustrades are perhaps inspired by Loggan's plate of Selden End (see p. 168), and the three-room design of Coimbra may be taken from the Bodleian division into Arts End, Duke Humphrey's and Selden End; the greater length and medieval lay-out of the central section at Oxford being rejected either as unsuitable or through a misunderstanding of Loggan's engraving.

John V dispatched to the University a large quantity of books on theology, philosophy, history, law and 'modern medicine'. From his death until the end of the century the collection grew slowly. In 1796 a copy of the Latin Bible printed at Mainz by Fust and Schöffer in 1462 was bought for 680,000 *reis*; it had failed to reach its reserve in a Paris sale four years earlier and had been sold privately to a Portuguese bookseller. It is the most valuable printed book in the library and, with the Gutenberg Bible in the Biblioteca Nacional in Lisbon, the only monument in Portugal of the first years of printing. A superb twelfth-century giant Bible, in a Parisian binding of the eighteenth century, was perhaps acquired at the same period. In 1806 the library received its most important single accession, the collection of fine and rare books formed in Lisbon by Monsignor Hasse. Among them was a manuscript *Chronicle of Dom Pedro* in the only binding known with the arms of the Marquis of Távora, the ancient and tragic family every member of which was executed in 1758 for an alleged attempt on the king's life. Shortly afterwards a member of the mathematical faculty bought in Holland a notable Hebrew Bible, almost certainly written in Portugal or Spain and carried to the Low Countries by a Sephardic exile. After 1834 the University received many books from the secularised religious houses, including part of the library of Coimbra's largest monastery, Santa Cruz, where the city's first printing-press had been set up in 1530 by Germão Galharde.

A modern library building was completed in 1961 and John V's library, which remained the chief reading-room until 1926, is now used only for special functions. The University receives a copy of every book published in Portugal; its present holdings number over a million volumes.

The Mafra Library is an impressive vaulted room, eighty-eight metres long and cruciform in shape, built between 1717 and 1730 by Johann Friedrich Ludwig. Although the room was used at least as early as 1751 by the Franciscan friars for whom the king created it, it seems to have been furnished only with temporary shelving; and it was not until the Franciscans were replaced in

ABOVE *The Canary Isles depicted as parts of a shellfish. Illustration to Lorenzo Torriani of Cremona's* Description and history of the Canary Isles, *written for Philip II of Spain in the second half of the sixteenth century.* BELOW *Luis de Camões,* Os Lusiadas, *printed in Lisbon in 1572; the rare first edition of the most famous Portuguese poem.*

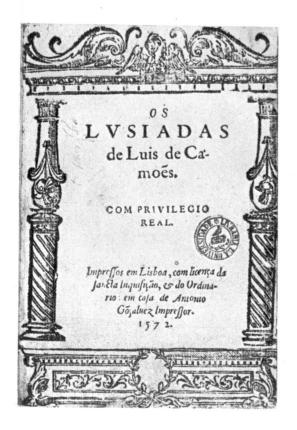

1771 by Augustinians that the latter commissioned Manuel Caetano de Sousa to design the existing cases. (They proved too baroque for William Beckford's taste in 1787; he considered them 'clumsily designed, coarsely executed, and darkened by a gallery which projects into the room in a very awkward manner'.) The friars' return five years after Beckford's visit interrupted plans to have the cases gilt and they have in consequence remained a faded white. The library's effect is muted by comparison with Coimbra and depends for its colour and sparkle on the gilt spines of the bindings; many of them are said to have been executed in the monastery and have the name MAFRA across the foot of the spine. The books, 38,000 in all, remain exactly as arranged by the first librarian of the restored Franciscans, Fr João de Santa Anna, whose manuscript catalogue, still in use, was completed in 1819. They are shelved by subject, folios in the lower cases, smaller books in the gallery. Editions of the Bible occupy the convex case at one end of the room; other sections are devoted to civil and common law, theology (both scholastic and polemical), liturgy, church history, lives of the saints, sermons and constitutions of religious orders. Lay subjects include Greek, Latin and Italian literature, literary history and bibliography, medicine, philosophy and mathematics. Most of the books are of the seventeenth or eighteenth century, many, bought in Paris, still bearing the arms of their earlier owners, but there is a handful of incunabula, and the most valuable book is probably the rare first edition of Gil Vicente's *Obras* (1562), a copy lavishly scored through by an ecclesiastical censor.

In spite of its late foundation, this is very much a monastic library, with a similar range of subject to St Gall or Admont.

ABOVE *The ancestry of Jesus: the initial L of St Matthew's Gospel in a twelfth-century giant Bible.* BELOW *Interior of the Library of Mafra built between 1717 and 1730 by Johann Friedrich Ludwig (Ludovice).* OVERLEAF *Coimbra: the University Library built by King John V of Portugal in 1717–28. The library is divided into three rooms of equal size.*

British Museum

LONDON

Brought into existence by Parliament against the Prime Minister's advice, and free from apparent purpose or planning in its early growth, the British Museum, like the British Empire, is an example of the national ability to create impressive institutions in a fit of absentmindedness. It had no single founder and was called into being by the death on 11 January 1753 of the ninety-two-year-old physician and former president of the Royal Society, Sir Hans Sloane. Sloane left a house in Chelsea crammed with a lifetime's accumulation of curiosities – natural history specimens, stuffed animals, shells, fossils, minerals, insects, coins and medals, classical antiquities, and a few Oriental and American-Indian objects, besides about 3,400 manuscripts and a library over-optimistically estimated at fifty thousand volumes – with an expression of his desire 'that these things, tending many ways to the manifestation of the glory of God, the confutation of atheism and its consequences, the use and improvement of physic and other arts and sciences, and benefit of mankind, may remain together and not be separated, and that chiefly in and about the city of London . . . where they may, by the great confluence of people, be of most use.' His will placed the collections in the care of over seventy named trustees, who were to offer them to the King for £20,000.

'You will scarce guess how I employ my time,' Horace Walpole wrote to Sir Horace Mann, 'chiefly at present in the guardianship of embryos and cockleshells. Sir Hans Sloane is dead and has made me one of the trustees to his museum. . . . He valued it at fourscore thousand; and so would anybody who loves hippopotamuses, sharks with one ear, and spiders as big as geese! It is a rent-charge to keep the foetuses in spirit!' Horace Walpole's letter was dated two days after the receipt of the news that the King declined the purchase. The next step was to approach Parliament, and on 6 March the trustees' petition was delivered to the House of Commons.

Henry Pelham, the First Lord of the Treasury, moved that the petition should 'lie on the table' – in other words, that no action should be taken – but he was overruled and the House debated

S. Slaughter. Portrait of Sir Hans Sloane. OPPOSITE *Alexander O'Driscoll, after Elijah Shaw. The entrance to Montague House from Great Russell Street, c. 1840.*

ABOVE *St Elizabeth with the infant John the Baptist; from an English eleventh-century hymnal in the Cotton collection.* BELOW *Top, the Harrowing of Hell; Bottom, St Mary Magdalene and the Risen Christ; from a twelfth-century Psalter written at St Swithun's Priory, Winchester, in the Cotton collection.*

the subject on 19 March. It was soon evident that members favoured acquiring the Sloane museum on the terms of Sir Hans's will. Pelham, and the Speaker, Arthur Onslow, then drew their attention to two other collections: the English historical manuscripts and books saved from the wreck of the monastic libraries by Sir Robert Cotton in the reigns of Queen Elizabeth and James I, and presented to the public by his grandson in 1702; and the 7,660 manuscripts brought together by Edward and Robert Harley, first and second Earls of Oxford, which could be bought from the second Earl's widow and daughter for £10,000. Meanwhile the Cotton manuscripts were homeless, temporarily lodged in Westminster School since the destruction by fire twenty-two years earlier of Ashburnham House.

The House did not take long to reach a decision. They resolved to buy the Sloane and Harleian collections and add them to the Cotton manuscripts in suitable premises, the necessary money to be raised by lottery. An Act to this effect received the royal assent on 7 June 1753. Two years later Montague House in Bloomsbury was acquired as a 'general repository' for the collections. In 1757 George II gave the royal library, which, besides Archbishop Cranmer's and Isaac Casaubon's books, incorporated a substantial group of fifteenth-century histories and romances written and illustrated in Flanders for Edward IV. On 15 January 1759 the British Museum was opened to the public.

Partly because the collections were thought to be held in accordance with the terms of the testators' wills, and partly so that the Museum should not lack influential friends, a board of trustees was instituted by the Act such as W.S. Gilbert might have invented to satirise the Victorian establishment. Three principal trustees, the Archbishop of Canterbury, the Lord Chancellor and the Speaker of the House of Commons, were to be supported by the Lord High Admiral, the Lord Steward, the Chancellor of the Exchequer and several other ministers, the Lord Chief Justice and two more judges, the Presidents of the Royal Society and the College of Physicians, six trustees appointed by the Sloane, Cotton and Harley families, and fifteen more elected by the *ex officio* trustees. These busy officers of Church and State did not confine themselves to a policy of general supervision. From the beginning they insisted on controlling the *minutiae* of administration, meeting four times a year to receive the officers' applications for leave of absence and to 'overlook and examine the bills of tradesmen'. As late as the 1950s no purchase of more than £50 could be made without their approval. It is amazing that the system lasted unchanged until 1963, and a tribute to the national love of books that in spite of this unwieldy constitution the library grew in a century to be the greatest in the world.

The first years of the Museum were as calm and idyllic as the situation of Montague House, in an eight-acre garden on the edge of open country extending to the picturesque village of Highgate. The senior officers, all doctors or clergymen, were required to attend only two days a week, and readers numbered no more than five or six a month. One of the earliest, Thomas Gray the poet, wrote in August 1759 of passing 'four hours in the day in the stillness and solitude of the reading-room, which is uninterrupted by anything but Dr Stukeley, the antiquary, who comes there to talk nonsense and coffee-house news.' The 1753 Act had provided an income of £900 a year to pay salaries and expenses, but there was no provision for purchases; and although the Museum had acquired with the royal library a theoretical right to a deposit copy of every book registered at Stationers' Hall, in practice little was received. 'The British Museum, sir, is rich in manuscripts,' John Wilkes informed the House of Commons in 1777, 'but it is wretchedly poor in printed books.' Nevertheless, important additions were made by gift or bequest: the Thomason tracts, over 22,000 pieces relating to the Civil War, presented by George III in 1762; David Garrick's collection of plays, bequeathed in 1779; the cabinet of Greek and Latin classics, fine bindings and early printing chosen by the Reverend C. M. Cracherode (1799); and the magnificent library of George III, totalling 65,000 volumes and 868 boxes of pamphlets, given by George IV in 1823. By this time new readers amounted to five hundred a year, and the reading-room offered an animated scene of students standing, book in hand, warming their backs in front of the fire, and 'Bond Street Dandies enveloped in fur and lambswool'.

This easy-going amateurish institution was to be entirely transformed by an Italian doctor of law, Antonio Panizzi, who joined the staff in 1831 as Extra Assistant in the Department of Printed Books. The events of Panizzi's life were intensely dramatic: the death sentence passed on him *in absentia* for sedition against the Duke of Modena; his arrival in England in 1823 as a destitute fugitive; his promotion in 1837 to be Keeper of Printed Books over the head of a senior colleague; the jealousy and intrigues of Sir Frederic Madden, Keeper of Manuscripts, and the Reverend Josiah Forshall, Secretary to the Trustees; his vindication by the Royal Commission of 1847–50 and Forshall's collapse with signs of incipient madness; and his triumphant appointment in 1856 to be principal librarian – these incidents might almost have come from the libretto of a romantic opera.

Panizzi's aim was expressed in the trustees' report to the Treasury of 1845. It was 'a public library containing from 600,000 to 700,000 printed volumes, giving the necessary means of information on all branches of human learning, from all countries, in all languages . . . capable for some years to come of keeping pace with the increase of human knowledge.' This ambition, largely realised during Panizzi's Keepership, must be contrasted with the state of affairs when he entered the Museum. Holdings of printed books were then about 240,000, but although they included many rarities and the Greek and Latin collection was particularly strong, there were glaring deficiencies in all other classes: no foreign music, hardly any foreign literature except Italian and Spanish, no copy of Keats's 'most popular poems', and an almost total lack of first editions of Defoe, Richardson, Sterne, Fielding and Smollett.

Panizzi set out to correct this situation in three ways. From

The opening of a manuscript of Bonaventura's Life of St Francis, *copied in Florence in 1504. The miniature shows the author seeing a vision of St Francis, while St Thomas Aquinas is entering the room. From the Harley collection.* BELOW *Sir Anthony Panizzi, by 'Ape', 1874.*

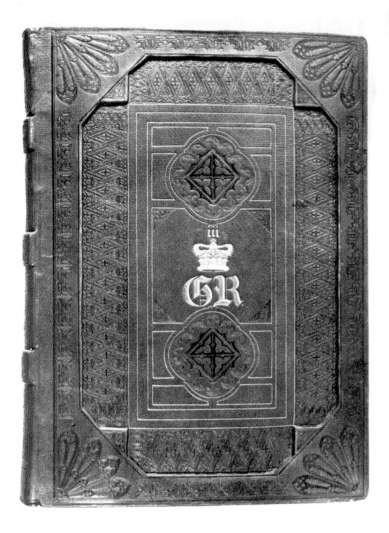

Binding of brown morocco by the Buckingham Palace Bindery for George III, c. 1815.

1850, when the responsibility became his, he insisted on the strict enforcement of the Copyright Act; defaulting publishers were prosecuted, and in six years the intake of deposit copies trebled. Secondly he persuaded the Treasury, through the trustees, to increase the annual purchase grant from £1,000 to £10,000 ('. . . when you have given three times as much [as Napoleon promised Van Praet], say £100,000 in ten or twelve years, then you will begin to have a library worthy of the British nation'). This was a handsome sum at a period when book-prices had not fully recovered from the post-Waterloo depression and before American competition had begun to be felt, and it was used for purchases on the largest scale. Continental books were obtained chiefly through Asher of Berlin, whose network of agents covered the whole of Europe, American books through Henry Stevens of Vermont. Panizzi's instructions to Stevens were to supply the Museum 'with *everything* – e.g., all historical works, general and local, even to all the little histories of churches and parishes – all school books – theology – science – *Belles lettres* – Reports. Laws. All Pub[lic] Documents of the General Government, as well as all those of the individual states. All periodical literature – Topography, – Indians, &c. In short, all American books of all kinds.' Finally, Thomas Grenville's library of twenty thousand volumes, bequeathed in 1847 as a result of the collector's friendship with Panizzi, added many splendid rarities.

This flood of accessions provoked acute problems of storage. By 1851 Panizzi could use only £2,000 of his annual grant owing to the lack of space for further purchases. Sir Henry Ellis twice applied to the Treasury to buy extra land and houses on the Museum's east side. No answer was received to either request,

and the officers were in despair when Panizzi hit on a brilliantly simple solution: a circular reading-room to be erected in the central quadrangle with book-stacks at each corner. The suggestion was adopted and the building, completed in 1857, provided shelving for a million volumes and seats for five hundred readers. The inaugural breakfast on 2 May 1857, at which Panizzi – by then principal librarian – entertained the political and literary establishment (Sir Frederic Madden pointedly absented himself) was the crowning point of his career.

The Museum lost its natural history specimens to South Kensington in 1881. Otherwise it is still Sir Hans Sloane's cabinet of learning and curiosity vastly expanded, with material which in other capitals would stock three museums as well as a library. In theory the latter still covers 'all branches of human learning, from all countries, in all languages'. In practice, however, it has been in retreat from Panizzi's ideal since the purchase grant was cut by forty per cent in 1886. How long can it continue to play both roles? It is currently growing at the rate of 130,000 volumes and 575,000 parts, or one and a half miles of shelving, a year. Shortage of space will force a fundamental change sooner or later. What this will be is still uncertain. The trustees' proposal for a massive extension of the buildings to the south has been rejected by the Government. Instead in 1969 a committee under Dr F.S. Dainton recommended the library's removal to a different site as a separate unit and the independent creation of a National Library of Science and Invention. Thousands of readers of all nationalities use the Museum and benefit from its astonishing profusion of rare books, especially in the fields of literature and history. They will all wish it well in its present perplexities.

Sir Robert Smirke's portico on the south front of the British Museum, and his sketch for an alternative façade.

247

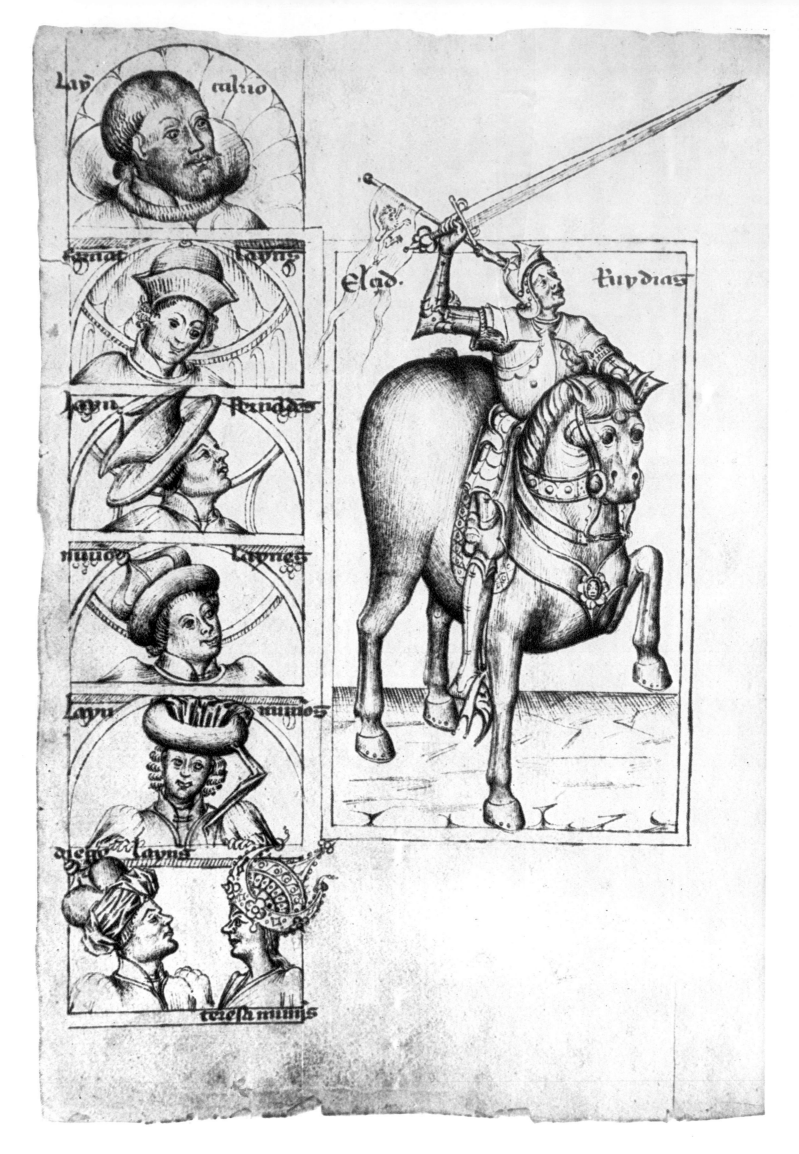

Palace Library

MADRID

The Royal Library in Madrid, now known as the Biblioteca de Palacio, was the creation of the Bourbon dynasty. When Philip v, the first Bourbon king, reached Spain in 1700 he found about eight thousand volumes assembled by Philip iv. Philip v added some books brought from France and gave the collection to form the Royal Public Library, the nucleus of the present Biblioteca Nacional, keeping back, however, two notebooks of Leonardo da Vinci which were not transferred until the nineteenth century. The Royal Public Library was housed in an annexe and so escaped the fire of Christmas Eve 1734, which totally destroyed the old Hapsburg palace. In the Italianate *Palacio de Oriente*, built on the same site to plans by Juvara and Sacchetti, no provision was made for a library, and for the greater part of the eighteenth century such books as the royal family owned were contained in bookcases scattered through the state-rooms and corridors. Philip v recovered one precious family manuscript, a book of Hours written and richly illuminated in Paris about 1460 for Queen Juana Enríquez of Aragon, Ferdinand the Catholic's mother, which Philip iv had presented in 1642 to Cardinal Teodoro Trivulzi. A century later it was bought back from the same Milanese family through the good offices of Farinelli, the king's castrato confidant.

The palace seems to have remained more or less empty of books until Charles iii succeeded his brother. In 1760, the year after his accession, a charmingly written and decorated catalogue of his collection lists 824 works in 2,153 volumes. It is very much a ruler's working library; history, law, religion, horses and warfare are the chief subjects. There are no books acquired for the sake of their typography or illustration, 'a very ancient Gothic codex' (not otherwise identified) being the only entry that is not strictly utilitarian in content. A censor – perhaps the King's confessor – has marked *Prohibido* against the Koran in Arabic, Le Maistre de Sacy's translation of the Bible into French (1730), and a few other titles. In 1782 a Supplement recorded 453 additions, a rate of accession of only about twenty works a year; among them was the masterpiece of Spanish eighteenth-century printing, the Ibarra

ABOVE *Queen Juana Enríquez of Aragon kneeling before the Virgin and Child; from a Parisian book of Hours, c. 1460.* OPPOSITE *The Cid Ruy Diaz and some of his contemporaries, an illustration to the paper manuscript of a fifteenth-century Spanish translation of the* Genealogy of the Kings of Castille *by Alonso de Cartagena, Bishop of Burgos.*

edition of Sallust (1772), illustrated by Maella, the Spanish translation being by Charles III's younger son, the Infante Don Gabriel. A handful of American manuscripts were acquired in the last months of the reign. Besides eight vocabularies of Arawak, Carib and other Amerindian languages, compiled by missionaries on the king's instructions, there is a delightful series of watercolours of Peruvian flora and fauna, and of Creole and native dress, customs and pastimes, collected and presented by Baltasar Martínez Compañon, Bishop of Trujillo in Peru.

At Charles III's death there were perhaps two thousand works in the library. By 1801, thirteen years later, when José Angel Alvárez Navarro, the sub-librarian and an accomplished calligrapher, finished elegantly penning a new catalogue, there were over twenty thousand, installed in cases of rare American woods in a series of six small rooms, whose ceilings were frescoed by Maella and Bayeu with appropriate scenes from mythology. A book collector had come to the throne in the person of Charles IV, Goya's patron and butt. This monarch, gullible and good-natured, did not strike his contemporaries as intelligent: '[It] was not a difficult matter [to change the subject of conversation] with poor Charles IV,' the Duchess d'Abrantès relates in her Memoirs, 'it was only necessary to say that a dog was running past, and the thing was accomplished.' His library, however, seems to have been a constant interest. It owed its rapid increase to three major acquisitions, the most important being the purchase of the collection, rich in incunabula and early woodcut books, formed

Two illustrations from Alonso de Cartagena's Genealogy of the Kings of Castille. ABOVE *Ferdinand IV with stylish footwear.* BELOW *Alfonso VIII of Castille, with his English Queen Eleanor appearing at the top left. At the lower left is depicted St Louis, King of France.*

in the previous century by Diego Sarmiento de Acuña, Count of Gondomar, Spanish ambassador to James I. One of the most famous private libraries in Spain since the dispersal of the Conde-Duque de Olivares's books, it had remained intact in family ownership at Valladolid. In 1798 the Colleges of San Bartolomé and of Cuenca in Salamanca University were suppressed and their manuscripts confiscated for the royal library; all those still in Madrid were recently returned by General Franco's orders to Salamanca, with the single exception of Francisco López de Caravantes's *General account of the provinces of Peru, Tierra Firme and Chile,* dedicated to Philip IV. Finally in 1807 the Secretariat of Grace and Justice of the Indies surrendered to the palace a valuable collection of manuscripts about America, among them the autograph text of Fray Bernardino de Sahagún's *Universal history of the matters of New Spain* [*c.* 1577], not printed until 1829. State papers found in unauthorised hands were requisitioned and books bought from many private owners, for example Don Francisco Bruna, a judge of the Audiencia of Seville, from whom came St Augustine's *City of God* printed by Jenson (Venice 1475), and Rocha's pattern-book for tailors (*Geometría y traza perteneciente al oficio de sastres,* Valencia 1618), a work of great rarity.

Although badly educated by an intriguing Basque canon of Saragossa (he was made to study only one hour a day), Charles IV's heir, Ferdinand, Prince of the Asturias, early developed a genuine interest in reading. Booksellers' bills record the sale to

Ferdinand III receiving the keys of Seville after conquering the city; from Alonso de Cartagena's Genealogy of the Kings of Castille.

A Valencian binding of white silk with painted chinoiseries, made for presentation to Charles III in 1776.

E.167.

Este que aqui estàs mirando
Quien te parece que es!
Sin duda tu no lo ves
Que es ntro amable FERNANDO
Es el que se halla triunfando
Del monstruo mas ambicioso
Napoleon infame Corso,
Que puso en duras prisiones,
Y rompimos Españoles
Con un valór asombroso.

OPPOSITE *Scenes from Spain's American empire in manuscripts from the royal collection.* LEFT *Mummers dance dressed as condors, from a collection of Peruvian scenes given to Charles III by the bishop of Trujillo, eighteenth century.* RIGHT *American Indians and llama: the frontispiece to an account of the Spanish colonies in South America by the royal accountant in Peru, 1630–4.* ABOVE *Ferdinand VII crowned by Victory; illustration to a manuscript writing-book by Colonel Bruno Gómez of Saragossa, 1816.*

Amòr, cuya
inicial letra primera
tan dulce ſe preſenta al pronunciarla,
que tan ſolo la boca placentera
la anuncia bien y facil al dictarla:
del miſmo amòr eſ ſigno; puès dò quie^ra
que ſu grato placèr ò encanto para,
al que ſu aſpiracion ha poſeido
queda preſo en las redes de Cupido.

Caracter antiguo de eſtampilla.

ABCDEFGHIJK
LMNOPQRSTV
UXYZ.

Joſe Dominguez.

him of works such as Duhalde's *Description of the Chinese Empire*, a *History of the Golden Fleece* and a Spanish translation of *Robinson Crusoe*; and when he was only fifteen, Angel Navarro was paid to make an inventory of his books. In 1808 he was interned by Napoleon's orders with his brother Don Carlos and uncle Don Antonio in Talleyrand's château of Valençay. Long afterwards Talleyrand recalled the Spanish princes' arrival in an ancient coach 'that looked as if it dated from Philip v's reign'. Their host did his best to be agreeable.

I attempted to entertain them for some hours in the library, but without much success, although the librarian, Monsieur Fercoc, and I tried every means we could think of to engage their attention. After failing with the interest of the books themselves, we pointed out the beauty of the editions, then the works with engravings, finally even the subjects of the illustrations. I cannot describe to what degree all was unavailing. Their uncle, Don Antonio, who dreaded the effect on them of most books which form a fine library, soon thought of an excuse to make them return to their own apartments.

The pious Don Antonio, in fact, was shocked by the free illustrations to Talleyrand's editions of La Fontaine, Boccaccio and so on, and spent the years of imprisonment expurgating the library by tearing out the plates he considered indecent.

Although permanently short of money at Valençay, the Infantes were allowed to receive visits from dealers and devoted much time and effort to collecting. In 1812 they were described as having a good library, which increased every day, a laboratory, a pharmacy and an infirmary where they visited the patients daily. The following year a bookseller from Bourges was engaged to arrange and catalogue the books, and the governor of the castle reported that Ferdinand was occupied in translating Chateaubriand's *Le Génie du Christianisme*, Don Carlos in translating a work on chemistry, and Don Antonio in planting trees. Acquisitions of these years included a copy on vellum of Durandus, *Rationale divinorum officiorum* (Mainz 1459), the earliest printed book in Spain, a beautiful Parisian early fifteenth-century book of Hours, the death-mask of Henri iv of France, Breguet watches and musical instruments. When Ferdinand returned home in 1814 his books and works of art filled numerous packing-cases.

While the library was being augmented in France, it was suffering losses in Madrid. On 21 June 1813 the English and Spanish army under the Duke of Wellington defeated the French outside Vitoria and captured their entire baggage train. Among the spoil was Joseph Bonaparte's carriage, which proved to be full of looted property, including 220 paintings and thirty books. Most were from the royal collection and although chosen in haste and partly at random, they included three of its finest manuscripts, a Sallust and a Vergil, both splendidly illuminated, and an illustrated history of the Incas. When their ownership was recognised the Duke at once offered to return them, but Ferdinand generously refused to accept them back. 'His Majesty,' wrote the Spanish ambassador, 'touched by your delicacy, does not wish to

ABOVE *A vetinary surgeon sewing up the flank of a wounded hound while the King looks on: the boar that has gored it lies dead in the foreground. A miniature to the* Libro de Montería, *a late fifteenth-century treatise on hunting by Alfonso XI of Castille.* OPPOSITE *Alphabet written by José Dominguez for the Infantes Ferdinand (later Ferdinand VII) and Maria Isabela,* c. 1790–5.

deprive you of that which has come into your possession by means as just as they are honourable.'

In the later nineteenth century the library was greatly enlarged during the curatorship of a distinguished bibliographer, Manuel Zarco del Valle. A decree was passed during the first Spanish Republic to incorporate it into the library of the Cortés, but native powers of procrastination delayed any move until Alfonso XII became king and the decree was annulled. On 7 November 1936 when Moorish troops began their assault on Madrid across the Casa de Campo, the collection, moved during the regency of Queen María Cristina to the western side of the palace, was literally in the front line. Two hundred and fifty thousand printed books, 5,000 manuscripts, 250 incunabula, 2,000 musical scores and 1,500 maps had to be hastily evacuated, fortunately without loss. They are now arranged in twenty-four rooms, where the handsomely bound volumes in locked glass-fronted cases, brushed past by groups of tourists, seem like a Sleeping Beauty awaiting the return of a Bourbon Prince.

A Valencian binding of marbled calf with panels of flowers composed of spangles, made in 1788 for presentation to María Luisa as Princess of the Asturias. The book is an account of the subjects taught in the seminary of Valencia.
ABOVE RIGHT *Map of the world from a portulan atlas by Joan Riezo alias Oliva, Naples 1580. Russia and Moldavia have changed places and Scotland has become detached from England.*
BELOW RIGHT *The Palacio de Oriente, built for Philip V to designs by Juvara and Sacchetti.*

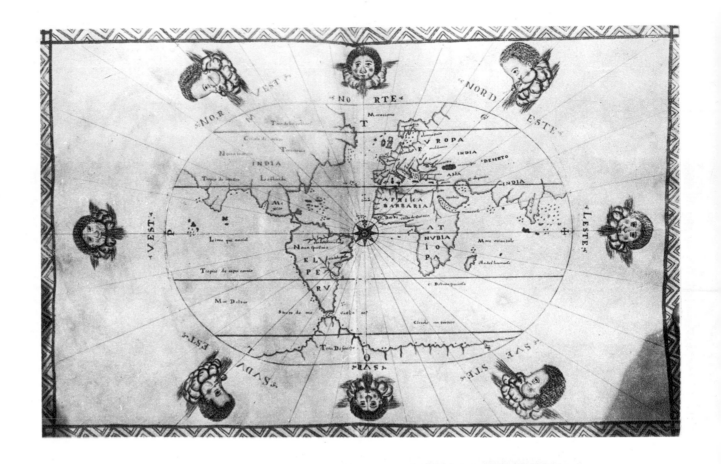

Bibliothèque de l'Arsenal

PARIS

ABOVE *The Bibliothèque de l'Arsenal, Paris.* OPPOSITE *Computists calculating the calendar, from the Psalter of Blanche of Castille; Paris, thirteenth century. Until the Revolution, this manuscript was one of the major relics of the Sainte-Chapelle.*

The eighteenth century in Paris was a golden age for book collectors. They were supplied by numerous expert booksellers and by frequent auction sales. Only an infinitesimal proportion of books passed out of circulation into the one public library, that of the king, and until Russian and English competition made itself felt towards the end of the century, scarcely anything was exported. On the contrary, the market was constantly refreshed by a flow of books from religious houses, by the production of *éditions de luxe* and by imports from abroad. As the century drew on, the tide of bibliomania mounted. Fortunes were spent, legacies engulfed as soon as received. Brancas de Lauraguais ruined himself on inlaid bindings and the works of Giordano Bruno. Girardot de Préfonds inherited a hundred thousand *livres* and at once paid a record price for the 1462 Bible. Baron d'Heiss, crippled by debts to booksellers, was obliged to sell his collection and immediately used the proceeds to start another. By the 1770s two collections were outstanding: those of the Duc de la Vallière and the Marquis de Paulmy.

Antoine-René de Voyer d'Argenson, Marquis de Paulmy, was born in 1722 into a family that for generations had held high office under the French crown. Two ancestors had been ambassadors to Venice, his grandfather was Keeper of the Seals, Lieutenant-General of Police and President of the Council of Finance, his uncle Minister of War, his father briefly Minister of Foreign Affairs. He himself was ambassador to Switzerland at the age of twenty-six, Secretary of State in the War Office, Minister of War for thirteen months, and ambassador to Poland and to Venice. He retired from public service in 1770 to live in Paris, where he occupied the former residence in the Arsenal of the Grand Master of the Artillery, an office abolished by Louis xv.

When the Marquis de Paulmy was eighteen, his father, the Marquis d'Argenson, wrote a description of his character.

He eats nothing but medicine, cakes and milk foods; he hates butcher's meat . . . he dislikes every kind of physical exercise. Since his childhood all his strength has gone into his mind, none into his imagination, his senses or his heart. . . . He likes comedies and is acquiring a

vast knowledge of them, but he only laughs at the wit, and never weeps at tragedies; at the saddest moments he admires the dramatist's art but feels nothing. . . . By degrees, as his links with society weaken, my son, without being hated, will not be loved, particularly when his nature becomes still colder and he offers society only what it obtains from a dictionary.

Composed, meticulous, invariably good-mannered, always correct, M. de Paulmy on his deathbed could assure his daughter, 'I have no dishonourable or dishonest action to reproach myself with. You may weep for me as a good father, a good friend and even as a good Christian,' and remembered to address his son-in-law, the Duc de Luxembourg, as 'Monsieur le Duc'. His passion for books, though deeply felt, was always under control. He had married a wife with an income of 45,000 *livres*, but had no money himself except his state pensions of 52,000 *livres*, reduced by Necker's policy of retrenchment to 46,000 *livres*. It was only by careful management, by abstaining from auction sales when prices were wild, and by skill in private negotiation that he succeeded in outlasting his competitors and profiting from the dispersal of their collections.

He already owned a considerable library in 1754, though it is probable these were mostly current works and included few rarities. About 1756 he bought the papers of the Arnauld family and four years later negotiated unsuccessfully for a group of Madame de Sévigné's letters. But his collection only entered the first rank after the death in 1764 of his uncle, Comte d'Argenson, from whose estate he purchased for 37,586 *livres* the 934 most precious books, printed and manuscript. These had been familiar to him from childhood and no doubt had influenced the development of his bibliophilic taste. They included magnificent examples of gothic illumination: Jean, Duc de Berry's *Terence*, known as the *Térence des ducs,* a sumptuous Italian copy of Roberto della Porta's *Romuleon,* and no less than forty volumes from the Librairie de Bourgogne, removed from Brussels after its capture by the French in 1746 and apparently given to the Minister of War by a certain Courchelet d'Esnans, who had been commissioned to search for French historical works in the occupied territories. There were rare printed books, such as the *Mozarabic Missal* and *Breviary* (Toledo 1500 and 1502), and presentation copies of Montesquieu's *De l'esprit des lois* and of Voltaire's *La Pucelle d'Orléans,* 1755, and *Poèmes sur la religion naturelle,* 1756. The last was accompanied by a letter headed *aux délices près de genève* and signed *le suisse V.;* 'I am not so impertinent as to beg a Minister of War to read them but present them to him very humbly and holily so that he may condescend to find a place for them among his books of devotion.'

Other purchases were made privately and at auction from the Duc de la Vallière: a choice from the library of a rich financier, Jean Milsonneau, including a manuscript of Petrarch's *Canzoniere* bound for Jean Grolier and the papers of Valentin Conrart, secretary of the Académie, 'an inexhaustible mine for literary history from Malherbe to the *Misanthrope*'; from his next-

OPPOSITE *A French translation of Terence's plays, written and illuminated in Paris in the early fifteenth century for Jean, Duc de Berry. It was one of a magnificent group of manuscripts which the Marquis de Paulmy bought from the estate of his uncle, Comte d'Argenson.* BELOW *Portrait of Jacopo Antonio Marcello, from his* Passio Sancti Mauricii, *Padua 1453.*

Cato senex, cōmis ancilla, Dauus seruus.

Cato.

R hic habitasse platea dictum est eth
lidem. que sele in honeste optauit pri
late hic diuinias. potius quam hone
ste in patria nupta niuere. cuis morte ea ad me
lege redicunt bona: sed quos perdonter in deo. sal

Qui vult venire post me abneget
semetipm tollat crucem suam
et sequatur me:—

Miniatures from a thirteenth-century collection of French poetry. ABOVE *The Three Living and the Three Dead.* BELOW *A Coronation.* OPPOSITE *Miniature illustrating the text, 'If any man will come after me, let him deny himself and take up his cross and follow me', from the prayerbook of Marguérite de Valois, who is shown on the left. Her husband, later Henri IV of France, is in the centre.*

door neighbours, the Celestine convent (discreetly entered in his catalogue only as 'a religious house'), an illuminated Bible they had been given by Louis d'Orléans, who had received it in 1397 from his brother, King Charles V, and a fine copy of the first Bible printed in France (Paris, Gering, Crantz and Friburger, 1476); Henry of Navarre's Protestant catechism, Jacopo Antonio Marcello's *Passio Sancti Mauricii* with miniatures of the school of Mantegna, and fifty-four other manuscripts from the Charles-Adrien Picard sale in 1780; the historical papers of Charles-Marie Fevret de Fontette, mostly exchanged with the *Cabinet des chartes* for Lacurne de Sainte-Palaye's collections on French literature; finally, in 1781, for 100,000 *livres*, the entire library of Baron d'Heiss, a retired officer ruined by his addiction to books. Paulmy kept three hundred manuscripts and many printed books from the d'Heiss collection, but the auction sale of the unwanted surplus provided sad evidence of the Baron's too indiscriminate enthusiasm; the manuscripts included nine Bibles, seven Breviaries, five *Romans de la Rose* and no less than seventy-seven books of Hours.

in eo loco ubi fuerant expositi conde urbis una menia animi
cupiditas inuasit. Quare igitur numitori auo suo albanum
regnum pacificum dimiserunt et romanam urbem condide
runt. Ad quam habitandam omnium conuicinarum multi
tudo gentium concurrebat. Post romam conditam inter sres
de imponendo nomine lis orta est. Sed p augurium romulusuicit.

Though the library's greatest treasures came from French collections, a wide net was spread for current works. Many purchases were made during Paulmy's embassy to Venice. Besides contemporary Venetian illustrated books, the dispatch of a case from Turin and other books collected on journeys through Italy are mentioned. Before returning home in 1770 he gave twenty-five *louis* and De Bure's *Bibliographie instructive* to a certain Abbé Luigi Baroni and dispatched him on a buying tour. But the Abbé had only failures to report: he found little or nothing in Lombardy, too many other collectors had been there first, and when on his way to sound out Consul Smith's widow about her husband's books, his coach overturned and broke his leg.

German publications were obtained through the bookseller Jean Néaulme of Altona. Catesby's *Natural History of Carolina*, 1754, and George Edwards's *Gleanings of Natural History*, 1758, were ordered from England and Horace Walpole sent the second edition of his *Catalogue of engravers* (Strawberry Hill 1765). Paulmy had made an ingenious arrangement to secure the same advantages in Paris as a copyright library enjoyed in England. French booksellers, authors and printers had a legal obligation to deposit eight copies of every new book; it appears from the correspondence of the Marquis's secretary, Pierre-Antoine Soyer, that one copy found its way to the police, who passed it on to the Arsenal.

The library was a general one, divided according to the current system into Theology, Law, Science and Art, *Belles Lettres*, History, and one heading more than was usual, Literary History. Each category contained valuable works but the collection's great strength was in French literature, especially medieval manuscripts and the scarce romances of the sixteenth century. Paulmy owned a few humanistic manuscripts but does not seem to have pursued the *editiones principes* of the classics, preferring the more reliable texts published by the Estiennes and later editors. His Italian holdings were extensive and he had a representative collection of over a hundred titles in English literature, from Chaucer to Macpherson's *Ossian*. Here is his comment on Pope and Warburton's edition of Shakespeare, 1747:

... he lived in a still barbarous century and could only judge antique models through bad English translations; he was ignorant, a libertine and by profession an actor; he wrote his comedies to earn a living and please the common people; nevertheless genius shines through his works which are sometimes sublime. His faults are those of his century and his condition, and his talent is probably his own.

A poem in Croat and a hundred Oriental manuscripts should perhaps be ascribed to a fondness for curiosities which the Marquis de Paulmy shared with Samuel Pepys, but felt obliged to disguise in the Age of Reason. His father had disapproved of collecting altogether: a taste for fine editions, masterpieces of typography, was one thing – he could even understand searching for the first books printed in every language – but to go further was abuse and folly. The son's partial apologia is to be found in the introduction to his theological catalogue. Since 'the science of salvation', he wrote, is the most important of all, a man of the world, a layman, only needs in his library a Bible, a good catechism, a book of Hours and the best collection of sermons. But a savant 'curieux de bons ouvrages' may go further. 'The study of the Human Spirit's progress, even of its errors, and the study of history are the principal objects of attention of someone forming a library'; theology has a bearing on these subjects. In this way the collector felt that he had justified his four to five thousand volumes on religion; his Life of Jesus Christ in Chinese, his works on Our Lord's umbilical cord venerated at Châlons-sur-Marne, the Holy Tear of Vendôme and the Sacred Shroud of Campiègne, and his treatises on the correct dimensions of the ecclesiastical tonsure and the right of clerics to wear wigs.

Paulmy's main interest was in texts, but he was by no means insensitive to a book's appearance. Although Carolingian and romanesque miniatures seemed to him 'ridiculous', 'of the worst possible drawing', he was one of the first European collectors to appreciate gothic illumination and rightly called the *Térence des ducs* 'of the greatest beauty'. His taste in book illustration was old-fashioned and the artists he admired had nearly all made their reputations in the previous century: Abraham Bosse, Claude Mellan, Charles Le Brun, Robert Nanteuil, Sébastien Le Clerc, Hyacinthe Rigaud, Bernard Picard, Callot, Sadeler, Hollar. Cochin's work was praised, but he thought Piazzetta, who had died twenty years before the note was written, 'very modern, illustrious in this century in Venice where the arts are in decline' and Romeyn de Hooghe 'a forceful draughtsman but his works are disagreeable'. He approached everything English, even the art, with cautious respect: 'Hoggart [Hogarth] était d'un génie tout à fait anglais'. He found Pyne's *Horace* [London 1733-7), 'un très bel ouvrage' and Baskerville was almost the only printer for whose work he expressed admiration. He appreciated luxurious bindings, but normally preferred to economise by buying books in sheets and having them simply bound in marbled calf by Anguerrand, or after 1775, Bradel. The elaborately gilt red morocco portfolio made to hold Madame de Pompadour's present of her etchings was a rare exception.

Paulmy read all, or nearly all his books. The great majority are annotated with critical remarks and details of the author's life and of other editions. His ambition seems to have been to produce a general bibliography, a revised and amplified version of De Bure's *Bibliographie instructive*, and by a process of extracting and vulgarising to make his collection available to the public, rather as Algarotti had popularised Newtonian astronomy in his *Newtonianismo per le donne* (1737), which Paulmy owned in a French translation. Two enormous but unfinished works were the result: the *Bibliothèque universelle des romans*, discontinued after appearing for three years at the rate of sixteen volumes a year, and *Mélanges tirés d'une grande bibliothèque*, which ran to seventy volumes.

Men of letters were allowed free use of the library; on one occasion when the royal librarian was absent his deputy found it

OPPOSITE PAGE BELOW *The building of Rome, from Roberto della Porta's* Romuleon, *written in Italy, c. 1500.* OPPOSITE PAGE ABOVE *Woodcut representing a theatre, from an early sixteenth-century edition of Terence in French.* BELOW *Edward Tyson,* Orang-Outang, sive Homo Sylvestris; or, the anatomy of a Pygmie, *printed in London in 1699. The Marquis de Paulmy's catalogue note reads: 'The description of a kind of monkey so like man that it makes the reader reflect furiously'.*

Red morocco binding with the Marquis de Paulmy's arms; a collection of Madame de Pompadour's engraved work which she gave to the Marquis in 1756.

easier to direct enquirers to the Arsenal than to search for what they wanted himself. (But books were never allowed out and the single recorded exception was disastrous: a volume of costume plates lent to the Duc de Luxembourg and 'miserably torn' by his children.) Paulmy was anxious that the collection should continue to be preserved as a public library after his death. He first offered it to Louis XVI with the condition that he should be made royal librarian; but, like Sir Thomas Phillipps's similar proposal to Oxford University a century later, this was refused. The solution was a sale in 1785 to the king's brother, Comte d'Artois, retaining the use of the books for his lifetime and with the tacit understanding that the collection should form a second royal library, accessible to scholars. The price was 400,000 *livres*, to be paid in eight annual instalments of 50,000 *livres*, but before even receiving the first instalment the Marquis made another huge purchase: the remainder of the Duc de la Vallière's collection, amounting to 80,000 volumes.

At his death in 1787, the Arsenal held about 160,000 volumes. The Comte d'Artois added 30,000 of his own and installed an ex-bookseller, Saugrain, as librarian. On 14 July 1789, when a mob swarmed from the Bastille to the Arsenal to sack this residence of the most unpopular royal prince, Saugrain saved the collection by making the porter change into the king's uniform, thus persuading the crowd that it had called at the wrong address. Since then the Bibliothèque de l'Arsenal has been a national library, although returned to the titular ownership of the Comte d'Artois (later Charles X) under the restored monarchy. It was allowed a pick of confiscated books during the Revolution and obtained not less than fifty thousand volumes in this way, notably the Psalter of Blanche of Castille, a major relic of the Sainte-Chapelle since the thirteenth century, and the archives of the Bastille. During the librarianship of Charles Nodier from 1822 to 1844, a brilliant coterie of intellectuals met in his salon: Victor Hugo, Alexandre Dumas, Lamartine, Alfred de Musset, Balzac, Sainte-Beuve, Alfred de Vigny, Delacroix and Liszt came to hear their host talk on every subject from entomology to steamboats. ('He knows the history of the Estiennes, the Alduses and the Manutiuses,' wrote Gustave Planche, who clearly did not.) In 1860–3 the transfer to the Bibliothèque Nationale of the Marquis de Paulmy's Oriental manuscripts, Chinese books, prints (including Jean Duvet's *Lapocalypse figurée*, Lyons 1561), drawings and medals destroyed the integrity of the founder's collection, without (one would imagine) benefiting the larger institution to a corresponding degree. Since then the original nucleus of plays has swelled by judicious acquisitions, by the gift of three hundred thousand volumes from Auguste Rondel in 1925 and the recent purchase of Edward Gordon Craig's collection into the richest theatrical library in the world. The Arsenal receives deposit copies of all literary and dramatic works published in France and now possesses 1,800,000 printed volumes and 11,800 manuscripts, of which 2,728 comprise the Bastille papers.

One of the Marquis de Paulmy's salons in the Arsenal. The clock belonged to the abbey of St Victor in Paris until the Revolution.

John Rylands Library

MANCHESTER

ABOVE *Illustration to Aesop's* Fables *(Naples, Francesco del Tuppo, 1485).* OPPOSITE *The main hall of the John Rylands Library, seen from the gallery. The building, by Basil Champneys, was completed in 1899.*

The John Rylands Library owes its existence and its distinctive composition to four remarkable people: three collectors, George John, second Earl Spencer, Alexander, twenty-fifth Earl of Crawford and Balcarres, and his son James, the twenty-sixth Earl; and a benefactress, Mrs John Rylands.

Earl Spencer, born in 1758, belonged to one of the great Whig territorial families, a class then richer than many sovereign princes. He received the usual classical upbringing of an educated Englishman of the day, entered politics after Harrow and held office as First Lord of the Admiralty from 1794 to 1801, where he was largely responsible for giving Nelson the independent command in the Mediterranean which led to the victory of the Nile. After a spell as Home Secretary in 1806–07 he retired from public life to devote himself to his duties as land-owner, magistrate and colonel of the Yeomanry, and to his library.

His earliest purchase of a rare book was of Caxton's prose translation of the *Distichs of Cato* in 1789. The year after he bought the splendid collection of first editions of the Greek and Latin classics formed by Count Károly Reviczky, a Hungarian nobleman in the Imperial diplomatic service, mostly at the La Vallière and other French sales of the previous decade. From Caxtons and classical first editions his interests spread to embrace early and fine printing in general, blockbooks and early woodcut illustration, Italian poetry, Aldines, Elzevirs and editions of the Bible.

Spencer had a remarkable memory and a keen eye for type, capable of recognising instantly books from the press of Ulrich Han in Rome or Petrus Caesaris in Paris. He paid generous sums for books of importance; twenty years after his death the price of Caxtons stood at only thirty per cent of its level during his lifetime. In the 1790s he still took collecting lightly and agreed with the Duke of Roxburghe at the Mason sale of 1798 not to bid against him but to toss for the lots afterwards. The determination of the dedicated collector became evident in later years. On hearing that his nephew, the Duke of Devonshire, intended to compete for the Merly copy of Caxton's *Book of divers ghostly*

matters, he made sure of the book with an unbeatable bid of £200 'or still more'. At the auction sale of the Duke of Roxburghe's library in 1812 Spencer 'in the full heighth of the Roxburgian fever' (as he later remarked ruefully) defeated stiff competition to win five Caxtons; but the first dated edition of Boccaccio's *Decameron* (Venice, Valdarfer, 1471) was lost to the Marquess of Blandford at £2,260 after an epic struggle lasting 112 bids. It was a price that echoed round Europe, the highest paid for a printed book until that date, or for long afterwards. The defeat rankled and attempts to secure the only other complete copy, privately owned in Milan, were unsuccessful. Patience and persistence were eventually rewarded. In 1819 the Marquess sold his library and Spencer obtained the *Decameron* for only £918.

In 1802 Thomas Frognall Dibdin, a young clergyman with a passion for fine books, sent Spencer a copy of his *Introduction to the Knowledge of Rare and Valuable Editions of the Greek and Latin Classics.* Spencer replied politely, offering to show the author his 'old editions', but declined the dedication of the second edition. The acquaintance did not mature into a closer friendship until in 1811 Dibdin proposed publishing an account of Spencer's library. The collector welcomed the idea, advanced money to finance the publication, read the manuscript and suggested improvements, and rewarded Dibdin with 'a small box containing 4 Pints of the best Tokay' and similar flattering attentions. The catalogue appeared between 1814 and 1823 in seven stately volumes with type facsimiles, engraved illustrations and much enthusiastic description. In return Dibdin rendered his patron valuable services, both in locating books and in undertaking special commissions. He travelled to Stamford to buy Caxton's edition of Lydgate's *The lyf of Our Lady* from a grocer, Octavius Gilchrist (the first approach was unsuccessful and Spencer who, like Dibdin's other correspondents, seemed to find the clergyman's facetious style catching, lamented 'that [the owner] did not partake more of the melting Quality of his Sugar'). In the same year (1813) Dibdin persuaded Thomas Johnes of Hafod, the translator of Froissart and Monstrelet, to sell Spencer the Alchorne library with its three Caxtons. 'Remember, how noble and manful it is to make sacrifices when they are required to be made!' he exhorted the vacillating proprietor.

Besides following the chief auction sales, Spencer bought heavily from English booksellers, especially Edwards of Pall Mall, London, who sold him a Gutenberg Bible, and three Caxtons extracted from the Chapter of Lincoln Cathedral. Other books came from English private owners. His brother-in-law, the Duke of Devonshire, let him choose a few volumes from Chatsworth; Charles Williams gave up his *Godfrey of Boloyne* (Caxton, 1481); and the Hon. Charles Jenkinson surrendered leaves lacking from Spencer's copy of the Thirty-six Line Bible. Even during the Napoleonic Wars books arrived from the Continent and bids on French sales were sent, with some reluctance ('I am a little afraid of trusting to Renouard'), to A.-A. Renouard, the bibliographer of the Aldine Press. Many great rarities were

ABOVE *Dido directing the building of Carthage: illustration to Boccaccio's* De claris mulieribus *(Ulm, J. Zeiner, 1473).* OPPOSITE *Joshua: from the first edition of the Bible in Danish (Copenhagen, L. Dietz, 1550).*

Et septim? angl's effudit
fialā suā mae eꝛ et exiuit uor magna detem
plo a thꝛono dicens fᶜᵐ eſt Et fᶜᵃ sunt fut
gura et uoces et tonitrua et terremotus
factus eſt magnus q̄ lis nūꝗ fuit ex quo
hoīes Et ceperūt fuy trat tabo terre
motus et sic magnus eſt facta eſt ciuitas
ꝩes in ptes et ciuitates gentiū ceciderūt Et
babiloū magna ciuitas uēt ĩ memoꝛiā
ante deū dare calice uini ĩ dignaꝯis ire
eius Et omis insula fugit et montes nō
sunt inuēti Et grādo ꝗ

obtained through Alexander Horn, an English dealer living in Germany, notably the *editio princeps* of Vergil (Rome 1469) and Turrecremata's *Meditationes* (Rome, Ulrich Han, 1467), the first illustrated book printed in Italy – perhaps also the Mainz Psalter of 1457, which like the Turrecremata came from a Bavarian religious house. Another 'valuable helpmate' (in Spencer's phrase) in procuring rare works was Count D'Elci, an Italian connoisseur also engaged in building up a collection of classical first editions.

By 1818 Spencer had only eight major desiderata and Dibdin was dispatched on a Continental tour in search of them. In Stuttgart the King of Wurtemberg consented to exchange two early editions of Vergil for modern theological books to an equivalent value. More purchases were made from the Munich Library, from Professor May of Augsburg, St Peter's, Salzburg (the motherhouse of Admont), and the Capuchins of Rossau in Vienna. Spencer visited Naples a year later and bought the Duke of Cassano-Serra's collection of early Neapolitan imprints, thus securing the extremely rare *editio princeps* of Horace (Naples, Arnoldus de Bruxella, 1474). The duplicates from this and other block transactions were disposed of in nine sales between 1798 and 1823.

By the year of Spencer's death (1836) the library comprised over forty thousand volumes and was shelved in five adjoining rooms at Althorp, the family seat in Northamptonshire. 'A Shetland pony might be conveniently kept, in ready caparison,' Dibdin suggested, 'to carry the more delicate visitor from one extremity to the other.' Here were fifteen incunable editions of Vergil and seventy-eight of Cicero, among which Gibbon exhausted a morning in 1793; fifty-seven books by Sweynheim and Pannartz, the first Italian printers; fifty-five Caxtons, three of which were unique; four books printed by Pfister and part of a fifth, the only examples of his press in England; fourteen blockbooks, one of which (*Apocalypse I*) was printed in 1451 (as Mr Allan Stevenson has recently proved from the watermarks) and is therefore the only surviving blockbook to antedate printing with movable type; over eight hundred Aldines; all three editions of Dante printed in 1472; collections of Boccaccio, Petrarch and Ariosto; and a splendid array of early Bibles. There could be no doubt that Renouard was correct in calling it 'the finest private library in Europe'.

Alexander, Lord Lindsay, was born in 1812 and succeeded as twenty-fifth Earl of Crawford and Balcarres in 1869. He was a precocious collector, covering one wall of his room at Eton with incunabula and early editions of the classics. Book lists jotted down when he was nineteen include such unusual works as Coutinho's *Journey to Mazagam* (Lisbon 1629) and Johannes Schildtberger's captivity in Turkey. The same notes show the foundations being laid of his astonishing bibliographical knowledge: 'At Wardour St stall look at Ariosto – the edn Venice 1584 – has 52 engravings by Girolamo Porro – rarest of all edns – 34th plate almost always deficient – cancelled and replaced by

OPPOSITE '*The seventh angel poured out his vial into the air*': an illustration to a fifteenth-century blockbook Apocalypse *from Lord Spencer's Collection.*

273

Portrait of Marco Polo; illustration from his Travels *in German (Nuremberg, Creussner, 1477).*

dupl. of 33ᵈ.'

'I had . . . in my earliest youth . . . proposed to myself as an object the development of our library into one worthy of our family,' he wrote to his son in 1865, 'not a mere bibliomaniacal *congeries* of undigested accumulation, but a library of intrinsic excellence, to contain the most useful and interesting books old and new, in all walks of literature . . .' Bibliographies and literary histories were studied and an ideal catalogue drawn up. In the 1850s the process can be observed operating at full pressure. Lists of desiderata were going out to London dealers; to Bernard Quaritch, the German immigrant bookseller in Castle Street, Leicester Square; to Charles Frederick Molini, who signed himself 'Agent to the Institute of France and General Agent', in King William Street; to H.G.Bohn in York Street: lists of French genealogy and provincial history, of the Edda and of sagas, of Italian books on art. From time to time there is a note of urgency. Persan's *Recherches historiques sur la ville de Dôle* is starred: 'this Lord L. is much in want of', and before the Stuart de Rothesay sale of 1855, 'For the American books, especially those marked with a double cross, Lord L is prepared to give Mr B[ohn] almost an unlimited commission.' In spite of the inevitable disappointments and delays ('the only means of getting Russian books,' he was informed by Quaritch, 'is by ordering them from such a bookseller in Leipsic, who has a correspondent at St Petersburg; – it will therefore be an uncertain and slow operation'), the library at Haigh Hall, Wigan, quickly grew to over fifty thousand volumes. 'Books came pouring in, on all subjects from all parts of the world,' his son recalled, 'far quicker indeed than it was possible to shelve them: room after room had its walls covered and old portraits in the passages were hung in the bedrooms and replaced by books.' It was the most erudite private library to be formed since the seventeenth century and in its grand design Oriental literature had an essential place. In the 1860s two collections of Arabic, Persian and Turkish manuscripts were acquired in England and the Van Alstein Chinese books in Belgium. Subsequently with the help of an agent in Pekin, the Far Eastern section was built up to eight thousand volumes in Chinese and one thousand in Japanese.

James Lindsay, the twenty-sixth Earl, had already assembled a distinguished group of scientific books, later presented to the Royal Observatory at Edinburgh, before succeeding his father in 1880. Besides adding to the general library, he devoted his attentions to several specialised collections: broadsides and proclamations, jewelled bookbindings, states and issues of De Bry's *Voyages*, tracts on the Reformation, the French Revolution and the English Civil War. Fine illuminated manuscripts were acquired to illustrate the history of script and miniature painting. In 1893 he bought in Rome the Borghese collection of papal bulls and proclamations, and in Egypt in the winter of 1898–9 demotic and Arabic papyri newly unearthed from the ancient rubbish-dumps of the Fayum, while Coptic and Greek papyri were purchased for him by two Oxford dons, Arthur Hunt and

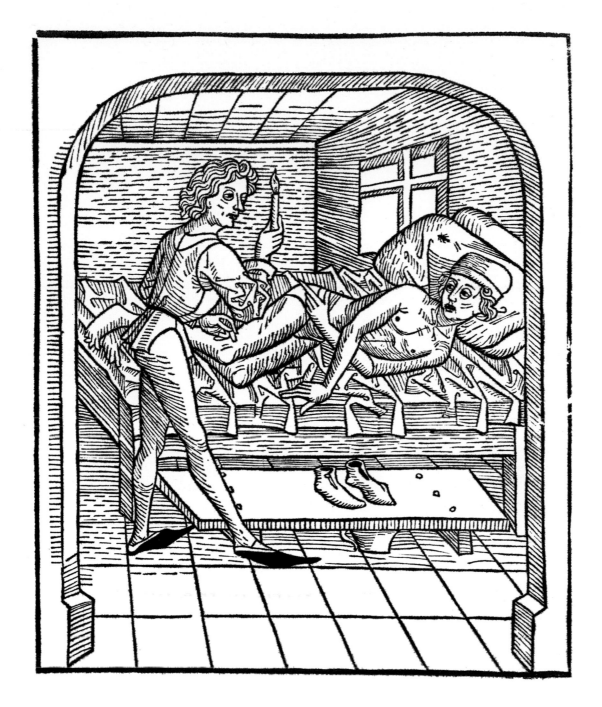

Bernard Grenfell. The twenty-fifth Earl had been his own
librarian, bibliographer and secretary. His son employed a
librarian, J.P.Edmond, and six assistants. The catalogues they
compiled were privately printed and distributed to British and
foreign libraries and learned societies.

In 1892 an article appeared in *The Times* giving the news that
Earl Spencer proposed to sell the Althorp library. A new figure
now enters the story. Enriqueta Augustina Tennant was born in
Havana in 1843, the second of five children of a Yorkshireman
and his Cuban wife. Her father died when she was five and his
widow returned to England with her family. Years of hardship
followed; a reference to Miss Tennant's 'splendid fortitude under
circumstances which always test human quality and strength'
no doubt applies to this period. In her early twenties she was
engaged as secretary by John Rylands, a Manchester manu-
facturer and businessman who from modest origins had amassed
a fortune of nearly three million pounds. When he was widowed

275

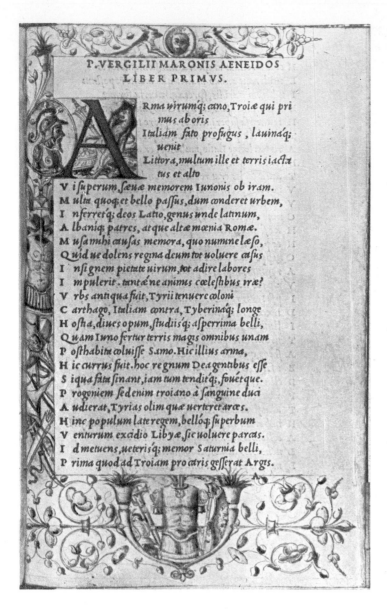

for the second time in 1875, she became the seventy-four-year-old millionaire's third wife.

Dr Joseph Parker, a Congregationalist minister, has left an entertaining account of the Rylands' life at Longford Hall, Stretford. John Rylands travelled to his office every day, returning in the evenings for a game of bowls in summer, or of billiards in winter. He was a Liberal in politics, a Nonconformist in religion and a generous contributor to charitable causes. Busts of Bright, Cobden, George Thompson and other Free Trade heroes filled the hall; Nonconformist ministers were frequent guests. The fare was apt to be Spartan. Their 'hospitable but abstemious host', whose wine was celebrated for its nastiness, drank only champagne himself and had 'the old-fashioned habit' of keeping a bottle on the floor at his right hand. The rules that had brought him success in business were applied to other areas of life. Fruit and vegetables supplied from the garden to the kitchen were charged for. 'This is the only way,' the millionaire informed Dr Parker, 'by which you can really tell whether a garden pays or not.' The Bible composed a large part of his reading, but did not satisfy him in its existing form. He wished to make it as convenient to consult as a stock list, and subsidised for free distribution an edition with each paragraph numbered consecutively for easy reference and a comprehensive subject index.

It was perhaps her husband's habit of giving books to indigent preachers that decided Mrs John Rylands, after his death in 1888, to found in Manchester a library for theological students in his memory. Dr Green, secretary of the Religious Tract Society, was engaged to buy appropriate works and passed the commission on to his son, John Arnold Green. In the course of visiting London booksellers the younger Green made the acquaintance of A.B.R. Railton, manager of Henry Sotheran & Co.'s branch in the Strand. So it happened that when the article announcing the Althorp library's sale appeared, Railton, after consulting Green, cut it out and sent it without comment to Mrs Rylands. Her response was encouraging. Railton then called on Edward Grose Hodge, the senior partner of Sotheby's, who was acting for the owner, and was given a week's option at £220,000. Railton's valuation of the library amounted to £193,127 and an offer of £210,000 was accepted. By prompt action Mrs Rylands had made a sound bargain. An American agent was waiting to see Hodge when Railton called, and Lenox Kennedy would have given three hundred thousand pounds to secure the collection for the New York Public Library.

The building in Deansgate, Manchester, to hold the Spencer collection and other books was not completed until 1899. Basil Champneys, the architect, created a minor masterpiece of late Victorian gothic, with pleasant variations of scale and a large hall with flanking bays gleaming with gilt morocco spines, which succeeds in being both impressive and intimate.

The Library was still almost wholly deficient in medieval manuscripts to balance the Althorp printed books. In the meantime however the Haigh Hall library's financial future was

Jra plane 7 stupenda sapie tue dispositō bōe ihe
su·ut p icremēta tempoz icremēta tue dilectōnis
oñderes.Transiturus q̄dē ad patrē·cū tēpus tue passio
nis istaret·cenā cū apostolis tuus mira caritate affluente
celebrasti·in qua legalib) epulis expletis·7 eoz pedib)
ablutis memoriā facies mirabiliū tuorū·micors 7 mi
serator dñs·sacramentū corporis 7 sanguis tui summa
tractās caritate nobis consecrasti ut coleretur iugiter p
misteriū·qō semel offerebatur i pretiū. VJude ut tāti be
nefitij·iugis i nobis meōria pseueraret corp) tuū i abū
et sanguinē tuū i potū·sub spetie pais 7 uini sumēdū
fidelib) dereliquisti.O clemētie magnitudinē·o iaudita
dilectio.Bene quidē de te pulcro serōe euāgelista.Johā
nes ait.Qō cū dilexeris tuos usqz i finem id ē usqz ad
maximū caritatis excessū dilexisti·totū te i eoz dilecti
onē effūdēs Corp) i abū sāguinē i potū·anima i pretiū

The Last Supper: from J. de Turrecremata's
Meditationes (Rome, Ulrich Han, 1467), the
first Italian illustrated book.

277

Joseph and Potiphar's wife. Drawing by James Tissot for his illustrations to the Bible in French (Paris 1904). Given to the Library by Mrs Rylands. OPPOSITE *Statues of Mrs John Rylands and her husband survey the Library.*

beginning to preoccupy Lord Crawford. Income from land was declining, the prices of rare books rose steadily, while cataloguing and printing must have involved substantial costs. In 1887 and 1889 it had already been necessary to sell the Gutenberg Bible, the romances of chivalry and other treasures of the collection to redeem twenty-five thousand pounds worth of mortgages.

In July 1901 Railton cast a fly over J.P.Edmond by remarking that 'an American gentleman' (perhaps he intended to suggest Pierpont Morgan) wished to buy the manuscripts at Haigh Hall. Edmond passed the news on to Crawford, who wrote to Sotheran's: 'Is the matter really serious? for it is a large matter.' A period of confused but intense activity followed. Crawford named a price, £155,000, which he 'felt confident no one would give', and apparently received an assurance that the collection would remain in England. Mrs Rylands was interested but uncertain. 'Has the owner purposely named a prohibitive sum, not caring whether the MSS be sold or not?' Was the collection 'offered as a *whole*, and not one weeded out, so to speak, of some of its finest examples?' And what exactly did it consist of? The last question was not easy to answer, as there was no printed catalogue. Crawford could only provide a list of totals: 663 Western manuscripts, 2,425 Oriental, 464 Chinese and 231 Japanese (the two last categories including printed books), plus an unknown number of papyri. (Some of the latter were not even in England but on loan to Dr Karabacek in Vienna.) Railton succeeded in reassuring his client, and by 31 July, although Mrs Rylands declared herself still 'somewhat in the dark', agreement had been reached. It only remained for *The Times* to report the sale (Dr Henry Guppy, the Rylands librarian, wired in amazement to Edmond: 'Is Times announcement correct? I have heard nothing and am anxious') and for the volumes to be packed under Railton's supervision (Edmond was amused to see that he carefully rubbed out any prices marked on the flyleaves) and delivered to Longford Hall. Thither Edmond was summoned a fortnight later. 'I was very glad to find that the lady appreciates her purchase,' he told Crawford, 'she is going over every one and reading the descriptions in the catalogue. I don't think she will be in any hurry to give them to the John Rylands Library.'

The Crawford connection, so fortuitously brought about, was of lasting benefit to the Library. In 1924 the twenty-seventh Earl presented the French proclamations and broadsides. In 1946 when Haigh Hall was given up, his son, the present holder of the title (a Trustee of the Library), deposited on semi-permanent loan the Reformation and French Revolutionary tracts, the Borghese papal bulls and proclamations, the De Bry voyages, the family papers and the largest collection of English tracts outside the British Museum. Grenfell and Hunt had continued to hunt for Egyptian papyri on the library's behalf. In this way a papyrus fragment of St John's Gospel of the first half of the second century AD was acquired in 1920, the earliest manuscript of any part of the New Testament to have come to light, and a most appropriate possession for a library founded to advance theological studies.

Bibliothèque Spoelberch de Lovenjoul

CHANTILLY

ABOVE *Viscount Charles de Spoelberch de Lovenjoul.*
OPPOSITE *Chantilly: the Duc d'Aumâle raises his hat to the Lovenjoul Library.*

'It's almost a Benedictine work!' Raymond Nacquart, the son of Balzac's doctor, remarked. It was a comparison that readily suggested itself, between the Maurist fathers' monuments of erudition and Charles de Lovenjoul's minutely detailed bibliographical studies of French authors, and if it contained an element of exaggeration, this was due to the unexpectedness of a rich Belgian viscount, with the appearance of a cavalry officer, devoting his time to such an occupation. He himself was more modest, inscribing one book to a relation of his wife's 'with the threat of intolerable boredom if he risks opening these pages'.

Viscount Charles-Victor-Maximilien-Albert de Spoelberch de Lovenjoul was born in Brussels on 30 April 1836. His parents belonged to the high Belgian nobility, with a large modern town house in the Boulevard du Régent and a castle at Lovenjoul, near Louvain, where the young Charles, their only child to survive infancy, formed his first collection – of butterflies. He grew up with the characteristics of his social class but detesting their lack of intellectual interests and their favourite pastimes, shooting and racing. He was tall and slim, with waxed moustaches, impeccably dressed and proud of his small hands and feet, a devout Catholic and with aristocratic good manners, but also intelligent, restless, voluble, nervous and untiringly industrious (he had a carriage fitted with a makeshift desk so that – like Federigo Borromeo – he could read and write on a journey 'in order not to lose time'). His education was perfunctory; although his life was devoted to the written word, he knew no Latin or any foreign language, and even in French literature paid small attention to any century earlier than his own. He was devoted to his mother and did not marry until she died, when he was nearly forty. No similar feeling is recorded for his father, to whose memory a virulent essay *On Idleness* seems to have been addressed.

By the age of seventeen Lovenjoul owned 259 books, and during the following two years he was buying an average of eight titles a week. Walter Scott was his earliest favourite, in French translation like his other foreign authors: Dante's *Inferno*, Heine's *Reisebilder*, *Uncle Tom's Cabin* and *The Scarlet Letter*. There were a

The autograph manuscript of George Sand's Elle et Lui.

few children's books of history and travel (the last that is heard of either subject in the library), and the remainder were contemporary novels and poetry: Théophile Gautier and George Sand as they appeared, Lamartine, Stendhal, Henri Monnier, Émile Souvestre and La Comtesse Dash. Balzac made his first appearance (misspelled *Balsac*) as a contributor to *Le Diable à Paris*; 'le Bibliophile Jacob' (Paul Lacroix, curator of the Arsenal Library, whose bibliographical works he took as models for his own), as the author of *Soirées de Walter Scott à Paris*. He owned many Belgian pirated editions and no rarities.

As time went on, though his purchases covered the whole range of contemporary fiction, he concentrated increasingly on three authors: Gautier, George Sand and Balzac. Regular visits to Paris twice or three times a year started in 1856. The days were spent in bookshops, the evenings at the theatre. His collection had already taken a new and significant turn. Realising that he could never possess the Romantic School complete unless he owned their serials and journalism, he began to buy runs of old newspapers and to subscribe to current ones. His first major *coup* was the purchase in Paris in 1860 of the entire contents of a *cabinet de lecture*, a circulating library, where subscribers were entitled to read the papers in return for a small annual fee. It belonged to a certain Lecoq and was situated in the Rue Sainte Anne, but the panache of the Viscount's gesture was rather diminished by a reduction in the price offered from four to three thousand francs after his first figure had been accepted.

He scrutinised these periodicals with close attention and developed a high standard of expertise in identifying his authors' anonymous contributions on stylistic grounds. Michel Lévy, of the publishing house of Lévy Frères, met him in 1865 and at once realised his usefulness to the firm's programme of reprinting Romantic authors. A lively correspondence started. 'Thanks to you,' Lévy wrote on 7 April 1865, 'my edition [of Balzac] will leave all others far behind,' and in the following years he appealed for Gérard de Nerval's and Berlioz's contributions to periodicals, for everything Gautier had written on Nerval and for help in preparing his defence against a charge of theft of literary property. Printing of Balzac's *Complete Works* (1869–75) was held up until Lévy could visit Brussels to decide in consultation with the Viscount how the four volumes of *Oeuvres diverses* should be composed.

Lovenjoul owned no original manuscript until the purchase in 1875 from Sainte-Beuve's former secretary, Jules Troubat, of George Sand's correspondence with the great critic, adding from the same source a year later over seven thousand letters received by Sainte-Beuve from other writers. Once launched on the pursuit of manuscripts he applied himself to the chase with his customary thoroughness. His annual expenditure on books, which had averaged 5,100 francs from 1858–74, rose to over 9,000 francs in 1875–6 and to 12,500 from 1877 onwards. Initially he concentrated on autographs of Gautier and George Sand, with a few representative contemporaries, and traded in his first Balzac letters soon after buying them in part exchange for the manuscript of Gautier's *Le Tricorne enchanté*. But the opportunities following Madame Balzac's death in 1882 proved irresistible. At her sale he was outbid for the manuscript of *Eugénie Grandet* (now in the Pierpont Morgan Library) but bought the *Histoire des Treize*, *César Birotteau*, *Le Lys dans la Vallée*, *Le médecin de campagne* and six others for 11,176 francs. Balzac's letters to his wife were excluded from the auction. Many were bought privately from his step-daughter, Countess Mniszech, by Paul Lévy, Michel's nephew, but others had been carried off with the furniture by her indignant creditors, and Lovenjoul discovered thirty-five in neighbouring shops, one just as a cobbler was about to light his pipe with it.

Lovenjoul met Théophile Gautier in Brussels in 1871, the year before his death. The poet was amazed and enchanted by his knowledge. 'You alone,' he wrote, 'can one day undertake the reconstruction and complete publication of my works,' and he addressed an unfinished sonnet to him:

> Moderne est le palais mais le blason ancien,
> Peint par Van Dyck au coin des portraits de famille . . .

Portrait of George Sand, by Alfred de Musset, 1833.

To George Sand, the second of his idols, he was introduced in Paris by the publisher Calmann Lévy in 1875. Noël Parfait, Lévy's partner and previously the elder Dumas' secretary, arrived half an hour before the time of the appointment to warn her against his 'excess of bibliomania', but in fact collector and authoress were delighted with each other, and Lovenjoul was allowed to call next day to continue ferreting through a drawer-full of papers. An amicable correspondence followed, although his spate of questions and apologies provoked her to begin one letter 'Dear Bibliophile' and sign it 'G.S.Bibliophobe'. She invited him to her house at Nohant and only her death in 1876 prevented the visit.

He had previously been too timid to approach private owners, but in the 1880s, as the grip of his obsession tightened, he sought out everyone who might have preserved any scrap of paper relating to his heroes. Balzac's cook resisted his advances for two years but finally succumbed. Caroline Marbouty, who had accompanied Balzac in male dress on a journey to Turin in 1836 and served as the model for *La Muse du Département*, read him a chronicle of the trip which she claimed had been dictated by the deceased author's spirit. He was given an introduction to Mme Sabatier, Baudelaire's 'White Venus', to whom Gautier had addressed several highly obscene letters, and on successive evenings he listened to her current lover read aloud these bawdy documents while she knitted placidly by the light of the same lamp. Her reluctance to part with the 'precious tokens of affection' was overcome and he acquired Gautier's pencil portrait of her as well. Countess Mniszech became an enthusiastic, though not entirely disinterested ally in his search. In 1887 a *petit bleu* reached him from her: 'At midday to-morrow I shall have *Le Père Goriot* . . . [My cousin] offers me a thousand francs cash.

A sheet of caricature studies of dancers by Théophile Gautier; signed 'Theophilos' in Greek.

Bring me 1,500 for it and the manuscript is yours.' It speaks highly for Lovenjoul's tact and powers of persuasion that he obtained the manuscript for exactly a thousand francs.

For, although of great wealth, he was careful never to pay too much. His accounts were meticulously kept; even in 1882, the year of the Balzac sale and of his largest expenditure, he did not fail to record the purchase of pamphlets by Dr Louis Fiaux costing fifty centimes. 'Few transactions – and I often handle more important ones,' Étienne Charavay, the doyen of Parisian autograph dealers, wrote after a particularly thorny negotiation, 'have given me so much trouble as this, and never have autographs been so bargained over. . . . You complain of the price of the correspondence. I have more right to complain, as you are pitiless in denying me any profit that I might have made.' Another letter of Charavay's (18 November 1882) introduced the collector to the workings of the dealers' ring at French auctions. 'The letter of George Sand was sold for five francs at the Cocheris sale as the result of an agreement between me and those who wanted it. In the knock-out (*refait*) I obtained it for twenty-five francs and send it enclosed. It's very cheap at this price and I am pleased with my arrangement, as if I'd bid it up at the sale and anyone suspected it was for you, we'd have been made to pay double.'

To hold his collection Lovenjoul constructed an eccentrically narrow and high room in his Brussels house, windowless and lit by a glass roof; enthusiastic visitors thought it resembled a gothic cathedral. Books, nearly all in wrappers (as he cared neither for bindings nor association copies), were ranged round a gallery; manuscripts, unbound in file covers, were concealed behind the pale grey doors, panelled in carmine, of two rows of tall cupboards, their topmost shelves reached from ladders mounted on rails. Here the collector spent as much as fifteen hours a day, extracting the last grain of significance from his documents. His wife, who married him when she was twenty-three and 'swore before the nuptial altar' (in Madame Simone André Maurois's words) 'to be faithful, obedient and a bibliophile', divided her time between helping her husband and compiling an immense work of her own, *La Belgique charitable*, published under a pseudonym in 1893.

une aigle d'or planait sur sa tête sacrée!

le jeune Piot las d'être Don Juan Piot de Marana
imite celui que la pudeur m'empêche de nommer les
aigles viennent manger sur son chapeau; à l'instar
du grand homme; il parle d'un brusque et saccadé
et quand il se lave la figure l'univers doit faire silence

Lovenjoul's first published work, *Notes sur Alfred de Vigny*, appeared in three numbers of the *Courrier du Commerce* in October 1865; his second, *Étude bibliographique sur George Sand*, in *Le Bibliophile Belge* the following year. Both were signed 'Le Bibliophile Isaac' in imitation of Paul Lacroix's pen-name. His *Histoire des Oeuvres de Honoré de Balzac*, 1879 (second edition 1886), and *Histoire des Oeuvres de Théophile Gautier*, 1887, earned him a solid scholarly reputation. His attitude to his chosen authors was protective and proprietary. He omitted Balzac's attacks on Belgium from Lévy Frères' edition of the *Oeuvres diverses* and although all the library's holdings are now made available, as late as 1949 André Maurois was refused access, in accordance with the testator's wishes, to George Sand's most intimate correspondences.

Lovenjoul's character held a strange dichotomy. In Paris he was gay and charming, a keen theatre-goer and something of a *bon vivant* (among his papers is the menu of what must have been a cheerful dinner: Potage à la Lovenjoul, Champignons farcis de publicité, Boeuf à la Théophile Gautier, Poulet Jules Lévy, Lapin Balzac . . .). His French friends were warmly welcomed in the sanctuary of the Boulevard du Régent; Paul Lévy wrote of 'the happy time I passed in your amiable company, the most intelligently agreeable time I can remember'; and foreign scholars received generous help. But in his own country he behaved like a morose hermit. One boyhood friend, his doctor and Eugène Gilbert, son of a professor at Louvain, were the only compatriots he received. His rejection of his father developed into a policy of non-participation in all aspects of Belgian life. He never held public office, refused an offer from Émile Verhaeren to contribute to a national anthology of prose-writers, and declined election to the Académie Belge.

His wife's early death in 1902 broke his spirit. During his tragic last years his powers of concentration failed and a history of George Sand's works, long projected, remained unwritten. He died in 1907, bequeathing his collections to the Institut de France with certain conditions: they were to form a separate entity, known as the Bibliothèque Spoelberch de Lovenjoul, attached to the Chantilly estate which the Institut had received from the Duc d'Aumâle; sightseers were forbidden; no book or document might be lent or exhibited.

A former convent in the Rue du Connétable in Chantilly was bought to house the library. Six hundred and fifty-nine boxes of books and papers and 818 bundles of newspapers were delivered there in 1910, containing over fifty thousand printed volumes, substantially complete runs of all French periodicals since 1815, and besides the great collections of Balzac, Gautier and George Sand, letters or manuscripts of Musset, Vigny, Barbey d'Aurevilly, Baudelaire, the two Dumas, Mérimée and Gérard de Nerval. Georges Vicaire, the first librarian, performed a herculean task of arrangement, classification and cataloguing; innumerable dossiers were put in order and bound; the grey and carmine cupboards were brought from Brussels and an exact

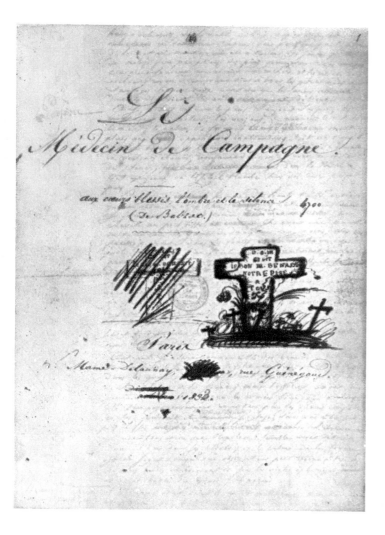

The autograph manuscript of Balzac's Le Médecin de Campagne, *written in 1833.*

replica of the 'sanctuary' installed; and by 1914 the library was ready for students.

In his first manuscript transaction, with Jules Troubat, Lovenjoul was content to receive only the letters 'having some value as autographs' and made no claim on the unimportant letters or those 'from women' which the vendor proposed to burn. In time however he came to realise that anything relevant was worth preserving. He bought not only Balzac's manuscripts and letters, but letters to him and to his family, documents concerning his houses, furniture, servants, lawsuits, publishers, service in the national guard and final illness, his business correspondence, bank statements and bills. His library is the archetype of the modern research collection (Texas University is the outstanding contemporary instance) which aims to illuminate the mysteries of literary creation by accumulating the completest surrounding documentation. The student is given his choice and can attach what relative significance he wishes to a corrected draft and an unpaid laundry bill.

The library opens three times a year for ten days at a time. This may seem a meagre allowance for reading, but the régime is in practice so appropriate for a specialist collection that one wonders why it has not been imitated elsewhere. Experts in allied fields arrive in Chantilly together, and there are moments when the room buzzes with friendly greetings and animated discussions. André Maurois described working there with his wife in 1949, when the library had neither heating nor electric light (both since provided). 'Those icy and laborious days have remained in our memories as hours of unforgettable enchantment. The presence of so many foreigners, come from the five continents to study the great French Romantics; the universal character of the cult; the moving ardour of the pilgrims, everything made us live in a state of strange enthusiasm. We understood that erudition may be passionate and research a sacred frenzy.'

ABOVE *Théophile Gautier's*, Le Capitaine Fracasse; *the incomplete autograph manuscript.* BELOW *The Viscount de Lovenjoul's 'sanctuary': the portraits are of Balzac's father, Lovenjoul himself (over the door) and Madame de Berny.*

Pierpont Morgan Library

NEW YORK

ABOVE *The entrance to the Library on Thirty-sixth Street.* OPPOSITE *The Holy Family at the fireside: from the Hours of Catherine of Cleves, Utrecht, c. 1435. The anonymous artist was a master of realistic detail.*

J. Pierpont Morgan (born in 1837) had been interested in autographs as a schoolboy; an orange card with President Fillmore's signature was his first acquisition, and a set of the signatories of the Declaration of Independence is almost the only notable feature in the catalogue of his library printed in 1883. Soon afterwards he was given the manuscript of Sir Walter Scott's novel *Guy Mannering* by his father, but it was only after the latter's death in 1890 that a New England sense of propriety let him feel free to collect on a grand scale. Most of the purchases were made during leisurely annual visits to Europe. In 1896 he bought in London a Gutenberg Bible on vellum and the four Shakespeare Folios, adding on his next visit the manuscript of Keats's *Endymion*. In 1899 two complete collections were acquired, the George B. de Forest French literature, and the personal 'library of leather and literature' of a London bookseller, James Toovey, notable for its magnificent run of Aldines, its fine bindings, Balbus's *Catholicon* (Mainz 1460) – the first printed book on any branch of secular learning – and the *Book of St Albans,* 1486, the first English sporting book.

In 1900 he bought the library of Theodore Irwin of Oswego, New York. This contained the Hamilton Gospels on purple vellum of the tenth century, a French manuscript Apocalypse that had belonged to Jean, Duc de Berry, four Caxtons and a second copy of the Gutenberg Bible, the Old Testament only. (A third Gutenberg Bible and the 1462 Bible were added from the Huth collection in 1911.) In the same year he obtained in London the Mainz Psalter of 1459 on vellum, the third dated book and – until recently – the only copy in America, and the autograph manuscripts of *Don Juan,* cantos 1–5, and eight other works by Byron which the poet had given to Countess Guiccioli.

In 1902 the library received, at a cost of £130,000, its greatest accession, the collection of Richard Bennett in Manchester, with twenty-four Caxtons, the Subiaco *Lactantius,* 1465, another copy of the *Book of St Albans* and a magnificent series of early illustrated books and French and English gothic manuscripts. Most of these had belonged to William Morris. The Ashburnham Gospels, a

288

Eus in aduitorniu meu
intende. Dne ad adiuua
du me festina. Glo
ria pri. Erat erat. ymnus
pristum suis iderbus
uirginali lacte pauit.
Et in panius pauperib;
inuolutu comportauit. abisq

be holden for folye, ffor the droptes and lawes by whiche
the iugementes be made and that by rayson & after right
ben kept and
mayntened in
ye court of kyn-
ges of princes
and of barons
come & procede
of Rethoryque,
Of this scien-
ce were extrayt
and drawen the
lawes and de-
crees whiche by nede serue in alle causes/and in alle righ-
tes & droptes/Who wel knewe the scyence of Rethoryque/
he shold knowe the right & the wronge/ffor to do wronge
to another who so doth it/is loste & dampned/& for to do
right & reson to every man / he is saued & geteth the loue
of god his cre-
atour/

Here foloweth
Arsmetryque
& wherof it pro-
cedeth. ca. Cº

O he fourth
scyece is
called arsmetri

Endymion Book 1st

A thing of beauty is a joy for ever:
Its loveliness increases; it will never
Pass into nothingness; but still will keep
A bower quiet for us, and a sleep
Full of sweet dreams, and health, and quiet breathing.

[autograph manuscript of Keats's Endymion]

ninth-century manuscript in a jewelled binding, was an acquisition of the same year, followed in 1903 by William Blake's drawings for the Book of Job and the John Edward Kerr collection of French romances of chivalry.

By this time a new library building was urgently needed. The small basement room in Morgan's house at 219 Madison Avenue, where the treasures were kept, had become so crowded 'that it was difficult to get into it and find anything; books, pictures and manuscripts were piled on the floor, after every table and chair had been filled' (Satterlee). Charles F. McKim was chosen as the architect and the building was completed in 1906 on Thirty-sixth Street next to Morgan's house, with which an underground passage connected it. Mrs John Rylands, envisaging the ideal library as a creation of the Age of Faith, placed her books in a replica of a medieval college; Pierpont Morgan looked for his model to the Italian Renaissance, the age of merchant princes. The façade, of Tennessee marble blocks, was inspired by the Palazzo del Tè in Mantua, with the blocks fitted together in the ancient Greek manner. He was warned '. . . it would cost a small fortune, and no one would see where the additional money went'. 'How much extra?' Morgan asked. 'Fifty thousand dollars,' McKim replied. 'Go ahead.' (Wayne Andrews). Bronze doors led to a domed marble hall; on the left was the West Room, Morgan's study, with red damask walls and a ceiling from a palace in Lucca, in the centre a small librarian's room, on the right the great East Room with books on three levels and a Flemish tapestry of the 'Triumph of Avarice'. It has been justly called 'one of the Seven Wonders of the Edwardian World' (Francis Henry Taylor).

There were all-night meetings in the library during the financial crisis of 1907. On the evening of 2 November the heads of the national banks were assembled in the East Room, Morgan with his advisers was in the librarian's office, in the Study were the presidents of the trust companies. The latter were unhappily debating Morgan's proposal to raise a fund of twenty-five million dollars. At quarter to five in the morning Morgan walked in holding a written agreement and handed a gold pen to their leader. ' "There's the place, King," he said, "and here's the pen." King signed. Then they all signed.' (Frederick Lewis Allen.)

The impetus of Morgan's collecting did not slacken. The disinterred codices of a ninth-century Coptic convent and Lord Amherst's Egyptian and Greek papyri entered the library, so did his fifteen Caxtons, including *The Myrrour of the Worlde* (1481), one of the two first English illustrated books. The manager of the London booksellers J. Pearson & Co. wrote to announce 'a unique Caxton . . . I regard the discovery of this Caxton . . . as the greatest literary and topographical [sic] discovery made in England within living memory.' The book so described (the same letter offered 'the grandest Renaissance binding in the world') was Caxton's Sarum *Horae* (1477), the first English prayerbook and the first English book printed on vellum, otherwise unknown except for a fragment in Oxford. To the Caxton collection was added the only complete copy of Malory's *Morte d'Arthur* (1485) from the Hoe sale of 1911.

Morgan's taste in books was very much the same as that of the aristocratic collectors whose activities were publicised by Dibdin, with an added interest in nineteenth-century literature and in the papyri which had just begun to be discovered in quantity in Egypt. He also pursued two other types of quarry: English and American literary manuscripts, ranging from Pope's *An Essay on Man*, Dickens's *A Christmas Carol* and Wilkie Collins's *The Moonstone* to works by Du Maurier and Hardy bought from the authors; and volumes of royal or famous provenance.

A young Princeton cataloguer recommended by Morgan's nephew, Belle Da Costa Greene, had been engaged as librarian. Miss Greene, whose taste and scholarship later became legendary, was at pains to protect her employer from extravagant demands. She prolonged negotiations for the Gospels of Countess Matilda of Tuscany with the heirs of Sir Thomas Phillipps for seven months until the asking price of £10,000 had come down to £8,000. But when Morgan was in Europe her influence waned. We find her writing in December 1912 that she hears Mr Morgan bought a manuscript Persian bestiary in London in June; where had it been delivered, as she had not yet been able to locate it? An Italian dealer who had complained that she did not answer his letters took advantage of Morgan's presence in Rome to show him a group of books. 'Mr Morgan bought all the 27 wonderful volumes I had the honour of presenting,' he reported to her. 'he liked them enormously and exclaimed more times, in examining

ABOVE *The first edition of the Old Testament in Hebrew, printed by Joshua Salomon in Soncino in 1488.* OPPOSITE *Saul defeating the Ammonites; Saul anointed by Samuel; Sacrifice of peace offerings; from a volume of Old Testament illustrations presented in 1607 by a papal mission to Shah Abbas of Persia: France, thirteenth century.*

Quiter Samuel Saulem que prcreto unxerat coram omni populo ungit in Regem.
et cum summa leticia ipse samuel quam populus sacrificant.

ABOVE *Two elephants from Ibn Baktīshū's* Advantages derived from animals, *in Persian. Maragha (Persia), c. 1295. Bought in London by Pierpont Morgan in June 1912.*

them, "wonderful".' Among them was Cicero, *De Oratore* (Subiaco, before 30 September 1465), the earliest book printed in Italy of which copies have survived.

Pierpont Morgan died in Rome in 1913, leaving the library to his son J.P. Morgan. In 1924 the latter created it a public reference library, vested in trustees, with an endowment for maintenance. The younger Morgan added many important manuscripts to the collection. Thackeray's *The Rose and the Ring* joined all that survives of the manuscript of *Vanity Fair*. Medieval manuscripts were acquired from English owners: the French thirteenth-century *Old Testament Illustrations*, a present from a Polish cardinal to Shah Abbas of Persia, from the Phillipps Trustees; four manuscripts in jewelled bindings, once the property of Weingarten Abbey, for one hundred thousand pounds from the Earl of Leicester; a group of manuscripts from the estate of Sir George Holford and an eighth-century English Psalter from the Marquess of Lothian. Six manuscripts of great beauty were bought at the sale in London in 1919 of Henry Yates Thompson's collection, together with the illuminated vellum copy of a Venetian *Aristotle, 1483*, which the owner had called 'The Most Magnificent Book in the World'. 'I am, personally, *quite* opposed to buying the Aristotle at any such ridiculous sum as £6,000,' Miss Greene wrote acidly, 'but I shall put it up to Mr Morgan ... I should *very* much like a copy of the *book* itself on vellum, but do not particularly care for this "Most Beautiful Copy In The World".'

J.P Morgan died in 1943; Miss Greene retired in 1948. The purchasing value of the endowment was greatly reduced. An era of honourable inactivity seemed to lie ahead. That nothing of the sort occurred was due to the talents and energy of the library's second director, Frederick B. Adams Jnr. He organised an Association of Fellows whose subscriptions and special contributions financed new purchases. Miraculously, in a period of increasing scarcity and export control, he maintained the momentum and quality of accessions. Two of the most important were the Dutch Hours of Catherine of Cleves and the Constance Missal. Whether or not the latter is the earliest printed book, antedating the Gutenberg Bible by two or three years, as some claim, may long be debated; but its acquisition from the Capuchin convent of Romont in Switzerland (of four known copies it is the only one

LEFT *Pentecost, from the Missal of Abbot Berthold of Weingarten. One of four manuscripts in jewelled bindings bought from the Earl of Leicester in 1926. Written in Weingarten in the first quarter of the thirteenth century.* OPPOSITE *Aristotle's* Opera, *printed in Venice in 1483 on vellum and illuminated by a Venetian artist for Petrus Ugelheimer, a German merchant. Henry Yates Thompson, its former owner, called this 'the most magnificent book in the world'.*

Uoniam quide intelli-
gere τ scire cotingit circa omnes sciecias: qua-
rum sut principia cau-
se τ elementa ex horum
cognitione. Tuc enim
opinamur cognoscere
vnuquodqz: qum causas pmas cognoscim':
τ principia prima: τ vsqz ad elementa. Manife-
stum quide quot τ que sunt circa principia scientie q de natura est prius determinare tetandu.

Uoniam dispositio scientie: τ certitudi-
nis in omnibus vijs habetibus principia: τ causas τ elementa: no acquirit nisi
ex cognitione istoru. Credimus eni in vnaquaqz
rerum ipsam scire: qum sciuerimus causas eius
simplices: τ prima principia eius: donec perue-
niamus ad elementa eius. Manifestu est q in scie-
tia naturali etia oportet primo querere determi-
nationem principioru eius.

Lo.s. Incepit hunc libru a causa propter qua fuit cosi-
deratio hui' sciecie in cognitione causaru reru
naturaliu: τ dixit: qm dispositio .i. qa declaratu
est in posteriorib' q dispositio sciecie certe in oibus artib'
demonstratiuis psideratib' de rebus habetibus vna quatuor causaz: aut plures vna: aut omes: no acquirit nisi ex
cognitione causaru. τ no intedebat per scientia τ certitudi-
nem nomina synonyma: qm noia synonyma no vsitant i
doctrina demonstratiua: sed intendebat dispositione sciecie certe τ est sciecia pfecta. Sciecia eni alia est pfecta: τ est
illa que est p causam: alia est impfecta: τ est illa que e sine
causa: τ intedebat p vias artes speculatiuas: q dicunt vie
qa cosiderane in eis vadit a determinatie rebus ad res in
determinatas: τ p res terminatas. τ dixit pncipia: aut causas: aut elementa: qa artiu speculatiuaru aut suaru partiuz
sunt queda q psiderat de reb' simplicib' carentib' pncipijs
τ hec est dispositio sciecie psideratis de primis pncipijs cu
iuslibet entis. τ dixit principia: aut causas: aut elementa: p-
ter diuersitate modozu quor causaz. τ intedebat p pnn-
cipia in hoc loco causas agetes τ mouetes: τ p causas: fines: τ p elementa causas q sut ptes rei .s. materia τ forma
τ q hic vtit hoc noie principiu ppie: τ similit hoc nomie
causa: qa sut nomia synonyma qum vsitent coiter. τ sicut
mihi videt exposuit ipse Alex. τ intedebat Arist. per huc
sermone docere q no oes artes psiderat de omnib' causis:
sed queda psiderat de causa formali tm. τ mathematicis:
queda de trib' causis .s. motore τ forma τ fine: τ est scientia diuina. τ queda de quor causis: τ est sciecia nalis. τ qa

hoc no fuit manifestu in hoc loco: induxit sermone in forma dubitatiois: τ .d. bñtibus principia: aut causas: aut elementa .i. qm ide sequil siue ponat q ille res habeat principia agetia: aut finalia: aut elemetaria: aut oia: τ impossibi-
le est ut hec coiunctio aut sit sicut copulatiua: na dispositio
certe scie inuenit in reb' bñtibus causas quasda p scie-
tia illaru causaru: sicut inuenit in bñtib' oes causas. τ qn
posuit hac ppositione induxit testimoniu ad verificandu
illa: q fere induxit in posteriorib' analecticis: τ .d. credimus eni in vnaquaqz reru τc. τ signu eius qd dixim' q dispositio scie certe de aliq no acquirit nisi ex cognitioe cause cu est: qm ois qui dicit se scire aliqd: no dicit hoc nisi
qn sciuerit illud p suas oes causas ppinquas τ remotas:
τ hoc inuenit in omi qui aliqd scit in veritate: aut fm esti-
matione: τ q in ista ppositione pueniut oes psiderates
adeo q etia sophiste ut dixit in posteriorib'. D.d. qm sciuerimus causas eius simplices: τ intendit ut videt causas
existetes in re primas no copolitas: τ sut prima ma: τ vltima forma. que eni sunt pret prima materia τ vltima forma cuiuslibet reru naliu: sut materie coposite: τ forme coposite. D.d. τ pma principia: τ intedit h ut videt p prima
principia: primas causas q sut extra rem .s. primu ag: ne: τ
vltimu fine omniu reru. D.d. donec pueniam ad elementa eius: τ intedit h p elementa causas existetes in re propin-
quas τ essentiales. τ innuit p hoc qd dixit: q doctrina or-
dinata est incipe a cognitione causaru primaru rei cogno-
scende pfecte. Deinde intedere ad cognitione aliaru causa-
rum remotaru fm ordine: donec pueniat ad causas ppinquas: τ fm hoc h hoc noie causa: τ elementi alio mo
ab eo q vsus est illic pus fm suu more in habedo modica
sollicitudine de nominib'. τ qum posuit hac maiore ppositione in hoc sermone .s. vicente q sciecia certa de rebus
habetibus causas τ elementa no acquirit nisi ex cognitioe
causaru τ elementozu eoru: dimisit minore ppositione: τ
induxit coclusione qua intedit p huc sermone: τ dixit ma-
nifestum est q in sciecia nali τc.i. manifestu est: qm ex hoc
sequif q qui vult largiri scientia de natura oportet ipsum
pius querere determinatione causaru reru naliu habe-
tium causas τ elementa. τ iste sermo coponif sic: oia nalia
habent causas τ elementa: τ oia habeia causas τ elementa
no sciunt nisi ex cognitione causaru τ elementozu: g oñia
nalia no sciunt nisi ex cognitione suaru caru τ elementoz.

Innata est aute via ex notiorib' nobis τ certioribus incertiora nature τ notiora: no enim sut
eadem nobis nota τ simpliciter. vnde quide ne-
cesse est fm hunc modu pcedere ex incertiorib'
nature: nobis aute certioribus incertiora nature τ notiora.

Et via ad illa est de rebus notioribus τ ma

not in a Continental public library) has been an outstanding service to American bibliographical scholarship.

It is part of the library's unique attraction that it has resisted the temptation of growth for its own sake. Although it owns so many famous and magnificent volumes, it is still not much larger than Lord Spencer's collection in 1836 and retains the easy atmosphere of a private house where the books are to be enjoyed as much as studied. As a focus of bibliophilic taste and scholarship its influence has been incalculable and continues to grow.

BELOW *The Constance Missal. Some experts consider that it was printed by Gutenberg c. 1450; others believe it to be the product of a Basle press of as late as 1471.* RIGHT *The East Room. The frescoes are by Harry Siddons Mowbray; the bronze Cupid is Hellenistic: the sixteenth-century tapestry is Flemish and represents the Triumph of Avarice.*

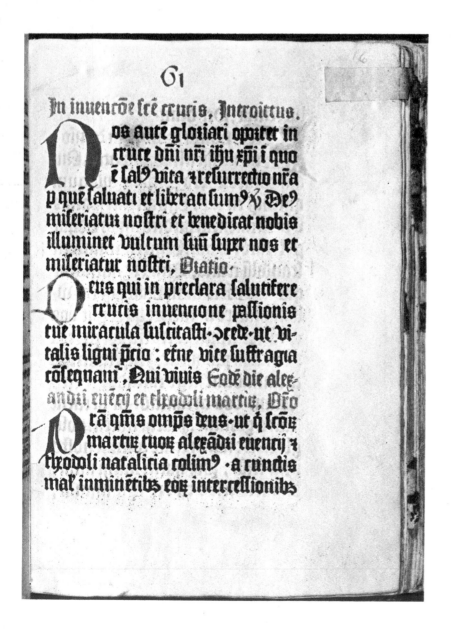

Henry E Huntington Library

SAN MARINO CALIFORNIA

Henry Edwards Huntington. OPPOSITE *Palms, fountains and statues in the gardens of the Huntington mansion.*

In 1905 a certain William D'Alton Mann produced a book called *Fads and Fancies of Representative Americans.* Among the rich and eminent flatteringly described was a fifty-five-year-old business-man who had made a fortune in the development of California, Henry Edwards Huntington. After observing that he was a director of forty corporations – thirteen railway companies, the remainder divided amongst banking, express, land, lumber, coal and iron, copper, steamship, shipbuilding and so on – William Mann continued, 'He is a great reader of books, and in his personal and social relations with men he is fun-loving and a good deal of a joker with specially intimate friends.' There was no further mention of a library.

Twenty years later Huntington was admitted to hospital in Philadelphia for an emergency operation. Duveen and Rosen-bach, the two dealers who dominated the market for works of art and rare books respectively, hurried to his bedside. Seeing their anxious faces, the millionaire is said to have asked, 'Do I remind you of anyone? . . . Jesus Christ on the Cross between the two thieves.' Between these two incidents, Huntington's progress had been meteoric.

Three phases can be discerned. By 1909 he had assembled a large but commonplace collection of literature, Kelmscott Press books and illustrations by Alken, Rowlandson and Cruikshank, his first major appearance on the bibliophilic stage being at the Henry W. Poor sales of 1908–9 where he bought 1,600 lots. The second phase was marked by the decision to limit himself to 'the history and literature of the English-speaking peoples', in manuscripts, or in first or early editions. His business experience in an age of vast takeovers and mergers had given him a propen-sity for grandiose, lavish and decisive action. These methods were now to be applied to his hobby.

The library of Elihu Dwight Church of Brooklyn was the first trophy of the new policy; bought in 1911 for a million dollars, it contained twelve Shakespeare folios, thirty-seven quartos, the first editions of *Lucrece, Love's Martyr* (one of two copies known) and the *Sonnets,* the unique copy of the first American collection of

laws (*The Generall Lawes of the Massachusetts*, 1648) and the autograph manuscript of Benjamin Franklin's *Autobiography*. Two weeks later took place in New York the first of four sales of Robert Hoe's library, the finest in the United States at that time. George D. Smith, bidding for Huntington, secured 5,500 lots totalling over one million dollars, headed by the Gutenberg Bible on vellum ($50,000, a record price; before Hoe owned it, it had belonged to the Earl of Ashburnham, and earlier had 'disappeared' from Mainz University during the Napoleonic Wars). But at the sale Huntington lost Malory's *Morte d'Arthur* (Caxton 1485) to Morgan at $42,800 and the unique *Helyas Knight of the Swanne* to Mrs McCormick at $21,000. The following year he bought Beverly Chew's collection of English poetry, 1,600 volumes for $500,000; in 1913 the Washington letters and documents of Grenville Kane, one for each year of the statesman's adult life; soon after, the Lincolniana of Ward Hill Lamon, once the President's law-partner in Illinois.

By now American sources alone were unable to satisfy the collector's appetite. His next acquisitions were from the Duke of Devonshire, the Chatsworth Caxtons, twenty-five in number, and the Kemble plays – over 7,500, including one of two surviving copies of *Hamlet*, 1603, and 111 volumes of play-bills. In 1915 he bought, this time in the United States, Frederick Robert Halsey's English and American literature. Two years later Sir Montague Barlow of Sotheby's sold him (through G.D. Smith, Huntington's invariable agent) the Earl of Ellesmere's Bridgewater House library, founded by Sir Thomas Egerton, Queen Elizabeth I's Lord Keeper and James I's Lord Chancellor. Extremely rich in English books of the sixteenth and seventeenth century, with presentation copies of Chapman, Marston and Captain John Smith, it also included twelve thousand manuscripts, of which the most famous was the illuminated Ellesmere Chaucer, and the manuscript plays accumulated by John Larpent, the Lord Chamberlain's censor from 1778 to 1824.

Collecting on such a scale caused dismay and some sharp comment in rare book circles. E.H. Dring (of Quaritch's) to an American librarian, 5 December 1916: 'I hear to-day that Mr Huntington has bought the Britwell Americana from G.D. Smith. I can hardly credit it.' American librarian to E.H. Dring, 24 December 1916:

You have evidently forgotten that I told you when I was in London, that Smith bought the Britwell because he heard of the numerous commissions Huntington had given. Had I been H's librarian, I should have resigned at once when he took over the entire collection; the really amusing part is that he is re-selling over eighty per cent of it at the Anderson Auction Company here in January. He has lost all standing in *every* one's eyes here as a *collector* . . .

This exchange introduces the series of sales of the incomparable library of English literature and works on American travel from Britwell Court, Buckinghamshire, held at Sotheby's from 1916 to 1927. The first section Huntington bought complete before the auction. Before the next section was offered George D. Smith had

ABOVE *William Caxton presenting a book to Margaret of York, Duchess of Burgundy. A unique engraving in the Chatsworth copy of Lefèvre's* Recuyell of the historyes of Troye, *printed in Bruges by Caxton and Colard Mansion in 1475 – the first printed book in English.* OPPOSITE *The travelling library of Sir Thomas Egerton, Lord Ellesmere, Lord Chancellor, 1615. Forty-four volumes in a special box. The list of contents is divided into Theologians; Philosophers; Historians and Poets.*

For it is ernest to me by my feith
That feele I wel what that any man seith
And yet for al my smert and al my grief
For al my sorwe labour and meschief
I koude neuere leue it in no wise
Now wolde god my wit myghte suffise
To tellen al that longeth to that art
And nathelees yow wol I tellen part
Syn that my lord is goon I wol nat spare
Swich thyng as that I knowe I wol declare

¶ Heere endeth the prologe of the Chanons yemannes tale

¶ Heere bigynneth the Chanons yeman his tale

With this Chanon I dwelt haue seuen yeer
And of his science am I neuer the neer
Al that I hadde I haue lost ther by
And god woot so hath many mo than I
Ther I was wont to be right fressh and gay
Of clothyng and of oother good array
Now may I were an hose vp on myn heed
And wher my colour was bothe fressh and reed
Now is it wan and of a leden hewe
Who so it vseth soore shal he rewe
And of my swynk yet blered is myn eye
Lo which auantage is to multiplie
That slidynge science hath me maad so bare
That I haue no good wher that euere I fare
And yet I am endetted so ther by
Of gold that I haue borwed trewely
That whil I lyue I shal it quite neuere
Lat euery man be war by me for euere
What maner man that casteth hym ther to
If he continue I holde his thrift y do
For so help me god ther by shal he nat wynne
But empte his purs and make hise wittes thynne
And whan he thurgh his madnesse and folye
Hath lost his owene good thurgh iupartie
Thanne he exciteth oother folk ther to
To lesen hir good as he hym self hath do
For vn to shrewes ioye it is and ese
To haue hir felawes in peyne and disese
Thus was I ones lerned of a clerk
Of that no charge I wol speke of oure werk
Whan we been there as we shul exercise
Oure eluysshe craft we semen wonder wise

died and Dr Rosenbach had moved in to secure Huntington's custom. Subsequent Britwell sales were dominated by Rosenbach bidding mainly for his chief client. Having failed to obtain the second section privately, he bought five-sixths of the sale, over three-quarters of the third sale, five-sixths of the fourth. The latter included a book modestly catalogued as Philip Pain's *Daily Meditations; or Quotidian Preparations for and Considerations of Death and Eternity*, Cambridge 1668. Rosenbach recognised that the place of printing was not Cambridge, England, but Cambridge, Massachusetts, and the insignificant octavo was the unique copy of the first volume of verse printed in New England. He bought it, and passed it on to Huntington at the purchase price of fifteen pounds, plus ten per cent commission.

The 1920s saw the addition of Americana in large numbers, and of 5,400 incunabula acquired in large blocks from Rosenbach or a German dealer, Otto Vollbehr – the highest total of any American library at that date, though exceeded since by the Library of Congress. They also witnessed the third phase of the collector's development: the acquisition for their research value of British muniments and family papers – the papers of James Campbell, fourth Earl of Loudoun, Commander-in-Chief in America from 1756 to 1758, those of his successor in the American command, General James Abercromby, the cartulary and muniments of Battle Abbey (bought with twenty English medieval manuscripts from Rosenbach for $32,000 cash and sixty first mortgage bonds of the Safety Insulated Wire and Cable Company), the Hastings family papers (mostly from Leicestershire), and those of the Temple, Grenville and Brydges families (originally at Stowe in Buckinghamshire). Huntington is estimated to have spent twelve million dollars on his library – probably below the real figure, as *The New York Times* reported in 1917 that he had already spent six million, and his bills from Rosenbach alone after that date totalled $4,333,610.

From about 1915 all purchases were sent to Huntington's house in New York, where a staff of twelve headed by George Watson Cole (who had compiled the Elihu Church catalogue) tried to find space for themselves and essential reference books in a former billiards-room and worked against time to keep up a card index and sort out duplicates. The latter were discarded in fifteen auctions, but the hectic pace made mistakes inevitable, such as the sale of the copy of Milton's *Comus*, 1637, which had belonged to John Egerton who played the elder brother when the masque was first performed at Ludlow Castle on Michaelmas night 1634. From the catalogue-room special rarities went up to the library on the first floor, a long room lined with bronze bookcases, with a double desk for the collector and his secretary, Charles II armchairs and a safe containing the Gutenberg Bible, Ellesmere Chaucer, Franklin autobiography and Shakespeare Folios.

The remaining books were repacked for dispatch to San Marino. This was a 550-acre property eleven miles from Los Angeles (though now engulfed in that vast conurbation), which Huntington had bought in 1902. Here, in a Louis Seize mansion

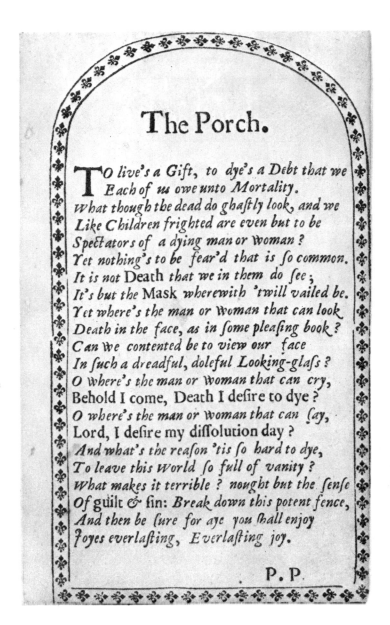

The Porch.

To live's a Gift, to dye's a Debt that we
Each of us owe unto Mortality.
What though the dead do ghastly look, and we
Like Children frighted are even but to be
Spectators of a dying man or woman?
Yet nothing's to be fear'd that is so common.
It is not Death that we in them do see;
It's but the Mask wherewith 'twill vailed be.
Yet where's the man or woman that can look
Death in the face, as in some pleasing book?
Can we contented be to view our face
In such a dreadful, doleful Looking-glass?
O where's the man or woman that can cry,
Behold I come, Death I desire to dye?
O where's the man or woman that can say,
Lord, I desire my dissolution day?
And what's the reason 'tis so hard to dye,
To leave this World so full of vanity?
What makes it terrible? nought but the sense
Of guilt & sin: Break down this potent fence,
And then be sure for aye you shall enjoy
Joyes everlasting, Everlasting joy.

P.P.

OPPOSITE *The Canon's Yeoman; from the Ellesmere manuscript of Chaucer's* Canterbury Tales: *late fourteenth century.* ABOVE *Philip Pain's* Daily Meditations, *printed in Cambridge, Massachusetts in 1668. The unique copy of the first volume of verse printed in New England.*

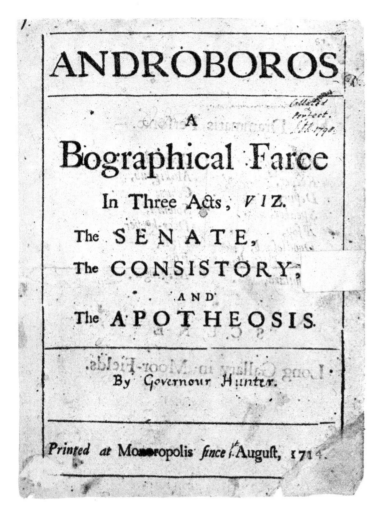

Androboros, *by Richard Hunter, Governor of Virginia; printed in New York, 1714. The unique copy of the first play printed in America.*

full of French furniture and English pictures, at the centre of a park with statues and vistas, palms, avocados and cycads, a Japanese garden and eight acres of exotic succulents, his life was surrounded by that magnificence which millionaires fifty years ago could still enjoy unabashed. A colonnaded building to hold the books was completed beside the mansion in 1923, and in this the library was at last assembled.

Huntington's own papers have not been made available to a biographer, and behind the pious references to 'the Founder' his personality remains elusive. Tall, broad-chested and with a white moustache, his appearance in photographs is part military, part avuncular. His ability in business was of course outstanding. 'Will take one hundred eighty-five items not in my collection banks closed to-day will cable forty-two thousand pounds Tuesday.' This was the sort of cable he sent. His passion for books was sincere and intense, and he normally read and marked all catalogues himself. But in spite of his interest in English history, he did not care for foreign travel and visited England only once. Apart from incunabula and Spanish-American documents, only books in English were admitted into the collection; even the Continental books in the Bridgewater library were discarded. His own education ended at sixteen and he is said to have observed wistfully at the end of his negotiations with Beverly Chew that he would double the price if he could acquire Chew's knowledge with his books; but in practice he resented the requirements of research, grudging money for works of reference and obliging his cataloguers to economise by writing collations on the backs of used envelopes.

His last care was to plan a mausoleum in the park where his body might lie beside his second wife, a remarkable lady previously married to his uncle. He died in 1927. The library, which had already been vested in trustees, then comprised 175,000 printed books and two million documents and other manuscripts, 6,500 American imprints earlier than 1800, and eleven thousand English books printed before 1641 including twenty-nine Shakespeare folios and seventy-three quartos, among them the first edition of every play except *Pericles* and *Titus Andronicus*. The incunabula, shelved together in a single vault, many of them copies from central European abbeys in medieval bindings, others bound in eighteenth-century morocco from the aristocratic libraries of France and England, are unforgettably impressive.

'Acquisitions were made so rapidly,' the first number of the *Huntington Library Bulletin* acknowledged in 1931, 'that when the period of tremendous purchases came abruptly to a close, no member of the staff could hope to have more than a confused impression of the total contents.' The first twenty years after the founder's death were spent in equipping the library to serve as the great research institution it now is. Since then a policy has been followed of adding English text manuscripts, modern literature and Continental books. The present holdings are five hundred thousand volumes, of which about half may be classed as rare books. There have been many agreeable discoveries: the Library proves to own the autograph manuscript of the *Polychronicon* of Ranulph Higden, a fourteenth-century monk of Chester, and a manuscript of Richard Rolle's *The Pricke of Conscience* marked up for a printed edition, the unique copy of which is also at San Marino. Huntington's foundation of the first great assemblage of rare books on the American west coast had another happy result. William A. Jackson, the chief architect of Harvard's rare books collection (see p. 199), grew up in the next town and as a boy used to mow George Watson Cole's lawns. Dr Cole gave him the entrée to the collections, then in full spate, a chance that certainly provided a powerful inspiration, and was perhaps the decisive influence in Jackson's choice of a librarian's career.

Possibly the first illustration of a pineapple: from the autograph manuscript of Gonzalo Hernández de Oviedo's Natural History of the Indies, *c. 1539–48.* BELOW *The Huntington Library.*

on the television screen, and drawing a deep
~~then occasion deep breath~~ breath of the
new perfume smiled in infantile ecstasy.
"Pope," she ~~whispered~~ murmured distractedly "oh, so
like it... when you ..." She closed her
eyes & sighing leaned back on the pillows.

~~Pope~~

~~He had ~~that~~ the remembrance ~~out~~ that~~

~~Linda had flung open~~

"Linda," ~~he whispered~~ the savage spoke imploringly. "Don't you
know me?" He had ~~start~~ tried ~~back these~~ hateful
tried hard, had done his best; why ~~would~~ ~~not~~ she allow him
memories ~~latin she~~ ~~should not~~ allow him
to forget? He squeezed her limp hand almost with
violence, as though he would force her
to come back from this ~~odious~~ dream
of ignoble pleasures, from these hateful memories of
~~a hateful past~~ back into the present, ~~the~~
~~the awful~~ ~~significant~~ appalling ~~but~~ and
~~sublime reality~~ back into reality:
the appalling present, the awful reality,
but sublime, but significant, but
desperately important precisely because so fearful
of the imminence of that which made them so fearful
of ~~their fearfulness~~. "Don't you know me, Linda?"
~~he~~ ~~Linda?~~
He felt ~~on~~ the faint answering pressure
of her hand. Her lips moved. "Pope," she
whispered again, and it was ~~like~~ ~~he had a~~
& it was as though ~~also~~ he had ~~received~~
pail-full of ordure thrown in his face.

University Library

AUSTIN TEXAS

The most prominent person at Sotheby's sale of nineteenth- and twentieth-century literature on the morning of 8 November 1960 was a New York bookseller, making his third appearance in the London auction-rooms. He was not conspicuous because of his appearance (which hinted at disguise: dark glasses, black rain-coat buttoned to the chin – later explained as the result of over-sleeping; below the raincoat was nothing but a pyjama top) nor from the way he bid, but from the amount he was willing to pay and from his habit of buying every lot he bid for. That day he bought 173 letters of Robert Southey for £1,950, five of Oscar Wilde for £220 and the autograph manuscript of D. H. Lawrence's *Etruscan Places* for £2,000. It was by now generally known that in making these purchases he was acting for the University of Texas, which was engaged in a programme of acquisition such as had not been seen in the USA since Henry E. Huntington's death. The previous June, after buying half the total value of a sale at Sotheby's, including every lot of a T.E. Lawrence collection, he had secured the major part of a charity sale held at Christie's to raise funds for the London Library, notably the manuscript of E.M. Forster's *A Passage to India* for £6,500.

The following May he bought over sixty per cent of the next sale of modern literature, letters of the Pre-Raphaelites, Shaw, Yeats and D.H. Lawrence, manuscripts of Swinburne, Whitman, Edward Johnston the calligrapher, Maurice Baring and Stephen Spender. Edith Sitwell's manuscripts and notebooks were acquired in three later sales for £17,928, Graham Greene's for £14,550. Apart from these purchases at auction, an even larger quantity of material had been bought privately, in many cases directly from the author: J.B. Priestley, David Garnett, Robert Graves, Compton Mackenzie, C.P. Snow, Stephen Spender, A.A. Milne, A.P. Herbert, Hugh Walpole and John Lehmann; while in America the papers of Christopher Morley and Joseph Hergesheimer, and the Sinclair Lewis collection belonging to his first wife were bought, and those of Tennessee Williams given. Acquisitions on this scale affected the whole market. Prices rose sharply (the £6,500 paid for *A Passage to India* was nearly three

ABOVE *Dr Harry H. Ransom.* OPPOSITE *Aldous Huxley's* Brave New World. *The author's type-script with manuscript insertions.*

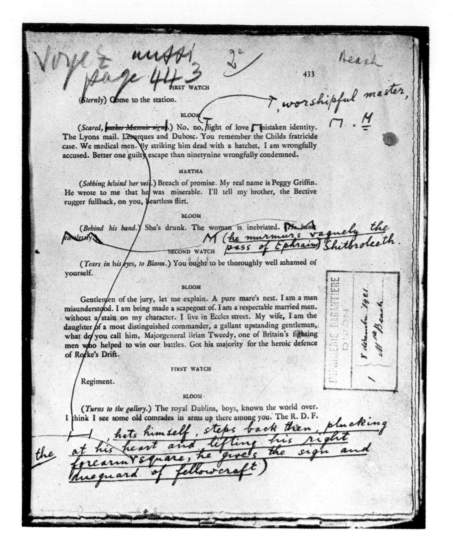

ABOVE LEFT *James Joyce's* Ulysses: *page proof with autograph corrections.* ABOVE RIGHT *T.E. Lawrence's* The Arab Revolt; *the earliest surviving draft, c. 1921, of* The Seven Pillars of Wisdom. BELOW LEFT *D.H. Lawrence's* Sons and Lovers, *the autograph manuscript titled 'Paul Morel'.* BELOW RIGHT *Somerset Maugham's* Cakes and Ale, *the autograph manuscript.*

times the previous English record for a modern manuscript) and other institutions were concerned that all recent literary material might escape them. The Arts Council set up a special fund to acquire living poets' notebooks, the British Museum was happy to pay £5,000 for the manuscript of Virginia Woolf's *Mrs Dalloway*, and the Bibliothèque Nationale intervened to prevent the export of the great Proust collection belonging to the writer's niece. Authors, who were the chief beneficiaries of the process, regarded it more benevolently.

The best American universities [Cyril Connolly wrote] will not only pay for what an author has written but what he has tried to throw away; his note-books, correspondence, false starts; they will sort it all out for him and accept material which is never to be shown and provide him with copies and even resident facilities for writing his autobiography.... He can look the milkman in the eye. It is probably the best thing that has happened to writers for many years.

The man responsible for this huge programme of acquisition was a former member of the English department, at the time holding the office of Dean of the College of Arts and Sciences, later President of the University, Harry H. Ransom. By 1956 he had become convinced of the advantage to undergraduate and graduate students of a research collection of original manuscripts. The University Library at that time had strong holdings on Texas history and Latin America. Its English literature was based on the collections of George A. Aitken, a specialist in the eighteenth century, and of a Chicago businessman, John Henry Wrenn, both acquired soon after the First World War. The latter had suffered a disastrous loss of prestige when it was discovered that Wrenn had been the chief dupe of Thomas J. Wise and owned most of his forgeries and several Stuart plays which Wise had completed with leaves stolen from the British Museum copies. Ransom decided that while opportunities of building on the earlier holdings should be taken whenever possible, the main effort would have to be in a new field, where competition was less intense and it was possible to achieve a pre-eminent position – the twentieth century in England and America. This is an area, Dr Ransom considers, 'in which several disciplines interact, particularly literature and science', and so of special value to the University. He won over the President, Logan Wilson, and persuaded the State legislators to vote the necessary funds. By the autumn of 1956 the programme was ready to take off.

Two years later a single coup raised the collection to the level of international importance; this was the purchase of the major part of the library formed over thirty years by T.E. Hanley of Pennsylvania, particularly rich in D.H. and T.E. Lawrence, Shaw, Eliot, Pound, Joyce, Yeats and Dylan Thomas. At an early stage Ransom had set himself the goal (based on the needs of one English course) of acquiring the manuscripts of Conrad's *Victory*, *A Passage to India* and Aldous Huxley's *Brave New World*. By 1964 all three were at Austin and an exhibition of that year, *A Creative Century*, read like a roll-call on Parnassus. Here were the manuscripts or the author's corrected typescripts of Shaw's

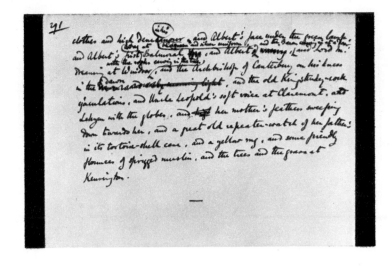

ABOVE *Lytton Strachey's* Queen Victoria, *the last page of the autograph manuscript.* BELOW *E.M. Forster's* Passage to India, *the autograph manuscript.*

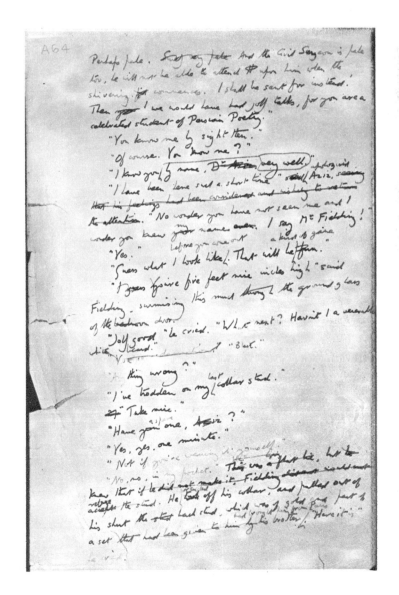

LEFT *Edith Sitwell, by Paul Tchelitchew.* ABOVE RIGHT *Max Beerbohm's Edwardian Parade, from his house at Rapallo. Left to right: Edward VII; unidentified; Joseph Chamberlain; Henry James; Lord Rosebery; Reggie Turner; Andrew Pinero; William Rothenstein; George Moore; Rudyard Kipling; Lord Burnham; Winston Churchill.* BELOW *The Humanities Research Centre, Texas University.*

Pygmalion, Auden's *The Age of Anxiety,* Beckett's *Waiting for Godot,* Norman Douglas's *Looking Back,* Conan Doyle's *A Scandal in Bohemia,* T.S. Eliot's *The Dry Salvages,* Faulkner's *Absalom, Absalom!,* Graham Greene's *The Power and the Glory,* Hemingway's *Death in the Afternoon,* D.H. Lawrence's *Sons and Lovers,* the earliest surviving draft of T.E. Lawrence's *The Seven Pillars of Wisdom,* Sinclair Lewis's *Arrowsmith,* Somerset Maugham's *Cakes and Ale,* Arthur Miller's *Death of a Salesman,* Lytton Strachey's *Queen Victoria,* Oscar Wilde's *Lady Windermere's Fan,* and much else – for example Colin Wilson's correspondence with T.S. Eliot about *The Outsider.* These visible witnesses of the great creative writers of the century at work are accompanied by a display of literary portraits, supported by a vast archive of printed books, letters and related material, and housed in spacious comfort in a handsome limestone building, completed in 1960, with colonnaded walks around the ground and top floors reminiscent of a Roman villa of the later Empire.

Texas is like an active volcano; it is impossible to tell in which direction it will erupt next. The whole of Evelyn Waugh's library, shelves, furniture and all, has recently been transported to Austin. There have been great additions in the field of scientific history – two large collections, one American, the other from Munich, the papers of Sir William Herschel (1738–1822), the astronomer, and his son, Sir John, and the Gernsheim photographic archive. An extension backwards in time has netted a poetical commonplace book of Robert Herrick, the Brudenell manuscript of *The Canterbury Tales,* a fourteenth-century codex of Dante and the first printed edition (Foligno 1474), an eleventh-century compendium of astronomical texts written by an abbot of Tegernsee, and much else besides. But these older trophies, splendid though they may be, are peripheral to the library's main strength. It is on the great twentieth-century archive that its lasting reputation will be based. Texas's collections are not restricted to the members of the University but are open to all scholars, and future biographers and literary historians are likely to travel to Austin as inevitably as students of Balzac now visit Chantilly.

FURTHER READING

CAPITULAR LIBRARY, VERONA

G.B. Carlo Conte Giulari, *La Capitolare Biblioteca di Verona*, Verona 1888.

A. Spagnolo, *Le scuole accolitali in Verona*, Verona 1904.

R. Sabbadini, *Le scoperte dei codici latini e greci ne' secoli XIV e XV*, 2 vols, 1905–14.

G. Ongaro, *Coltura e scuola calligrafica veronese del secolo X*, Venice 1925.

Teresa Venturini, *Ricerche paleografiche intorno all' arcidiacono Pacifico*, Verona 1929.

E.A. Lowe, *Codices Latini antiquiores*, Oxford 1934, etc, Vol. IV.

Augusto Campana, "Veronensia," in 'Miscellanea Giovanni Mercati', Vol. II, *Studi e Testi*, No. 122, Città del Vaticano 1946.

Giuseppe Billanovich, 'Petrarch and the textual tradition of Livy,' *Journal of the Warburg and Courtauld Institutes*, XIV (1951), 137–208.

Giuseppe Billanovich, 'Dal Livio di Raterio al Livio di Petrarca,' *Italia medioevale e umanistica*, II (1959), 103–178.

Giuseppe Turrini, *La Biblioteca Capitolare di Verona*, English and Italian editions, Verona 1962: reprinted in *Italia medioevale e umanistica*, V (1962), 401–423; reprinted with illustrations under the title *Millennium scriptorii veronensis*, Verona 1967.

Giuseppe Turrini, *Indice dei codici capitolari di Verona redatto nel 1625 dal Canonico Agostino Rezzani*, Verona 1965.

Delisle's letter is in the Bibliothèque Nationale, Paris, ms.n.acq.fr.13033, 105–106.

ABBEY LIBRARY, ST GALL

The literature on the St Gall library is enormous: a comprehensive bibliography is given by Duft and Meyer (see below). The following are some of the most useful works.

F. Weidmann, *Geschichte der Bibliothek von St Gallen*, St Gallen 1841.

G. Scherrer, *Verzeichnis der Handschriften der Stiftsbibliothek von St Gallen*, Halle 1875; *Verzeichnis der Incunabeln der Stiftsbibliothek von St Gallen*, St Gallen 1880.

J.E. Sandys, *A History of Classical Scholarship*, 1908, Vol. I.

Paul Lehmann, *Mittelalterliche Bibliothekskataloge Deutschlands und der Schweiz*, Munich 1918, I, 55–146.

Adolf Merton, *Die Buchmalerei in St Gallen*, 2nd edn, Leipzig 1923.

J.M. Clark, *The Abbey of St Gall as a Centre of Literature and Art*, Cambridge 1926, Vol. VII.

E.A. Lowe, *Codices Latini antiquiores*, Oxford 1934 etc, Vol. VII.

A. Bruckner, *Scriptoria medii aevi Helvetica*, Geneva 1936–8, Vols II, III.

Johannes Duft and Peter Meyer, *The Irish Miniatures in the Abbey Library of St Gall*, Berne and Lausanne 1954.

Alfred A. Schmid, *Die Buchmalerei des XVI. Jahrhunderts in der Schweiz*, Olten 1954.

The translation, on p. 27, of the poem in the Irish Priscian (cod. 904) is by Professor Myles Dillon in *The Celtic Realms* by M. Dillon and Nora Chadwick (London: Weidenfeld and Nicolson, 1967), p. 233.

Gall Kemly's woodcuts were removed from his books by the St Gall librarian Fr Ildephons von Arx in 1824 and bound together in a volume. All were described and reproduced by a later librarian, A. Fäh, in Paul Heitz, *Einblattdrucke des fünfzehnten Jahrhunderts*, Vol. III, 1906. In 1930 the Stiftsbibliothek sold the collection for 150,000 Swiss francs (about £7,500) to the firm of Hollstein and Puppel, who offered them for sale by auction in Berlin on 7 November 1930. The catalogue describes forty-one as *unica*. Although the British Museum and the city of Basle were among the purchasers, the sale was not a success and most lots appear to have been bought back by the auctioneers.

STATE LIBRARY, BAMBERG

P. Ruf, *Mittelalterliche Bibliothekskataloge Deutschlands und der Schweiz*, Vol. III, p. 3, Munich 1939.

Hans Fischer, *Die Königliche Bibliothek in Bamberg und ihre Handschriften* in *Zentralblatt für Bibliothekswesen*, Jahrg. 24, 1907.

E.A. Lowe, *The Beneventan Script*, Oxford 1914.

Paul Lehmann, 'Die Institutio oratoria des Quintilianus im Mittelalte,' in *Philologus*, 89, 1934.

Arthur Allgeier, 'Das Psalmenbuch des Konstanzer Bischofs Salomon III in Bamberg,' in *Jahresbericht der Görres-Gesellschaft 1938*, Cologne 1939.

H. Weber, 'Geschichte der gelehrten Schulen im Hochstift Bamberg,' in *Berichte des historischen Vereins Bamberg*, 42, 1879.

F. Leitschuh and H. Fischer, *Katalog der Handschriften der K. Bibliothek zu Bamberg*, 3 vols, Bamberg, Leipzig 1887–1912.

ABBEY LIBRARY, ADMONT

P. Jakob Wichner, O.S.B., *Geschichte des Benediktiner-Stiftes Admont*, 4 vols, Graz 1876–80.

P. Jacob Wichner, O.S.B., *Kloster Admont in Steiermark und seine Beziehungen zur Kunst*, Vienna 1888.

P. Jakob Wichner, O.S.B., 'Zwei Bücherverzeichnisse des 14. Jahrhunderts in der Admonter Stiftsbibliothek,' *Zentralblatt für Bibliothekswesen*, Beiheft 4, 1889.

F. Wickoff and M. Dvořák, *Beschreibendes Verzeichnis der illuminierten Handschriften in Österreich: IV, Die illuminierten Handschriften in Steiermark: I. Teil, Die Stiftsbibliotheken zu Admont und Vorau von Paul Buberl*, Leipzig 1911.

Dr Adalbert Krause, O.S.B., *Die Stiftsbibliothek in Admont*, Linz n.d.

E. van K. Dobbie, *The Manuscripts of Caedmon's Hymn and Bede's Death Song*, New York 1937 (for the St Gall and Admont MSS).

The library's catalogue of manuscripts is available on microfilm from University Microfilms Ltd.

DURHAM CATHEDRAL LIBRARY

Catalogi veteres librorum ecclesiae cathedralis Dunelm. Catalogues of the library of Durham Cathedral at various periods, from the Conquest to the Dissolution, Surtees Society Publications, Newcastle 1838, No. 7.

C.H. Turner, 'The Earliest List of Durham MSS,' *Journal of Theological Studies*, XIX (1918), 121–132.

H.D. Hughes, *A History of Durham Cathedral Library*, Durham 1925.

E.A. Lowe, *English Uncial*, Oxford: Clarendon Press, 1960.

N.R. Ker, *Medieval Libraries of Great Britain*, 2nd ed., London 1964.

P.S. Allen, 'Bishop Shirwood of Durham and his Library,' *English Historical Review*, XXV (1910), 445–56.

The quotation from Humfrey Wanley on p. 59 is from *The Diary of Humphrey Wanley 1715–1726* by C.E. and Ruth C. Wright, London: Council of the Bibliographical Society, 1966 II, 227. The quotations on p. 57 are from N.R. Ker, *English Manuscripts in the Century after the Norman Conquest*, Oxford 1960; by permission of the Clarendon Press. The quotation on p. 55 is from R.A.B. Mynors, *Durham Cathedral Manuscripts*, 1939; by permission of the Dean and Chapter of Durham and the Clarendon Press, Oxford.

MONASTERY OF ST JOHN, PATMOS

Richard Pococke, *A Description of the East*, London 1745, II, 2, p. 31.

E.D. Clarke, *Travels in Various Countries of Europe, Asia and Africa*, London 1810–23.

I. Sakkelion, *Patmiake Bibliotheke*, Athens 1890.

Charles Diehl, 'Le trésor et la bibliothèque de Patmos au commencement du 13e siècle,' *Byzantinische Zeitschrift*, I (1892), 488–525.

Giovanni Mercati, 'Per la storia dei manoscritti greci,' *Studi e Testi*, No. 68, Città del Vaticano 1935.

D.J. Geanakoplos, *Byzantine East and Latin West*, Oxford: B.H. Blackwell Ltd, 1966 (for Margounios).

The Institute of Byzantine Studies, Athens, is preparing a revised edition of the library catalogue.

BIBLIOTECA MALATESTIANA, CESENA

R. Zazzeri, *Sui codici e libri a stampa della Biblioteca Malatestiana*, Cesena 1887.

A. Campana, 'Le biblioteche della provincia di Forlì,' *Tesori delle biblioteche d'Italia: Emilia e Romagna*, Milan 1932.

D. Fava, 'La biblioteca di Pio VII,' *Accademie e Biblioteche d'Italia*, Anno 16, Rome 1942.

D. Fava, 'La biblioteca Malatestiana nei cinque secoli della sua storia,' *Accademie e Biblioteche d'Italia*, Rome 1952.

A. Campana, 'Origine fondazione e vicende della Malatestiana,' *Accademie e Biblioteche d'Italia*, Rome 1953.

A. Domeniconi, 'Ser Giovanni da Epinal,' *Studi Romagnoli*, X, Faenza 1959.

A. Domeniconi, *La Biblioteca Malatestiana*, Udine 1962.

THE VATICAN LIBRARY

Eugène Müntz and Paul Fabre, *La bibliothèque du Vatican au XVe siècle*, 1887.

Eugène Müntz, *Les arts à la cour des papes*, 1882.

Eugène Müntz, *La bibliothèque du Vatican au XVIe siècle*, 1886.

P. Batiffol, *La Vaticane de Paul III à Paul IV*, 1890.

Pierre de Nolhac, *La bibliothèque de Fulvio Orsini*, 1887.

Isidoro Carini, *La Biblioteca Vaticana*, 1892.

E. Tisserand, 'Bibliothèques pontificales,' *Recueil Cardinal Eugène Tisserand*, Louvain, n.d.

E. Tisserand and E.W. Koch, *The Vatican Library*, Jersey City 1929.

Studi e Testi (a series published in the Vatican City and devoted to discoveries in the library).

Léopold Delisle in *Journal des Savants*, juillet-août 1892.

BIBLIOTECA MEDICEO-LAURENZIANA, FLORENCE

Fortunato Pintor, 'Per la storia della libreria Medicea nel Rinascimento,' *Italia medioevale e umanistica*, III (1960).

E. Piccolomini, 'Delle condizioni e delle vicende della Libreria Medicea privata dal 1494 al 1508,' *Archivio storico italiano*, Ser. 3, XIX–XXI (1874–5).

C.S. Gutkind, *Cosimo de' Medici*, Oxford 1938.

K.K. Müller, 'Neue Mittheilungen über Janos Lascaris und die Mediceische Bibliothek,' *Zentralblatt für Bibliothekswesen*, I (1884), 333.

R. Sabbadini, *Le scoperte dei codici latini e greci ne' secoli XIV e XV*, 2 vols, Florence 1905–14.

B.L. Ullman, *The Origin and Development of Humanist Script*, Rome 1960.

Giuseppe Zippel, *Niccolo Niccoli*, Florence 1890.

N. Anziani, *Della Biblioteca Mediceo-Laurenziana di Firenze*, Florence 1872.

D. Fava, *La Biblioteca Nazionale Centrale di Firenze*, Milan 1939.

James S. Ackerman, *The Architecture of Michelangelo*, London 1961.

Filarete's phrase is quoted by E.H. Gombrich, 'The Early Medici as Patrons of Art' in *Italian Renaissance Studies*, ed. E.F. Jacob, London: Faber, 1960.

The provenance of Cosimo's *Pliny* (Laur. 82, 1–2) is given in an erased note at the end of each volume, visible under ultra-violet rays. I am indebted to the kindness of Dr Filippo Di Benedetto for this reading:

Prima (Secunda) pars librorum Plinij conuentus lubecen-[sis] *prouincie saxonie ordinis predicatorum/concessa gherardo de boeriis (?) hon*[orabi]*li* [viro ?] *lubecen*[si] *ad exscribendum.* In fact, like many other codices that passed into the possession of the humanists, it was lent for copying and never returned.

ROYAL LIBRARY, BRUSSELS

C.P. De La Serna Santander, *Mémoire historique sur la bibliothèque dite de Bourgogne*, Brussels 1809.

P. Namur, *Histoire des bibliothèques publiques de la Belgique*, Vol. I, 1840.

A. Voisin, *Documents pour servir à l'histoire des bibliothèques en Belgique*, Gand 1840.

Victor Tourneur, *Coup d'oeil sur l'histoire de la Bibliothèque Royale de Belgique*, Brussels 1939.

There is a large literature on the Librairie de Bourgogne; the following may be found helpful.

G. Doutrepont, *La littérature française à la cour des ducs de Bourgogne*, Paris 1909.

C. Gaspar and F. Lyna, *Philippe le Bon et ses beaux livres*, Brussels 1944.

L. Delaissé, *Miniatures médiévales de la Librairie de Bourgogne au cabinet des manuscrits de la Bibliothèque Royale de Bruxelles*, Brussels 1959.

La miniature flamande. Le mécénat de Philippe le Bon (exhibition catalogue), Brussels: Bibliothèque Royale, 1959.

La Librairie de Philippe le Bon (exhibition catalogue), Brussels: Bibliothèque Royale, 1967.

BIBLIOTECA COLOMBINA, SEVILLE

Henry Harrisse, *Fernand Colomb, sa vie, ses oeuvres*, Paris 1872; *Grandeur et décadence de la Colombine*, Paris 1885; *La Colombine et Clément Marot*, Paris 1886; *Excerpta Colombiniana. Bibliographie de quatre cents pièces gothiques*, Paris 1887; *Toujours la Colombine*, Paris 1897.

Servando Arbolí y Faraudo and others, *Biblioteca Colombina: Catálogo de sus libros impresos*, 7 vols, Seville 1888–1948.

Archer M. Huntington, *Catalogue of the Library of Ferdinand Columbus reproduced in facsimile from the unique manuscript in the Columbine Library of Seville*, New York 1905.

R.G. Howarth, ed., *Letters and the Second Diary of Samuel Pepys*, London 1932, p. 327 (Pepys's letter to Wanley).

BIBLIOTHÈQUE DE LA VILLE, SÉLESTAT

A. Horawitz, 'Beatus Rhenanus, Eine Biographie,' *Sitzungsberichte der Kaiserlichen Akademie der Wissenschaften*, Wien, LXX, 189–244: 'Des Beatus Rhenanus literärische Tätigkeit,' *ibid.* LXXI, 643–90, also LXXII, 323–76; 'Die Bibliothek und Correspondenz des Beatus Rhenanus zu Schlettstadt,' *ibid.* LXXVIII, 313–40.

A. Horawitz and K. Hartfelder, *Briefwechsel des Beatus Rhenanus*, Leipzig 1886.

J. Geny and G. Knod, *Die Stadtbibliothek zu Schlettstadt*, Strasbourg 1889.

A. Renaudet, *Préréforme et Humanisme*, Paris 1916.

J. Walter, *Ville de Sélestat. Catalogue Général de la Bibliothèque Municipale . . . Incunables et XVIme siècle*, Colmar 1929.

P. Adam, *L'humanisme à Sélestat*, Sélestat 1962.

(For the charge that Beatus destroyed manuscripts: Prof. Giuseppe Billanovich in *Italia medioevale e umanistica*, II (1959), 171.)

BIBLIOTHÈQUE NATIONALE, PARIS

Léopold Delisle, *Le cabinet des manuscrits de la Bibliothèque impériale*, 3 vols, Paris 1868.

T. Mortreuil, *La Bibliothèque Nationale, son origine et ses accroissements*, Paris 1878.

Alfred Franklin, *Précis de l'histoire de la Bibliothèque du Roi*, Paris 1875.

Henri Omont, *Catalogues des manuscrits grecs de Fontainebleau sous François Ier et Henri II*, Paris 1889.

Henri Omont, *Anciens inventaires et catalogues de la Bibliothèque Nationale*, 5 vols, Paris 1908–21.

Tammaro de Marinis, *La biblioteca napoletana dei Re d'Aragona*, Milan 1952, I, pp. 195–8.

E. Quentin Bauchart, *La bibliothèque de Fontainebleau et les livres des derniers Valois à la Bibliothèque Nationale*, Paris 1891.

Henri Lemaître, *Histoire du dépôt légal*, Paris 1910.

A.E. Armstrong, *Robert Estienne*, Cambridge 1954.

T.F. Dibdin, *A Bibliographical Antiquarian and*

Picturesque Tour in France and Germany, London 1821, II, pp. 130–133.

Edward Edwards, *Memoirs of Libraries*, 2 vols, London 1859.

The quotation on p. 130 is from E.A. Lowe, *Codices Latini Antiquiores*, Oxford 1939: by permission of the Clarendon Press.

BAVARIAN STATE LIBRARY, MUNICH

Johann Christian von Aretin, *Beyträge zur Geschichte und Literatur*, 9 vols, Munich 1803–7.

T.F. Dibdin, *A Bibliographical Antiquarian and Picturesque Tour in France and Germany*, London 1821, III, 256–321.

Otto Hartig, *Die Gründung der Münchener Hofbibliothek*, Munich 1917.

Waldemar Sensburg, *Die bayerischen Bibliotheken*, Munich 1926.

Die Bayerische Staatsbibliothek in den letzten hundert Jahren, Munich: Sonderdruck aus der Heimatzeitschrift 'Das Bayerland', 1932.

AUSTRIAN NATIONAL LIBRARY, VIENNA

Josef Stummvoll, ed., Ernst Trenkler, Franz Unterkircher, etc., *Geschichte der Österreichischen Nationalbibliothek. Erster Teil: Die Hofbibliothek 1368–1922*, Vienna 1968 (all published; two more volumes promised).

Angelo Rocca (*Bibliotheca Apostolica Vaticana a Sixto V Pont. Max. in splendidiorem . . . locum translata*, Rome 1591) says of the Emperors Maximilian II (1564–76) and Rudolph II (1576–1612) 'quorum ille Viennae Bibliothecam instituit nobilem, hic vero in dies auget et exornat.'

Lazius' description of his visit to Ossiach is from his introduction to Abdias, *Liber de passione*, Basle 1552: quoted by Hermann Menhardt, 'Die Kärntner Bibliotheksreise des Wolfgang Lazius,' *Archiv für vaterländische Geschichte und Topographie*, 24/25 Jg., Klagenfurt 1936, 100–12.

Logan Pearsall Smith, *The Life and Letters of Sir Henry Wotton*, 2 vols, Oxford 1907.

Edward Browne, *An Account of Several Travels through a Great Part of Germany*, London 1677.

LIBRARY OF THE ROYAL MONASTERY, EL ESCORIAL

Charles Graux, *Essai sur les origines du fonds grec de l'Escurial*, Paris 1880.

P. Eustasio Esteban, O.S.A., 'La Biblioteca del Escorial, apuntes para su historia,' *La Ciudad de Dios*, XXVII (1892), 182–92, 414–24, 596–606; *ibid.* XXVIII (1892), 125–38: XXXI (1893), 591–96.

P. Guillermo Antolín, O.S.A., 'Historia, procedencias, organización y catalogación de la Biblioteca de El Escorial,' in *Catálogo de códices latinos de la Biblioteca de El Escorial*, 1910–23, I, i–liii; V, 1–330.

P. Julián Zarco, O.S.A., 'Biblioteca y bibliotecarios de San Lorenzo el Real de El Escorial,' *Catálogo de mss castellanos de la Biblioteca de El Escorial*, 1924–9, I, ix–cxxxiii.

Documentos para la historia del monasterio de San Lorenzo el Real de El Escorial, Vol. VII, 1964.

The quotation from Madden's letter on p. 162 is taken from A.N.L. Munby, *Phillipps Studies*, Cambridge University Press, 1951–60, IV, 100.

BODLEIAN LIBRARY, OXFORD

W.D. Macray, *Annals of the Bodleian Library*, Oxford, 2nd ed., Oxford 1890.

Sir Edmund Craster, *History of the Bodleian Library 1845–1945*, Oxford University Press, 1952.

G.W. Wheeler, ed., *Letters of Sir Thomas Bodley to Thomas James*, Oxford 1926.

[E.W.B. Nicholson and others,] *Pietas Oxoniensis in memory of Sir Thomas Bodley, Knt*, Oxford 1902.

Trecentenale Bodleianum, Oxford 1913.

G.W. Wheeler, *The Earliest Catalogues of the Bodleian Library*, Oxford 1928.

Roberto Weiss, *Humanism in England during the fifteenth century*, 2nd ed., 1957 (on Humphrey Duke of Gloucester's Library).

Bodleian Quarterly Record (later *Bodleian Library Record*), *passim*: the translation of part of Burton's mourning poem is by R.T. Milford in *BQR*, I, 1914.

TRINITY COLLEGE, DUBLIN

John K. Ingram, *The Library of Trinity College, Dublin*, London 1886.

T.K. Abbott, 'The Library' in *The Book of Trinity College, Dublin 1591–1891*, Belfast 1892, 147–81.

J.P. Mahaffy, 'The Library of Trinity College, Dublin: the Growth of a Legend,' *Hermathena*, XII (1903), 68–78.

Sir Edward Sullivan, 'The Library of Trinity College, Dublin,' *The Book-Lover's Magazine*, VII (1908), 1–12.

J.G. Smyly, 'The Old Library: extracts from the Particular Book,' *Hermathena*, XLIX (1935), 166–83.

Friends of the Library of Trinity College, Dublin, Annual Bulletin, 1949, 1951, 1952, etc.

Maurice Craig, *Dublin 1660–1860*, London 1952, 94–6.

William O'Sullivan, 'Ussher as a collector of manuscripts,' *Hermathena*, LXXXVIII (1956), 34–58.

William O'Sullivan, 'The donor of the Book of Kells,' *Irish Historical Studies*, XI, 41 (March 1958), 5–7.

H.W. Parke, *The Library of Trinity College, Dublin*, Dublin [1959].

Arthur Rau, 'Portrait of a Bibliophile, XIII: Henry George Quin, 1760–1805,' *The Book Collector*, XIII, No. 4 (Winter 1964), 449–62.

The quotation on p. 180 is taken from Maurice Craig, *Dublin 1660–1860*, Cresset Press, 1952.

The final quotation is adapted from Professor Myles Dillon's translation of a marginal poem in the St Gall Priscian: M. Dillon and N.K. Chadwick, *The Celtic Realms* (London: Weidenfeld and Nicolson, 1967), p. 233.

BIBLIOTECA AMBROSIANA, MILAN

P.P. Bosca, *De origine et statu Bibliothecae Ambrosianae*, Milan 1672.

A. Ceruti, *Lettere inedite di dotti italiani del secolo XVI*, Milan 1867.

A. Ceruti, 'La Biblioteca Ambrosiana di Milano' in *Gli Instituti scientifici, letterari e artistici di Milano*, Milan 1880.

A. Ratti, 'Ancora del celebre cod. ms. delle opere di Virgilio già di F. Petrarca,' *Società Storica Lombarda* (1904), 217–42.

A. Ratti, *Guida sommaria*, Milan 1907.

A. Ratti, 'Manoscritti di provenienza francese nella Biblioteca Ambrosiana di Milano' in *Mélanges Emile Chatelain*, 1910.

Paolo Bellezza, *Federigo Borromeo*, Milan 1931.

A. Barera, *L'opera scientifico-letteraria del Card. Federico Borromeo*, Milan 1931.

G. Morazzoni, *L'Ambrosiana nel terzo centenario di Federico Borromeo*, Milan 1932.

A. Saba, 'La Biblioteca Ambrosiana,' *Aevum*, Anno VI, fasc. 4 (Oct.-Dec. 1932).

A. Rivolta, *Catalogo dei codici Pinelliani dell' Ambrosiana*, Milan 1933.

Constituzioni del Collegio e della Biblioteca Ambrosiana tradotte dal dottore Francesco Bentivoglio, Milan 1933.

E.A. Lowe, *Codices Latini antiquiores*, Oxford 1934, etc., Vol. III.

Maria Luisa Gengaro and Gemma Villa Guglielmetti, *Inventario dei codici decorati e miniati, secc. VII–XIII, della Biblioteca Ambrosiana*, Florence 1968.

HARVARD UNIVERSITY LIBRARY, MASSACHUSETTS

A.C. Potter, *Library of Harvard University: Descriptive and Historical Notes*, 4th ed., Cambridge, Mass., 1934.

William A. Jackson, 'The Importance of Rare Books and Manuscripts in a University Library,' *Harvard Library Bulletin*, III (1949), 315–26.

Edwin Wolf 2nd with John Fleming, *Rosenbach*, London: Weidenfeld and Nicolson, 1960.

William A. Jackson, 'Contemporary Collectors XXIV: Philip Hofer,' *The Book Collector*, IX (1960), 151–64, 292–300.

W.H. Bond, 'William Alexander Jackson 1905–1964,' *Harvard Library Bulletin*, XV (1967), 7–36.

The Houghton Library 1942–1967, Cambridge, Mass., 1967.

Henry James's description on p. 196 is from *Selected Letters of Henry James* [edited with an introduction by Leon Edel], London: Rupert Hart-Davis, 1956.

HERZOG AUGUST BIBLIOTHEK, WOLFENBÜTTEL

Otto von Heinemann, *Die herzogliche Bibliothek zu Wolfenbüttel*, Wolfenbüttel 1894.
Otto von Heinemann and others, *Die Handschriften der Herzoglichen Bibliothek zu Wolfenbüttel*, Wolfenbüttel 1884– (continuing).

PEPYS LIBRARY, MAGDALENE COLLEGE, CAMBRIDGE

Bibliotheca Pepysiana. A Descriptive Catalogue of the Library of Samuel Pepys. I: *'Sea' Manuscripts* by J.R. Tanner; II: *General Introduction* by F. Sidgwick and *Early Printed Books to 1558* by E. Gordon Duff; III: *Medieval Manuscripts* by M.R. James; IV: *Shorthand Books* by William J. Carlton. London, Sidgwick & Jackson, 1914–40.
A complete catalogue is soon to be published. The quotations are mostly from H.B. Wheatley's edition of the Diary, London 1893–9, or *Letters and the Second Diary of Samuel Pepys*, ed. R.G. Howarth, London and Toronto (Dent), New York (Dutton), 1932. Pepys's opinion on Noah's Ark is printed in *Samuel Pepys's Naval Minutes*, ed. J.R. Tanner, Navy Records Society, Vol. LX (1926). His draft reply to a letter on the Durham fragments was published by Sir Owen Morshead in *The Times* (17 February 1926).

YALE UNIVERSITY LIBRARY, NEW HAVEN, CONNECTICUT

Edwin Oviatt, *The Beginnings of Yale*, New Haven, Conn. 1916.
Robert Dudley French, ed., *The Memorial Quadrangle*, New Haven, Conn. 1929.
Wilmarth S. Lewis, *The Yale Collections*, New Haven, Conn. 1946: *Collector's Progress*, London: Constable, 1952.
Edwin Wolf 2nd with John F. Fleming, *Rosenbach*, London: Weidenfeld and Nicolson, 1960.
The Yale University Library Gazette, 1926– (continuing).

COIMBRA AND MAFRA

Grande Enciclopedia Portuguesa e Brasileira, Vol. IV, p. 651.
José Ramos de Bandeira, *Universidade de Coimbra*, Vol. I, Coimbra 1943, pp. 166–80.
Carlos de Azevedo, 'Some Portuguese Libraries,' *The Connoisseur Year Book*, 1956.
James Lees-Milne, *Baroque in Spain and Portugal*, London: Batsford, 1960, pp. 174–194.
André Masson, 'Le décor des bibliothèques anciennes en Portugal et en Espagne,' *Bulletin des bibliothèques de France*, 7e année, 2 (février 1962), 87–99.

BRITISH MUSEUM, LONDON

Edward Edwards, *Lives of the Founders of the British Museum*, London 1870.
G.F. Barwick, *The Reading Room of the British Museum*, London: Ernest Benn, 1929.
Arundell Esdaile, *The British Museum Library*, London: George Allen & Unwin, 1946.
G.R. De Beer, *Sir Hans Sloane and the British Museum*, Oxford University Press, 1953.
C.B. Oldman, 'Sir Anthony Panizzi and the British Museum Library,' in *English Libraries 1800–1850*, London 1958.

C.E. Wright, 'The Elizabethan Society of Antiquaries and the Formation of the Cottonian Library,' in *The English Library before 1700*, ed. Francis Wormald and C.E. Wright, University of London, The Athlone Press, 1958.
C.E. and Ruth C. Wright, *The Diary of Humfrey Wanley 1715–1726*, 2 vols, London: The Bibliographical Society, 1966. (Wanley was the librarian of the Harley Library.)
Edward Miller, *Prince of Librarians* [Panizzi], London: André Deutsch, 1967.
Panizzi's instructions to Henry Stevens are contained in a letter from Stevens to Jared Sparks of 27 March 1846, now at Harvard; quoted by I.R. Willison, 'The Development of the United States Collection, Department of Printed Books, British Museum,' *Journal of American Studies*, 1 (1967), 1.

PALACE LIBRARY, MADRID

Catálogo de la Real Biblioteca, 9 vols, Madrid 1898–1935 (with introduction by the Conde de Las Navas).
Matilde López Serrano, *Biblioteca de Palacio. Encuadernaciones*, Madrid n.d.
M.I. Hernández, *Antecedentes y comienzos del reinado de Fernando VII*, Madrid 1963.

BIBLIOTHÈQUE DE L'ARSENAL, PARIS

Henri Martin, *Histoire de la Bibliothèque de l'Arsenal: Catalogue des manuscrits de la Bibliothèque de l'Arsenal*, Vol. VIII, Paris 1899.
Auguste Rondel, *Catalogue analytique sommaire de la collection théâtrale Rondel*, Paris 1932.
Michel Salomon, *Charles Nodier et le groupe romantique*, Paris 1908.
The account is largely based on the Marquis de Paulmy's manuscript catalogue, MSS Ars. 6279–6297, and the correspondence with Soyer, Baroni and others in MS Ars. 6408.

THE JOHN RYLANDS LIBRARY, MANCHESTER

T.F. Dibdin, *Bibliotheca Spenceriana*, 4 vols, London 1814–15.
T.F. Dibdin, *Aedes Althorpianae*, 2 vols, London 1822.
T.F. Dibdin, *A Descriptive Catalogue of the Books printed in the fifteenth century, lately forming part of the library of the Duke of Cassano Serra*, London 1823.
T.F. Dibdin, *A Bibliographical Antiquarian and Picturesque Tour in France and Germany*, 3 vols, London 1821.
T.F. Dibdin, *Reminiscences of a Literary Life*, 2 vols, London 1836.
Earl of Crawford and Balcarres, *Bibliotheca Lindesiana: Catalogue of the Printed Books*, Vol. I (Introduction), 1910.
Henry Guppy, *The John Rylands Library, Manchester: A Brief Historical Description*, Manchester 1906.
Henry Guppy, *The John Rylands Library, Manchester: A Brief Record of Twenty-one Years' Work*, Manchester 1921.
Henry Guppy, *The John Rylands Library, Manchester: 1899–1924*, Manchester, London 1924.
Henry Guppy, *The John Rylands Library, Manchester: 1899–1935*, Manchester 1935.
Bulletin of the John Rylands Library, Manchester, 1903–8 and 1914– (continuing).

Quotations from letters of the second Earl Spencer and T.F. Dibdin are from MSS Eng. 71 and Eng.

915 in the John Rylands Library and MA 2254 in the Pierpont Morgan Library, New York. The account of the purchase of the Althorp books and the Crawford MSS is based on documents in the John Rylands Library and among the private papers of the Earl of Crawford and Balcarres.

BIBLIOTHÈQUE SPOELBERCH DE LOVENJOUL, CHANTILLY

Alice Ciselet, *Un grand bibliophile: le Vicomte Spoelberch de Lovenjoul*, Paris and Brussels: Éditions Universitaires, 1948.
Max Deauville, 'Charles de Spoelberch de Lovenjoul' in *Revue générale belge*, No. 72 (October 1951).
Christophe Ryelandt, *Le Vicomte de Spoelberch de Lovenjoul et George Sand*, Brussels 1958.
André Maurois and others, *Hommage au Vicomte Spoelberch de Lovenjoul*, Académie Royale de Langue et dé Littérature Françaises de Belgique, Brussels 1958.
Georges Vicaire, *Chantilly, Bibliothèque Spoelberch de Lovenjoul* in *Catalogue général des manuscrits des bibliothèques publiques de France*, Vol. LII, Paris 1960.

The quotations from Raymond Nacquart, Michel and Paul Lévy, Jules Troubat, Mme Sabatier, Countess Mniszech and Étienne Charavay are from Spoelberch de Lovenjoul's correspondence in the library.

PIERPONT MORGAN LIBRARY, NEW YORK

Belle da Costa Greene, *The Pierpont Library. Review of the activities and acquisitions of the Library from 1930 through 1935*, New York 1937.
Herbert L. Satterlee, *J. Pierpont Morgan, an Intimate Biography*, New York: Macmillan, 1939.
Frederick Lewis Allen, *The Great Pierpont Morgan*, New York: Harper & Row, 1949.
Frederick B. Adams, Jr, *First [-Fourteenth] Annual Report to the Fellows of the Pierpont Morgan Library*, New York 1950–67.
Wayne Andrews, *Mr Morgan and his Architect*, New York: Pierpont Morgan Library, 1957.
Francis Henry Taylor, *Pierpont Morgan as Collector and Patron*, New York: Pierpont Morgan Library, 1957.

HENRY E. HUNTINGTON LIBRARY, SAN MARINO

Robert O. Schad, 'Henry Edwards Huntington,' *The Huntington Library Bulletin*, No. 1 (May 1931) (re-issued separately 1963).
The Huntington Library Bulletin, 1931–7.
The Huntington Library Quarterly, 1937– (continuing).
Carl L. Cannon, *American Book Collectors and Collecting from Colonial Times to the Present*, New York 1941.
Roland Baughman, 'Henry Edwards Huntington,' in *Grolier 75*, New York: The Grolier Club, 1959.
Edwin Wolf 2nd with John Fleming, *Rosenbach*, London: Weidenfeld and Nicolson, 1960.

UNIVERSITY LIBRARY, AUSTIN, TEXAS

The Library Chronicle of the University of Texas, 1944– (continuing).
Cyril Connolly, 'The Egghead Shrinkers,' *The* [London] *Sunday Times*, 15 April 1962.

REFERENCES

133 Prayerbook of Maximilian I. Augsburg, Hans Schönsperger the elder, 1513. 2° impr. membr. 64, f. 55b.

134 Gratian, _Decretum._ Mainz, Peter Schöffer, 1472. 2°. L.Impr. membr. 1a.

135 Orlando di Lasso, Penitential Psalms, 1565. Cod. mus. A, vol. II, p. 3 detail.

136 Left: Kleinodienbuch. Cod. icon. 429, f. 1b.
Right: L. Surius, _Der erste Theil bewerter Historien der lieben Heiligen Gottes._ Munich, Adam Berg, 1574. 2° V.SS. C. 129a, upper cover, detail.
Below: Tournament book of William IV. Cgm. 2800, pp. 10–11.

139 Above: Paul Hektor Mair, _Fechtbuch._ Cod. icon. 393, pt. VII, fig. 3.
Below: Book of Pericopes. Clm. 4452, ff. 131b–132.

140 Hartmann Schedel, _Liber antiquitatum._ Clm. 716, f. 6.

141 _Eyn Manung der cristenheit widder die durken_ (Mainz 1454). Rar. 1, f. 5.

VIENNA

143 Cod. 2835, f. 2b (= MS Ambras 331).

144 Cod. 8329, f. 10.

145 Cod. min. 53, vol. 2, no. 57.

146 Above: Cod. ser. n. 2669, f. 91.
Centre: Cod. ser. n. 2664, f. 17.
Below left: Cod. ser. n. 4711, f. 4.
Below right: _Ambraser Heldenbuch._ Cod. ser. n. 2663, f. Vb.

148 Above: Sir Thomas Browne, _Religio Medici . . . the sixth Edition._ London, for Andrew Crook, 1669. *LXIX. N.171, upper cover.
Below: Cod. 338, f. 34 detail.

149 Blaeu, _Atlas Major,_ vol. 44, pl. 10.

EL ESCORIAL

151 Codex Aureus. Vitr. 17, f. 2b.

152 St Theresa of Avila, _Libro de la Vida,_ 1565–6.

153 Book of Hours of Philip II, 1568. Vitr. 2.

154 Apocalypse. Vitr. 1, f. 8.

155 Beatus of Liebana, _Explanatio in Apocalypsim._ &.II.5, f. 134.

156 _Codice Vigilano._ d.I.1, f. 17.

157 Alfonso X, _Cantigas de Sta. Maria._ T.I.1, f. 182.

158 Boccaccio, _Las mujeres illustres._ Saragossa, Pablo Hurus, 1494. 11.IV.23.

159 Aesop, _Vita et Fabulae._ Saragossa, Juan Hurus, 1489. 32.1.13.

160 Beatus of Liebana. &.II.5, f. 120.

161 Breviary of Isabella the Catholic, _c._ 1480. b.II.5.
Left: f. 251b.
Right: f. 534.

BODLEIAN

167 Above: _The Mirroure of the Worlde._ MS Bodley 283, f. 59 detail.

169 Nizami, _Laila and Majnun._ MS Pers. d. 102, p. 65.

170 Above: _The seuerall notorious and lewd cousnages of John West and Alice West,_ 1613. 4°G.8. Art BS 5.

Below: William Goddard, _A mastif whelp with other ruff Islandlik Currs_ (1599?). 4°G.8. Art BS 4.

171 Above: _Looke up and see wonders,_ 1628. 4° C.16. Art BS 6.
Below: Thomas Dekker, _O per se O,_ 1612. 4° G. 8. Art BS 13.

172 Book of Hours, Rouen _c._ 1460. MS Auct. D. Inf. II. 11, f. 44b.

TRINITY COLLEGE, DUBLIN

176 Left: Matthew Paris, _Vita S._
–7 _Albani._ E.1.40.
Above: f. 55b detail.
Below: f. 59 detail.

177 New Testament and Psalter. A.1.1, f. 24b detail.

179 William Caxton, _The veray true history of the valliant knight Jason._ Antwerp, G. Leeu, 2 June 1492. FF. hh. 53 (3).

180 Missal from the convent of St Agnes at Delft. K. 2. 32, f. 214b detail.

181 Johannes Hevelius, _Machina coelestis._ Danzig 1673. OO. aa. 36.

182 Book of Durrow. A.4.5, f. 85b.

183 Botanical drawings by Nicolas Robert. V.2.26, f. 22.

184 Above left: Shakespeare, _Works,_ 1784. Quin 35, upper cover.
Above right: M. Accursio, _Coryciana._ Rome 1524. Quin 111, lower cover.
Below left: L. Tansillo, _Il Vendemmiatore_ (Paris 1790?). Quin 117, upper cover.
Below right: Hieronimo Morlini, _Novellae._ Naples 1520. Quin 95, lower cover.

185 Book of Armagh, vol. I, f. 90.

AMBROSIANA

187 _Vitae archiepiscoporum Mediolanensium._ H 87 Sup, f. 1.

188 Galileo Galilei, _Il Saggiatore._ Rome 1623.

189 Galileo Galilei, autograph letter. S P 47.

190 Al-Gāhiz, _Kitāb al-Hayawan._ D.140 Inf.
Above: f. 23.
Below: f. 5.

191 Above: Thomas à Kempis, _Contemptus mundi._ Amakusa 1596. S P 20.
Below: Francesco Rivola, _Dictionarium armeno-latinum._ Milan 1621. S.M.B. VI. 2.

192 Rhazes, _Opera chirurgiae._ D 120 Inf, f. 42b detail.

193 'Ambrosian Iliad'. F 205 Inf.
Above: f. 23.
Below: f. 29.

195 Petrarch's Vergil. S P Arm. 10. 27, f. 1b.

HARVARD

197 _Prague Missal._ Leipzig 1522. Typ 520.22.262F.

198 Below: Giuseppe Galli Bibbiena, Sketchbook. f. MS Typ 412.

199 Vitruvius, _Gli oscuri et dificili passi._ Mantua 1558. *H525–259F.

200 Right: _Usatges de Barcelona e Constitucions de Cataluña._ Barcelona, Père Miquel, 1495. Typ 41–14 Inc 9550. SF*.
Left: Edward Lear, _The Owl and the Pussycat._ 6 MS Typ 55. 14.

201 Pablo Picasso, _Eaux-fortes originales pour des textes de Buffon._ Paris, Martin Fabiani, 1942. Typ. 915. 42. 69201.

WOLFENBÜTTEL

203 Gospels written at Helmarshausen, 1194. Helmst. 65, f. 23b.

204 _Totentanz_ (Ulm, Johann Zainer, _c._ 1488). 19. 2 (4293) Eth. fol.
Above: f. 2.
Below: upper row f. 17b; f. 6b. lower row f. 10b; f. 19.

205 Alexander Cortesius, _Laudes Bellicae_ (Padua?, _c._ 1480–90). 85. 1. 1. Aug. fol., f. 3.

208 Wolfram of Eschenbach, _Willehalm._ 30. 12. Aug. fol., f. 91.

209 Above: Codex Arcerianus. 36. 23. Aug. fol., f. 56b.
Below: Thomasin von Zerclaere, _Der wälsche Gast,_ 1408. 37. 19. Aug. fol., f. 34.

210 Ulrich Boner, _Der Edelstein._ Bamberg, Albrecht Pfister, 1461. 16. 1. Eth. fol.

PEPYS

212 The Anthony Roll. PL 2991.

215 Below: G.F. Hildanus, _Lithotomia vesicae,_ translated by N.C. London 1640. PL 792.

216 Above: _London's Dreadful Visitation,_ 1665. PL 1595.
Below: Will Stokes, _The Vaulting-master._ Oxford 1652. PL 1434 (7).

217 Above: Stephen Hawes, _The example of virtue._ London, Wynkyn de Worde (1510). PL 1254 (2).
Below: Sir Richard Maitland, _Poems,_ 1586. PL 1408, f. 134.

218 Above: Francisco de Quevedo, _Satiras graciosas._ Seville 1677. PL 1545, no. 35.
Below: _The Most Pleasant History of Tom a Lincoln,_ 1682. PL 1192 (18).

219 Above left: Wycliffite New Testament, PL 2073; centre, _Ornamento nobile per ogni gentil matrona._ Venice 1620, PL 2097; right: Capt. D. Newhouse, _The whole art of navigation,_ 1685, PL 1863.

219 Below: 'Habits de France'. PL 2295, pl. 16.

YALE

222 Tacitus belonging to Matthias Corvinus. Yale MS. 145, upper cover.

223 Sir Thomas More, _Utopia,_ Louvain 1516. If M81 r. 516.

224 Above: _Speculum humanae salvationis._ Yale MS. 27, ff. 31b–32.
Below: Engraving by T. Johnson, 1745, reprinted 1911. (Yale University Art Gallery, A.P. Stokes Collection).

226 The 'Bay Psalm Book', Mlm 405. 640b.

227 Gutenberg or 42-line Bible. (Mainz 1454–5).

228 Alfred J. Miller's scenes of William Steward's expedition to the Far West. Withington 342.

229 J.J. Audubon, _The Birds of America,_ 1827–38. SS y 13g. 31.

231 James Boswell, _The Life of Samuel Johnson,_ autograph MS. Boswell Papers M 144.

COIMBRA AND MAFRA

236 Above: Antonio de Beja, _Contra os juizos dos astrólogos._ Lisbon, Germão Galharde, 1523. R–14–10.
Below left: _Regimento dos Contos do Reyno_ Lisbon 1708.
Below right: Ludolphus of Saxony, _Vita Christi._ Lisbon, Valentim Fernandes and Nicolas of Saxony, 1495. R–67–11.

237 Above left: _Cronica do condestabre de Portugal._ Lisbon, Germão Galharde, 1526. R–28–2.
Below: _Regra statutos e diffuçoẽs da ordem de Sanctiaguo._ Sétubal 1509. R–31–30.

238 Above: Lorenzo Torriani of Cremona. (_Description and history of the Canary Isles_). MS 314.
Below: Luis de Camõens, _Os Lusidas._ Lisbon, A. Gonçalvez, 1572. RB–32–4.

BRITISH MUSEUM

244 Above: English hymnal. Cotton Caligula A XIV, f. 20b.
Below: Psalter. Cotton Nero C.IV, f. 24.

245 Above: Bonaventura, _Life of St Francis._ Harley 3229, f. 26.

246 Latin Bible. Nuremberg, A. Koberger, 1477. C.10.d.3, upper cover.

246 Robert Smirke. Sketch. Depart-
–7 ment of Prints and Drawings.

MADRID

248 Alonso de Cartagena, _Genealogia de los reyes._ 2–Ll–2, f. 147b.

249 Hours of Juana Henríquez, f. 37b.

250 Alonso de Cartagena. 2–Ll–2.
Above: f. 179b.
Below left: f. 171b.

251 Above: _Ordenanzes de la Real Maestranza de Cavalleros de la Ciudad de Valencia._ Valencia 1776. I–E–4, upper cover.
Below: Alonso de Cartagena. 2–Ll–2, f. 165b.

252 Left: Baltasar Jaime Martínez Compañon. _Aguadas de los Indios de Trujillo, etc._ Vit. sal. III.
Right: Francisco López de Caravantes, _Noticia general de las Provincias del Perú, Tierra Firme y Chile,_ 1630–34.

253 Bruno Gómez, _El magnífico tabernáculo de N.S. del Pilar de Zaragoza,_ 1836, f. 4.

254 José Domínguez, Calligraphic alphabet. II–1961.

255 Alfonso XI of Castille, _Libro de monteria,_ f. 34b.

256 Antonio Miralles y Anglesola, _Examen literario,_ Valencia 1788. X–62, upper cover.

257 Juan Riezo or Oliva, _Cartas de marear,_ 1580.

ARSENAL

259 Psalter of Blanche of Castille. MS 1186, f. 1b.

260 Jacopo Antonio Marcello, _Passio Sancti Mauricii,_ 1453. MS 940, f. 38b.

261 Terence, _Comodiae._ MS 664, f. 36b.

262 'Instruction en la religion chrestienne'. MS 5096, f. 1b.

263 French poetical collection. MS 3142.

Above: f. 311b detail.
Below: f. 229 detail.

264 Above: *Therence en francoys.* Paris, Antoine Vérard, n.d. Rés. Fol B. 1388, a iii verso.
Below: Roberto della Porta, *Romuleon.* MS 667, f. 10 detail.

265 Edward Tyson, *Orang-Outang, sive Homo Sylvestris.* London 1699. 4° S 2606, fig. 1.

266 Madame de Pompadour, *Oeuvre.* Rés. 419 Estampes, upper cover.

JOHN RYLANDS

268 Aesop, *Fables.* Naples, Francesco del Tuppo, 1485. 18392.

270 Boccaccio, *De claris mulieribus.* Ulm, Johann Zainer, 1473. 15996.

271 Bible in Danish. Copenhagen, L. Dietz, 1550. 20650.

272 Apocalypse IV. 16119.

274 Marco Polo, *Buch des edlen Ritters und Landfahrers Marco Polo.* Nuremberg, Creussner, 1477. 18148.

275 *Das Buch der Weisheit.* Ulm, Lienhart Holle, 28 May 1483. 19048.

276 Above: Vergil, *Opera.* Venice, Aldus Manutius, 1501. 3359.
Below: Hebrew *Haggadah.* Hebrew MS 6, f. 15.

277 J. de Turrecremata, *Meditationes,* Rome, Ulrich Han, 1467. 17251.

278 James Tissot, Drawing for illustration to *La Sainte Bible,* Paris 1904. R 16279.

CHANTILLY

282 George Sand, *Elle et Lui.* E. 790.

283 A. de Musset, Portrait of George Sand. E 956, f. 14.

284 Above: Théophile Gautier, *Magdeleine de Maupin,* Oct. 1834. C 516 bis, f. 16.
Below: Théophile Gautier, Caricatures of dancers. C 516 bis, f. 38.

285 Théophile Gautier, Caricature of Eugène Piot. C 516 bis, f. 47.

286 H. Balzac, *Le Médecin de campagne.* A 137.

287 Théophile Gautier, *Le Capitaine Fracasse.* C.415.

PIERPONT MORGAN

289 Hours of Catherine of Cleves. M 917, m-p. 151.

290 Vincent of Beauvais, *Mirror of the World.* Westminster, William Caxton (1481). PML 776.

291 John Keats, *Endymion.* MA 208.

292 Hebrew Bible, Soncino 1488. PML 21590.

293 Old Testament Illustrations. M 638, f. 23b.

294 Above: Ibn Baktishū, *Manāfi al-Hayawān.* M 500, f. 78b.
Below: Berchtold Missal. M 710. f. 64b.

295 Aristotle, *Opera.* Venice, Andrea de Asola, 1483. PML 21194-5, vol. II.

294 Constance Missal. PML 45545.

HUNTINGTON

300 HM 124576.

301 Above: HM 18538.
Below: HM 62222.

302 EL 26 C9, f. 200.

303 Above: EL 1142, f. 207.
Below: HM 4700, sig. A2 (p. 3).

304 HM 18568.

305 HM 177. Gonzalo Hernández de Oviedo y Valdés, *Historia general y natural de las Indias,* vol. 2, f. 46.

INDEX